Professional specialists, using market research and promotional campaigns, have come to dominate public communication. The modern public of the Enlightenment, based on free discussion, has, in Leon Mayhew's terms, been replaced by a "New Public," subject to mass persuasion through systematic advertising, lobbying, and other forms of media manipulation. Professor Mayhew examines this sociological development in terms of discourse and social influence, offering an original theory which bridges Talcott Parsons and Jürgen Habermas. Most importantly, he shows how the rhetorical techniques of the professional communicators are designed to avoid having to defend their claims, thereby precluding meaningful discussion of public issues. As a result, institutions providing forums for good-faith, two-way discourse no longer exist, community through communication cannot be achieved, and the social order is unstable.

# The New Public

**Cambridge Cultural Social Studies**

*General editors:* JEFFREY C. ALEXANDER, *Department of Sociology, University of California, Los Angeles, and* STEVEN SEIDMAN, *Department of Sociology, University at Albany, State University of New York.*

*Editorial Board*
JEAN COMAROFF, *Department of Anthropology, University of Chicago*
DONNA HARAWAY, *Department of the History of Consciousness, University of California, Santa Cruz*
MICHELE LAMONT, *Department of Sociology, Princeton University*
THOMAS LAQUEUR, *Department of History, University of California, Berkeley*

*Titles in the series*
ILANA FRIEDRICH SILBER, *Virtuosity, charisma, and social order*
LINDA NICHOLSON and STEVEN SEIDMAN (eds.), *Social postmodernism*
WILLIAM BOGARD, *The simulation of surveillance*
SUZANNE R. KIRSCHNER, *The religious and Romantic origins of psychoanalysis*
PAUL LICHTERMAN, *The search for political community*
ROGER FRIEDLAND and RICHARD HECHT, *To rule Jerusalem*
KENNETH H. TUCKER, *French revolutionary syndicalism and the public sphere*
ERIK RINGMAR, *Identity, interest and action*
ALBERTO MELUCCI, *The playing self*
ALBERTO MELUCCI, *Challenging codes*
SARAH M. CORSE, *Nationalism and literature*
DARNELL M. HUNT, *Screening the Los Angeles "riots"*
LYNETTE P. SPILLMAN, *Nation and commemoration*
MICHAEL MULKAY, *The embryo research debate*
LYNN RAPAPORT, *Jews in Germany after the Holocaust*
CHANDRA MUKERJI, *Territorial ambitions and the gardens of Versailles*

# The New Public

## Professional communication and the means of social influence

Leon H. Mayhew
*Professor Emeritus of Sociology, University of California, Davis*

CAMBRIDGE
UNIVERSITY PRESS

PUBLISHED BY THE PRESS SYNDICATE OF THE UNIVERSITY OF CAMBRIDGE
The Pitt Building, Trumpington Street, Cambridge CB2 1RP, United Kingdom

CAMBRIDGE UNIVERSITY PRESS
The Edinburgh Building, Cambridge, CB2 2RU, United Kingdom
40 West 20th Street, New York, NY 10011-4211, USA
10 Stamford Road, Oakleigh, Melbourne 3166, Australia

First published 1997

Printed in the United Kingdom at the University Press, Cambridge

Typeset in 10/12½ Monotype Times

*A catalogue record for this book is available from the British Library*

*Library of Congress Cataloguing in Publication data*

Mayhew, Leon H.
    The new public: professional communication and the means of
social influence / Leon H. Mayhew.
        p.     cm. – (Cambridge cultural social studies)
    ISBN 0 521 48146 5 (hb). – ISBN 0 521 48493 6 (pb).
    1. Public relations.    2. Communication – Social aspects.
    3. Influence (Psychology)    4. Manipulative behavior.    5. Persuasion
(Psychology)    I. Title.    II. Series.
    HM263.M3124    1997
    659.2–dc21    96–49355    CIP

ISBN 0 521 48146 5 hardback
ISBN 0 521 48493 6 paperback

# Contents

# Preface

*The New Public* began to take shape in 1988, when, faced with several
months of bed rest, I entertained myself by watching the American electoral campaign on television. In the course of watching and reading
about the campaign, I became convinced that one element of sociologists' longstanding response to the radical critique of mass society
requires substantial revision. Critics of the notion of mass society assert
that the mass public is not so vulnerable to manipulation by elites as
might be imagined. Messages of elite communicators can be rejected or
reinterpreted by the public as its members pass their views from one
member to another within their private groups and circles. The "two-step
flow of communication" is still present and can thwart the intentions of
influential spokespeople, but what about the reverse flow of communication from the public to its leaders? Are the views of the public transmitted along comparable lines of social organization? I contend that the
rationalization of public persuasion and its consequent domination by
professional communicators erodes the social organization of public
opinion. Rationalized techniques employed in systematic campaigns rely
on market research to learn what the public believes and wants, or what
is likely to prove persuasive. In consequence, public opinion loses its
social moorings; it becomes less organized by social groups that create
and transmit public views and more affected by what market research
determines to be hot-button appeals.

An initial attempt to explore these ideas appeared in my 1992 essay,
"Political Rhetoric and the Contemporary Public." Jeffrey Alexander's
welcome invitation to submit a contribution to the Cambridge Cultural
Social Studies series allowed me to expand this thesis by examining the
rationalization of rhetorical means in the light of theories of social influence and discourse, especially the ideas of Talcott Parsons and Jürgen

Habermas. Their fertile insights allowed me to see the New Public as generating either *inflated influence* or *unredeemed discourse*. These two concepts, though born of very different conceptual schemes, are closely related, so much so that Parsons' concept of influence as a generalized medium, roundly criticized by Habermas, can be revised to build a useful bridge between structural and critical sociology.

Jeffrey Alexander is well aware of his contribution to this project. I deeply appreciate his wise assistance. Others may not know how much they have affected my work. I learned Parsonian sociology directly from the late Talcott Parsons, but Jürgen Habermas' thought was introduced to me later, during a sabbatical quarter in Berkeley in the spring of 1983. I place Jean Cohen, who first taught me about Habermas, at the head of the list of those whose contributions to my education made this book possible, but who might well issue modest disclaimers in response to any expression of gratitude on my part. Perhaps she will think that I still do not have it quite right, but if I do not, the fault is mine, not hers. In any event, she had more influence than she realized.

Other gracious individuals have helped me more than they know. Both academic colleagues and professional practitioners have illuminated my project with suggestions, leads, caveats, ideas, information, and ephemeral printed material. In this respect, I especially thank Don Abbott, Fred Block, Beth Capell, Greg Clark, Wally Clinton, Glenn Cowan, Clay Chandler, Bruce Hackett, Robert Jackman, David Jacobson, John Lofland, Charles Lacey, Frank Mankiewicz, Thomas Mann, Roland Marchand, Michele McCormick, Mark Melman, John Roemer, John Finley Scott, Gary Segura, Richard Sinopoli, Andrew Skalaban, Roger Strauss, Wilson Smith, Michael Sununu, and John Vohs. Bruce Jentelson, Director of the Washington Center of the University of California, Davis, deserves a special place among this group. He and the staff of the Center made my stay in Washington both pleasant and productive.

I am grateful to UC Davis for making this project possible. A grant from the campus administration greatly facilitated my work, and, as always, the proficient and generous staff of the Shields Library assisted me every step of the way.

Finally, I am grateful for my family's support. Families are often thanked primarily for their patience. In my case, family contributions were active and substantive. My sons, Jonathan Mayhew and Stewart Mayhew, provided challenging ideas and advice, often from opposite sides of the great divides of contemporary political and intellectual thought. Her proximity to New York City allowed my daughter Deborah Mayhew to make valuable inquiries on my behalf. My wife Janet helped me in more ways than I can possibly list, ranging from accomplishing tasks that I cannot easily manage, through innumerable corrections of the manuscript, but most of all through her unfailing support.

# PART I

*Rhetoric and the integration of society*

# 1

## Public influence in modern society

The complexities and intricacies of modern society are disturbing and perplexing. As observers we wonder how cohesion is possible in societies that can no longer be integrated by uniform adherence to conventional norms, and as citizens we search for public policies that can effectively include diverse people with disparate interests in a single societal community. We are tempted to conclude, with Yeats, that the center cannot hold.

What is this "center" that is losing its grip? Some observers assert that there is a special sector of society with specifically integrative functions, a sector variously identified as the public, societal community, or civil society, or possibly located in particular institutions such as law or voluntary association. Others question the authenticity of integrative institutions, even in democratic societies, charging that these institutions are mere covers for class and state domination. They doubt the independence and autonomy of so-called integrative institutions and deny that such institutions can provide moral guidance for society. This dispute goes beyond abstract sociological theorizing about social integration, for what is at stake are conceptions of the social foundations of democratic social orders.

In the traditions of democratic theory, hopes for a vital center have rested on establishment of a properly organized public life. Self-guidance of a modern society depends on a public capable of discussing and resolving issues and forming an effectual collective will. The ideals of public discussion were well stated by the Enlightened philosophers in the eighteenth century, but by the mid twentieth century, many critical thinkers had concluded that prospects for enlightenment in the modern world were dim. Horkheimer and Adorno, in their influential book *The Dialectic of Enlightenment* (1972 [1947]), saw the rise of the "culture industry" as transforming communicated meaning into standardized, manipulable bits, which could no longer be tools for forging authentic public culture. Fifteen years later, Jürgen Habermas, (1989 [1962]), heir to the traditions of Horkheimer and Adorno and the Frankfurt school of critical thought, examined the outcome of the public life inaugurated during the Enlightenment and concluded that its premises had failed in the nineteenth century when elites refused to allow the emerging working class access to public space. In the twentieth century, the rise of technical, instrumental reason threatened to vitiate the process of public discussion. These trends became apparent in American political communication and campaigning in the late 1950s and, accelerating over the next thirty-five years, brought about the forms of public life that I refer to in this book as the New Public.

### The New Public

In the New Public, communication is dominated by professional specialists. The techniques employed by these specialists are historically rooted in commercial promotion, but beginning in the 1950s, rationalized techniques of persuasion born of advertising, market research, and public relations were systematically applied to political communication. As this movement took flight in the 1970s and exploded in the 1980s and 1990s, political consultants, media specialists, public opinion pollsters, professional grassroots organizers, specialized lobbyists, focus group organizers, specialists in issue research, and demographic researchers burgeoned in numbers and established increasingly specialized roles. Political consultants now specialize in fields as narrow as strategies for countering negative advertising. The experts of the New Public have brought us the often impugned methods of civic persuasion that now dominate public communication: sound-bite journalism, thirty-second political advertising, one-way communication, evasive spin control by public figures who refuse to answer questions, and the marketing of ideas and candidates by methods developed in commercial market research.

Some of these roles have become conjoined in new approaches to public influence. Lobbying, though an old profession, now uses new methods that integrate the specialized contributions of market research, pollsters, purchased policy research, partisan studies done in "think tanks," and the efforts of other agents of communication not previously involved in shaping public opinion, such as public accountants. Political consulting has also flourished, integrating a similar array of differentiated contributions. The systematic conjoining of the expertise of varied political specialists has produced professional "grassroots" lobbying, often called astroturf lobbying, for it creates the appearance of support by artificial means, not by grassroots discussion. It has also promoted a process that I refer to as "the certification of facts." Professional political operatives now orchestrate the testimony of experts to create the appearance of factual foundations for political positions.

These new specialized techniques suggest manipulation and furnish evidence for critics who proclaim the decline of the public, and judge democratic institutions, including elections, to be a sham. Political communication, say the critics, merely manufactures consent, rather than allowing discursive formulations of policy in the public interest. When influence is fully paid for and serves a process of reaching compromises among powerful private interests, it is not realistic to call the sphere of influence a guiding "system" or to claim that influence is the currency of a differentiated integrative realm, emancipated from political and economic pressures. Influence cannot be idealized if it is cooked in the back rooms of influence specialists who manipulate behind the scenes rather than in settings designed for truly public discourse. Rhetoric calculated by experts belongs in the category of fraud – a type of coercion. To the critics, this rhetoric is surely not rational argument but the "cookery" of which Plato so disparagingly spoke.

The public is not a realm of complete consensus. It is an arena of conflict and debate, sometimes polite, sometimes rancorous, often indecisive. Like the economy and the polity, the public works imperfectly. Just as economic and political systems fail to match the overblown expectations of ideological defenders of free market economies and expert bureaucracies, so does the public often fail to produce consensual and effective answers to integrative questions. The public engages in contesting and creating meaning, not in applying norms to the resolution of conflict by simple acts of deduction that are accepted by acclamation. Nevertheless, the integrative significance of public life cannot be dismissed, even in the atmosphere created by the institutions of the New Public. In the course of public discussion – persuasive discourse founded on influence rather than force – people find ratification of identities, they reinforce or discover memberships and meaningful attachments to groups larger than the groups that bear their primary solidarities. Opinions are shaped and mobilized in the service of collective action, and situationally specific norms are created. Insofar as these processes work, people are able to resolve their conflicts without eliminating their differences or each other. Still, faced with the challenges presented by the New Public, serious discussion of public life must reassess the theory and practice of public discourse. Even when the terms of discourse are dominated by professional specialists, these specialists do not then constitute the public. The public still includes both the influential and the influenced, but by weakening trust in *influence*, professional domination alters the organization of social life by undermining the ties between citizens and the connections between citizens and their leaders.

The aim of this book is to trace the origins and development of the New Public and to diagnose its social consequences in the context of a theory of democratic influence. I will look to the roots of the New Public in the classical liberal public, which I view as a key factor in the emergence of modernity, particularly the rise of modern solidarity. Placing the New Public in these theoretical and historical contexts brings two competing views of the contemporary public arena to the fore. One view, illustrated by Habermas' call for a new ethics of discourse, derides late twentieth-century public life as utterly at odds with the classical ideals of public discussion. The other, more forgiving approach accepts less than fully rational debate as inescapable. Abbreviated discussion is a necessary element in the organization of the systematic influence by which the public will is created. This approach is illustrated by the systems theory of Talcott Parsons. I then propose to bridge Habermasian conceptions of pure *discourse* and Parsonian conceptions of *systematic influence* by arguing that while economies of time and effort do require abridged, token arguments, systems of influence cannot be stable unless citizens can effectively insist on straightforward defense and amplification of token rhetorical claims in two-side public forums. Indeed, the key failure of the New Public as we know it is the lack of such forums. Public leaders employ rhetorical techniques that discourage two-sided dialogue and do what they can to avoid challenges in open forums.

The concerns expressed in this book are not new. They stem from a number of independent but related themes that began to move to the foreground of social and political analysis in the middle of this century. As early as the 1920s, John Dewey, in *The Public and its Problems* (1927, 142), complained that the modern "Great Society" has destroyed the small communities of former times without replacing them with a "Great Community." Hence, the public is in eclipse and will remain so until this larger community is rebuilt through communication of "the signs and symbols without which shared experience is impossible." For Dewey, shared experience is the *sine qua non* of public deliberation, for only the actual cooperative experience of the whole community allows a group to come to self knowledge and self governance. Party machinery, expert bureaucracy, and anonymous social relations do not allow authentic communication, nor can people identify with specific issues outside of their relations within communities. In short, modern society provides no social foundation for public life.

Distress about the specific impact of the professionalization of communication management in American public life emerged in the late 1950s. Stanley Kelley's *Professional Public Relations and Public Power* (1956) sounded an early warning about the growing use of consultants with backgrounds in public relations and advertising to prominent positions in campaign management. In 1956, Kelley could not foresee the extraordinary growth of specialized and variegated forms of political and public relations consulting. At that time, generic public relations and advertising experts were just beginning to turn their attention to new styles of campaign design based on the use of television, but Kelley believed that this trend might well presage a separation of the actual process of government from political life as carried out in manipulated electoral contests.

Early criticism of the New Public was not limited to Americans writing about developments in the United States. Habermas' first major publication, *Structural Transformation of the Public Sphere* (originally published in Germany in 1962) included an interpretation of national elections in the late 1950s in both Germany and the United States. Habermas saw elections in the new mass public as dramatized spectacles designed to stage a (non)public image of consent, spectacles far removed from the authentic public dialogue that the nascent public sphere had produced in eighteenth-century Britain. In contrast, Parsons (1966, 1967) was persistently more optimistic about the capacity of modern societies to meet the challenge of social integration. He argued that the modern public remains at the center of a specialized system of social integration. Organized as a "societal community," modern integrative systems are separate, differentiated institutional spheres comparable to the economy and the political system, but integrated by social influence rather than by money or power. Opinion is organized through *social* processes of association and debate. When aggregated as demands for appropriate social policies, public opinion can provide integrative resources to regulate the conflict and competition that drive political and economic life.

Since 1980, a number of scholars and journalists have examined particular aspects of the New Public in the United States. To cite a few prominent examples, Sabato (1981) and Luntz (1988) have chronicled the rise of political consultants; Blumenthal, in *The Permanent Campaign* (1980) reports that modern techniques of campaigning have come to affect the means of governance; and Ricci (1993) has provided a remarkable account of the impact of new political trends, including the politicization of think tanks, on the proliferation of intensely partisan special interests.

## Social influence and social integration

*Influence and rhetoric.* Arguments about the efficacy of the public turn on the question of whether public discussion is sufficiently independent of other strong forces – most notably power and wealth – to constitute a guiding integrative force in its own right. Accordingly, debates about the integration of democratic society inevitably lead to questions about persuasion, its nature, its role in society, and its relation to the basic distinction between reason and coercion. Democratic theory presumes that questions of public policy should be resolved by mutual persuasion rather than by force. In the good society, free citizens *influence* each other by persuasive argument. This conception of social life affirms *rhetorical* ideals, so differences of opinion as to whether there is an "integrative system" easily become disputes about whether supposedly free and rational discussion is, in fact, polluted by latent coercive forces, disguised by misleading rhetoric. Such arguments are often murky because of the ambiguous theoretical status of rhetoric as the means by which influence is exercised.

"Influence," in this context, refers to affecting the actions of others by means of persuasion. Persuasion may or may not be fully rational, but the term "influence" clearly excludes coercion by threat and inducement by payment; its resources are social. This usage comports with a common dictionary definition of influence as "power to sway based on prestige, ability, wealth, or position."[1] Unfortunately, this standard definition is silent on the matter of argument. Does influence imply presentation of some sort of argument? Yes, for how else can the resources behind its "sway" be conveyed to an audience? Perhaps mere gesture, appearance, uniform, or demeanor are the limiting cases of "argument." They are oblique rhetorical references to arguments that *could* be made. When a physician's white coat and professional manner suggest that expertise is behind the coat and objectivity and trustworthy concern is behind the manner, patients believe that, if necessary, compelling reasons could be advanced for diagnoses and prescriptions. We can speak, then, of the *rhetoric* of white coats as *tokens* of argument. If persuasion does not include argument, however slight, it is hard to see how influence can be distinguished from power or force. Influence invariably employs rhetoric in order to present its aims and to support those aims with reasons, however poor or sketchy. The study of influence is therefore unavoidably tied to concepts of rhetoric.

Influence, in turn, derives its crucial role in sociological theory from the support it provides to processes of social integration. Integration involves resolving conflict, coordinating cooperation, suspending self interest, and promoting cohesion and loyalty. None of these dimensions of order can be achieved by strict adherence to detailed rules established in advance, nor can such rules be fully enforced by even the most strict surveillance and discipline. Even markets, for all their flexible capacity to bring together willing buyers and sellers, require an infrastructure of both facilitating rules and networks of loyalty and trust between long-term trading partners. Sustaining and drawing upon these underlying supports requires the nudges and reminders, displays of good faith, and acts of persuasion that we call *influence*. In daily activity and in the larger affairs of community and state, social life is ordered by a process of addressing people and talking them into accepting and believing and doing. When such talk is a matter of obtaining consent and not a matter of issuing binding commands backed by force, it is called influence.

*Differentiation and integration.* In asking whether public discussion could provide a control center for society, we reenter a conversation inaugurated by Emile Durkheim, whose search for the sources of "organic solidarity" continues to animate contemporary discussion of the public sphere (1933 [1893]). Challenges to integration come in many forms: inequality between classes or status groups produces latent or manifest conflict; cultural differences and intergroup hatred undermine the cohesion of the larger society; failures to coordinate complexity generate confusion and failures of mutual expectations, which include experiences as varied and discouraging as economic failure (e.g. unemployment), bureaucratic frustration, and loss of faith in society's capacity to provide security, guidance, and meaning. Cross cutting these and other integrative problems is the generic challenge of role differentiation – the intense division of labor – which becomes elaborate and intricate in modern societies. How, Durkheim asked, can a society organized around narrowly circumscribed occupational roles achieve solidarity? When society was more homogeneous, its integration could be attributed to likemindedness – common consciousness that guaranteed action in unison and solidarity across the whole group. Arguing that this linkage was like the direct connections between molecules, he called premodern solidarity "mechanical." Solidarity in a modern society requires coordination of differentiated activity, which is more like the integration of functionally differentiated parts of organisms. Hence the notion of "organic solidarity" entered sociological discourse as a term for the special forms of integration that replace the normative unification of traditional society.[2]

Durkheim believed that mutual recognition of interdependence would be as fecund a well-spring of solidarity as recognition of similitude. Organic solidarity should emerge naturally among interdependent contributors to common work, whose intense interaction would reveal their profound dependence on networks of social relations and give rise to a cooperative type of regulative norms. Durkheim eventually set aside his initial concept of organic solidarity (Lukes 1973, 166–7; Pope and Johnson 1983). A theory of role differentiation cannot fully explain integrative problems located in groups and institutions. Analysis of modern society as a system of occupational roles must clearly place these roles within a larger structure of group interests and conflicts stemming from class divisions, cultural diversity, regional differences, and the interests of the state. The many levels of organization between occupation and society cannot be slighted.

The concept of differentiation applies not only to roles but to institutions and to sectors of society comprised of clusters of related institutions. Banking, for example is a differentiated institution within the economy and legislatures are differentiated institutions within the polity. If the economy and the polity are fully differentiated, well-integrated, boundary-maintaining packages of institutions, they can be called *subsystems* of a larger society, and particular functions can be attributed to them. This is the theoretical strategy employed by Parsons' system-theory of society. He applies the theory of differentiation embodied in the notion of the division of labor to the division of functions between subsystems of society.

According to Parsons, specialization allows for emancipation of effort from ascription to subsidiary needs. Differentiation, whether of roles or of institutions or of subsystems, enhances the capacity of societies to perform the varied functions essential to collective life, functions with different imperatives requiring different modes of organization. Ongoing social life involves radically different functions: production and allocation of resources; organizing and controlling power in the interest of achieving collective goals; coordinating the activities of varied groups and individuals with diverse, sometimes conflicting, interests and aims; reproducing culture and socializing the members of society to common values, social motives, and group loyalties. In traditional societies these functions are fused and generally ascribed to kinship. In the process of modernization, new structures break free of the matrix of kin and clan, and the members of society are free to assume specialized roles within institutions adapted to the exigencies of performing specialized functions – market economies and states, for example (Parsons 1961; 1966; Mayhew 1968; Alexander 1990). In Parsons' view, the same logic applies to *integrative* functions. Modern societies include a complex of integrative institutions, comparable to the economy or the polity, which function together as a differentiated integrative system.

The components of a differentiated integrative system include, for example, an independent legal system. Since normative order is one focus of social integration, a complex of specialized institutions devoted to interpreting and applying legal norms in a manner relatively free of political domination, and offering access and protection to a wide range of individuals and interests, can legitimately be regarded as a differentiated system with integrative functions. The work of the legal system is performed through an organized set of occupational roles within or connected to the legal profession, and the system is set apart from the larger system of roles and institutions in society by norms protecting the independence of courts and the legal profession. Institutional constraints, ranging from regulation of professional practice by bar associations, accreditation of law schools, and the status of attorneys as "officers of the court" to appellate review and constitutional law, help to insulate the legal system from direct political control or domination by economic interests, allowing the articulation of a legal process of normative interpretation within a social world of ongoing competition and conflict. The process of advising clients, writing legal documents, trying cases, and engaging in legal inquiry employs legal rhetoric to persuade people to pursue their interests within the flexible framework of a legal order. To the extent that this somewhat idealized picture of the legal system is accurate, it depicts a differentiated institutional sphere, a sector sufficiently insulated to be regarded as independent. According to Parsons, a social system functions more effectively when it has a differentiated legal system, because it is then organized to deal with integrative problems in their own terms, unencumbered by constraining responsibilities for making decisions that will also sustain wealth and power (Parsons 1977a, b).[3]

Not all observers take such an optimistic view of the possibilities of modernity. Critics assert that the notion that integrative institutions are differentiated in the sense that they overcome economic and political forces to create stable social integration is illusory; there are no effective controls on power and money and their destructive effects. Class conflict and the bureaucratic state are not overcome by a normative order, legal or otherwise. Nor is injustice, the ultimate obstacle to true social integration, removed by so-called integrative institutions.

While most observers would concede that the legal systems of many Western democracies enjoy a measure of independence and contribute to social integration, drawing a parallel between legal systems and the organized public is considerably more problematic. Public communication involves many specialized occupations, but the public lacks roles that are professionalized along the lines of law, medicine, or science. Nor does the organization of the public provide an array of tightly organized forums comparable to courts. Although elections are comparable to courts in the sense that they lead to binding decisions, mass electoral processes are diffuse and lack well-regulated forums for public debate. The rise of the New Public has made information-rich, issue-joining debate progressively difficult. The idea that the public is a specialized integrative system is not immediately compelling, but it should not be dismissed out of hand either. Clarification of this critically important issue is a principal concern of this book, for one of the promises of modernity is that a free public can settle divisive issues through mutual persuasion.

*Influence and communicative action.* Habermas is one of the critics who insists that there is no integrative system in the Parsonian sense. Moreover, according to Habermas this is not merely an empirical question: *there can, in principle, be no integrative system.*[4] This is precisely the point at which Habermas joins the issue with "systems-theoretic" approaches to modern society. Influence cannot be conceived as a system of forces. Self-regulating systems tend to equilibrium states, not by the intentions of their participants but by impersonal, systematic forces that exist in the economy in the form of markets and, to some extent, in political systems in the form of balances of power, so we can properly speak of *system integration.* But *social integration* cannot be achieved by self-equilibrating systems, for interpersonal cooperation is a matter of establishing meanings. Satisfying, consensual meaning cannot be produced in so-and-so many meaning units, comparable to units of money or amounts of force; it can only be achieved through communicative action, that is, action oriented to reaching agreement rather than attaining one's own instrumental goals. Habermas insists that Durkheim's organic solidarity, defined as the differentiation of uniform and traditional mechanical solidarity into a complex body of situational understandings, must be accomplished by discussion in ordinary language and not by offers of money or threats of power (Habermas 1987 [1982], 82–92). Since interpersonal influence must work through language, not impersonal sanctions, it cannot comprise a system. This debate about influence provides an indispensable background for understanding the issues presented by the New Public, and further analysis of social influence, its mode of operation, and the question of its systematic character plays a substantial part in this book.

*Culture and argument.* Whether one accepts as legitimate only rational discourse and the force of the better argument or, following Parsons, allows other rhetorical strategies as means of *bona fide* influence, the language of persuasion is deeply embedded in culture. Habermas' high valuation of the life world as the locus of socialization and the reproduction of culture and his corresponding critique of the intrusion of systematic forces into the life world imply that human relations and everyday persuasion are bound up in the fabric of meaning that we call culture. Concepts of persuasion that allow for rhetoric imply even stronger links to culture, for eloquent language is a cultural phenomenon. What counts as persuasive argument depends on culturally defined standards.

Whether persuasion is attributed to reason or to rhetoric, the cultural dimension of the process need not be conceived as fixed. Culture is created and contested. Language and the meanings it conveys have an inherently dynamic structure that moves according to terms implicit in its own logic, a logic decipherable by what Kenneth Burke (1961) calls "logology." Associations tie words together in chains of implication, including connections implied by the logic of opposition. When opponents contest meanings, the logic of binary opposition suggests arguments and counter arguments which can then cohere into ideologies. Language, like other tools, can shape the user, channeling creative efforts into well-worn modes of argument, even when expressing novel ideas. Recognizing the cultural aspects of influence does not commit us to viewing culture as a mechanism of stabilizing control. On the contrary, it is the innovative capacity of culture that makes influence a flexible means of swaying others, bringing them to new views within a framework of mutual intelligibility.

### Information: rational discourse and tokens

Because rhetoric depends on cultural symbols, rhetorical statements cannot be conclusively demonstrated. Their assertions express values and meanings that cannot be reduced to simple propositions. The meaning, for example, of a campaign promise is so contingent on unknowable future circumstances, unstated priorities, and contestable criteria as to resist definitive judgments as to whether it has been fulfilled. Accordingly when I speak of demands to "redeem" rhetorical statements, I do not refer to demonstrating their truth. To redeem a rhetorical claim is to respond to demands for clarification, specification, and evidence to the satisfaction of an audience that shares many of the speaker's values and presuppositions and relies on these common meanings to fill in the blanks.

Advocates of authentic civic discourse contend that public persuasion should be rational and redeemable, its outcomes governed only by the force of the better argument. Participation should be free and full, and full involvement in discourse implies that all assertions are subject to question and must be defended on demand by means of additional argument. By contrast, persuasion in the New Public offers brief bits of symbolic information and persuaders avoid answering questions both by making vague or indirect assertions that do not lend themselves to discussion and by speaking within structured situations that do not allow for challenges.

We might well ask why parties to civic discussion are willing to accept terms that do not allow them to participate on a rational basis. One answer would attack the utilitarian premises of the question, arguing that the participants are not free and rational to begin with. They are repressed by the power of persuaders and of the hierarchies that they represent. If this is the answer, then the process cannot properly be referred to as persuasive, for it employs power rather than influence. But there is another answer to the question of why people accept less than full participation and instead acquiesce to incomplete information, explanation, and argument. *There is not enough time*. Full discourse in which everything is always subject to question is impossible, for even in highly motivated groups time is not limitless; deadlines are imposed by the situation, and the participants have other things to do. The limits are yet more restrictive in groups whose members have plural interests and variable commitments to the matters at hand.

Since the pioneering work of Simon (1961 [1947]), Downs (1957), and Stigler (1961), economists have recognized that the limits of time and other costs create an *economics of information*. Rational actors accept informational shortcuts in order to *economize* their resources – to save time and money according to their priorities. Accordingly, people accept "bounded rationality" rather than insisting on perfect rationality. They seek informational shortcuts that offer low-cost approximations of what they would discover if they spent more time and effort searching for certain answers. Bounded rationality encourages rhetoric, makes people accept influence rather than investigate everything for themselves, and, establishes fertile ground for the weak discourse of the New Public. But does the public have limitless tolerance for hollow, unchallengeable claims?

I conceive rhetoric as relying on trust. Audiences are asked to accept abbreviated arguments, *tokens* of more ample arguments that could supposedly be supplied were time and opportunity available. Because of the limits of bounded rationality, people accept rhetorical tokens, but their trust is not limitless. Hyperinflated rhetoric leads to influence no longer backed by discernible realities and hence without a basis for sustaining trust. The safety valves that can protect the viability of civic discourse are public forums wherein civic leaders are asked to make good on their claims and promises. From a sociological standpoint, the public sphere does not depend on the unrealistic notion that rhetoric can be banished in favor of fully rational discourse on all issues at all times, but on the institutionalization of forums for the redemption of rhetorical tokens.

### Modern solidarity and *Gemeinschaft*

Twentieth-century views of the integration of modern society are deeply embedded in Toennies' contrast of *Gemeinschaft* and *Gesellschaft.* Toennies asserted that *Gemeinschaft* (or community) is founded on "natural" will and modern *Gesellschaft* (or society) on "artificial" will; the former creates social solidarity based on fellow feeling while the latter connects people by ties based on calculation of interests. Modern social trends expand society at the expense of community; industrialization, urbanization, and capitalist economy entail high levels of geographic mobility, weakening of kinship and local community, the growth of bureaucracy, and the unleashing of both self interest and *raison d'état.* For all Toennies' insistence that *Gemeinschaft* and *Gesellschaft* were not intended as value-laden terms, the rhetorical implications of his analysis are unmistakable. Modern societies are artificial and unnatural; they destroy community and create aggregations of people who are mere means to each other, not persons whose human association is valued in its own right. Social integration is fragile in a society that lacks an underlying community to provide loyalty, trust, credibility, reciprocity, and disinterested support for fair play.

The notion of breakdown of *Gemeinschaft* presents a historical image of modern social forces destroying traditional, stabilizing connections between people – villages, manors, parishes, extended family groups – and leaving nothing in their place but the cash nexus, bureaucratic domination, and individual, privatized lives. Little thought is given to the possibility that new institutions of solidarity emerge from the old, and behind this failure of imagination is an unstated assumption that solidary ties cannot be freely *chosen* but must be defined and fixed by an established order. The assumption that solidarity is necessarily grounded in fixed ties and obligations is a denial of modernity, a failure to consider the associational model of solidarity that has informed modern ideas of community from the Protestant reformation, through Locke and the enlightenment, to twentieth-century sociological critiques of the theory of mass society. Modern challenges to traditional solidarities are so pervasive and obvious that it is all too tempting to define the consequences of modernization as the destruction of community rather than to exercise the sociological imagination to construct a vision of the new forms of solidarity that replace the old.

Several branches of the sociological tradition have sought to salvage a modern concept of the social. Durkheim's concept of organic solidarity was directed to precisely this end. He insisted (*contra* Toennies) that modern society is no less social than traditional community. Its solidarity rests on interdependence rather than uniformity, and its self-interested contracts are integrated by a fabric of stabilizing normative institutions. Another approach looks to solidary ties within large-scale impersonal organizations and aggregations: the informal organization that make bureaucracy work; the personal loyalties that make it cohesive; or, in the public, the face-to-face interactions in which remote, faceless messages are interpreted and assessed; and to the networks that people use to mobilize others to engage in collective action. Yet another strand sees voluntary organizations as new substitutes for the traditional organizations that formerly provided cohesion to society, staking the effectiveness of democratic polity on a healthy associational life that anchors the solidarity of independent citizens with varied opinions and interests. Yet none of these concepts of modern cohesion comes fully to grips with the distinctive character of the social relations that replace *Gemeinschaft* in post-traditional society. They fail to illuminate solidarity as such, a term that usually connotes the ties that bind – memberships that connect people together in common league.

In this book I take the position that there is a modern form of solidarity that partially replaces the strong ties of kin, clan, local community, and traditionally defined deference hierarchies. Modern differentiated solidarity consists in processes of communication. A massive flow of person-to-person and group-to-group communication, both spoken face to face and transmitted through a wide variety of media, connects people to each other. People use these connections and the influence that they create to forge substantive agreements, to seek and give advice, and to establish working rules. In formalized settings, they are used to create laws and binding political decisions. Communication embeds interest-motivated, instrumental, economic relations in a setting of trust; if communication fails to establish sufficient trust, people break off old ties and seek to establish new socially grounded connections.

*Liberalism.* Following Parsons' term for describing separate, emancipated spheres of life, I refer to the emergence of new associational solidarities as the "*differentiation* of solidarity" (Mayhew 1990). Freedom of association and genuinely social solidarity can co-exist and support each other, but to understand this connection requires rethinking the ideology of liberalism, which played a crucial role in establishing the legitimacy of emancipated solidarity and in driving the process of modernization.

"Liberalism" is a protean term. Commentators speak of economic and social liberalism, contrast classical and modern liberalism, and refer generically to the modern capitalist state as liberal. Various ideologies are designated "rights," or "interest-group" or "welfare-state" liberalism. The term is sometimes used to label philosophical or political positions as strictly individualistic, as defenses of individual rights against all communal constraints, a position implied in Macpherson's (1962) grouping of classic liberals, including John Locke, under the rubric of "possessive individualism." I reject this usage. It is, I think, tainted by Toennies' false dichotomy between community and society and is, moreover, not consistent with the first premises of liberal philosophy as set forth in the writings of Puritan Protestants, Enlightened philosophers, and even some nineteenth-century economic liberals.

Liberalism is not antagonistic to community. Properly understood, liberal philosophy proclaims freedom to create community, not freedom from social constraints. Classic liberalism asserts the dignity and worth of the person and objects to *arbitrary* constraints on individuals. Such social constraints as are necessary must be established by a political community founded on the principle that human dignity demands self-governance, and that the deliberations of governance must allow for participation of all citizens, lest the worth of any individual be denied. Self-governing communities are valued, not denigrated as mere necessary evils. This understanding of liberalism will help us to grasp the force of liberal ideology in stimulating the differentiation of associational solidarity and the rise of the public.

### A preview

This first, introductory chapter has presented brief previews of the principal themes and premises of my approach to public life. Chapter 2 proceeds to ground my argument on the premise that rhetoric is the inescapable medium of public discussion. Although the persuasive sway of rhetoric pervades human communication and is deeply embedded in social organization, its theoretical status in sociology is ambiguous. It straddles the line between reason and coercion. Preliminary discussion of Talcott Parsons, Kenneth Burke, and Jürgen Habermas leads to the conclusion that although rhetoric can be institutionalized in relatively reasonable forums of discussion, there are limitations in the use of reason in rhetorical communication. Effective persuasion relies on appeals to social norms, on ties of solidarity, and on the cultural strength of eloquence. The development of the New Public has been largely driven by the instrumental rationalization of eloquence, so that messages are not left entirely to intuition and creativity, but carefully managed by techniques perfected through market research.

Chapter 3 moves from rhetoric as the means of persuasion to influence as *generalized* capacity to persuade. Parsons, true to his proclivity for normative and functional explanations, accounts for the generalization of persuasion by reference to the credibility of people who are accorded high status in systems of stratification. His approach leaves a murky and ambiguous role for rational argument and solidarity in the production of influence. I therefore suggest that the influence paradigm should stress the importance of affiliation and appeals to identification with groups.

Chapter 4 presents Habermas' critique of Parsons' theory of influence as well as counter arguments that might be employed in defense of Parsons' concepts. Habermas argues that influence must be based on authentic discourse, not on mere status or credibility. There can be no *system* for reaching interpersonal understanding or for steering opinion by means of impersonal, equilibrating mechanisms. Although it is possible to state important and useful arguments in Parsons' defense, Habermas does present a valid critical point: it is ultimately necessary to attach influence to persuasive reasons. This point is, in effect, a powerful warning against accepting the existence of influence systems as a guarantee that the forces unleashed by the New Public can be constrained by equilibrating processes.

Chapter 5 seeks to bridge the gap between Habermas' discourse theory and Parsons' systems theory by presenting a new paradigm for public influence. I suggest that the exercise of influence depends upon "warrants" comparable to the warrants of sincerity that Habermas attributes to participants in discourse. Effective influence requires those who aspire to possess influence to warrant their sincere intention to advance their common interests with the audience – their mutual solidarity. *Prolocutors* who gain the right to speak on behalf of solidary groups are able to warrant their solidarity and to establish their influence. Influence created in this way depends on two kinds of backing, *relational* backing, guaranteed by the validity of the *discourse* between persuaders and their audiences, and *system* backing, guaranteed by the strength of the underlying *solidary ties* on which the system of influence rests. This conception of influence leads to a reassessment of the systematic properties and independence of civil society within a modern social order and underscores the vulnerability of civil society to the instrumental rationalization of persuasion in the New Public. New practices undermine confidence in warrants of solidarity and bypass the grounding of society in its constituent groups. Without grounding, influence becomes inflated and integrative systems unstable.

The New Public is an extension of the modern public. In many ways the New Public retains the heritage of its roots in modernity, but in some respects, the rationalization of persuasive techniques challenges the cultural premises of modern solidarity. In chapter 6, the rise of the modern public, called here the "differentiation of rhetorical solidarity," is traced to its origins in sectarian Protestant thought and in the Republican ideal of civic virtue. The early history of modern solidarity and its legitimation by liberal ideas provides a backdrop for understanding the problematic consequences of the rationalization of persuasion in the New Public.

Chapter 7 traces the emergence of the New Public from its roots in the rationalization of public communication in the commercial sector. Advertising, market research, and public relations came to be organized around two principles with strong rationalizing force: *systematically planned campaigns* organize persuasive efforts around defined goals and strategies, and *systematic research* allows better prediction of how the public will respond to campaign messages.

Chapter 8 continues the narrative of the growth of the New Public by describing the export of techniques of rationalized persuasion to the political sector. The rationalizing force of systematic campaigns, now extended to elections, "grassroots" lobbying, and politicized policy analysis, has intensified the representation of plural interests into a new form of *hyperpluralism*, that excludes ordinary citizens from public debate and inflates influence by separating electoral politics from governance.

Chapter 9 returns to the problem of forums for the redemption of inflated influence – the point at which Parsons' concept of influence systems must be articulated with Habermas' insistence on the validation of claims through discourse. The institutions of the New Public are inflationary, yet few effective forums exist. The mass media do not provide for effective public discourse, nor do advocates and builders of civic dialogue, who work primarily at community and organizational sites, successfully attend to the aggregation of local dialogue in larger arenas. In this context, I discuss the possibility of establishing a national civic forum.

In the concluding chapter, I ask whether postmodern thought renders the influence paradigm obsolete. The rhetoric of the New Public is the rhetoric of presentation, a self-contained mode of argument which relies on employing just the right images or just the right words in a manner that thwarts critical analysis and places rhetorical tokens beyond redemption. This line of analysis runs parallel to the contentions of critics who assert that in the world of postmodern communication, messages are no longer referential and are therefore immune to critique. I argue that the hyperbolic claims of postmodern criticism are misleading, for the communication involved in cooperative activity continues to refer to objects and events in the world. Finally, some of the premises of postmodern thought are consistent with the paradigm of willed solidarity, for they call attention to new escapes from traditional ideologies and point to the possibility of inaugurating new solidarities and assembling new selves in the pursuit of novel forms of flexible, associational community.

# 2

## Rhetoric and reason

Public influence is delivered through rhetoric, which Aristotle defined as the available means of persuasion. Rhetorical persuasion is not entirely reasonable. In the Aristotelian formulation, rhetoric includes logical argument, but it also allows, as available means, appeals to the character of the speaker and the emotions of the audience. Rational discourse gains a foothold in public life only to the extent that society includes *specialized* public forums for mutual persuasion that require participants to engage in sincere, two-sided exchanges and to accept good arguments as grounds for decision. Such forums are rare in the New Public. Because of the crucial role of rhetoric in public influence, I introduce the study of influence in the New Public by reviewing the protean appeals of rhetorical practice.

### Rhetoric and the social order

In discourse about the good society, myths of origin are rhetorical terms for social cohesion. They represent, in rhetorical form, ideas about universal and ever present sources of social solidarity. For example, the myth of the great lawgiver, whether human or divine, asserts the enduring importance of normative rules in producing social order. The rhetorical force of such metaphors derives from the narrative appeal of what Derrida has called "the metaphysics of presence" – the notion in Western thought that our current experience both derives from and disguises the original events that, in all their foundational purity, lie behind the present moment (Derrida 1976 [1967]).

Social contract theories are myths of reason. They assert that the underlying grounds of society are the mutual obligations that rational people take upon themselves in return for the benefits of orderly self protection, social peace, and the achievement of collective purposes. The method of contract theory is to deduce the individual's rights and obligations from rational calculations of the costs and benefits of various social constraints. Individual rights are claims that no rational person would have been willing to barter away for the sake of forming society. At the opposite pole, myths of irrationality attribute the original social bonds to deep psychological forces, as in the case of Freud's story of a band of brothers joining to kill the father and thus held together in perpetuity by their common guilt. Even now, deep, unconscious psychic forces are the source of social bonds.

The myth of conquest, which refers metaphorically to the place of force in human society, has often been used as a critical rhetorical term. Society originated in conquest but must now be reconstructed on a rational basis. Herbert Spencer's account of social evolution from "military" to "industrial" society, together with similar conflict theories set forth in the nineteenth century by Bagehot, Gumplowicz, and Ratzenhofer are variants of the myth of original conquest. The rhetorical leverage of this general line of thought remains alive today in critical claims that force yet lurks behind all that had its origins in coercion. Again, a variant of the metaphysics of presence infiltrates rhetorical interpretations of social experience, giving primacy to a moment of origin and subordinating mere present appearance. Setting aside ongoing life in favor of unmasking sinister, contaminating origins remains an important theme in critical analysis. Though critical theory itself employs rhetorical methods, it tends to a cynical view of rhetorical modes of mutual influence, taking elements of unreason or coercion as defining the character of every social transaction and vitiating claims that social order is founded on consent.

Where in this array of primitive terms – norms, reason and unreason, force – does rhetoric fit? Rhetoric has its own myth of the origin of society. Cicero, writing in the first century BCE., and extolling the value of oratory to his fellow Roman citizens whose lives were steeped in public speech, asked this rhetorical question: "What is so admirable as that out of an infinite multitude of men, there should arise a single individual who can alone, or with only a few others, exert effectually that power which nature has granted to all?" Cicero goes on to claim that no other power could have assembled humankind, brought them to a civilized state of society, and established civil order and civil rights (Cicero 1970, 13–14).

Aristotle's classic definition of rhetoric as "an ability, in each particular case, to see the available means of persuasion" (Aristotle 1991, 36) has dominated conceptions of rhetorical study throughout the history of the subject, and "rhetoric," in the sense of what rhetoricians study, is defined as persuasive communication. Yet ever since Plato claimed that rhetoric is only a knack of making the worse appear the better cause – a form of "cookery" – rhetorical theories of social order have been under attack and the relation of persuasion to reason has been at best ambiguous.[1]

Whatever its relation to *rational* persuasion, rhetoric cannot be viewed as ineffectual; it is not realistic to treat it as the window-dressing of social life – as "mere rhetoric," to quote a common turn of speech. Persuasion is an ubiquitous feature of human conduct and a deeply rooted element of social organization. Accounts of society that locate persuasion in the very concept of social action have the best chance of capturing the role of the rhetorical in social conflict and social order, whether such accounts explicitly employ the term "rhetoric" or not. We will look, therefore, to three potentially illuminating approaches to the phenomena of rhetoric and persuasion, those of Talcott Parsons, Kenneth Burke, and Jürgen Habermas, viewing their contributions against a backdrop of traditional rhetorical theory as it grapples with the issue of reason and force.

### The matrix of the rhetorical tradition

Two dichotomies have dominated discussion of rhetoric since the classical age: (1) rhetoric is distinguished from logic or dialectic, that is *rational* modes of discussion, and (2) rhetoric is distinguished from *coercion*. Since Plato, rhetoric and rational discussion have been contrasted in order to denigrate rhetoric as manipulating, for personal benefit, the world of mere appearance – or mere words. To contrast rhetoric and coercion is usually to praise rhetoric, asserting that verbal persuasion is more social and certainly more civilized than violence. But skeptics doubt the sincerity of people's verbal commitments to the force of words rather than the force of violence, asking whether in avoiding direct force we merely accept fraud, another form of coercion, in its stead. These dichotomies form the matrix of attack and defense from which traditional rhetorical theory springs, and to this day discussion of rhetoric plays variations on these themes.

In traditional theory, rhetoric is defended as inescapably necessary. Reason can produce conviction but not persuade to action. The strength of rhetoric is required to change attitudes, compel attention, impress memory, and induce conduct. The value of this approach is its placement of rhetoric *outside* the realm of the cognitive capacities of mind and *in* the world of action, so that it bears directly on the study of society. Still, the defense of necessity is not altogether persuasive to those who would prefer to construct a positive defense that rhetoric is good in its own right. How then can rhetoric – persuasion by means not limited to strictly rational argument – be good? What is good rhetoric?

Plato, a forceful enemy of utilitarian rhetoric in *Gorgias*, describes good rhetoric in *Phaedrus* as true words inscribed in the hearer in the spirit of love, a theme followed for centuries by defenders of the rhetorical enterprise. Rhetoric is good when practiced by people of character who speak truth and pursue right ends. It is also good when the audience is sincerely addressed, and its persuasive power draws on the needs of those to whom messages are directed. This theme is in a direct line of descent from Plato's notion of love for the pupil. There is an ancient and continuing association of rhetoric and solidarity in the idea that ethical rhetoric brings people together.

Critics of the ethical theory of rhetoric argue that rhetoric cannot be defended by positing a normative quality that is not relevant to influence as it is actually exercised. The ethical conception affirms what good rhetoric would be if there was such a thing, but fails to make any sociologically interesting empirical observations about the real world of persuasion. In that real world, persuaders often achieve their self-interested ends by lying, misleading, concealing, and all manner of trickery. There is, however, an empirical assertion embedded in ethical theories of rhetoric which claim, implicitly or explicitly, that ethical persuasion is more effective than manipulation. In assessing the impact of the audience on messages and their acceptance, one can look to the vulnerability of the audience – ignorance or powerlessness – or to their values and their needs. When values and needs enter the foreground of the observer's field of view, the role of norms and of social solidarity become paramount in explaining successful rhetoric.

Other defenses of rhetoric emphasize the value of eloquence in its own right. Advocates of eloquence often treat tropic language, especially metaphor, as the defining characteristic of rhetoric. Metaphor is said to be a particularly human device. The literal language of science has its uses, but metaphor is the device by which humans grasp relationships and connections and make them understandable (Grassi 1976, 1980). Eloquence furnishes a link between culture and social participation. The rhetorical use of language allows speakers to be effective. It allows individuals to achieve personal identity and groups to achieve collective identity by learning and using the cultural tools of discourse. Rhetoric links shared culture with the terms of participation in public discussion.

Aristotle inaugurated another line of rapprochement between rhetoric and reason by defining the domain of rhetoric as the merely probable (Aristotle 1991, 42–5). Argumentation in daily affairs does not involve matters subject to strict deductive proof or thorough inductive study. This theoretical move allows the construction of modes of rhetoric to be conceived as methods of practical reason, an attractive option for twentieth-century philosophers and rhetoricians attuned to problems of argument and communication in the face of uncertainty, misunderstanding, and normative conflict (Richards 1936; Toulmin 1958; Perelman and Olbrechts-Tyteca 1969 [1958]; Perelman 1982 [1977]). A reasonable rhetorical framework provides tools for clarifying the grounds of argument and strategies for honest but effective persuasion. Rhetoric is indispensable for the pursuit of collective ends in a world not amenable to the application of pure logic, and a proper rhetoric would discipline arguments about opinion. These advocates continue to appeal to notions of how practical argument *ought* to be pursued.

### Rhetoric and social action: three views of persuasion

The matrix of rhetorical theory is not so "traditional" as to be obsolete, despite postmodern critiques that attack the dichotomies that have long defined rhetoric. Deconstructionist thought, looking to the metaphorical character of language, holds that the distinction between rhetoric and logic is invalid because all communication is rhetorical. Other theorists deny the distinction between rhetoric and force because all persuasion is based on force. Foucault, looking genealogically at the development of Western rationality, holds that the distinction between reason and force is illusory because reason itself has become a mode of systematic domination. Taken together, these views collapse the principal polarities that have animated discussions of rhetoric for centuries, but not necessarily in a manner productive for rhetorical analysis. "Rhetoric" becomes so universal a term as not to apply to anything in particular. If reason and coercion are one (and all), "rhetoric" has no independent significance. Nevertheless, even if the foregoing radical critique were granted, I argue that one remaining concept has prospects for illuminating the independent and irreducible functions of rhetorical communication: *rhetoric is the discourse of solidarity.*

Concepts of solidarity play a major part in the influential writings of Talcott Parsons, Jürgen Habermas, and Kenneth Burke, whose social theories bear directly on problems of rhetoric. Of the three, only Burke, a social and literary critic rather than a sociologist, explicitly places rhetoric at the center of his project, but his account of persuasion is profoundly sociological.[2] Ironically, Parsons and Habermas, who start from a sociological standpoint, seldom speak of rhetoric as such, but issues of persuasion are central to their interpretation of contemporary society, and the problem of rhetoric necessarily enters their thought through sundry back doors.

The concerns of traditional rhetorical inquiry are manifest in the theories of all of our three exemplars. Parsons emphasized the crucial importance of social norms in the acceptance of rhetorical messages and ultimately came to see persuasion as a central component of the social order. Burke's rhetoric centers on the dynamics of language and social solidarity as inescapable elements of persuasion, elements that ensure that communication will take rhetorical forms, for better or worse. Habermas, fearful of rhetoric as less than completely reasonable, nevertheless follows the rhetorical tradition in seeking to establish norms to define good communication: it would be unconstrained and, by testing all perspectives, would effectively create true solidarity.

*Talcott Parsons: rhetoric and the normative order.* Analysis of Parsonian theory will be prominent in later chapters, where discussion will turn to Parsons' treatment of the role of influence, a species of persuasion, in the integrative systems of modern societies. A preview is in order because, as we will later see, crucial ambiguities in his treatment of the concept of influence can be traced to earlier stances that he assumed as his basic position took shape in *The Structure of Social Action* (1937).

Parsons began with a basic paradigm of human action to use as a framework for analysis of the problem of order in society. He conceived action as employing *means* to achieve *ends* in the face of *conditions*. In the most minimal form of action theory, the utilitarian version, *norms* enter solely as criteria for the selection of means, and the sole norm is rational efficiency. According to Parsons, there are two categories of available means in social relations: reason and coercion. If rational efficiency is the only criterion for choice of means, there can be no guarantee that actors governed by the norm of efficient reason will select persuasion as a means when unregulated coercion would be more effective. Hence, pure utilitarian theory confronted a serious problem in explaining order, and Parsons proceeded to trace the consequent breakdown of nineteenth-century social theory and its replacement with sociological theories that gave normative order a more prominent position, allowing values and norms to regulate means and to structure human ends, too. Norms became an essential third category of grounds of potential order, beyond reason and coercion, which cannot by themselves produce an integrated society. This terse, capsule summary hardly does justice to the elaborate arguments that Parsons put forward, but it allows us to ask, Where, exactly, does persuasion fit into this basic scheme of categories? In the utilitarian scheme, it falls within the category of reason, but where does it fit when ethical norms enter the picture?[3] At the very least an additional dimension of persuasion has been added, for persons can be influenced either by providing rational grounds *or* by invoking norms.

One might respond that the role of persuasion is *not* ambiguous in the

Parsonian action frame of reference. The scheme is *analytical*; it is not intended to classify concrete acts of persuasion, but to identify theoretically relevant dimensions of social action. Persuasion (and its rhetorical means) is an empirical category, and individual acts of persuasion involve rational, coercive, and normative elements in varying forms and proportions. Indeed, for Parsons the normative element is always present. At one point he even states that "purely voluntary agreement is the limiting case" (1937, 660–1). Normative constraint is so deeply ingrained in the actor, and commitments to moral legitimacy and institutional frameworks are so strong, that norms must be considered constitutive of human personality and hence an indelible component of motivation to agree and conform.

One might ask whether all the analytical dimensions of the process of securing agreement were included in Parsons' early scheme of analysis, or if key aspects of persuasion were missing. I contend that affiliation – finding gratification in solidary association with other people – is a primary category of social relations. Parsons omitted emotional bonding, a category he later introduced as interpersonal "cathexis." Parsons may have ignored the endemic pervasiveness of motivation to affiliate to avoid begging the question of order. If so, this move was unnecessary, for interpersonal ties cannot be posited as a simple explanation of order in society. Bonding is as disruptive as it is integrative. For any two people to bond together is to exclude others from that special relationship, and the manifold patterns of interpersonal attraction within a group are as much a source of its division as its solidarity. Parsons need only have affirmed that affiliation, like economic interests or coercive sanctions, must be normatively constituted and regulated. Nor would it make sense to insist that reason and coercion are "primitive" terms referring to pre-social attributes and to argue *a priori* that seeking affiliation is a derivative product of social life, merely one of many ends that actors might seek. Only Parsons' preoccupation with the challenge of utilitarian economics, and his determination to advance a normative solution to the problem of order can explain his neglect of affiliation as an independent dimension of analysis by reducing solidarity to the force of normative rules.

The need for solidarity, as well as the search for it, provides a set of resources for persuasion. Just as rhetoric can appeal to reason, or suggest force lurking in the background, or invoke norms, so also can it invoke solidary ties. Indeed, I will argue that the affiliative basis of rhetorical communication constitutes its primary mode of persuasion and that Parsons began to recognize this in his later analysis of the role of influence in modern society. I dwell on this point at some length to ground my contention that Parsons' suppression of affiliation in his initial scheme, and his subsequent virtual reduction of affiliation to a normative definition, had long-term consequences that are apparent in ambiguity, confusion, and missteps in his later writings about *influence*.

The germ of Parsons' thought about the concept of influence is found in his interpretation of Durkheim's emphasis on moral authority. Moral authority evokes respect, and it is this strong emotion that establishes solidarity between the individual and society (1937, 428–9). In consequence of respect for society, its members are able to exercise moral authority over each other. In this line of argument, the suasion of moral authority can be seen as a species of influence backed by solidarity, and I suggest that Parsons saw this concept a starting place for his later analysis of influence and its role in the integration of social systems. He remained, however, profoundly wedded to normative interpretations of social phenomena, and the great weight he accorded to values and norms is apparent in the link between his later accounts of influence and his theory of stratification (Parsons 1954b).

Parsons' linkage of rhetoric and stratification follows a chain of connections bound together by the idea of prestige within a moral order. People who command respect have prestige, and prestige in turn is bestowed upon actors by society according to their status in the social order. Social status reflects the value that society places on the contributions of various social roles to the larger collective enterprise, and the process of valuation is governed by the society's value system. Or, taking the argument in reverse direction, values determine social status, status confers prestige, prestige implies respect, and respect is a resource for influence. By this account, the entire system of stratification can be regarded as a moral order within which exemplars of social values contribute to social integration by influencing others to conform to social norms, and, more generally, to adjust their conduct to society's integrative needs.

The idea that society is integrated by the persuasive sway of prestige and status has some merit, particularly in traditional, caste-like societies, in which each person is born into a ranked status group, each group is governed by status obligations and rules for kinship and marriage, occupation, property rights, authority, and daily life. This entire complex of membership and obligation is legitimized by a value system founded upon a generally accepted account of its origin and place within the cosmic order. Even in modern societies, prestige enhances persuasion, but the linkage between status and influence is attenuated when social status is more fluid. Citizens are free to accept or reject the contested authority of unofficial statuses, and a new question comes to the fore: how are people able to translate status into influence? In any event, Parsons' account of integration through the prestige of valued status clearly assimilates influence to a normative base.

Parsons' predilection for normative explanation, as manifest in what he called his "analytical theory of stratification" and in his linking of status to social influence, created analytical problems to the end. His mature theory of influence never fully clarified the respective roles of good argument and status in persuasion. This is far from a trivial problem of semantics, for Parsons ultimately came to see the value of treating the exercise of influence as an independent dimension of social integration, one that is particularly useful in the study of modern societies, but he was unable to exploit his insights for he could not entirely loosen the constraints imposed by his earlier system of categories.

In the rhetorical domain, the categories of Parsonian action theory – norms, reason, and coercion – are difficult to separate, and Parsons initially let solidarity remain in the background, assumed but not analyzed. Yet caste-backed rhetoric is fundamentally *about* solidarity. Whatever appeals are made to norms, this rhetoric is ultimately about whether the target of persuasion will become *outcast*. "Follow the ways of the caste" means "stay with us." Rhetorical messages ring changes on this theme: Join us. Follow me. Support us. Do not let us down. Is this pressure appropriately called an exercise of coercion, or of reason, or of normative constraint?

These problems are yet more perplexing in the modern context. The Enlightenment's modern ideals for public debate deplored the legitimation of inequality and privilege by implausible cosmic theories. "Superstitions," in the terminology of Enlightened thought, violate the cultural standards of Western rationality. Parsons implicitly recognized this problem in his original statement of the opposition of reason and coercion. He subdivided coercion into two primitive categories: force and *fraud*. The charge of fraud – trickery to make the worse appear the better – has been the principal count against rhetoric since it first came into the arena of philosophical discussion. Fraud, for Parsons, refers to ignorance on the part of one party to a transaction (Parsons 1937, 240). To attack ignorance was the basic program of the Enlightenment. Within this tradition and its modern offshoots, discussion and persuasion are not rational if they merely apply accepted norms and are not themselves subject to discussion. Rational discourse must involve a moment of critical reflection. Persuasion that suppresses reflection on the taken-for-granted social world is coercion, not persuasion.

The process of appealing for affiliation and support and responding to such appeals may, in premodern societies, follow lines of stratification and fix the links between social status and patterns of affiliation, but when new rhetorical cultures become differentiated, appeals can be based on solidary ties not given in systems of stratification and subject to rational appraisal. In modern societies, the independent significance of rhetorically created solidarity comes to the foreground; it is no longer possible to conceive rhetoric as appeals to norms and statuses without regard to substantive argument. Parsons recognized this problem and proposed a theory of modern influence that attempted to save stratification as the backing for persuasion, even in modern societies, but as we shall see in the next chapter, his sketchy analyses of the sources of social influence remained confused by his continuing insistence that status and prestige lie at the heart of persuasive influence. There is a normative dimension in the background of rhetorical appeals, but it is necessary to adopt a multidimensional approach that adequately recognizes the decisive role of open systems of social solidarity, systems whose participants persuade each other to unite by arguments backed by reasons beyond the normative authority of their status.

*Kenneth Burke: rhetoric, language, and solidarity.* Burke never loses sight of the symbolic nature of rhetorical discourse, the complexity of human symbols, or the solidarity to which symbols refer. In his "dramatistic" approach to human conduct, rhetoric is at the center from the outset, inextricably enmeshed in language and social action. *"Rhetoric . . . is rooted in an essential function of language itself, a function that is wholly realistic, and is continually born anew: the use of language as a symbolic means of inducing cooperation in beings that by nature respond to symbols"* (Burke 1950, 43; emphasis in original). Rhetoric in use is not, however, necessarily integrative and cooperative. It "deals with the possibilities of classification in its *partisan* aspects; it considers the ways in which individuals are at odds with one another or become identified with groups more or less at odds with one another" (22), and partisan rhetoric includes malice and lies and deliberate cunning (45). Moreover, while emphasizing that rhetoric does bring people together on common grounds, Burke also states that the realism of rhetoric is problematic. It is realistic for speakers to call upon the mutual identifications of people with each other in order to exhort them to cooperative action, but "the resources of identification whereby consubstantiation [recognition of common properties] is established between beings of unequal status may extend far into the realm of the idealistic" (46). It is from such idealism that magic and mystery come to engulf human relations. When unequals are conjoined by consubstantiation despite their relative lack of common identities, a dialectic of conflict and compromise ensues. Since humans tend not to accept a continuing dialectical jangle of interests, we seek instead some principle behind diversity, a mystical communal order and a corresponding set of mysterious terms for order, which become a vocabulary for rhetoric. There is rhetorical advantage in these "ultimate terms," for they embody magical unifiers for hierarchical orders.

We are back on familiar ground. Reason, coercion, and solidarity appear again as fundamental to the problematics of rhetoric. Rhetoric serves to unite (and also to divide by uniting *against*), but social status lurks in the background. Since Burke calls some rhetoric fraudulent, he apparently holds out a standard of reason against which rhetoric can be judged. Rhetoric between equals is, if not entirely rational, at least realistic, for it creates real solidarities as a basis for cooperation, but rhetoric between unequals drifts in magical directions. The distinction between coercion and reason is relative, a matter of the situational weight of different aspects of the larger category of rhetorical, symbolic action. Appeals to social order can be accepted on the basis of "faith to the extent that one accepts a given command, proscription, or statement as authoritative; reason to the extent that one's acceptance is contingent upon such proofs as are established by a method of weighting of doubts and rebuttals" (450).

Burke's analysis of rhetoric reveals an important aspect of rhetoric that did not emerge in the foregoing analysis of the Parsonian paradigm: Burke placed the rhetorical process directly in language as such. It is not just that language is used rhetorically; it is inherently rhetorical – intrinsically hortatory and oriented to action. He starts from the premise that "language is primarily a species of action . . . rather than an instrument of definition" (1968, 447) and that language is therefore always freighted with persuasive implications and motives. Secondary accounts of Burke's rhetoric sometimes fail to convey the subtlety of his linguistic approach. In the standard account, Burke is made to say that humans influence each other by calling attention to things they have in common and that this makes them identify with each other. The resulting "consubstantiation" or participation in common identities creates a solidarity that can be invoked to induce cooperation. Burke's thought does include these ideas, but he says more and he says it in ways that evoke the rich complexity of language in action. His core notions of identification and consubstantiation posit ever present, fluid processes of rhetorical connection between words and between actors. For example, his analysis exploits the ambiguity between identification *of* and identification *with*. "This is an excellent refrigerator" identifies an item. "This is *my* excellent refrigerator" identifies me with my refrigerator and allows me to participate in its excellence.

From simply identifying to identifying *with* is a large logical leap but a small psychological step, and just by using language we regularly move back and forth between merely identifying objects and connecting to them. This allows a persuasive speaker to draw upon the evocative psychological power of words. Words evoke other words by connotation, association, and implication, and chains of terms and images call up a dynamic process of multiple identifications.

Burke analyzes chains of terms under the heading "logology." In *The Rhetoric of Religion* (1961), he traces "tautological cycles of terms," from "order" to "command" to "disobedience" to "punishment" to "redemption," together with parallel and lateral cycles that include notions of setting apart, scapegoating, and vicarious victimage. He uses these cycles to follow connections between the terms of Biblical narrative, but they clearly have wider application to the terms used in the rhetoric of order – law, crime, punishment, exclusion – terms that control our thinking about social solidarity. Burke's cycles of terms are not all chains of deduction. Some terms call forth their opposites and provide rhetoric with names for opponents and victims. Independent of Saussure and the French structuralists, Burke not only made the linguistic turn, but began to identify the polarities by which actors identify themselves and their opponents as opposite sides within the same system of rhetoric.

For Burke, the solidary order is constituted by rhetoric in a manner not unlike the construction of the persuasive arenas of civil society by discourse itself. Solidarity requires a definition of who belongs to the group (Alexander and Smith 1993), not only by virtue of simple defining characteristics like birth, but in terms that define what makes them worthy members. In the rhetoric of democratic discourse, members who display, for example, that they are active, autonomous, and rational in their motives, open and truthful in their relationships, and that they participate in institutions founded on rules and laws are not only citizens but display citizenship. These rhetorical terms call out, by a logic of binary opposition, such contrary terms as passive, secret, deceitful, and arbitrary (Alexander and Smith, 1993, 292–5). Discourse then proceeds according to a structured logic of claims and accusations. Thus, civil society is embedded in the internal structure of discourse itself, and it is by the logic of this discourse that persuasive narratives, whether of myths or of daily affairs, are fashioned. Though Alexander and Smith are influenced by the French structuralists rather than directly by Burke, both schemes illustrate the possibility of a "linguistic turn" in our understanding of rhetoric as a cultural force that fuses social solidarity and opposition on the one hand and the logic of language on the other.

Burke's logology, with its suggestion that rhetorical terms cohere in cycles of implication, implies that rhetoric is affected by an inner dynamic at a cultural level. To engage in persuasive speech is to enter into a cultural realm with a logic of its own. Though rhetoric is embedded in social action, the meaningful, cultural elements of language display a dynamic process. Logology is the study of *systems* of symbols, which, when used rhetorically, embed the culture of words in action. Communicating requires that we organize our presentations "dramatistically." We speak dramatistically in the sense that our presentation, in speech, of motives and conduct is couched in dramatic terms as action set in scenes and performed by actors.[4]

Burke employs his own version of an action frame of reference to analyze the inherently action-oriented nature of human speech. His influential "dramatistic pentad" is best introduced in his own characteristically concise terms. Statements about motives, which provide a frame for interpretation of acts and intentions, always answer these questions: "what was done (act), when or where it was done (scene), who did it (agent), how he did it (agency), and why (purpose)" (Burke quoted in Gusfield 1989, 139–57). Emphasizing one or another of the terms of the pentad creates what Burke calls a "ratio." For example, a narrative that stresses the scene more than the act – a high scene-act ratio – suggests that action is implied, even justified by the environment, as in an intense depiction of a crime that gives special weight to description of the setting.

The dramatistic pentad refers to the fundamental grammar of the depiction of action, a grammar intrinsic to symbolic presentation, even within science. Gusfield, in a study of the presentation of social science research, employs the Burkean pentad to display rhetorical elements in the presentation of science. He points to the difference between research that depicts *drinking-drivers* rather than describing the problem as one of *drinking-driving*. "The first directs attention to the agent as the source of the act. The second frames the experience as an event, with the act as paramount." Though such research may be presented as descriptive and neutral, "the first, *drinking-driver*, is a call to transform the motorist. The second, *drinking-driving*, directs attention to the auto, the road, the event." (Gusfield 1989, 15, emphasis in original; see also Gusfield 1976).

Rhetorical structures affect more than the presentation of empirical research in sociology. The influence of rhetoric extends to the highest levels of abstract theory. I have elsewhere suggested that the term "society" operates rhetorically in sociological theory as a scene term (Mayhew 1984, 1,274–6). It is what Burke calls a "God term," an ultimate scene term with a very high scene-act ratio, which calls out action appropriate to the scene and stands as the final guarantor of value and validity. Society – as it once was, or as it is, or as it should be – implies standards for evaluation of the individual act. Strategic definition of "society," in the form of social theory, is essential to its effective rhetorical use.

Rhetorical usage is not a monopoly of the higher orders, used only as an instrument of domination by mystification. Burke points out that hierarchical terms are rhetorically powerful for Lenin, who argued that politics conducted through the play of varied interests is not proper for a proletarian party that knows the true transcending principles of its own historical march, the mysterious ultimate scene terms of its victory (Burke 1950, 189–97). This structure of argument is no less rhetorical for Lenin than for defenders of an established order. Rhetoric unites underdogs, too, and rhetorical cultures within excluded groups provide both tools for self defense and, equally important, cultural resources for individual and collective identity. To cite but one example, Gates (1988) has shown that the linguistic practice in the African-American community of "signifying" involves a complex rhetorical strategy. It is founded on modes of indirect discourse and irony that allow covert reversals of the dominant society's modes of influence and control. It can be used on the street in competitive talking games of the "dozens." It can be employed in preaching or in teaching children. In all these uses it offers modes of discourse that identify the dominated community as different from and opposed to the dominant society and identifies the speaker as a skilled and effective member of that community.

Contemporary social scientists, including students of professional communication in the New Public, continue to find Burke's concepts illuminating. For example, K. Olson (1995) has applied Burke's concept of literary form (Burke 1953, 123–83; see also Schudson 1995b, 53–71) to the presentation of news by the mass media. Burke sees literary form as a rhetorical device that employs dramatistic techniques to establish expectations as to how narratives will unfold. Fulfilling these expectations provides readers a gratifying experience and the writer is credited with having produced a credible story. Strong expectations are created by cycles of terms drawn together by both syllogistic and associative connections as well as by sheer repetitions of patterns. Olson shows that newspaper writers employ the same techniques to tell series of compelling stories that evoke an expected unfolding that readers anxiously await, but while readers of fiction hold authors responsible for outcomes that derive believable outcomes from their narrative forms, readers of newspapers hold the subjects of reporting responsible for properly playing their narrated roles. Public leaders become characters in dramas of conflict who must play out their roles in manufactured stories as well as their public responsibilities. In another recent application of dramatistic rhetorical thought, Blain (1995) puts Burke's "victimology" to good use. The oppositional logic of cycles of terms makes victims symbols of the injurious side of power. Accordingly, social movements make rhetorical use of victims as heroes, providing dramatic focus for presenting the injustice frames that provide hot buttons for mobilizing groups for collective action (Gamson 1992).

Burke does not advocate escape from rhetoric, for that would entail an alienating withdrawal from the embedded cultural life that allows us to find meaning and value in social activity. His rhetoric has been called "Ciceronian," one of a number of contemporary rhetorics that return to a classical ideal (Conley 1990, 304). Rhetoric is not merely instrumental, not just a way of tricking opponents with a flow of words, but a means of entering public life. Rhetoric integrates culture and eloquence by providing life-enhancing vocabularies for active social participation.

For Burke, our present challenge is not the inescapable presence of rhetoric in human communication, but the grip of positivism and scientism in contemporary life, a grip so strong as to make people imagine that science is above rhetoric and its predilection for the Babel of human contention. Science, too, can only be presented rhetorically, and to pretend otherwise only magnifies the authority of those who don the cloak of false objectivity and turn questions regarding human values into problems solvable by expert calculations.

### Jürgen Habermas: rhetoric and rational communication

Habermas' project, like Burke's, was undertaken in the context of a critique of the claims of science and of instrumental reason, which would reduce reason to means-ends calculations and politics to the decisions of experts (Habermas 1970; McCarthy 1978, 1–16). Following the "linguistic turn" in contemporary thought, Habermas starts with a theory of the nature of language, but he adopts a view of language very different than Burke's. For Habermas, language is not intrinsically hortatory; rather, language by nature seeks interpersonal understanding. "Our first sentence expresses unequivocally the intention of universal and unconstrained consensus."[5] Because of this optimistic notion of the *telos* of human communication, he is ready to dismiss traditional rhetoric as both unethical and dispensable.

Habermas, like both Parsons and Burke, employs an action frame of reference. Within this framework, he distinguishes two basic types of action, *purposive-rational* and *communicative*. The former is oriented to rational decision and the selection of technically effective means, the latter to reaching interpersonal understanding. When purposive rationality is employed in interaction, without regard for the requisites of true understanding, and for the purpose of achieving ends at the expense of other people, it is dubbed *strategic* action. The distinction between strategic and communicative action is at the center of Habermas' work and is the source of most of its critical leverage. It leads to a critique of economic and political institutions governed on scientistic premises that place them beyond the reach of citizens who should achieve agreement on the premises of their lives and work through "truly" communicative discussion.

In what sense can communication be "true"? For Habermas, communication has its own imperatives, and if attempts to communicate violate its intrinsic character, they are deformed and ineffective in producing actual and stable consensus. Communicative action cannot employ force. Indeed, any mode of persuasion that falls short of a strict standard of reciprocity is coercive, even if its persuasive sway is not directly based on force. A communicative speaker must make several good faith efforts: to be comprehensible, so that speaker and hearer can *understand* each other; to communicate true empirical propositions so that they can *share knowledge*; to state propositions that are normatively right, so that the hearer can *accept* them and *agree* on a common normative background; to speak truthfully, that is sincerely, so that the hearer can *believe and trust* the speaker. Moreover, all claims to comprehensibility, truth, rightness, and sincerity are subject to question and must be "redeemed in discourse," not merely backed by authority or strong assertion (McCarthy 1978, 272–357 Habermas 1984 [1981], 99–100). In authentic discourse, the force of the better argument is the only force employed or accepted.

The validity of claims are subject to redemption through discourse both for truth claims and for claims to normative rightness, because for Habermas both fact and value are within the realm of rational discussion. Values are not mere subjective preferences, beyond the reach of reason, for reason *means* the force of unconstrained argument. Habermas sets forth a version of a consensus theory of truth, with an essential qualification: a proper consensus must be produced dialogically and within the bounds of discussion that adheres to a strict set of discursive norms. Again, as in the case of Parsons, persuasion has been assimilated to normatively regulated appeals, this time at a philosophical level, in the form of a set of ideal norms for discourse; but, unlike Parsons, Habermas makes normative ends subject to rational choice by the same standards applied to empirical means. Both are validated by the same test: open scrutiny in the court of discourse, a court governed by norms drawn from the nature of communicative action – from the essential conditions of reaching informed, unconstrained agreement.

This conception excludes rhetoric, which traditionally allows a wide range of means of persuasion, short of direct force, to be employed. For

Habermas, rhetoric is indirect force. It does not operate within the ethic of discourse and must be excluded from the realm of reason that he seeks to reclaim. He is explicit on this point: a "peculiar ambivalence between conviction and persuasion . . . attaches to any consensus arrived at through rhetorical means." The equivocal character of rhetoric "evidences the element of force which to this day has not been removed from the determination of sociopolitical objectives – however much it is based on discussion" (Habermas 1980 [1973] , 183–4).[6]

To be sure, Habermas does not reduce all discourse to power. The move to reduce social influence entirely to domination was carried out by Michel Foucault, who saw coercive force not just in rhetoric but in modern discourses of reason, as well. His "genealogical" approach (so called after Nietzsche's *Genealogy of Morals*) reconstructs the historical development of modern reason as a system of rational surveillance, monitoring, discipline, and even compulsive self examination, in the interests of total social control (Foucault 1972; 1977), but Habermas wants to leave a place for reason within modernity. "Distorted communication," in which elements of coercion dominate, explains the lingering of historic forms of domination, but "communicative action," which is governed by an ethic of discourse, provides a form of liberating reason. The prominence of instrumental reason should not obscure the emancipating potential of communicative rationality. Foucault's approach risks sinking rationality so deeply as to preclude its use in redemptive critique (Habermas 1987 [1985], 238–93).

Nevertheless, to the extent that Habermas does limit consensus-building processes to conversations governed by discourse ethics, excluding rhetorical communication, he does assimilate rhetoric to force. The exclusion of rhetoric from processes of developing authentic consensus leads Habermas to speak of "merely empirical consensus" and "pseudo-consensus," which renders ambiguous the relevance of empirical study to questions of social integration. The study of how groups and individuals actually achieve and subsequently interpret agreements in the world as we know it is relegated to secondary importance in relation to analysis of how real agreements *ought* to be reached. The latter is the guiding impetus for critical theory, the former a mere documentation of what is. Critical theory unmasks ideological justifications and draws out motivating utopian implications, while empiricism implicitly justifies existing structures of domination.

In assimilating the category of ("true") interpersonal agreement to rational consensus and rhetoric to force, Habermas pays a price. Just as Parsons became entrapped in his normative presuppositions and was unable fully to develop his later notions of social influence, so Habermas is unable to develop a satisfactory conception of civil society (Cohen and Arato 1992). As we will later see, he is so determined to reject Parsons' conception of influence that he consigns the whole notion of influence to an inconsequential status. For Habermas, influence is merely a matter of short cutting full argument for reasons of convenience – for lack of time for complete discourse in the press of particular situations. This conception of influence, derived as it is from Habermas' conviction that only non-strategic communicative action can achieve agreements within the "lifeworlds" of actors who live in a world shaped by meaning, by-passes consideration of how influence actually works in social life: through *rhetoric* and the rhetorical amalgamation of reason, eloquence, appeals to established order, and pleas for solidarity.

The relation of influence to rhetoric, and of both these phenomena to social integration, is at the heart of the theoretical and interpretive problems raised in this book. Neither concept deserves the status of a residual category. Nor should we prejudge rhetoric and, bowing to popular parlance, accept the notion that rhetoric is, by nature and definition, detached from reality, reprehensible, and insincere.

### Limitations of reason in discourse

Our overviews of Parsons, Burke, and Habermas certainly do not exhaust the range and variety of contemporary views of discourse, but they provide a useful starting place for thinking about rhetoric and its place in modern society. Their ideas suggest important issues regarding rhetorical analysis as it bears on the principal concerns of this book: influence, social integration, and the modern public. These issues can be clarified by thinking of rhetoric as blending, in persuasive action, reason and four other elements of effective communication: *norms, solidarity, coercion,* and *eloquence.* Each of the four can be treated as analytically independent constraints on reason in rhetoric.

In the classical tradition, rhetoric consists in symbolic means of persuasion, excluding *direct* use of either force or payment. There are many techniques for symbolic persuasion and, given that persuaders do not scrupulously follow theories of rhetoric, but try to succeed by available means, rhetoric cannot be confined within a single concrete master category of such means. Concrete persuasive efforts employ mixed, composite appeals and only an analytical scheme can separate the strands. Rhetoric is not "essentially" covert force or embodied reason or mobilized prestige, but a complex process of persuasion by which people become convinced, or consent, or agree, or are moved to action. They respond to appeals that simultaneously invoke their moral commitments and their solidary ties, to their sense that persuasive messages are logical and accurate, and to the aura of wealth, power, and other forms of prestige. All of these appeals are clothed in stirring, eloquent presentations. People are also vulnerable to persuasion if they are without defenses – ignorant of alternative arguments, isolated from other people and alternative opinions, unable to distinguish emotional and realistic appeals. But there are no first principles for assuming that any of the modes of rhetoric are primary and the others derivative or subordinate. On the contrary, the plurality of human situations and ways of life, and the sheer complexity of human motivation, ensure that varied styles of persuasion will endure and that yet others are still to be created.

The union of varied, sometimes inconsistent, components of persuasive communication is well illustrated in Carruthers and Espeland's (1991) study of the origins and uses of double-entry bookkeeping. Demonstrating Burke's premise that all communication attempts to persuade, the authors show that modern bookkeeping, credited by Sombart, Weber, and Schumpeter with providing the foundations of rational business calculation at the very inception of capitalism, had rhetorical functions as well.[7] It not only allowed early capitalists to keep rational records; it also made them seem rational even if they actually kept haphazard, sloppy records. Merely keeping double-entry books rather than the older unsystematic narrative records of transactions, displayed character, a basis for trust. Double entry bookkeeping, with its elegant balance of debits and credits displayed its own form of eloquence. The rhetorical functions of modern bookkeeping, in which "accounts are a way of displaying the rationality of decisions and thus enhance their legitimacy" (61) are alive and well today. Accounts economically summarize and frame the activities of the firm, giving an impression of orderly enterprise strictly governed by rules of reporting; summary numbers still substitute for more detailed narrations, yet capsule summaries organized around sets of accounts necessarily provide but one among many possible versions of a complicated, messy background narrative. Carruthers and Espeland do not deny the useful instrumental rationality of double-entry bookkeeping. Its rhetorical functions do not destroy its character as a rational means, but it is clear that the use of double-entry bookkeeping in the social world of business is deeply embedded in normative rules, solidarity and trust, and eloquent expression that cannot be assimilated to its instrumental functions.

Many accounts of rhetoric do seek to assimilate the persuasive power of rhetoric to one or another of the dimensions of rhetorical communication, asserting the primacy of one factor and reducing other components to mere appearance or to derivative status. For example, to say that despite appearances, and whatever the participants believe, consent is always illusory – that behind consent are forces leading to coerced compliance – is to assimilate rhetoric to force and to deny the independent significance of other factors. Assimilating rhetoric to force justifies claims that reason merely masks coercion and that the underlying normative order was itself created by force, however many generations ago.

Assimilating rhetoric to one primary means is itself a rhetorical device for underscoring the importance of a persuasive factor for which advocates want to claim *decisive* importance. It is a technique of exaggeration, but it goes beyond mere overstatement by employing a *rhetoric of ultimacy*. As Burke suggests, to make our communication understandable we present even our most abstract concepts as dramas in which action flows in logical human terms and thereby becomes intelligible. Burke's dramatistic ratios speak to the particular interpretive slants that narrative presentation builds into rhetorical depiction. Intense description of the scene of action, with a high scene-agent ratio, suggests the power of the scene to explain the action that flows from it and to limit the range of possible decisions for actors. Ultimate scene terms are especially effective rhetorical devices for they suggest encompassing meaning, inescapable destiny, and orderly hierarchy. We cannot escape from God, or from History, or from the indispensable moral authority of Society. Hence the recurrence of these and comparable ultimate scene terms in human discourse. I propose, then, to avoid ultimate scene terms and to balance the independent factors of persuasion in relation to the rhetorical ideal of reasonable argument.

*Reasonable argument.* Reason is a cultural ideal. It is variably conceived as inherent in the logos of the universe, or as a method for individual inquiry, or as an agreed upon set of rules of argument and proof. The Renaissance view of "right reason," Descartes' view of the rational subject, and the modern conception of scientific method are profoundly different, but one least common denominator among culturally varied concepts of reason is the assumption that it is the same for everybody – if not for everyone in the world then at least for everyone in a communicating, truth-seeking group. That is, rational thought is *universalistic*; all who employ its methods will be led to the same truths. From a sociological standpoint, then, the key questions involve what, within a given group, are accepted as the methods and standards of reason, and to what extent are ideals of reasonable discourse institutionalized in actual discourse.

In the Western cultural tradition, there is by definition a reasonable moment in rhetoric, for the very notion of persuasion implies that the persuaders must provide good reasons and cannot simply rely upon authority or force. Yet institutionalization of the cultural ideal of rational argument is limited by realistic constraints attendant to actually making persuasion work – the conditions of successful persuasion in real social situations. Even when the participants in a discourse value rationality and employ it as a standard for argument, the exigencies of convincing others and securing their compliance lead to calls upon established *normative* commitments, in order to take advantage of preexisting readiness to comply; calls upon group loyalties, in order to mobilize the force of *solidarity*; references to the position or prestige of the speaker, in order to draw upon the *power* of hierarchy; the use of persuasive language – *eloquence* – to communicate effectively so that listeners can understand and be moved. In concrete persuasive performances, these four component elements are inextricably intertwined with rational argument. Indeed, the effectiveness of rhetoric often relies on the submerged, unrecognizable confluence of various species of appeal, the better to furnish concealed support for reasonable arguments. The use of blended rhetoric to garner support is not a product of a depraved and sinister streak in human nature and it is not limited to the protection of entrenched special interests. Ironically, the organization of group decisions around free and open discussion encourages rhetorical modes of persuasion, for autonomous participants who wish to prevail will not forswear the use of effective means in the interest of promoting a purely cultural conception of reason for its own sake. Nevertheless, once institutionalized, conceptions of reason then provide opportunities for rhetorical appeals to universalistic standards of good argument.

Rhetorical efforts are invariably responsive to the conditions of effective persuasion, but the ratios of its components vary from situation to situation. Some forms of rhetoric grant primacy to meeting reasonable standards; other situations ask for a rhetoric that is primarily about solidarity and therefore evokes appeals to loyalty. Elections call for a certain form of rhetorical appeal, face-to-face debate another, and membership drives for voluntary organizations yet different approaches. Journalism has standards that derive from its own social situation. There is, in other words, a *differentiation of rhetoric across rhetorical forums*. The potential for differentiation has decisive importance for the study of the public, for "reasonable rhetoric" can be given a sociologically relevant definition: *reasonable rhetoric gives primacy to persuasive appeals deemed reasonable according to cultural conceptions of reason in public discourse.* Such rhetoric is called "institutionalized" when rhetorical forums are established that constrain speakers to employ reasonable argument and to keep other appeals within fixed bounds. Forums that institutionalize reasonable rhetoric constrain discourse by requiring direct, public confrontation in debate governed by universalistic standards of demonstration. There are three prequisite conditions for the institutionalization of reasonable rhetoric: (1) at the cultural level, *universalistic standards* to allow the debate to be recognized as reasonable; (2) at the social level, *direct confrontation* to insure that issues are joined; and (3) *publicity* to constrain participants to conform to cultural norms of rationality. These definitions prove nothing about the reality of rhetorical reason or its requisite forums, but they do provide a starting place for a flexible approach to the sociological analysis of rhetoric in society, a multidimensional approach that recognizes the limits of reason and the functions of rhetoric without denying the possibilities of rational public discourse.

This conception of public reason is, in broad terms, consistent with Burke's definition of rational rhetoric and Habermas' notion of communicative rationality. When Burke notes that *reason* is employed in rhetoric "to the extent that one's acceptance is contingent upon such proofs as are established by a method of weighting of doubts and rebuttals" (1968, 450), he is stating, in capsule form, ideas about reason that Habermas also made central in his theory of communicative action. "Acceptance" and "rebuttal" are key terms. Rhetoric is not rhetoric without a moment of argument, and consent implies some opportunity to argue back. The rationality of persuasive communication cannot be definitively judged by a third party. If an argument is deemed rational by a disinterested referee, but is seen as irrational by the person being persuaded, the element of acceptance is not present. Rationality is a property of the interchange, not of the message in the abstract. We can speak, however, of procedural rationality and reckon as rational those persuasive interchanges that offer adequate opportunities for rebuttal and require persuaders to defend their claims. This is the idea behind Habermas' distinction between purposive-rational action, which amounts to the exercise of rational, administrative control over subjects treated as objects, and communicative action. Communicative rationality requires symmetrical obligations to provide opportunities for rebuttal and, in the face of rebuttal, to furnish additional compelling reasons until both parties achieve, through interaction, a rational consensus.

The centerpiece of Habermas' ongoing work is a valuable attempt to think through the conditions of rational communicative action, but it is misleading to insist that anything short of ideally rational consensus must be labeled rhetoric and equated with coercion. Nevertheless, we are indebted to Habermas for, as he would say, "thematizing" the issue of rational consensus, because his work draws attention to the vulnerability of social orders when forums for rational discourse are not available. The single most important question brought to the fore by the arrival of the

New Public asks whether there are, in the public arena, forums that institutionalize reasonable rhetoric in the face of the manipulative efforts of professional persuaders. Placing this problem in the foreground can lead to a critical reconstruction of inadequate approaches to social influence within publics that, satisfied with apparent equilibria among social interests, do not attend to distortions of collective reason in public life.

*Normative appeals.* There are normative components in the interests and attitudes that motivate social conduct. Persuaders and their audiences invariably bring preexisting norms to the rhetorical arena, so rhetoric speaks to the values and norms of audiences likely to accept persuasive messages to which they are already predisposed by their normatively formed attitudes. The obligation to abide by cultural standards of rationality in diagnosing social problems and advocating solutions may conflict with the need to make one's presentations conform to established substantive norms, especially when popularly accepted norms have not kept up with events and our changing understanding of society. Persuaders must therefore seek an effective balance between competing imperatives.

That motives have a normative component that literally constitutes human interests is Talcott Parsons' fundamental theoretical idea; it is his explanation of integration in a society that allows the self-interested pursuit of individual goals. The normative grounding of interests and action is no doubt an important source of social integration, but norms, even widely accepted and deeply institutionalized norms, are never adequate to ensure integration, because they cannot be specific enough to allow deduction of situational rules. Norms must be explicated, applied, and interpreted in concrete circumstances. In his later work, Parsons became increasingly cognizant of the need to expand his scheme to allow for diverse action, not literally called for or specified by norms, but legitimated by generalized values and regulated within normative frameworks (Mayhew 1984a). In the economy, the institution of contract provides the framework; creative entrepreneurs engage in adaptive economic action, integrating their contributions to the overall economy through the market. Such market systems are the hallmark of modernity, and it occurred to Parsons that other sectors of modern society are articulated by self-equilibrating markets and regulated by institutions comparable to contract (Parsons 1967a). Moreover, "media" function in other systems to facilitate transactions in a manner analogous to the role of money in the economy. For the integrative system the comparable medium is influence. Parsons came to suppose that there is a play of rhetoric in the public sphere comparable to the free pursuit of economic interests in the economy, grounded in normative constraints and structured by normatively driven aims, but nonetheless open to creative attempts to persuade others regarding appropriate and effective actions in varied situations. This whole system of persuasion is self equilibrating and, through its links to other social systems, has integrative force for the larger society.

Despite the legacy of Parsons' normative theory of stratification, the later Parsons made an important theoretical move toward a more differentiated theory of rhetoric, one that would allow for a partial detachment of persuasive reason from its constraints in an established normative order. According to Parsons (1961; 1968), the differentiation of modern society requires "normative generalization." In order to avoid the inflexibility inherent in detailed normative regulation, values and normative standards become generalized and so do the commitments of people to them. I have suggested above that the need to abide by cultural standards of rationality in advocating new policies often conflicts with the need to align rhetorical appeals with established substantive norms. When rational solutions to problems require substantial social change, the constraints posed by commitments to settled or traditional norms can be profoundly conservative. The generalization of norms allows for rhetorically contesting taken-for-granted rules; it becomes possible to appeal to new, ground-breaking interpretations of normative traditions. Norms become constraining as frameworks of legitimacy rather than as direct substantive limitations. It becomes possible, for example, to advocate civil disobedience in furtherance of some more generalized value that contradicts the law that should be broken. It becomes possible to engage in dialogue which, though still carried out as rhetoric and rhetorical counter claim, is more rational, because elements of the situation that were taken for granted have become subject to Burke's test of "such proofs as are established by a method of weighting of doubts and rebuttals."

*Solidarity.* Rhetorical appeals to *solidarity* are as necessary to persuasion as reasonable argument. Indeed, a claim to solidarity with the audience is implied in the notion of persuasion. If attempts to influence others cannot employ force, but must convince through argument, then what interest do others have in accepting the arguments presented to them? It cannot be presumed that reason, even if eloquently clothed, will impel others to accept arguments that run counter to their own interests just for the sake of sheer love of truth. Accordingly, rhetorical appeals must in some way align the interests of the speaker and the audience. The speaker can argue that what is advocated is in the listener's interests – that the listener may be assured that the speaker is sincere and not motivated solely by self interest, but has an interest in the listener's welfare; or the advocate may take a broader course and argue that the welfare of both speaker and listener are at stake because what is advocated is in the interests of a larger group that includes both of them. Whether the scope of common interest asserted is limited to the speaker and the listener, as in the case of a doctor-patient relationship, or extends to a larger group, as in the case of an attempt to mobilize support among physicians for legislation in support of their common professional interests, or extends to the public at large in the name of the public interest in health, or even to humane concerns in the interests of survival and common humanity, rhetoric appeals to solidarity and purports to strengthen the ties between people. It is this solidaristic dimension of rhetoric that Burke addresses in his account of identity and consubstantiation as the heart of the rhetorical process.

Solidarity necessarily involves normative components. It is impossible to speak of "self interest" and the "public interest" without normative overtones and, indeed, the establishment and maintenance of ties of solidarity are universally supported by values and norms. It is important to stress, however, that solidarity cannot be reduced to the norms that support it, any more than economic activity can be reduced to its normative regulation, or power to its legitimate use. Solidary ties – the interests of people in each other and their common fate – and, indeed, the manipulation of solidary relationships, from love to patriotism, for instrumental ends are part of the fabric of social life. Solidarity is an independent base for rhetorical appeal, and it is not possible to imagine a rhetoric that eschews reference to common interest in some form.

*Power.* By a strict definition rhetoric cannot be founded on coercion, for persuasion is conceived as an alternative to force, even its polar opposite. Certainly overt threat of violence is outside the bounds of what can meaningfully be termed rhetoric. Nevertheless, within a multidimensional conception of persuasion, it is necessary to recognize that real-world persuasion contains elements of coercion. Firstly, unstated but possible uses of force may lurk in the background of rhetorical discourse, intimidating participants, or at least providing a status-conferring aura of power on a persuader. Secondly, a persuader with superior knowledge faces a relatively ignorant opponent who cannot effectively argue and rebut. Within Parsons' categories, fraud is a form of coercion made possible by ignorance, a category of irrationality. In current usage, fraudulent appeals are not excluded from the category of rhetoric. On the contrary, its propensity to deceptive, misleading, and vacuous appeals is what makes rhetoric often seem an unreasonable mode of communication.

A third coercive element derives from the fact that the terms of rhetoric can, within any particular cultural setting, be biased in favor of one side. Culture provides vocabularies for argument, terms that furnish attached justifications, implied reasons, assumed imperatives, and implicit narratives to rhetorical pleas just by framing them in language. Counterclaims may appear strange, absurd, and against all reality and reason, just because they do not easily conform to the assumptions embodied in cultural presuppositions and linguistic forms. If we further presume that cultural advantage belongs to dominant social classes, perhaps deliberately created to provide a discursive edge, then we have the modern theory of ideology.[8] It is possible to interpret Habermas' theory as less a prescription for how everyday communication should be carried out than an archaeological method designed to show that current ways of thinking are distorted by past domination of discussion by powerful interests. This mode of analysis, in its posing of the question of what political policies rational people, engaged in free discussion, would have established, is a close cousin of social contract theory, indicating that Habermas' intense pursuit of reason makes him a true child of the enlightenment.

Even if we assume, for purposes of argument, that these theories of class domination are true – that power does penetrate the terms of rhetoric – it does not follow that rhetorical persuasion is completely coercive. If the terms of rhetoric are penetrated by cultural hegemony, so also are the terms of reason and of the normative order. Rhetoric is employed by the higher orders for domination and also by the lower orders for defense. It is employed *within* classes in competition for positions of leadership and on behalf of special interests. And it is used by critical theorists, including Habermas and all other advocates of liberation, on behalf of their causes. It employs normative, solidaristic, and reasonable appeals, rhetorically enhanced by eloquence, on behalf of its emancipatory claims. As long as there are opportunities to speak, reason enhanced by rhetoric retains its Foucauldian potential. The important questions for the sociology of rhetoric concern the institutional organization of critical discussion: What are these opportunities? How can they be effectively situated in well established institutions? In short, successful rhetoric includes a moment of coercion, more or less forceful according to circumstance and weakened to the extent that underlying, taken-for-granted assumptions are open for discussion. It is not possible, however, to examine every assumption in every discourse. Whatever one's cultural conceptions of reason, the exigencies of collective action require persuasive effort, even in radical, revolutionary discourse. Some causes seek the public good, others private interests; some causes favor the powerless, others the privileged. In any case, advocates seek to prevail by gaining and employing influence, and to gain such leverage, they must participate in hierarchical systems, deploying the resources of these systems in their rhetoric.

*Eloquence.* Rhetoric goes beyond the power of reason to convince by using eloquence to move. Rhetorical speech is not only intrinsic to language as a symbolic medium, it is a condition of its effectiveness in use, especially in a democratic society. The concept of eloquence is not rendered obsolete by modernity. As much as the modern critical temper disdains propaganda, demagoguery, and media hype, democratic theory still has a place for eloquence.

John Dewey, in *The Public and its Problems* (1927), attacked the elitism implicit in the "realist democracy" of such figures as Walter Lippmann (Westbrook, 1991). The realists thought the public too ignorant to play an active role in establishing policy. Policy must be made by objective, public-spirited citizens who must then manufacture the consent of the governed (Lippmann 1922). Dewey objected that even in the unlikely event that a public spirited elite could prevail over powerful interests, the outcome would be technocracy, not democracy, and that any policy formulated in this way would not embody the *experience* of the whole public. Hence, it would fail to express the public interest. Discussion is the means of democratic social life and all voices must be expressed and heard. According to Dewey, "social inquiry" that can hear and incorporate these voices into public opinion is the means of achieving active democracy.

Anticipations of Habermas are evident in Dewey's *The Public and its Problems*, but American pragmatism and European rationalism take quite different tacks in their approaches to the solution of problems of technocracy and the democratically constructed public interest.[9] Disembodied reason cannot grasp the raw experience of social groups, nor can it express experience *persuasively*. Social inquiry, which can aggregate and synthesize experienced needs, must be effectively communicated. For Dewey, "Communication of the results of social inquiry is the same thing as the formation of public opinion . . ." (Dewey 1927, 177). Yet the dissemination of properly informed social inquiry has it own imperatives: "Presentation is fundamentally important and presentation is an art" (183), not a scientific enterprise. As Dewey put it, "A newspaper which was only a daily edition of a quarterly journal of sociology or political science would have a limited circulation and a narrow influence" (183). Only incorporation of the eloquence of rhetoric into the discourses of public life will furnish persuasive appeal to reasonable argument.

Dewey's remarks on the public demonstrate American pragmatism's clear-headed understanding of the inescapable need for rhetoric and of the imperatives of persuasion (Shalin 1992). The culture of public discourse calls for reasoned discussion, but the expressive elements of culture also furnish the resources of eloquence – fluent, expressive, and moving language. If a persuader hopes to move an audience to conviction and beyond assent to action, expressive language, with its reliance on ambiguity, suggestion, connotation, and emotional appeal, then a full-range rhetoric is required. Because of the requisites of persuasion, in practice, reason takes the form of rhetorical rebuttal of rhetorical statement. Reason can only be realized in dialogue, and dialogue can only be institutionalized in society by providing strategically located public forums for expression and response, in which citizens speak freely about their socially located experience.

*Uncertainty and tokens of argument.* One final limitation on reason in rhetoric arises from the most inescapable constraints on every-day communication: time and effort. Aristotle distinguished logic and rhetoric by attributing certainty to logical argument and placing rhetoric in the uncertain realm of probability, the realm of questions we cannot be sure about. Rhetoric therefore has an open-ended quality, always open to question and to further argument and evidence. Yet time is a finite resource and efforts to persuade are costly. Persuaders have limited time and resources to speak and, equally important, audiences have limited time to listen. Even people who want to be well informed have other things to do and must economize their search for answers. In consequence, persuaders are not required to provide definitive arguments. Rhetoric employs adumbrated, sketchy arguments that amount to symbolic *tokens* of more extended arguments that the speaker purports to be able to expound if necessary. In attributing this element of discourse to the trivial matter of convenience, Habermas misses the profound and unavoidable significance of the token in persuasive argument. Tokens allow for strategic rhetoric that delivers suggestive cues but avoids confrontations that would require redeeming these tokens with more extensive arguments. It is this feature of rhetorical discourse that places the burden of sustaining rational standards of rhetoric on institutionalized forums for debate, especially in the professionally dominated arenas of communication in the New Public.

# PART II

## *Influence*

# 3

# Influence: capacity to persuade

The New Public is constituted by the rise of professional experts on persuasion. These experts aspire to more than particular acts of persuasion; they aim to build, and to help others to build, the general capacity to persuade that we call *influence*. Understanding the New Public and assessing its consequences therefore requires establishing a frame for thinking about the sources and uses of influence.

As public cynicism creeps into daily usage, the words, "rhetoric" and "influence" take on pejorative connotations. "Rhetoric," which once meant using words to urge to action has come to mean using words instead of action. "Influence," which once meant swaying by persuasive argument or by invoking trust, rather than by exercising power, is now used to label the power employed by insiders. In this usage, influence refers to fixing traffic tickets, or blocking legislation, or keeping names out of the newspaper. Such conflation of terms may simply reflect the fuzzy boundaries of categories of action in daily life, but failure to make clear distinctions obscures the diversity of ways that citizens affect each other's beliefs and conduct. Influence and power are analytically different processes. When an official's job is threatened if favors are withheld, this is an exercise of power, not influence. When a newspaper editorial changes people's opinions, or when a political speech affects how people vote, or when a public demonstration calls attention to a social cause, thereby signaling to others a measure of public support for that cause, that is influence.

To possess influence is to hold or to have access to resources of persuasion so that influence can be exercised on a regular basis across a broad range of situations. The resources of persuasion include prestige, knowledge (information and arguments), trust, charisma, rhetorical skill, and access to networks of communication, but do not include power or wealth as such. It is true that power and wealth are possible sources of prestige, but to secure compliance by direct application of power or by simple purchase is not persuasion. Persuasion works through rhetoric. Chapter 2 established the premise that rhetoric, with its focus on persuasion, is an appropriate starting point for thinking about influence, and my comments on three major contributions to locating persuasion in society yielded three first principles for a theory of influence:

Firstly, Parsons' well-developed argument that all motivation involves a normative element, including motivation to accept persuasive appeals, suggests that systems of influence are supported by a normative order. Norms not only make some arguments more appealing than others; the normative order accords prestige to persons of high status, which enhances their influence. Yet influence also requires argument, not just appeals to status. *A realistic theory of influence must analytically distinguish the separate roles of reputation and argument in persuasion.*

Secondly, Burke's presentation of rhetoric as a process of identification and consubstantiation suggests that an adequate account of how social orders are created and sustained by rhetorical language should allow a central place for persuasive appeals to social solidarity. *Influence can be defined as a process of affiliation.*

Thirdly, Habermas' argument that only discourse that provides reasons can be truly persuasive suggests the importance of identifying the rational component of influence. Open debate produces a gravitational force toward giving reasons, and, to the extent that reasons must be given, enhances rationality in public discussion. An adequate theory of influence must identify the factors that support or repress the dynamic of reason in public debate. *It is necessary to distinguish forums that support public rationality from those that suppress it.*

### Parsons' influence paradigm

In the later stages of his thought, Talcott Parsons addressed the concept of influence directly and, in his characteristic manner, developed a four-fold scheme for classifying what he called "ways of getting results in social interaction" (Parsons 1967b, 361). This scheme, which he called "the influence paradigm," deserves careful attention.[1] If his analytical distinctions are cogent, the scheme should illuminate the critical dimensions of public affairs. If his basic distinctions confuse fundamental issues, then these first missteps will multiply errors at each step of the analysis, and his overall scheme of interpretation will come to create a false picture of social life and politics in modern society.

Parsons' earliest approach to the dynamics of persuasion, set in the context of his theory of the structure of social action, gave privileged status to normative commitments. His later influence paradigm sought to differentiate more carefully the varied forms of attempts to affect the action of others.[2] He continued to employ an action frame of reference, beginning by positing actors in a social environment who select means to achieve ends, in this case means of affecting what others do. Means and ends are grounded in shared norms, which proscribe securing personal ends by unregulated, purely strategic force. Parsons then proposed categories for classifying the means of securing compliance by distinguishing the kinds of sanctions employed. The scheme generates a set of four modes of gaining ends in social interaction: inducement, deterrence, persuasion, and the activation of moral commitments. In the new paradigm, persuasion was accorded independent status as a special means of securing compliance, and the invocation of norms became one among several means. At first glance this appears to signal a major step toward recognizing the differentiation of persuasion (and social influence based on persuasion), but as we follow Parsons' line of analysis, it will become clear that the distinction between persuasion and normative pressure remained ambiguous.

The four types of sanctions are derived from two crosscutting distinctions. Sanctions may be *positive* or *negative* and they may work by changing the *situation* or by altering the targeted person's *orientations* to the situation. By "orientations" Parsons meant the actor's definition of and attitudes toward situations. In distinguishing between the positive/negative dimension and the situation/orientation dimension, Parsons was noting that people can be made to respond either by changing the balance of their available rewards and punishments or by being shown how to look at their situation in a different light.

The cross-classification of the two dimensions produces four means of securing desired outcomes from others:

### Situational sanctions
*Inducement* changes the actor's situation by offering positive sanctions, i.e. rewards.
*Deterrence* changes the actor's situation by threatening negative sanctions, i.e. punishments.

### Orientational sanctions
*Persuasion* changes the actor's definition of the situation by offering arguments that the proposed action, properly understood, will be good for her or him, i.e. compliance is in the interests of the person being persuaded, even without any changes in the balance of rewards. (This act

involves a positive "sanction" because a person thus persuaded *perceives* a benefit from compliance.)

The *activation of commitments* alters the other's definition of the situation by showing that non-compliance puts mental tranquility at stake. Failure to make good on a normative commitment risks guilt, shame, or dishonor. (A negative sanction is involved because the other perceives a negative change in the balance of rewards, even though the outcome is, as it were, self administered.)

To make this abstract paradigm concrete, imagine the following situation. Sally and Barbara are college roommates. Sally, who finds her economics course perplexing, is unable to complete an important homework assignment. Barbara, who is an excellent student of economics, could help. According to the paradigm, Sally has four basic options for getting Barbara to comply with a request for assistance. She can attempt to *induce*: "If you help me with my economics assignment, I will do the cooking for a week." Or she can attempt to *deter* a negative answer: "If you do not help me I will fail, and then I will be so upset that I will be very hard to live with." Trying *persuasion*, Sally might point out the intrinsic benefits of helping her: "Barbara, the best way to learn something really well is to teach it to others. If you help me with my economics assignment, you will also be teaching yourself more about your favorite subject." Finally, Sally might invoke Barbara's moral *commitments*: "Remember how I have helped you with every one of your essays for your English class. Now don't you think you should help me? You don't have to, of course, but I don't see how you could feel happy about it if you say no." The generic arguments employed in the four modes are: for inducement, "I will make it worth your while;" for deterrence, "I will make your life very unpleasant;" for persuasion, "This will be good for you;" and for the activation of commitments, "What I ask is right, and if you don't do it you will not feel good about yourself."

One can easily imagine a variation on one of Sally's approaches, one that Parsons did not directly consider, but that has important implications for the theory of influence. Suppose that Sally had not invoked the norm of reciprocity by reminding Barbara about helping with prior English assignments, but had made an indeterminate promise of a future reciprocating favor. "Barbara, do me this *favor*." Given a norm of reciprocity, Barbara would gain thereby an uncertain capacity to call for a reciprocal favor of an unspecified nature at an indeterminate time in the future.[3] According to some students of influence this is exactly what influence involves (Banfield 1961); it rests on an exchange of favors that establish mutual but ill defined and unenforceable obligations to reciprocate. The exchange of favors straddles the boundaries of the four-fold classification; it is partly a mode of vague inducements and threats, partly an evocation of norms. Yet in any relationship that is governed by a norm of reciprocity and provides opportunities to do favors, *favor-based influence* will be an important "means of achieving ends in interaction."

In practice, people who want others to comply use a variety of mixed methods, using all four techniques, mixed in different proportions and guises, some conveyed with a wink or a nod. Parsons understood that his scheme was analytical, not a set of categories for concrete classification, yet he asserted that this paradigm established, on systematic grounds, *exactly* four primary modes of affecting others' behavior. He also contended that the paradigm had strategic significance for constructing a theory of modern society, because it corresponds to a further claim that each of the four primary, analytically defined modes corresponds to a symbolic medium in which generalized capacities to affect others' conduct are lodged. *Money* is a generalized capacity to induce; it frees one from having to find a particular inducement that will appeal to a particular person and allows instead the use of a generalized medium that stands for value in general and can be used to secure any number of valuable things. Similarly, *power* is a generalized capacity to mobilize negative sanctions. *Influence* is a generalized capacity to persuade. Moral authority to define normative obligations and to call upon general commitments to broadly defined social values make *value commitments* a fourth generalized medium for affecting others' action. It is the generality of these institutionalized media that gives the modern social order its flexibility, for such instruments as money and legitimate power free actors from the constraints of barter and the direct show of force. Each of these generalizing media are embodied in concrete social institutions and each corresponds to one of the four analytical modes defined in the influence paradigm. Parsons thus turned an abstract scheme for defining dimensions into a guide as to how particular sectors of the institutional order work. It is necessary, then, to look closely at the paradigm to decide whether Parsons' initial derivation of the primary forms of affecting conduct produces a plausible set of generalized media, a set that represents the actual dynamics of modern societies.

### Persuasion and the medium of influence

Money can be readily viewed as a generalization of inducement, and it is not difficult to accept the basic idea that power is a generalized capacity to apply negative sanctions, even though the notion that power is a "medium," analogous in its social functions to money, is a less intuitive concept. The notion that influence is a medium is yet more problematic, and as we shall see in Chapter 4, it is Parsons' treatment of influence that attracts Habermas' critical attack and justifies, Habermas thinks, rejection of the four-fold system of media.

Let us reexamine the notion that influence, defined as generalized capacity to persuade, is a medium, starting with the definition of persuasion within the four-fold paradigm. Persuasion involves altering others' definition of the situation so that they come to see that complying with a request will be good for them – that, properly conceived, compliance is in their own best interest, independent of any reward or punishment administered by the persuader. I illustrated this idea in Sally's recourse to Barbara's proposed tutoring role as serving Barbara's own interests because of the learning that would flow from her teaching. This is a prototype of persuasion. Sally *argues* for an interpretation of the situation by proposing a *theory* of teaching and a representation of the *facts* of the matter. Let us now test the analytical scheme by asking how yet another plea to Barbara should be classified. Suppose Sally said, "Do this out of friendship; our friendship will be deepened by our studying together." I am asking, of course, "What about solidarity?" Barbara's appeal to friendship cannot be classified as one of the primary modes of getting results from others. It presupposes that there are norms governing friendship that call for altruism, assistance, and reciprocity; Sally is activating commitments to those norms. But Sally can also be seen as making an offer of affiliation, a form of inducement. This combination of normative regulation and personal gratification is consistent with Parsons' earlier treatment of interpersonal bonds in *The Social System*, where solidarity is defined as the institutionalized (i.e. normatively reinforced) "cathectic-expressive aspect of ego's integration with alter," that is, Barbara's and Sally's mutual emotional gratification (1951, 77). For Parsons, "*Every* role, insofar as it is *institutionalized*, involves a pattern of solidarity obligations," because "it involves membership in at least one collectivity" (98).

The stability of any group, even two roommates, requires normative regulation, including some norms that call for "collectivity-orientation" rather than "self-orientation." Solidarity is the stabilization, over time, of mutual gratification, through commitment of the partners to norms requiring some measure of control of immediate, self-interested gratification. These norms recognize the value of the group as such, over and above the immediate perceived interests of its members. Only by virtue of such norms can people ask, "Are you one of us?" or in the case at hand, "Are you my friend?" Yet solidarity is not without its inducements; the motivation for entering a solidary relationship is "gratification."[4] In principle, within the framework of this paradigm, the inducements to friendship are not different than the inducements to contractual relationships except as to the type of "gratifications" involved.

Solidarity plays a major role in Parsons' conception of influence, yet the exact place of solidarity in the paradigm is difficult to pin down. As he moved from persuasion as a means of influence, to influence as generalized persuasion, Parsons' initial emphasis on the role of argument in persuasion was displaced. It became difficult to locate the relative positions of argument, solidarity, and normatively defined social status in the play of influence. The problem starts in the original classification of ways of gaining results in social interaction, for solidarity does not exactly correspond to any of his four defined means. Solidarity can be an inducement, but it is also a potential threat. One need only note the powerful sanction of ostracism to make the point. Solidarity is also embodied in norms of loyalty, and so provides commitments that can be invoked in pleas for compliance. Persuasion also involves solidarity because successful argument requires showing that speakers and their audiences have a common interest – a basis for solidarity. This is true for Sally and Barbara, for appeals to worker solidarity among union members, or references to the national interest by politicians: through argument, the persuader makes the audience see that its interests correspond to what the persuader wants too.

There is nothing inherently wrong with a scheme that leads to the conclusion that so basic a sociological category as solidarity crosscuts the analytical dimensions of the mutual influence people have on each other. The problem arises in connection with the strategic theoretical reason that led Parsons to conceive the basic scheme. He wanted to isolate a set of four institutional means of ordering dynamic social systems that would explain the superior adaptive capacity of specifically modern societies. These four means are supposed to correspond to four basic analytical categories of interaction. Once he laid out the analytical scheme, he immediately announced his intention: "I should now like to suggest that this simple paradigm of modes of gaining ends in social interaction is matched by a paradigm of generalized media by which, in the appropriately structured interaction system, an enhanced capacity to gain such ends is made possible" (Parsons 1967b, 363).

Parsons' transition from persuasion to influence raises a serious question: which of the four media – each of them hallmarks of modernity – will correspond to modern social solidarity? Since none of the media correspond to a specific mode of getting results through solidarity, we must be attentive to the possibility that solidarity will be ignored or treated in residual and ambiguous ways, or in ways that change the terms of argument in midstream.

Money and power (conceived as generalized inducement and mobile capacity to empower people to get things done, respectively) are central institutional mechanisms of flexibility in modern society, but surely the institutions of modernity must include the forums wherein people influence each other by argument, debate, and propaganda. If the generalized media are, as Parsons claimed, the means by which dealing with others is freed from the constricting particularities of tradition, barter, and *ad hoc* political bargaining, then the freeing of opinion, establishing its contingent dependency on persuasion, must be recognized as the font of an equally important arena of adaptive mobility in society. Parsons clearly contemplated this argument, but he also subjected "persuasion" and "influence" to another line of analysis leading inexorably back to the center of gravity of his theoretical apparatus – a normative concept of rhetoric founded on a normative theory of social stratification. In explicating influence as a generalized form of persuasion, he began with a brief glance at *argument* (or "information") as the basis of influence (Parsons 1967b, 369), but quickly passed by that idea and moved on to the notion that it is *trust* that makes people accept arguments, and then concludes that reputation is the source of trust, status the source of reputation, and status the product of a system of normatively defined stratification. In summary, *influence allows the status order to organize public opinion.* This brief, skeleton argument fails to convey either the force of Parsons' argument or its precise routes, but it does point to the detour that left him unable to provide a convincing account of the "influence market," despite his powerful overall scheme for the analysis of modern society, and despite the promising start offered by the idea of generalized persuasion.[5]

*Flexibility and security.* Parsons' "media," which correspond to the primary modes of getting results in interaction, are generalized capacities to bring sanctions to bear. Money is a generalized capacity to induce, power to deter, and influence to persuade. They derive their effectiveness from their symbolic capacity to represent primary sanctions, which people are willing to accept instead of such real sanctions as goods and services, force, and detailed argument. The media allow great flexibility in social life for they dispense with the need to articulate the conduct of varied persons and groups by repeated negotiation of concrete particulars. Money lifts the burdens of barter and the limitation of exchange to ascriptively defined partners and readily available goods. Similarly, symbolic power eliminates the need to show force and to calculate its effectiveness at each use, rather than relying on acceptance of the right of persons with power to make binding decisions within abstractly defined limits. Organized symbolic power allows officials to issue orders without first asking themselves whether they have sufficient force at hand to deter violent resistance.

The media of exchange increase the degrees of freedom of choice. When markets are organized through monetary transactions, traders have an extended range of possible trading partners; they can choose to store value in the form of money, awaiting propitious opportunities. But to accept money is to accept risk, for the media, being symbols, have no intrinsic value. Those who accept symbolic tokens in lieu of what these tokens represent give up usable goods (or their own labor) for paper, or mere symbolic notations in records of accounts; or they trade their capacity to get what they want by their own use of force in return for defined delegations of power to make binding decisions within groups that organize collective power to achieve common ends.[6] In accepting influence, individuals give up making decisions based solely on their own limited experience in return for the benefits of trustworthy advice, gaining the advantage of a wider range of knowledge at the price of dependence on the views of others.

All the media depend on widely shared understanding of what they represent and on habitual trust in their effectiveness. As I read Parsons, the crucial lines of argument linking the primary modes of securing compliance to their generalized, institutional forms center on how trust is established to provide *backing* for the media. "Backing" refers to the underlying capacities of ongoing social systems to stabilize the value of media. If, for example, money is valuable and usable one day, and the next day rendered worthless by hyperinflation, then institutionalized trust in the medium of money is ruptured. The question, then, is what backs the value of money, stabilizes its worth, and makes it acceptable and usable. At a first level of security, money may be backed by objects with value in their own right such as precious metals or, in the case of money created by institutions of credit, by mortgaged or pledged properties held as collateral. At a deeper level, the value of money is backed by the productive capacity of the economy, its capacity to produce goods and services at a pace not outrun by growth in the supply of money. Parsons referred to unwillingness to look behind the immediate security backing of the various media – advocacy of the gold standard, for example – as "fundamentalism." The logic of money can be extended by analogy (some would say by metaphor) to the other media. Power is backed by force. Yet faith in the ability of a *system* of power relations to *control* force in order to secure the interests of the members of a society, is backed by the political capacity of organized institutions of power to support collective action in support of collective goals by providing legitimate force as necessary. Political capacity is not just a matter of having an army; it is a matter of articulating police powers, law, institutions of lawmaking, and access to legal redress in a complex system of use and control of force. These examples show that as analysis moves from the primary modes of affecting others' conduct, to the generalization of these modes as media, to the security backing of media, and finally to the ultimate, systematic backing of the media in society, it gradually moves away from pure types to amalgamations of all the factors that makes organization work. Yet money and power remain recognizable extensions of their primary basis throughout the analysis. Money remains a generalization of use value and power a generalization of force, even after recognition of the role of institutionalized norms in stabilizing their operation. The relation of influence to persuasion is more ambiguous.

*What backs influence?* In his principal exposition of the concept of influence, Parsons (1967b, 367) cast a brief glance at the possibility that the resources of argument provide backing for generalized capacity to persuade, but he made these remarks in passing, on the way to a different destination:

[It] seems that, to correspond to the intrinsic "want-satisfiers," which the economist calls "goods and services," there should be a category of intrinsic "persuaders." The most obvious member of this category is "facts" from which alter can "draw his own conclusions." Ego, that is, can persuade by giving alter information which, given his situation and intentions, will lead him to make certain types of decisions. It seems probable that information is the proper parallel to commodities, with a special type of information – the announcement of firm intentions of action on the part of significant others – the parallel to services.

In the same passage, he immediately abandoned this approach. Saying that influence as a symbol must be something yet more general, he proceeded to look for mechanisms that would signal that the persuader is to be *trusted*, rather than indicators that the persuader's *message* is *convincing* as such. At this point the direction of Parsons' argument substantially changed.

At first it appeared that Parsons was ready to ground influence directly on solidarity. He begins by positing an inherent connection between successful persuasion and underlying solidarity between partners in a persuasive transaction (Parsons 1967b, 368):

if . . . we are dealing specifically with social interaction, it seems reasonable to suggest that the most favorable condition under which alter will trust ego's effort to persuade him . . . will be when the two stand in a mutual relation of fundamental diffuse solidarity, when they belong together in a collectivity on such a basis that, so long as the tie holds, ego *could not* have an interest in trying to deceive alter . . .

He then points out that, in modern society, trust must extend beyond diffuse contexts of *Gemeinschaft* to the full range of mutual commitments that arise through freedom of communication. *Gemeinschaft*, then, is the gold standard of influence, and in modern societies a more complex systemic capacity is necessary, a capacity to create alignments on behalf of collective goals so that individuals with only relatively narrow connections can be united in stable networks of trust. This is a point of considerable significance, for it shows that Parsons was ready to grant that influence could be created by voluntary, purpose-specific alliances backed by solidary ties that do not preexist but are created by discourse – by "freedom of communication."[7] By definition such solidary ties must be created by rhetoric and not by merely pointing to existing structures. By implication, there must be room for argument as a constitutive element of modern social structure. Yet having said this, he immediately returned to the theme of normative regulation, emphasizing the normative contexts of discourse to the virtual exclusion of substantive argument. He suggested that just as the acceptance of money relies on its capacity to define value equivalences between different goods and services, and power rests on normative authorizations to use it, so the acceptance of influence rests on "normative justifications of generalized statements about information or intention (*not* their empirical validation)" (Parsons, 1967b, 369, emphasis in original). His argument regarding the grounds for accepting influence strongly assimilates persuasion to its normative supports:

The user of influence is under pressure to justify his statements, which are intended to have an effect on alter's action, by making them correspond to norms that are regarded as binding on both. With reference to items of information, justification is necessary, since influence is a symbolic medium. The function of justification is not actually to verify the items, but to provide the basis for the communicators' *right* to state them without alter's needing to verify them; for example, ego may be a technically competent "authority" in the field. With reference to intentions, justification may be regulated by various aspects of status that are regularly invoked to indicate that such intentions should prove trustworthy when stated by persons in the category in question. A very important category of the justification of influence is what is ordinarily meant by "reputation." The same statement will carry more "weight" if made by someone with a high reputation for competence, for reliability, for good judgment, etc., than by someone without this reputation or with a reputation for unreliability (369, emphasis in original).

This conception of the grounds for accepting influence is true to Parsons' definitions: to ask for more argument or for substantive grounds is to refuse to accept someone's influence. Arguing each matter out means resorting, in a persuasive dialogue, to the equivalent of barter in trade, shaping each particular plea to the situation in an *ad hoc* manner. The question, though, is whether an entirely normative, status-based conception of influence can portray the play of social and political rhetoric in modern societies. One cannot conceive, for example, of a meaningful electoral campaign solely oriented to competing claims to trust based on arguments about reputation, without regard to matters of political policy. Such a campaign would not conform to Parsons' own conception of the electoral process as an interchange between influence and power, with one of the categories of influence being the substantive demands of the public (Parsons 1967c, 350). Influence is a blend of necessary argument and appeals to be believed on trust, and the connections between these two modes of persuasion should be prefigured in the basic paradigm.

*Influence and stratification.* Parsons' easy recourse to prestige as the source of influence leaves an impression that he viewed social status as the sole foundation of social integration and leads some critics to place Parsons in the Hegelian tradition of finding civil society in the old order of estates (Cohen and Arato, 1992). But Parsons' views were more complex than his frequent reference to prestige and the order of stratification might suggest. Passages that appear to reduce influence to normatively defined prestige must be compared with passages that refer to the importance of backing influence with good argument. In his principal exposition of the concept of influence, he defined the "inflation" of influence as "the extension of *claims to authoritative diagnosis of situations that cannot be validated by solid information* and declarations of praiseworthy intentions that will not be backed up by actual commitments when the occasion arises" (1967b, 382, emphasis supplied). The matter of what backs influence remained equivocal and murky.

Parsons was not entirely satisfied with the initial formulation of his ideas about influence as originally published in 1963. The influence paper ended on an apologetic note, referring to his work as "very tentative indeed" and as not more than "the barest approach to the very complicated problems in this area." When "On the Concept of Influence" was republished in 1967, he noted in an introductory comment that he did not consider his analysis of influence to be as well developed as his prior analysis of power and that further progress would depend on "clarification of a whole range of problems concerning the integrative processes of social systems" (355). His next opportunity to clarify the analysis of influence was provided by *The System of Modern Societies* (1971). The theory of "societal community" presented in that book was designed to locate the "integrative processes of social systems" in a differentiated integrative subsystem, comparable to the economy or the polity. The economy organizes the production of goods and services, and the polity organizes the regulation and mobilization of force, while the integrative system organizes the solidarities attendant to membership in the community. Influence is the currency of this integrative system. But *The System of Modern Societies* was a slim volume intended as an advanced textbook and did not furnish a good vehicle for developing an expanded technical presentation. The ambiguities remained. At one point Parsons emphasized that influence requires persuasion in the strict sense (14), but he also unequivocally equates influence with prestige and locates it in systems of social stratification (14; 121), avoiding the question of the relation between the force of substantive rhetoric and its legitimation by the status of the persuader.

*Culture and the generalization of influence.* Was Parsons' dismissal of "information" as the backing for persuasion and return to a status-based theory warranted? In his abrupt reversion to a status-based theory of influence, Parsons did not not pause to consider the role of culture in the generalization of influence. He might, at this point, have argued that modern persuasion is generalized as influence through expertise and that the social organization of knowledge allows the production of convincing knowledge, but requires *both* the crediting of expert roles and the provision of forums for rational discussion. He could have begun a more general inquiry into the role of cognitive rationality itself in the generalization of persuasion. Or perhaps he could have explained the generalization of influence by calling on the concept of frames of reference. In defending abstract sociological theory, he had himself emphasized that the meaning of facts are always contingent upon a generalized frame of reference. Later, Erving Goffman (1974) developed the notion that perceptual frames can shift or "change key" very quickly, as when we decide that a scene is playful rather than serious. Changing frames allows actors to interpret, define, and label their experience. Frame analysis has since proved a useful tool in several contexts. Social movements can convert and mobilize their adherents by providing new contexts for evaluating their experience and its implications (Snow et al. 1986). The press influences opinion by placing events in or out of frames that define them as mainstream or peripheral (Entman and Rojecki 1993). Gamson (1992) reports that among groups of ordinary citizens talking politics, framing issues as matters of injustice often led groups to identify a victimized "we" and to see a need for collective action. Framing messages is, in fact, one of the principal means by which professional communicators sell their messages in the New Public.

Parsons' methodological appreciation of philosophical "frames of reference" could have suggested that persuasion is symbolically generalized through placement of rhetorical messages in a frame. One might even suppose that examining the generalizing force of perceptual frames would be an inviting strategy, because persuasion works, according to Parsons, on "the definition of the situation." Moreover, frames are clearly institutionalized as cognitive components of social motivation. General frameworks of definition legitimize obligations so that actors want to do what they have to do. Most theories of ideology and hegemony imply that the institutionalization of general concepts provides resources of influence to elites and other advocates of the mainstream.[8]

Perceptual frames exemplify the capacity of rhetorical culture to generalize rhetorical strategies. Symbols are the stuff of culture, symbols that by their generality refer to that which cannot be experienced literally and directly. A person cannot experience all the roses in the world, past, present, and future, but can understand the notion of the class of roses and can follow deductions about what must be true of something if it is a rose. People do not experience love as if it were literally a rose, but through metaphor they can generalize from properties in common and understand lines like "My love is like a red, red rose" or the significance of presenting (rhetorically) red roses on appropriate occasions. Symbols provide the generalized frames that give, even alter, the meanings of particulars, and symbols cohere in the deductive and associative chains of implication that Kenneth Burke treats under the rubric of logology. Symbols can stand for large complexes of meaning that are economically expressed by tokens that merely suggest them. Yet such tokens implicitly promise that given time or the right occasion, a more expansive spelling out would be possible: "For now, here is a rose; later I will demonstrate the sincerity of my presentation." In short, cultural symbols are well adapted to the tasks of rhetorical generalization. Yet Parsons did not explore this path to the generalization of persuasion into influence, but opted to focus instead on the messenger's right to be trusted.

All the media ultimately rest on trust. Why, in the case of influence, did Parsons move directly to trust as the base of the operation of the medium, barely lingering on the phenomenon of generalized persuasion as a mode of casting arguments? He apparently wanted to move as quickly as possible to establish a theoretical niche for influence that would allow him to recognize the undeniable role of status in making messages believable, and, in this way, to link his new theory of influence to his long-term interest in demonstrating that social stratification is at the heart of social integration (Parsons 1954b). His argument is, in effect, that the participants in social systems will accept the allocation of resources to productive groups and to necessary projects if they are justified by the statements of people who are believable by virtue of their social status. That such processes do exist and that they must be incorporated into the theory of society is not at issue. What is at issue is the role of substantive argument in establishing and supporting the credibility of proposals backed by generalized persuasion or influence. Parsons' specific exclusion of substantive argument as the grounding for influence is clearly stated at a crucial step in his argument – the point at which he begins to define the sources of trust in arguments presented by others.

### The analytical status of reputation

Criticism of the reduction of influence to status cannot ignore the empirical importance in everyday activities of reliance upon status as an indicator of reliability. A realistic account of how influence works cannot ignore the fact that people regularly accept on faith, without independent verification, the pronouncements of others. Confidence in reputation and prestige, in perceived common interests, and in the good faith of others is a pervasive background force in daily life. It is manifest in events as varied as visiting a physician, buying groceries, or asking a stranger for directions. Indeed, it is a component of looking at a published map instead of asking a stranger for directions. In a world of imperfect information, acceptance on trust is so pervasive that "influence," in the sense of substituting confidence in reputation for actual information, can hardly be viewed as a specifically modern institution. It is an indispensable substitute for massive investments in personal investigation and endless discussion prior to any action whatsoever. What is modern is the rise in the legitimacy of asking for evidence and refusing to limit one's decisions about accepting the interpretations and suggestions of others to recognition of their standing in the status order. Nor is the *system* of influence disturbed by requests for further evidence and argument. Such requests are not parallel to refusing money and demanding objects of value instead. Asking doctors for a second opinion is not analogous to asking them to accept furniture in payment. On the contrary, the stabilization of systems of influence depends on the existence of constant flows of confirming information. The parallel between money and influence is suggestive but limited, and the theory of influence must proceed by direct inquiry into its workings, not by mere analogy. There is, though, an element of the inner workings of economic systems that does provide an instructive approach to the relation between influence and information.

*Influence and imperfect information.* Recent economic theory suggests the value of treating reputation as a substitute for direct information and, by implication, analytically separating a component of influence based on information (i.e. evidence and argument) from a component based on prestige-backed *tokens* of information. Accepting the representations of others without direct verification is common and essential in economic life. Reputation, which can be defined as an expectation of quality in a market where there is not reliable information (Shapiro 1982), comes into play when trading partners have asymmetrical information, as in the sale of used cars, where owners know more about the reliability of their cars than prospective buyers. Akerlof (1970), in his seminal paper on the "market for lemons," uses the market for used cars as a prototype for analysis of asymmetrical information. Starting from the assumption that the quality of used cars varies, and that the lower the quality of a given car, the more likely it will be offered on the market, Akerlof shows that under the strict conditions of asymmetry, if the marketplace is completely competitive according to the purely economic motivations assumed in price theory, there will be no equilibrium price for any car. The market will break down. When deficiencies in information place special emphasis on trust, "counteracting institutions" arise: guarantees, warranties, brand names, standardized franchises, licenses, academic degrees, and awards and prizes are among the counteracting institutions Akerlof mentions. Trust is particularly important in the extension of financial credit, for informational asymmetry arises when the intentions of debtors to repay or the true quality of their investment projects are uncertain (Leland and Pyle 1977). Akerlof devotes a section of his analysis to an explanation of the concentration, in developing nations, of credit institutions in particular family and clan organizations, citing the value of solidarity as a ready-made source of warranty.

The effect of unreliable information in economic markets has also led to substantial work in economics on "signaling." Beginning with a remarkable paper by Spence (1973) on signaling in job markets, economists have developed the notion that signals of reliability must be more difficult ("costly," in economic terms) for unreliable signalers than for reliable signalers or everyone would send the same signals. Hence job seekers invest in degrees, and entrepreneurs convince lenders of the worth of their projects by investing their own money in them (Leland and Pyle 1977). These economic studies provide a clear and illuminating perspective on the analytically separate and independent status of information and reputation in the process of economic inducement, which though normally mediated by money, is dependent on influence, too. Each has an independent force. Reputation has an impact even in purely rational, cost-benefit driven systems, but market participants try to overcome the uncertainties implicit in reputation alone by seeking strong informational indices of reliability.

The importance of reputation among participants with asymmetrical access to information is also apparent in political systems. Economic models of politics, beginning with Downs' (1957) "economic theory of democracy," closely tie influence to information. For Downs, those who exercise "leadership" are able to "influence voters to adopt certain views as expressions of their own will" (87). Influence is possible because voters are uncertain and access to information is costly. In Downs' strictly economic model, the "tastes" of rational citizens are taken as a given, and if everyone had access to information they would not need leaders to advise them on political decisions. Investment in direct access to information always costs time or money, and it is not rational for citizens to make greater investments in personally gathering information than the value of expected payoffs. Accordingly, they delegate much of their gathering and evaluation of information to others. There is, then, an agency relationship between citizens, as principals, and the agents they rely upon for information. Like all principals, citizens must trust those to whom they have delegated responsibility, so they look for indicators of reliability: personal knowledge of the agent's character and good faith; the agent's credentials as a professional information specialist; knowledge that the agent represents an interest group with which the agent can identify – that is, paradoxically, knowledge that the source of information is biased, but in the right direction.

A parallel duality operates in economic, political, and social persuasion. Fully adequate information is often too costly. Lacking full information, the targets of persuasive communication must rely to some extent on the reputation of the persuader, yet, not wanting to accept "cheap talk," they seek to allay the uncertainties implicit in reputation by seeking information about reliability, too.[9] One cannot imagine a system of influence – regular, effective persuasion among an organized group – that is utterly dependent on calling upon reputation alone as the guarantee of sincere discourse. In any system that permits different points of view, persuaders cannot repeatedly insist, "Don't ask for reasons, just believe; don't ask where we are going, just follow me there." As in the case of economic transactions, the participants in systems of influence seek informational indices of reliability apart from the status of the persuader. They ask for reasoned argument, for explanation, for facts, and for indicators of sincerity. They expect to be able to redeem tokens of information in convincing items of direct information. It is neither plausible nor productive to think of influence as simply a system of normatively defined rights to expect others to believe one's messages. Yet, as we will later see, the need for redeeming tokens in extensive argument and information is not well served by the professional practice of influence in the New Public or by the mass media that carry influential messages.

### Influence, affiliation, and solidarity: toward a new paradigm

Parsons defined influence as generalized persuasion, but variously identified its sources and backing as sound argument, solidarity, normatively defined rights to make pronouncements and to be believed, prestige and reputation, and systems of status that bestow prestige. These common features of social life do contribute to social integration and to social conflict, too. The theory of influence need not pick one or another of these factors as the true essence of influence, but an adequate account of influence should sort out the respective roles of its several components and specify the relations of these components to each other, starting with a paradigm of persuasion that leads directly to accounts of the forms of differentiation that support integration in specifically modern societies. I will start from the premise that *persuasion entails an offer of affiliation*, and from this premise proceed to ground a theory of social influence, its sources and effects, its role in society, and its characteristic pathologies.

The influence paradigm can be substantially strengthened by asserting the inherent connection between influence and affiliation at the outset. Viewing attempts to persuade as offers of affiliation and defining the acceptance of persuasive appeals as acts of affiliation has two principal strengths: firstly, it clearly distinguishes persuasion from force or purchase, a distinction that goes to the roots of liberal political theory; secondly, it calls attention to the dynamic character of persuasion. Persuasion and influence do not just affect minds, they set alliances. The constant play of persuasion in society reinforces existing social connections, and hence reproduces existing social structures. At the same time, persuasion creates new connections, adapting common interests, alliances, and solidarities to new circumstances.

Treating influence as a bid for affiliation does require an adjustment in the Parsonian paradigm, for it implies that persuasion involves a special form of inducement, not just a detached, abstract attempt to change alter's definition of the situation.[10] The Parsonian influence paradigm, despite its problems, does call attention to an affiliative element in persuasion. Since persuasion must work by pointing to or redefining existing interests, it involves convincing others that what the persuader wants is *already* in their own interests. But what interest motivates the persuader? Unless we assume that persuaders are working against their own interests, the motive for persuasion must be to align interests – to point out a common interest that forms a basis for an affiliative solidarity. Parsons understood this implication and built upon it from time to time, but by regularly reverting to his long-term interests in social stratification and social control, he obscured the creative scope and impact of influence: *influence does not just produce conformity to the demands of the existing order; it creates new social structures.*

Parsons' early treatment of influence was tied to the problem of social control (Parsons 1954a). Influence is a form of social capital that is mobilized when people are brought into line by calling upon obligations inherent in their membership in the collectivity. A passage in *Economy and Society* (Parsons and Smelser 1956, 49) provides a telling illustration of Parsons' initial linkage of influence, solidarity, and social control. Comparing wealth, power, and solidarity, the authors write:

Power is the generalized capacity to mobilize the resources of the society, including wealth and other ingredients such as loyalties, "political responsibility," etc., to attain particular and more or less immediate collective goals of the system. Correspondingly, solidarity is the generalized capacity of agencies in the society to "bring into line" the behaviour of system units in accordance with the integrative needs of the system, to check or reverse disruptive tendencies to deviant behaviour, and to promote the conditions of harmonious co-operation. (emphasis supplied)

This passage presents solidarity as a central element in the ongoing integration of social systems, but suppresses the link between solidarity and the adaptive features of modern social organization. Power and wealth mobilize; solidarity constrains. The theory of influence must also account for the success of social movements directed *against* established features of a social system. Influence is created and mobilized on behalf of efforts to change social systems and to reintegrate them on altered terms. When this occurs, the key feature of influence is its capacity to create and to mobilize new solidarities.

By the time Parsons presented his foundation paper on the concept, he had begun to make room for affiliation and the creation of solidarity as core elements in the process of influence:

attempting to influence is to a degree an attempt to establish a common bond of solidarity, on occasion even to bring the object of influence into a common membership in a collectivity. Thus, being subject to mutual influence is to constitute a "we" in the sense that the parties have opinions and attitudes in common by virtue of which they stand together relative to those differing from them (1967b, 370).

I see here the germ of a possible articulation of Parsons' structural sociology with Kenneth Burke's ideas about the rhetoric of identity and division, a melding that offers great promise for understanding the operations of influence in modern and postmodern society.

## Forms of affiliation

The relation of influence and affiliation can be further clarified by moving through a series of empirical forms of influence, beginning with the influence exercised by persons in professional roles, a prototype for the status-based, reputational approach to influence (Parsons 1954b).

*Professional influence.* Physicians, for example, rely on occupational prestige to diagnose and prescribe, using the rights bestowed on their professional role to achieve compliance by orders alone, without supplying a complete medical school education to each patient. As Parsons would have it, commitment to a common interest is provided by the "collectivity orientation" of the physician, a normatively defined interest in their patients' health. Physician and patient form a small collectivity with a special type of solidarity, and the stability of the entire system of medicine rests in part on this system of roles. A physician's entry into a course of diagnosis and treatment involves an implicit offer of affiliation. The physician's sway is exercised through influence, not force, and it is possible for the patient to reject treatment and to break off the relationship. The physician's diagnosis and prescription entail an offer to aid the patient and include an affirmation, whether stated or not, that the relationship is solidary in the sense that both participants are in league toward the same end – that the physician has no dominant ulterior primary motive. The patient must decide whether to trust the physician's commitment, and may in fact not develop adequate trust to sustain the relationship. A patient may not understand a physician's diagnosis and medical advice; the physician may put off the patient's request for clarification and the patient may, in return, lose confidence, become suspicious and distrustful, and seek help elsewhere, refusing the physician's offer of affiliation.

Notwithstanding the relative strength of other-oriented, ethical norms in certain aspects of the medical profession, in both medicine and in the larger occupational order, professionalization is a means by which occupational groups assert jurisdiction over a domain of practice and establish controls on entry (Freidson 1970; Larson 1977; Collins 1979; Abbott 1988). Economic interests often dominate commitments to ethical practice and to the protection of the public. Collectivity orientation is a variable, relatively strong in some professions, less so in others. The crucial question for students of the New Public is whether such fields as public relations, which aspire to professional status, have in fact established effective ethical standards in support of the public's interest in accurate representation, a matter that will be taken up in chapter 7.

*Voluntary association.* The formation and support of voluntary associations provides a clear view of influence as an offer of affiliation. Suppose, for example, that a considerable number of patients lose faith in conventional medicine and its mainstream practitioners and seek alternative paths to therapy and health. These patients may be drawn to aggressive nutritional therapies, or to mind-body programs, or perhaps to holistically inclined physicians within the medical establishment. Those who choose alternative paths to health care, whether as patients or practitioners, are likely to join associations formed to promote their activities and beliefs and to defend themselves against attempts to debunk, restrict, or even prohibit their alternative forms of practice. Midwives, for example, work to legitimize their practice, to create favorable public images of their work, and to avoid legal restrictions that would award a strict monopoly to licensed medical doctors (Litoff 1978). Forming associations allows midwives and their supporters to speak with a relatively unified voice. Associations can seek to affect public opinion and policy and, at the same time, provide assistance to their members in the form of education, advice, and mutual support. When the leader of such an association ask others to join or urges members to participate, she is clearly making an offer of affiliation, and to the extent she is successful, she is building a base for influence. Associations that seek to influence public opinion and legislation are dependent on the support of members who voluntarily commit themselves to a common interest in response to an offer of affiliation.

Since Mancur Olson's (1971) path-breaking work on collective action, social scientists have been concerned about the implications of the "free-rider" problem. Why will people engage in voluntary effort on behalf of collective aims if they can receive the same benefits by letting others do the work? Olson stressed the motivational force of side benefits in the form of personal economic incentives for joining and staying in organizations. Others have pointed to the importance of "social capital" (Coleman 1990), the "features of social life – networks, norms, and trust – that enable participants to act together more effectively to pursue shared obligations." Voluntary organizations may offer strong solidary incentives. Wuthnow's (1994) study of support groups in the United States is particularly interesting in this respect. Forty percent of the US population report participation in small groups that meet regularly to provide care and support for each other. Wuthnow estimates that 25,000,000 Americans participate regularly in 3,000,000 such groups ( 59–76) and finds that their involvement creates profound communal feelings. Such groups illustrate the continuing importance of voluntary solidary association within a modern, supposedly depersonalized society. To the extent that such groups create a reservoir of organized solidarity, they provide resources for rhetorical appeals and a base for influence.

*Election campaigns.* In democratic nations, citizens are directly exposed to attempted influence each time elections are held. The logic of affiliation is evident in the typical format of appeals to the electorate. Voters are told that candidates will work for the voters' interests; they are asked to join in an effort to achieve common ends. Such appeals cannot be effective unless voters believe that a candidate is approaching them with some measure of sincerity, which implies that the candidate actually shares the voters' aims and beliefs and feels a degree of solidarity with them. That promises are not always kept and that candidates are cynical are staple maxims of popular belief, but that does not alter the logical form of electoral discourse. Jaded popular beliefs have not led candidates to appeal to common opinion by promising that they will do whatever will be in their own personal interest, that they are not to be trusted, and that they therefore deserve the electorate's support as the very model of a modern politician – the exact sort of person voters have always supported in the past. Campaign rhetoric, honest or not, invariably takes the form of offers of affiliation.

Electoral campaigns bring an additional element to the discussion of the role of affiliation in influence, for candidates' offers of affiliation are typically contested by other candidates. The governing norms of the electoral system call for competing offers of affiliation, which underscores the voluntary character of association within a democratic polity. Voluntary association is not limited to electoral politics; it extends to any arena in which leaders (or would-be leaders) extend offers of affiliation to like minded others who can join together in mutual support or to promote and defend their group's interests. Translated into the vocabulary of influence, leaders attempt to influence groups so that the groups can influence the larger society. While this commonplace proposition is not novel, it underscores the contested character of influence and the theoretical significance of competing bids for affiliation.

A leader who makes a competitive bid for affiliation in support of a cause draws upon all the resources of rhetoric, establishing solidarity with the audience and, in so doing, appeals to claims that support his or her credibility and trustworthiness, appeals grounded in status, reputation and prestige – attributes that place the leader in a solidary relation with the audience and display indicators of credibility. These attributes may be achieved, that is earned by past success, and displays of virtuous self sacrifice on behalf of the group, or they may be generalized indicators of status, such as position in a respected stratum. Whatever the indicator of status, a competitive bid for affiliation must go beyond announcing the attributes of the bidder.

One cannot imagine contested elections in which candidates restrict themselves to calling upon normative rights attendant to their status, claiming that those rights endow their claims to represent the electorate without reference to information regarding how these interests will be well secured by the candidate. Political discourse in electoral settings or in any other context where leaders ask for support, from advancing the causes of social movements to lobbying legislators, requires both reputation and information, but it is not correct to assert that reputation (or prestige) is the *generalized* foundation for social *influence* while substantive argument is the situational content of mere persuasion in *particular* instances. Such a theoretical strategy would overlook the generalizing capacity of cultural presuppositions, knowledge, ideology, and frames of reference in persuasive discourse – symbols that link leaders and followers through the cultural affinities supplied by rhetorically addressed appeals.

*Personal influence.* The theory of personal influence – influence exerted face to face, among friends and neighbors, colleagues and co-workers – has enjoyed paradigmatic status for half a century and, with the current prominence of network theory in sociology, is stronger than ever.[11] Recognition of the importance of personal influence originally emerged in studies of the impact of the mass media on the public, especially in studies of the presidential elections of 1940 and 1948 (Lazarsfeld, Berelson, and Gaudet 1948; Berelson, Lazarsfeld, and McPhee 1954). The discovery that most citizens were influenced directly by other people and that the messages of the mass media were filtered through a two-stage flow, first from the media to opinion leaders and then to others by personal influence, led to further studies of the source of opinions on other political matters and on consumer preferences (Katz and Lazarsfeld 1955; Merton 1968, 441–74). Again, networks of family, friends, and co-workers were shown to provide pathways for personal influence.

Current research, employing more sophisticated approaches to mapping and measuring networks and their impact, continues to demonstrate the importance of direct person-to-person influence, even in world-historical events propelled by mass action. Recent studies have shown, for example, that the shape of networks of personal ties explain the outcome of the final showdown between the Medici and the oligarchs in Florence in 1433 (Padget and Ansell 1993), and that interpersonal networks were the prime route for mobilizing street action in both the Paris Commune of 1871 (Gould 1993) and the East German Revolution of 1989 (Opp and Gern 1993). The older studies of personal influence and more recent studies of the mobilization of networks share a common stance: to understand the way that underlying social forces are played out in ongoing social life we must penetrate the formal level of organizations, social roles, and abstract categories of social status to study the substrata of people's actual lives (Padget and Ansell 1993; Somers 1993). Life is lived in proximity to others, among groups or circles that are relatively close to or distant from each other in social space. Personal influence on people's opinions and acts is the primary form of influence, and such influence flows through networks of connections that are strong or weak, stable or transient, latent or mobilized.

We will return to the personal-networks paradigm again because the concept of a two-step flow of communication needs revision in the light of emerging modes of producing influence in the New Public, whose specialized practitioners try, in effect, to overcome the embedding of opinion in primary groups. In the present context, personal influence is especially interesting for the light it casts on the close relations between influence and affiliation. One of the strengths of the concept of personal influence as it gained strength in the 1940s and 1950s was the convergence of studies of face-to-face influence within social circles and the then burgeoning interest among both sociologists and social psychologists in the study of small groups, which brought to the paradigm of personal influence a whole panoply of concepts invoked to explain the effects of group members on each other: group pressures to conform, cohesion, attraction to like-minded others, friendship in communication networks, group climates, leadership, strength of attachment, and the manipulation of group dynamics to achieve change (Katz and Lazarsfeld 1955, 13–115; Aronson 1995, 23–115). This conceptual apparatus, which has been supported in a long line of continuing research, is entirely consistent with defining influence as an affiliative process. People are influenced by others with whom they have solidary ties, who have similar views, who can be trusted. Influential people mobilize such ties, urging or suggesting actions and views that will reinforce or enhance their ties to those they influence.

The concept of mobilization marks a significant change in tone attendant to change from the initial notion of personal influence to more recent network studies, especially studies applying network theory to the explanation of social movements. The leaders of social movements seek to create solidary ties to followers and to mobilize these ties in action – to mobilize affiliations – but when it comes time to encourage group action, it is necessary to rely on networks of known and trusted grassroots leaders to mobilize their affiliations with particular people. In summary, coming to hold a belief and to take action founded on beliefs is more than a matter of intellectual persuasion; it involves looking to others for guidance, receiving advice and encouragement, and through this process, creating and enhancing interpersonal connections.

*Prolocutors: speaking for solidarity.* Existing and potential patterns of group solidarity provide generalized bases for influence. Persuaders can appeal to similarly situated persons, who, whatever the differences in their particular circumstances, have common identifications as members of groups: as physicians or working people or women or senior citizens or Southerners, or ultimately as members of a societal community – Americans or Japanese or Brazilians. Common interests that are not current bases for common identifications can become bases for solidaristic identification through rhetorical appeals. In Marxist terms, classes in themselves can become classes for themselves as they become aware of their common fate and align themselves as a self-conscious group. What is true for the working class is true for any common interest that emerges in the process of politics. The solidarity of groups and the strength of solidaristic identifications wax and wane as they become more or less salient in social and political arenas. The public alters its internal structure as issues come in and out of public attention, and solidary ties are promoted, strengthened, mobilized, and then allowed to decay. For example, were the institution of tenure for college teachers to be seriously challenged, we might expect the salience of identification with the profession to increase, loyalties to be mobilized, existing professional groups and leaders to be strengthened, group pressures to be placed on professors to pull together, and new leaders and groups to emerge. All these groups and leaders would claim to represent – *to speak for* – college professors.

Claims to speak on behalf of groups are an especially important resource for the generalization of influence. To assert that one speaks for a larger group is to place the solidarity of that group behind attempts to persuade both members of the group and others for whom the interests of the group have consequences. I refer to leaders who come to speak for groups as *prolocutors* (Mayhew 1990). For example, Jesse Jackson is a prolocutor. Insofar as he has achieved the capacity to make others believe that he speaks for Afro-Americans, he can persuade black citizens to follow his lead and politicians who depend upon black voters to heed his advice. His influence is sufficiently generalized to allow him to speak out effectively across an extraordinary range of political and economic issues, even issues of identity such as what label Afro-Americans should use to identify themselves.

Jesse Jackson did not become a prolocutor and achieve his influence by election or by official appointment; he achieved this status by asserting it, and his prolocutor's influence is confirmed by being followed, or even when he is simply not repudiated. Garnering influence by this route involves acquiring a status, and one might ask whether my argument has come full circle by treating influence as a form of prestige. It is important to reaffirm at this point that prestige is a resource for influence. My argument is that prestige is not bound to well-defined, fixed statuses and that those who have prestige do not necessarily acquire normatively defined rights to be believed. It would be misleading to attempt to subsume the prestige of prolocutors under the general heading of social stratification. The prolocutor does not occupy a defined role in the larger society with a given amount of prestige assigned to this role by a system of normatively defined levels of respect. A prolocutor need not achieve this position by mobilizing an already high status in society; people who assert that they speak for a group may start with statuses earned in or ascribed to other roles, but with or without prior stores of prestige, the achievement of the special prestige of prolocutorship is dependent on a group's indications of trust and acceptance of would-be leaders who purport to act on their behalf. The establishment of the prolocutor's status is created by successful rhetoric. It does not simply derive from a system of stratification operating in the background and granting persons in systemically defined roles the right to be believed. It is created and sustained in an ongoing process of assertion, persuasion and ratification, that is, an ongoing process of influence. Status is as much a consequence as a source of influence. Influence is produced by a process of building solidarity and identity, which are founded on meanings, which in turn are created by credible rhetoric. Credibility is supported by prestige, but when meanings are contested, prolocutors' assertions must ultimately be defended by effective argument. This issue is crucial in Habermas' critique of the Parsonian concept of influence, an argument to be treated in greater detail in chapter 4. Systems, Habermas says, can reproduce the material world of production, but they cannot create meaning.

*Public Influence.* When advocates seek to influence opinion and policy by open appeals for general support, they do so in the name of the public, addressing their arguments to the public interest. However strongly public appeals are reinforced by private influence outside the public view, and however much a particular political campaign, lobbying effort, social movement, public relations campaign, or bid to change the public's views on current issues might direct its appeals differentially to particular groups or segments of the population, any effort that aspires to broad support must generalize its message beyond the concerns of its most interested clientele. Since public appeals must be justified by reference to the public interest, a gravitational pull toward public justification is inherent in the rhetoric of public debate. Air-traffic controllers must appeal to the public by reference to the public safety, not by naked appeals for more jobs for union members. Opponents of governmental health programs cannot expect to prevail by explaining that doctors will be better off financially if their fees are not limited by regulations; they must appeal to the public health. Businesses lobbying for lower taxes employ economists to show that taxes will inevitably be passed on to the consumer. The inclusive population, referred to as the public, or as citizens, voters, taxpayers, consumers, or working people, or by national designations (e.g. Americans) or, as simply "the people," is invoked rhetorically to mobilize broad bases of support. Obvious as this point might seem, its broad implications can transform our understanding of political processes. For example, one of the limitations of class-based politics follows from difficulties in universalizing claims to an audience that does not fully identify with class designations. Recent research on the embattled issue of working-class consciousness in nineteenth-century England suggests that movements attempting to draw on working-class interests, e.g. the Chartist movement, couched their appeals broadly in order to enhance their numbers, referring to "the people" rather than to the "working class." They expressed an English populism that affected the substance of workers' self consciousness (Joyce 1991). What some would label "mere" rhetoric is a response to the conditions of successful social action and, in turn, affects people's conceptions of themselves and their interests.

Driven by the advice of public relations and communications experts, breadth of appeal has become a condition of successful influence in the New Public. This has accelerated several long-term trends in the structure of public debate: public influence comes to the fore when private, favor-based influence can no longer succeed without incorporating new techniques that employ the rhetoric of public interest; more resources are invested in creating certified "objective knowledge" in support of purportedly public claims; experts create new types of organizations devoted to establishing public claims on behalf of clients. All these trends are products of efforts to broaden the base of a specifically modern form of solidary appeals – appeals based on invitations to belong to and support the public, rather than merely to remain loyal to traditional group affiliations.

It is this dynamic relation between influence and broadly binding solidarities that Parsons had in mind in stating that the exercise of influence builds consensus by justifying variable obligations, performances, and rewards in the name of contributions to a common interest, a common interest that coheres in societies at the level of the entire "society conceived as a community" (Parsons 1966, 121). Accordingly, rhetorical appeals gravitate to the language of public interest when competitors in national debate bid for support by claiming identification with groups that purport to represent the public interest and, ultimately, by claiming personal identification with the public itself. Hence the long-standing notoriety of Charles Wilson's apparently backwards claim that "what's good for General Motors is good for the country," and hence the persistent claim of American presidents since Woodrow Wilson that the President is the spokesperson for the whole people.[12]

The dynamics of persuasion through public appeals illustrates the logic of influence. Because persuasion must rest on convincing others that proposals are in their own interests, and because trust in the persuader requires that the audience believe in the sincerity of the persuader, the entire process rests on a perception that the persuader shares the aims of the persuaded. Setting forth a suggestion predicated on an appeal to common interests amounts to asking another to join in a common identity or a joint effort. Accepting such a suggestion is, in effect, a ratification of the persuader's claim to common ground. An attempt to persuade is a bid for affiliation, asking for either a new connection or the reinforcement of an old one. Acceptance of the bid completes an act of persuasion and creates or strengthens a bond, however slight or transitory. The bonds of persuasion may be very strong, effectively linking co-followers with each other and to their leaders in common cause. Leaders who have a general capacity to forge the bonds of persuasion possess influence, and to the extent that their appeals unite in the name of the interests of a whole community, they exercise public influence.

### Culture and social systems in the generalization of persuasion

Parsons' proclivity for reducing influence to the mobilization of social status stems from his desire to construct a symmetrical theory. He conceived influence as a medium in the social system and, accordingly, wanted to locate the process of generalizing persuasion in social systems. Since social roles are a principal constituent of social systems, it is at least convenient to attach influence, conceived as capacity to persuade, to the prestige of roles. His search for one ultimate and *social* source of the generalization of persuasion led him to neglect the role of argument, and more generally, to slight the interplay of social and cultural factors in the generation of influence.

To recapture the several analytical strands of the theory of social influence requires another look at rhetoric, for all the components of rhetorical appeal furnish modes of generalization. Normative appeals to an order of values, solidaristic appeals to and on behalf of members of groups, references to positions in a status order, and the use of eloquent styles that embody culturally resonant meanings are all employed to generalize particular persuasive strategies into generalized, socially structured influence. Viewed in this context, it becomes apparent that culture is the generalizer *par excellence*. Culture, which includes the tools of language and logic, is inherently suited for extending the reach of the particular. Argument involves saying that this is like that, or that something else belongs to a category governed by general rules. For example, in the Parsonian scheme, institutionalized norms are part of the social system, but normative argument works by providing grounds for generalized appeals, freed from the limits of the particular situations of individual members of the audience. To the degree that norms are generalized, applicable as abstract obligations to all members of a group or to all members of a definable portion of the group, a persuasive address can, in its normative appeals, sway general audiences across a broad range of particulars. The discourse of normative rhetoric has a generalizing effect achieved by absorbing the persuasive situation into a larger pattern of concepts and rules.

The aura of authority and status are also important rhetorical resources, because capacity to persuade by implicit or explicit reference to authority transcends particular instances. Criticism of Parsons' notion that prestige is the main means for generalizing persuasion does not deny that hierarchy plays a part in influence. On the contrary, implicit and explicit appeals to hierarchy, appeals to be believed because of who one is, are one analytical component of influence and of the rhetoric by which it is delivered. The question is not whether prestige plays its part, but what are the relative roles of prestige and argument and how are they articulated.

Achieving generalized capacities to speak on behalf of groups is a crucial instance of the interaction of culture and society in the generalization of influence. Prolocutors cannot simply point to their positions in the occupational order to demonstrate that they represent solidary groups. They must use generalizing rhetoric to construct accounts of common interest designed to create a sense of solidarity among groups of potential followers. Once created, this solidarity must be continually reaffirmed by ratification, a process that requires prolocutors to construct new occasions for new messages. Professional practitioners in the New Public are well aware of the requisites of building and maintaining support for people and organizations that purport to speak on behalf of groups. For example, the recent proliferation of professional firms that create "grassroots" organizations from the top down highlights the danger, inherent in rhetoric, of *overgeneralization*, which builds representations of solidarity on overextended rhetoric that does not match the underlying structure of group interests and capacities for collective action. This leads to inflated, even false, claims of common interest and to public distrust of the process of representation.

# 4

# Habermas and Parsons: critical issues regarding influence

Jürgen Habermas has proposed an elaborate and complex critique of Talcott Parsons' work. Moreover, the body of Parsonian thought that Habermas addresses itself involves legendary complications. To disentangle the various strands of Habermas' argument and of Parsons' potential lines of rebuttal requires a clear understanding at the outset as to what the argument is about: it is about the integration of modern society. Habermas asks whether there is today a *social* sphere – a realm of specifically social institutions, outside the workings of money and power – that can steer society through the upheavals and stresses of modern life. For Habermas to reckon a coordinative steering mechanism as "social," it must be founded on mutual understanding. On these grounds, his answer to the question posed is decidedly negative. Such *system* integration as money and power might achieve by coordinating markets and bureaucracies does not count as *social* integration, which must be founded on the legitimate social relations that people undertake to form cultures, build character, and collectively resolve social problems.

Habermas has discussed this central question in a number of related texts, but in *Philosophical Discourses of Modernity* (1987b [1985] 358, 360–1) he makes particularly clear and unequivocal statement:

specialized subsystems such as economy, state, education, science, etc. are symmetrically related to one another, but their precarious equilibrium is not capable of being regulated for society as a whole ... Modern societies no longer have at their disposal an authoritative center for self reflection and steering ... As a matter of fact, today politics has become an affair of a functionally specialized subsystem; and the latter does not dispose over the measure of autonomy relative to the other subsystems that would be required for central steering, that is for an influence that comes from it and goes back to it.

Habermas not only asserts that ostensibly integrative structures do not integrate and do not govern adaptive change; in principle they *cannot*. Self regulation within a whole society requires achieved consensus, developed through a process of communicative understanding. No specialized discourse, removed from direct public debate, can construct such understanding. If people are to be persuaded, not regulated, by influence, its messages must be conveyed by honest discourse. A system that brings people into line by generating compromises among competing forces, not negotiating what is right but measuring the relative strength of demands, and strengthening or diluting demands by mere symbolic gestures, cannot produce stable public agreement. His analysis, is, in effect, a condemnation of the New Public, wherein new methods of rationalized symbolic persuasion, based on knowledge of how to affect aggregate opinion by superficial, unanswerable, one-sided messages, employ a mode of influence that is the very opposite of communicative action (Habermas 1989 [1962]).

Habermas' *The Theory of Communicative Action* (1984 [1981]; 1987a [1981] ), hereinafter referenced as TCA I and TCA II, provides detailed arguments for his position. This carefully crafted, two-volume work is a remarkable achievement. In a leisurely but cumulatively powerful exposition, Habermas situates both his social theory and his diagnosis of the times within the history of sociological thought. His thoughtful and appreciative reinterpretations of major social thinkers – Weber, Durkheim, Mead – creates an integrated and rhetorically effective presentation of an evolutionary account of the emergence of rational social organization, an account that takes rational communication as the defining feature of reason in society. Then, in a long critique of Parsons, Habermas describes how structural sociology, by a series of missteps, lost its purchase on the fundamental problem of social integration in contemporary society.

Habermas is clearly addressing the central problem of sociological theory. How is a highly differentiated society reintegrated? He specifically identifies the problem of social and functional integration of modern society – organic solidarity as defined by Durkheim – as the central question. He will not, however, credit any solution to the problem that accepts mere functional integration of activity – through economic markets, for example – as an answer. To be reckoned true *social* integration, the new moral order that replaces mechanical solidarity must be founded on achieved consensus on postconventional norms.

Parsons chose a similar starting point. He asked how, in a modern, highly differentiated society, is organic solidarity grounded in a moral order? Parsons found his answer in various processes of institutionalized public life, including most notably, "influence" and "value commitment," terms that he uses in specialized, technical senses. Habermas, too, favors an integrative role for the public, provided that public institutions are recreated as forums for proper rational discourse, but he cannot accept Parsons' formulation of the role of modern social influence in the integration of modern societies. Parsons' tolerant recognition of market-organized, impersonal communication came uncomfortably close to accepting the institutions of the New Public.

The influence of Parsons' work on the substance of *The Theory of Communicative Action* is manifest, but Habermas' regard for Parsons is highly ambivalent. He says of Parsons, "The body of work he left us is without equal in its abstraction and differentiation, its social-theoretical scope and systematic quality" and goes on to warn that "no theory of society can be taken seriously that does not at least situate itself in relation to Parsons" (TCA II, 199). Yet Habermas is apologetic about including a substantial section on Parsons. Other comparable sections are devoted to Weber, Durkheim and Mead. These figures are also found wanting in various respects, but Parsons alone is accorded extensive attention primarily on the grounds that we are to learn from his mistakes. Nevertheless, Habermas' own efforts parallel the Parsonian scheme in some respects, even making direct contact at several points, and not just because both work within a common tradition of thought.[1]

Habermas, like Parsons, begins with classifications of modes of action, a strategy that derives from their common participation in the Weberian tradition. All three thinkers employ strategies designed to define the rational and to locate rationality in structures of social action. Habermas accepts the three-fold division of action into cultural, social, and personal levels, but having adopted this three-fold paradigm, merges all three in the "lifeworld," the realm of interaction in which participants, in a taken-for-granted manner, reproduce cultural knowledge, social integration, and personal identity (Habermas TCA II, 137–8). His depiction of the realm of socialization, social coordination, and the reproduction of meaning portrays a social order rather like Parsons' integrated social system, as set forth in the early fifties (Parsons 1951), except that Habermas denies that the concept of system is an appropriate description of the ordering of this sphere. Nevertheless, Parsons' social system, like the lifeworld, is clearly engaged in the integrated reproduction of culture, solidarity, and personal identity in a consistent whole.

Habermas has also come to view structural sociology as the most advanced theoretical framework available and, within that framework, he emphasizes structural differentiation as a central dynamic force in a process of social evolution that tends to separate functionally diverse spheres. Tensions derive from incompatible fusions of radically separate spheres of action and from the contradictory requisites of appropriate action within these awkwardly intermixed spheres. Political and private realms have been fused, to the detriment of public life; the lifeworld, with its requisites of communicative action, has been breached and disrupted by the economy and the state, which operate by exchanges of money and power that operate *systematically*, without regard to authentic communication. Systems are outside the lifeworld, and Habermas deems it wrong to include the whole of social relations under the rubric of "system." Nevertheless, much of his analysis looks familiar to students of structure-functionalism. Indeed, some critics, approaching from radical directions, charge that Habermas has already given up too much to the functionalist paradigm by allowing that the economy and polity operate as systems coordinated by money and power.[2] Habermas even constructs charts using arrows to designate interchanges between spheres of society, diagrams reminiscent of Parsons' interchange paradigms of the sixties. However different their specific interpretations and their underlying intellectual strategies and attitudes, Parsons and Habermas converge in a tradition of differentiation theory.

Among the many points of convergence and divergence between Parsons and Habermas, one issue goes to the heart of the two authors' varied approaches to modernity. Parsons asserted a symmetrical set of societal subsystems – economy, polity, societal community – each differentiated from the others and each producing its own parallel forms of modernized "communication": money, power, and influence. Influence, the medium of integrative communication is organized within the societal community and provides an integrative resource for the entire society. Habermas, explicitly in opposition to this claim, divides the realms of society along different lines, opposing *lifeworld* and *system*. The lifeworld is an integrative sphere in which knowledge and meaning are sustained, solidarity established, and identities shaped through communication in language; economic and political realms are organized as functional subsystems, integrated by functional interdependencies and steered by money and power, outside the lifeworld's sphere of communicative action. Linguistic discourse in search of inter-subjective understanding cannot be integrated as a merely functional system and therefore cannot be treated as parallel to systems organized around money and power. Neither influence considered as medium of communication nor the societal community considered as a system can integrate the lifeworld or, for that matter, the larger society. This deliberately dualistic scheme, in which system integration by such mechanisms as markets or bureaucratic rules, is radically opposed to social integration by direct, linguistic communication oriented to achieving understanding, defines the fundamental disagreement between these two theorists.

### Parsons' false steps

Habermas claims that as Parsons moved from "action theory" to a "systems" approach, he uncoupled lifeworld and system. He then subsumed under systems theory elements of social life that can only be understood in an interactional framework – as relations among subjectively aware people who address their conduct to mutual understanding. Habermas believes that this misstep was inherent in Parsons' initial approach of his action frame of reference. Parsons' first wrong move was to construct an action scheme bound to a means-ends paradigm that retained the subject-object dualism implicit in positivism. Had he taken *intersubjective interaction* as a basic category of action at the very outset of his project, he could have treated the "interpretive accomplishments of participants in social interaction" as the foundation of social order, rather than simply assuming values and norms as given (TCA II, 213–15). From his misconceived starting point, Parsons found it difficult to give communicative action its proper due.

Parsons' second misstep occurred as the focus of his analysis progressively moved from the logic of action to the logic of systems. Along the way, culture came to be treated as a systemic environment for social interaction instead of an integral part of a lifeworld formed through communicative action (TCA II, 215–25). First, while still fully committed to an action frame of reference, Parsons made cultural values a part of the (external) situation of actors; then, as the logic of systems took over, he made culture itself a system in its own right, with its own imperatives and logic, external to the social system. When considered as a "boundary-maintaining system" that must sustain its own structures, rather than as an aspect of social life, culture becomes cut off from the lifeworld. Culture comes to be portrayed as a remote problem for people rather than a context and resource for their daily lives. Employing a metaphor from the Marxist tradition, Habermas refers to Parsons' treatment of culture as a "reification" (TCA II, 219). If culture is placed outside of interaction, it appears to be made *for* people rather than produced and reproduced *by* them through their communicative action in pursuit of shared meaning.

A third allegedly false step completed Parsons' transition from action theorist to systems theorist through and through. Following the logic of systems, Parsons divides the systems of action and their subsystems and sub-subsystems into exactly parallel entities, each with its own version of his fourfold scheme of functional requisites, each with its own inputs and outputs, and, most significantly, its own media for packaging and generalizing these outputs. At this point it became impossible to distinguish system and social integration, for integration becomes entirely a matter of an orderly flow of resources from system to system, so that each system can carry out its due functions.[3] Lifeworld and system have become thoroughly decoupled.

Parsons' ambitious systems theory, in its quest for symmetry, became more and more strained, its parallels confused and stretched, particularly the parallels between what he called the four "generalized media." Power, influence, and value commitment became exactly parallel to money, so that the system-integrating capacities of money and the concepts of markets, inflation, deflation, factors of production – all the useful concepts of economic theory – can be applied to other exchanges in the social system. Habermas contends that money, power, influence, and value commitment are not much like each other and cannot operate in the same way. Money has, for Parsons, become a mere metaphor allowing apparently consistent discussion of very unlike social phenomena. Habermas' criticism of Parsons' theory of generalized media, particularly influence, can be viewed as an account of the fourth and culminating Parsonian misstep, one that thoroughly vitiates his project, making it impossible for him to see the characteristic pathologies of modern society, even in its democratic formats, and allowing him to see a specifically social guidance in societies where no such guidance exists.

### The critique of influence

For Habermas, Parsons' false conceptualization of influence on the model of money (TCA, II, 256–82), in order to include influence among the exchange systems of modern society, is the source of his misinterpretation of modern social relations and of his blindness to the uncoupling of system and life world. Moreover, his concept of influence, by relying upon the institutionalization of prestige, puts an inegalitarian status order at the center of the modern social order and therefore makes such an order unjust in principle.

Habermas's closely argued and brilliantly devised critique of the concept of influence (TCA II, 256–82) is not to be taken lightly. His attack proceeds against several main openings. He notes that the concept of influence, conceived as a parallel to money, is an overgeneralization; the similarities between money as prototype and the other media are overdrawn, stretched, and ultimately metaphorical. He argues that influence cannot be a medium by Parsons' own definition of this concept. Parsons tried to derive the four media of the social system from the action frame of reference and then apply them to functions in the social system, but did not recognize that this created an unwieldy mix: offers of money and imperative commands are types of sanctions that can be understood within a functionalist logic of automatic systems, but affecting others' orientations to their situations requires communicative action and cannot be achieved by applying standardized sanctions. Habermas' main line of attack follows from a principle of communicative action: generalized symbolic media, which perform their coordinative functions in systems that operate automatically, through equilibrating forces that are beyond the ken of individual participants – in markets, for example – cannot resolve issues that require direct communication in ordinary language.

The burden of Habermas' project in *The Theory of Communicative Action* is a critique of functionalist reason. The historical rationalization of the economy and the polity have followed the functionalist logic of systems, but the unfinished work of reason, the rationalization of the lifeworld, must be accomplished by a specifically communicative rationality that is called into play when functional systems (and other modern trends) impinge upon the lifeworld and require its repair. This mending cannot be accomplished by appeal to conventional norms. The construction of the new order must proceed by reaching a rational consensus in a dialogue that consists in giving good reasons and subjecting them to validating discourse. Habermas is committed at the outset to opposing any notion of an integrative process that operates systematically by the exchange of merely acceptable tokens of opinion.

*Grounding the media in the lifeworld.* Habermas follows Parsons' basic pattern of exposition of the media, starting with money as the clearest example and model of a medium, and progressing to the other media, drawing parallels and analogies, but Habermas' belief that these analogies become forced as they are applied first to power and then to influence leads to a continuing thread of argument regarding the need to reconnect the media to the lifeworld. The media exert functionally organized forces outside the everyday awareness and consciousness of the participants in the lifeworld, above their heads and behind their backs. Media must be reconnected to the lifeworld, so that people can have confidence in them – so that they can become "institutionalized." The problem of reconnection becomes progressively difficult as we move beyond the boundary of money and the economy into the realms of power and influence.

Parsons accurately described the properties of money that make it useful as a medium; it is as a mode of communication that abstracts from the particularities of *ad hoc* exchanges by supplying a commensurate measure of value, thus facilitating market organization and a complex, differentiated economy. Money can be measured, transferred, and stored; hence, it can be circulated and invested. These properties enable its institutionalization in the sense that everyone can understand and accept money's value, independent of what they might want to do with it. Money has no semantic value and is not dependent on consent. It is validated by things, not meanings. In the typical standardized and circumscribed situation in which it is used, money contains its own motivation within itself and can therefore carry a prestructured message in the form of an offer, to which one can respond with a simple yes or no, enough or not enough. This, says Habermas, is why money "steers" conduct and can play a functional role in a steering system.

Habermas goes on to concede that Parsons was right to point to the parallels between money and power as media. There are important differences with significant theoretical consequences, but power does steer conduct in political systems. Power is not quantifiable; it substitutes definable powers of office for an abstract *amount* of power. It cannot be as readily deposited, for it easily erodes and is more tied to the person who exercises it. It cannot be circulated with ease, for it is not institutionally anchored in the law of contract, but in hierarchically organized offices. Still, power has use value for the holder and it offers to those who accept its commands the benefits of participation in a system that can achieve collective goals. It is also prestructured within its standardized situations, so that it carries its own intrinsic sanctions and is answered by either compliance or non compliance.

Power cannot be as readily institutionalized in an instrumental system because it is not as calculable. According to Habermas, the most important limitation on the simple calculation of power is that it is differently attached to the lifeworld. It requires *legitimacy*, an additional element of confidence that must be anchored in the normative order. There is an asymmetry between offers and commands in that a person taking orders is in a structurally disadvantaged position and needs validation that collective goals will in fact be realized by compliance. Whereas *private* interests are mediated by offers of money and need no external validation, one who is asked to comply with direction must be able to ask for validation that the *public* interest will be served. This calls for consensus in the community, which must be communicatively secured, without the assistance of steering mechanisms.

The direction of Habermas' argument is now apparent. Each step that Parsons took beyond money as the prototype for a medium, trying to liken communication codes to money so that they could be placed in the subsystems of society in a symmetrical manner, took him further away from the strict criteria established by the prototype. The proposed media become less *measurable*, *disposable*, and *depositable*. Hence these so-called media cannot freely circulate. There are not standardized situations in which people can calculate whether to say yes or no to offers or orders without prior discussion of the meaning of the situation. Institutionalization becomes problematic, for people cannot depend on the usability or worth of the medium and because the meanings of the messages conveyed by the medium cannot be reattached to the lifeworld. There is no institutional apparatus to tell people what these messages mean and whether they are true. To put the matter in a homely way, I can take a check to the bank and learn that five dollars means five dollars and be given cash for the check, but there is no place to take the promises of a politician.

By the necessary criteria, power qualifies as a medium, barely, and with qualifications. Influence does not. Apart from its unquantifiable vagueness, and the problems of circulation attendant to those problems, influence fails the test for even more fundamental reasons. True media must be backed by real values with empirically motivating power; that is they must contain intrinsic sanctions. To steer conduct, a medium must provide real, immediate motives that can replace rational motivation by reasons. "Institutionalization of a medium should not give rise to additional expenditures of communication and should not create additional risks of disagreement" (TCA II, 272). But influence contains no intrinsic sanctions and it can only be redeemed by reasons to be supplied by additional discussion, with potential for new disagreements.

We have now arrived at the heart of Habermas' rejection of Parsons' concept of influence, an objection that derives directly from his underlying ethical theory. He is ready to accept that media operate in the realms of instrumental and strategic action, wherein people calculate advantage in accordance with instrumental reason. In these arenas, media that carry intrinsic sanctions can affect the situation on which actors predicate their conduct. Benefit-cost ratios can be calculated in relation to positive and negative sanctions, but answers to questions that arise in the lifeworld cannot. Interpretations of the cultural meanings of situations, of the morality of courses of action, of justice between contending parties, of right and wrong ways of solving integrative problems – these are not amenable to solution by the application of sanctions and, accordingly, they fall outside the realm of media *by definition*. Parsons had defined influence as generalized capacity to persuade and had classified persuasion as directed not to the decision making environment, but to the actor's orientation to the meaning of the situation. For Habermas, this theoretical move (rightly) puts persuasion outside the realm of sanctions. Parsons' definition of "sanction" is sufficiently abstract to call persuasive acts sanctions, but Habermas insists that such a broad definition of "sanction" runs counter to our intuitive notion that persuasion must rest on reasons, not sanctions. Habermas emphatically puts the point, "[Parsons] does not consider that *the concept of sanction cannot be applied to yes/no responses to criticizable validity claims*" (TCA II, 278–9, emphasis in original).[4]

In sum, the arena of persuasion in the lifeworld is governed by the logic of communicative reason, not the logic of instrumental reason. The logic of communicative reason is one of giving reasons and redeeming them in argument, and only the force of the better argument can prevail. This process cannot be abridged by mediated messages without semantic content, messages that give no reasons yet ask us to believe interpretations and to act accordingly.

Habermas concedes that phenomena somewhat akin to influence do exist, stating that there "are indeed forms of communication that bring about a reduction in the expenditure of energy and in risks attending mutual understanding," but these forms achieve their effectiveness in a manner very different from money or power, because they do not uncouple interaction from lifeworld contexts of shared cultural understanding, valid norms, and responsible motivation. "They cannot replace ordinary language in its coordinating function, but only provide it with relief through abstraction from lifeworld complexity" (TCA II, 276–7). I take it that Habermas refers here to the overgeneralization, abridgement, and truncated argument of everyday discourse. He also concedes that prestige is "generalized" but it cannot be calculated and cannot, therefore, be a true medium. Its backing is not sufficiently institutionalized to allow people to understand and rely upon quantities of it, especially in modern societies, where prestige systems are fluid. In passing, Habermas briefly refutes (as obviously false) the empirical "assertion that the medium of influence is institutionalized in the system of social integration, that is in a public sphere established through the mass media, where the influence of journalists, party leaders, intellectuals, artists and the like is of primary importance" (TCA II, 275). There is, in other words, such a thing as influence, but it is not appropriate to characterize it as a medium.

These considerations lead Habermas to say that influence can, of course, be *interpreted* as a medium, and treated like a deposit of money or power, a deposit that "could be redeemed in such real values as reasons and justifications;" but such an interpretation would be "forced." Using such deposits strategically would be possible *only when we make manipulative uses of non-manipulable goods*" (TCA II, 275, emphasis in the original). Again, Habermas' ultimate objection to the concept of influence is its implication, in his mind, of a component of strategic action in an arena reserved for communicative understanding.[5]

Habermas does not deny that persuaders substitute tokens of status and prestige for reasoned argument or that people regularly accept such substitutes, but he does not think that this makes prestige a medium. Rather, the generalization of prestige has a "structure-forming" effect, which leads to the creation of status orders that put some people in a position to succeed in making strategic arguments, giving them disproportionate weight in the formation of social policy (TCA II, 280).[6] For Habermas this is not a process of social integration, but a problem for social integration. Inegalitarian discourse is a contradiction in terms, and only discourse can integrate a *modern* society. The continual emergence of novel problems of coordination in modern society outrun the integrative capacity of unproblematic conventional norms, and new norms and institutions must be created through processes that build rational motivation through reasoned discussion.

By allowing systems theory to crowd out his original action frame of reference, Parsons worked himself into a position from which he could not properly depict "social pathologies" as such; pathologies become redefined as technical imbalances, input/output deficits, or inflation or deflation – within a system that will reach equilibrium through self-corrective measures. Things will take care of themselves. Such an approach fails to see through benign macrostructural descriptions to the problems people actually experience in the lifeworld (TCA II, 284–94). Some critics would extend this point and contend that Parsons was prone to dismiss peoples' personal problems in the lifeworld by a strategy akin to blaming the victim. Some of Parsons' writings suggested that as society becomes more differentiated, people are not prepared for the new levels of personal maturity required by upgraded expectations for deferred gratification, objectivity, and indirect grounding of their needs and values. Parsons sometimes appeared to dismiss social criticism as a form of seduction of the critic by the plaintive, possibly neurotic, cries of immature people.[7] It is hardly surprising that a critical theorist would see Parsons as providing an inadequate diagnosis of our time.

Habermas' underlying criticism of Parsons, underneath the critique of media-based integration, is that Parsons' functional logic left him no leverage for criticism of the established social order. Parsons' well-known evolutionary optimism, his placement of American society at the forefront of benign evolutionary movements, and his critique of critique are not merely manifestations of a personal worldview. His diagnoses are built into the theoretical and conceptual apparatus that he employs, an apparatus that, by subordinating experience in the lifeworld to self-correcting systems, loses its capacity to support a critical stance. For Habermas, failure to provide built-in capacity to erect a critical platform ultimately disqualifies any edifice of theory in the human sciences.[8]

This criterion for adequate theory is the starting point for Habermas' critique of Parsons, and it is this starting point that leads Habermas to reject the concept of influence. Influence, conceived as a medium that substitutes for linguistic discourse, is not communication at all, for it fails to include the possibility of critical communication – authentic communication that requires all validity claims to be redeemed in discourse.[9]

### A Parsonian response

Since Talcott Parsons is no longer among us to ponder and respond to Habermas' critique, any construction of what he might have said in response is necessarily speculative. The following construction of a "Parsonian response" is designed to clarify issues and to provide a fresh starting point for thinking about influence in modern society. This constructed response cannot be fashioned in strictly Parsonian terms, working solely from Parsons' literal words and his particular modes of exposition. Rather, I will draw upon the resources and intents of the Parsonian scheme (as I understand it) to state a provisional counter argument to Habermas' critique of the notion of influence as medium, reserving for chapter 5 an exposition of a revised concept of influence-as-medium in a version designed to incorporate some of the genuine concerns and insights embodied in Habermas' work.

*Sociology and philosophy.* Parsons' account of influence and Habermas' attack on it were part of larger intellectual enterprises so different in their roots, conceptions, and aims that an actual debate between the two would probably have led to their talking past each other rather than joining issues. Habermas is first and foremost a philosopher engaged in the construction of justification for a universalisitic moral order.[10] From his Frankfurt Inaugural Lecture in 1965, reprinted in *Knowledge and Human Interests* (1971), to *Application and Justification* (1993), he has sought a new formulation for transcendental justification of moral judgments, a contemporary restatement of Kant's universal categorical imperative. His aim is to replace Kant's "monological" method, which reconstructs how a rational individual subject must think about moral life, with a "dialogical" method founded on the inherent requirements of communicative action. Following the "linguistic turn" in philosophy, it is necessary to secure moral thought by reference to the inherent implications of language – its necessary presupposition that communicative understanding can be achieved only if the participants in dialogue follow the inner logic of ideal speech.

Neo-Kantian as his formal philosophical approach might be, the animus of Habermas' project is Marxian, its roots in the critical theory of the Frankfurt school. It proceeds on egalitarian lines to show that the universalization of interests implied by full participation in truly communicative action inevitably leads to standards of justice that preclude exploitation of one class by another. Rational discourse cannot lead a dominated group to accept their exploitation as just.

Despite his encyclopedic (even imperialist) intellectual tendencies, Parsons was in the first instance a sociologist, not a philosopher. Sociology does not justify norms. Norms must be recognized as empirical facts with definite social consequences. Parsons was a member of the early cadre of sociologists who sought to justify sociology as an autonomous scientific discipline separate from philosophy or history or the other social sciences. Each social science has its own particular focus on a component of the scheme of social action; for sociology, it is the normative component, the component that orients social actors to common standards and thus allows coordinated action to take place and stable societies to form. The project of sociology is to establish a typology of norms, depict the special contributions of various types of norms in social integration, and explain how such integration is sustained by processes of socialization and social control.

In building his paradigm, Parsons privileged the empirical studies of the founding sociologists over equally illuminating philosophical traditions, most notably the work of the Scottish moralists and the naturalized Hegelian idealism of the American pragmatists. In his early years, Parsons was engaged in a struggle to legitimize positive sociology through a theoretical project designed to place sociology next to economics in the landscape of social science paradigms. Within the action frame of reference, economics studies the economizing of means, and sociology studies common values and the normative regulation of means. Both disciplines adopt a scientific perspective and neither are adjuncts of philosophy. Throughout his career, he never departed from his central concern with the empirical normative order and how it is brought to bear on human conduct.[11]

I do not mean to draw tight disciplinary boundaries around philosophy and sociology nor to assert that such boundaries could contain the scope of Habermas' and Parsons' broadly conceived work. Habermas constantly seeks to situate his moral philosophy in the empirical course of social development and in the moral maturation of personality. Hence his interest in the historical process of differentiation and rationalization, as pictured by Weber, Durkheim, and Parsons, and the stages of moral consciousness as proposed by Piaget and Kohlberg (Habermas 1979; 1990 [1983]). His writings on these matters are not ancillary digressions but integral components of his overall argument. When working in these areas he incorporates sociological and psychological perspectives that must be taken quite seriously. Indeed, in my judgment, *The Theory of Communicative Action* will take its place as a classic of sociological "grand theory" in the tradition of the figures whose works constitute his starting points. Moreover, Habermas himself could well object that the theory of communicative action is a reflexive, *critical theory* that transcends the distinction between sociology and philosophy, "a social theory concerned to validate its own standards." (TCA I, xxxix; see also Schnädelbach 1991.) Conversely, Parsons was a moral philosopher *malgré lui.* Despite his consistent efforts to distinguish empirical facts from value judgments and to deny that sociology could supply the latter, it is difficult to read his writings on the evolution of society without concluding that he believed implicitly that the course of social evolution, as he constructed it, validates the value of a liberal moral order founded on personal maturity, free choice, and loyalty to community ideals. Notwithstanding the broad-ranging, boundary-crossing character of their work, their respective roots and starting points would, in any direct confrontation, have led to a impasse, with Habermas proclaiming the *ought* and Parsons countering with the *is*. This is the classic confrontation of ideology and utopia.

*An empirical conception of influence.* Habermas' approach excludes, *by fiat,* instrumental and strategic action from the realm of specifically social coordination and integration. He accomplishes this by definition, in order to provide a foundation for his moral philosophy, citing as grounds that no *valid* social order can be based on instrumental conduct. Social order depends on the legitimation of conduct, and legitimacy requires achieved consensual validation, not mere success or victory. But what about empirical social orders? Are they in fact constructed of complex congeries of instrumental action designed to achieve success in private ends, strategic action designed to prevail over others, and consensus-seeking action designed to forge acceptable normative regulation? Parsons would surely answer these questions in the affirmative. Indeed his underlying scheme of sociological theory was from the outset intended to explain how such an order of mixed motivation is possible.

In *The Structure of Social Action* (1937), in his early essays, and in *The Social System* (1951), Parsons argued that all action is normatively regulated, even instrumental action. Instrumental, utilitarian conduct is not only normatively regulated, it is normatively grounded, in that instrumental rationality is a value. The norms deriving from this value call upon people and organizations to act both rationally and according to their self interest, within the framework of institutional arrangements that fix ground rules to limit the scope and means of action. Institutions facilitate the matching of complementary interests and guide the interpretation of interest-matching agreements. This state of affairs – the institutionalization of rationality – is not the natural state of humankind, but a historical achievement, the product of centuries of development of motivational structures and institutional arrangements. Such, says Parsons, are the lessons of Weber's studies of the Protestant ethic and Durkheim's insights into the non-contractual elements of contract. In an economic market, people seek gain, not justice. This is what they are supposed to: otherwise the market will not work. Contractual partners calculate their own interests, but they know that fraud is not a proper means of bringing contracts to a conclusion and that the meanings of the terms of their contracts are defined by the law. Human arrangements are amalgams of instrumental and ethical motives, individual interests and collective norms.

Habermas might well respond that so it is with contracts in the economy, but what of the procedures by which the laws of contractual relations are enacted? Are they too an admixture of instrumental and ethical discourse? When it comes to establishing the moral frameworks of public policy, is it then necessary to engage in open and sincere discourse aimed solely at reaching just understandings? No, for normative framework is produced by the same amalgamated combinations of types of action as private agreements. The same process of matching complementary and common interests occurs. Individuals and groups with particular interests propose normative standards, in the form of laws, or new interpretations of laws, or social policies, in various forums: courts, legislatures, boards, associations, or the public at large. The parties to disputes negotiate working agreements and compromises, often appealing to the public interest and urging public action, even while engaged in strategic action in the pursuit of interests. The procedural framework of normative debate is not formed to ensure that everyone has a chance to speak without constraint. On the contrary, the rules of public discourse are generally designed to reduce the range of admissible evidence and argument, limiting matters at issue, qualified witnesses, and specified time lines on the premise that complex issues cannot be resolved unless the information available is limited by judgments of relevance and rules of order. Hence, some observers sympathetic to Habermas' utopian communicative ideals complain that forums for public airing of governmental decisions, public hearings on planning issues for example, fail to provide for unconstrained communication, in part because of inhibiting procedural rules (Kemp 1985). Even the everyday practice of public planning tends to employ formalized and depoliticized expertise rather than creating organization designed to enable democratic communication (Forester 1985). Habermas' (1996) recent work on law suggest that he now recognizes the legitimating functions of some less than ideally discursive procedures.

In summary, Parsons would object to a dualistic scheme that radically contrasts functional systems and the lifeworld. He would insist on analytically identifying the respective places of various types of action within all the sectors of society, rather than classifying sorts of action as belonging to one or another concrete sector of social organization. There cannot be parts of society that are normatively organized and others that are not, some that allow for self-interested conduct and others that do not.

This does not mean that the forms of normative regulation are identical in all societies or in all the sectors of a society. With modernization and increasing complexity, normative order becomes less prescriptive. People are allowed to create their own circumstantially suitable arrangements and to *specify* general normative constraints to the situation at hand. The scheme of specialized media of communication was developed in order to systematize a scheme for understanding how this process of situational specification of ordered arrangements is possible and how it differs in the various realms of social life. Baum's (1976b, 533) outline of this development in late Parsonian thought is instructive:

> By the early 1960's it had become quite clear that the emphasis on values and norms, no matter how differentially specified and subjected to a ramified complex system of normative mechanisms, was insufficient . . . [It was] found that the freight that normative specification was to carry proved too heavy. Some more generalized mechanisms of control had to be found. These are generalized symbolic media.[12]

In the social worlds we all inhabit, every act cannot be determined in advance by social structures. We must constantly improvise, constructing courses of action that seem practical and right. We look for clues that will help us to understand and to act despite our uncertainty about how to cope with a changing world. We need to coordinate our action with others so that we do not face that world in imitation of Robinson Crusoe. Since the normative order to which we have been socialized cannot answer all questions, we look to others for advice. *Whenever we accept advice or take suggestions, or adopt the opinions of others, without verifying for ourselves that what we are told is sound, we have been influenced.* Social life without influence is inconceivable, for no one has the resources of time, knowledge, or experience to substitute personal investigation of every questionable matter for placing one's faith in others. This is true in every society, no matter how traditional, but it is especially important in modern societies when conventional norms provide fewer answers and the body of culture and preserved knowledge far outruns any person's experience and grasp.[13] It is true in the lifeworld as well as in specialized economic and political systems.

*Habermas' acceptance of empirical influence.* Habermas concedes this elementary point. In a set of "Intermediate Reflections" on the uncoupling of systems from the lifeworld (TCA II, 179–85), he amply expresses his understanding that prestige and influence do play a crucial role in the life-world. Moreover, he rests this understanding on several premises entirely consistent with a functionalist conception of the workings of the special-ized media of communication: the need for simplification and abstraction from the overwhelming complexity of the full range of potential informa-tion; the need to credit others' good will before it has been demonstrated, which makes social arrangements dependent on advances of trust; the evo-lution of generalized communication into specialized media. His exposi-tion of these points is presented with such clarity as to merit select quotation, so that there can be no doubt as to his position on the reality and significance of truncated communication backed by trust and credit, and so that the distance between Parsons and Habermas can be accurately gauged.

He begins by accepting Parsons' contention that modernity necessarily involves actors in sending and accepting generalized messages that are the prototypes for the formation of media:

If we begin with simple interactions within the framework of everyday commu-nicative practice and inquire after *generalized motives* that might move alter to a *blanket* acceptance of ego's interaction offers, we come across trivial [*sic*] elements not tied to any special presuppositions: the prestige ego enjoys and the influence he exercises. When a prestigious or influential person takes the initiative, he can count on receiving a certain "advance" of trust or confidence, which may be paid out in a readiness for consensus and obedience that goes beyond any single situation (TCA II, 179) . . . In the wake of the differentiation between action oriented to mutual understanding and to success, two sorts of *relief mechanisms* emerge in the form of communication media that either condense or replace mutual understanding in lan-guage. We have already come across prestige and influence as primitive generators of a willingness to follow; the formation of media begins with them . . . The problem of reducing the expenditure of communication and the risk of dissensus can be resolved on the next level when prestige and influence no longer only induce a readi-ness for consensus and a willingness to follow, but are themselves generalized. They come to form generalized media. (TCA II, 181–2)

In these passages Habermas falls just short of accepting influence as a medium, but, at the same time, he prepares the way for his critique of Parsons' particular formulation of the concept of influence by noting that influence is fundamentally different from money and power, because the use of influence in persuasion cannot be separated from ordinary discourse, *in language, within a lifeworld context.* This medium, if medium it be, cannot be uncoupled from culturally and normatively grounded social life.

The generalization of the influence that attaches to rationally motivated trust in the possession of knowledge – whether cognitive-instrumental, moral-practical, or aesthetic-practical – cannot have the same effect. Where reputation or moral authority enters in, action coordination has to be brought about by means of resources familiar from consensus formation in language. Media of this kind cannot uncouple interaction from the lifeworld context of shared cultural knowledge, valid norms, and accountable motivations, because they have to make use of the resources of consensus formation in language . . . (TCA II, 183) By contrast those media of communication such as reputation and value commitment, which decontextualize and focus, but do not replace, processes of reaching understanding, relieve interaction from yes/no positions of criticizable validity claims only *in the first instance.* They are dependent on technologies of communication, because these technologies make possible the formation of public spheres, that is, they see to it that even concentrated networks of communication are connected up to the cultural tradition and, *in the last instance,* remain dependent on the actions of responsible actors. (184–5, emphasis in original)

I should like to lay special stress on Habermas' emphasis on the phrase *"in the last instance,"* for it suggests that the principal argument between Parsons and Habermas might be less about the concept of influence than the question of what is its ultimate, "last instance" backing. This point will be at the center of my attempt to bridge the gap between these two theorists.

### The family of specialized media

Habermas can concede that influence based on various forms of status and prestige does in fact affect opinion and conduct, and yet be entitled to ask whether it does so as a *functional medium,* or just as a common means of supplementing discourse by abbreviating claims to expert knowledge or to speak for common interests. To qualify as a medium that permits a functional system to operate, Parsons must be able to show that it meets his criteria for a generalized medium. He must show that influence can be generalized in a manner that provides for its use as a *code* that represents *quantities* of some sort of credibility and trust that can be readily *transferred* and *stored* in a market-like structure of *sanctions*.

Parsons' and Habermas' use of money as the prototype for a specialized medium can be a source of confusion. In some ways money offers a good starting point because of its familiarity and because it so clearly legitimizes a further look at economic theory as a paradigm for media interchanges, using such concepts as deposits, inflation, and deflation. It was, after all, in the context of the preparation of *Economy and Society* (Parsons and Smelser 1956) that the interchange paradigm was initially formulated. On the other hand, to start with money is to burden one's exposition with serious vulnerabilities, for nothing is quite like money. It becomes easy for any critic, including Habermas, to point to the fact the other media are not exactly like money and to gain the upper hand against concepts that are bound to look analogical, even metaphorical, as indeed many of Parsons' arguments do.

The media are better discussed as a family, of which money is a member, but not the defining member. This avoids confusing the expository strategy with the concept. The defining characteristics of the concept of media are not identical in their application to each specific type. Their structure varies according to the imperatives of the realms from which they derive. Were it not so, money, with its exact quantifiability, ready transferability, and exceptional abstraction from intrinsic meaning, would dominate all the systems. Everything would simply be bought and sold. But everything cannot be for sale, for each differentiated subsystem has its own particular function and must sustain its own integrity. The unique structures of each media protect their differentiation.

To summarize in a vulgar and oversimplified, but instructive illustration, money cannot buy love. Habermas would agree. In a sense, this metaphor is at the heart of Habermas' objection to the misuse of the concept of generalized media. Highly abstracted media, like money, cannot, with a mere market transaction, create and deliver complex motivational resources that have their own conditions of production and acceptance. Solidarity, for example, is dependent on cultural meanings, interpersonal bonds, and socialized identities that cannot be abstracted from the lifeworld. Similarly, commitments to work within bureaucratically structured organizations are purchased by money (and directed by power), but at a cost of meaning to workers whose personal motivations, produced in the lifeworld, do not correspond to the abstracted, functional organization of the workplace (TCA II, 318–73). But the fact that market transactions mediated by money cannot insure proper direction of all the necessary resources of social life does not imply that various activities within the lifeworld must renounce specially adapted media – influence, for example – to guide the creation and application of consensual resources for social integration. This, in effect, is the Parsonian response to the claim of radical discontinuity between system and lifeworld.

*Four clarifying distinctions.* Four analytical distinctions will prepare the way for clearer thought about the somewhat slippery concept of generalized media and the confusion that sometimes arises from their overlap in concrete instances. First, it is important to distinguish the use of money to facilitate actual *exchanges* from its use to make *valuations.* For example, it is possible to calculate the economic value of a spouse's unpaid domestic labor, but were household contributions literally a form of wage labor, with actual exchanges transacted in money, the marital relationship would be quite different. Money's powerful capacity for apparently exact measures is often used to make quantitative *estimates.* Many of the dollar values used in the economy are not records of exchanges but accounting records and forecasts produced by rules of accounting and formulae for predicting future values, especially income streams, which found estimates of the present value of capital. This capacity of money to provide a common language of valuation allows for substitution of resources without actual concrete exchange, which brings us to a second distinction, that between *exchange* and *interchange.*[14]

The interdependence of different media are often expressed in the capacity of actors to substitute one medium for another. Firms, for example, are in a position to choose alternate means of maximizing income, some based on money, some on influence, some on power, and some on knowledge. Consider the use of unenforceable commitments in the financial industry. "Confidence letters" and "comfort letters" are written by investment bankers to increase the resources that might be drawn upon in support of a project. Such letters are not legally enforceable, but the organizations that issue them do place reputation at stake and will often make good on them if necessary. These instruments have value, and clients will pay for them. Economic analysis of this type of credit instrument demonstrates that reputational capital and financial capital are interchangeable. Faced with the question of whether to backstop a loss by a failing enterprise, the issuer of an unenforceable letter of promise can elect to pay and lose *financial* capital or not to pay and thus lose *reputational* capital. To lose reputational capital is no small thing, for it is to build reputation that issuers undertake to supply this form of backing in the first place. In making their choice of which form of capital to forego, issuers will also take into account *information* losses that might be attendant to liquidating financial capital to make good on the instrument, for partial liquidations might involve liquidation of portions of the organization itself, losing the information that is stored therein (Boot, Greenbaum, and Thakor 1993). The authors do not conceive this particular example to be an illustration of an interesting but exotic business practice. It is a paradigm case for business decisions made every day: whether to establish or accept obligations backed by potential force of law, or to rely instead on funds of reputation created by networks of trust, or to create mixed types of arrangements. The very choice provides greater flexibility in the means of coordinating economic affairs. The use of money as a means of expressing estimates of value allows decision makers to use monetary values (derived from projected future income streams) as a common unit of evaluation of quantities of money and other media – power (enforcement), influence (reputation), and access to information.

Third, we must distinguish *simple* from *compound* uses of media. In a simple transaction mediated by money a particular good, say a loaf of bread, may be exchanged for cash, but in more complex actions, the media are usually compound. For example, a business firm convicted of criminal fraud (by state power), may suffer some monetary losses in fines and some reputational losses in prestige (influence). Reputational losses can be estimated in dollars, but these losses are not in the first instance dollar losses as such.[15] Compound transactions are another source of what media flows in and out of the sectors of society in patterns of interchanges. In this case, the convicted business firm loses reputational influence and the legal system gains power (capacity to make believable threats to prosecute), but not by a literal exchange.

Finally, it is useful to distinguish the use of media in the strictest sense, in which given quantities of media "speak for themselves,"( in that the worth, credibility, or validity of the media are not problematic) and the use of media in cases where supplementary linguistic communication is necessary in order to clarify problematic elements of the situation. Exchanging cash for a loaf of bread is an uncomplicated use of a medium, but unproblematic illustrations should not be considered normal and the use of supplementary language abnormal. On the contrary, whenever money in the form of credit instruments is involved, as it is in complex economic transactions, linguistic supplementation is normal, for the parties must reach understanding regarding the reliability and value of the monetary medium being offered. This ranges from the simple matter of the proper endorsement of checks to very complex negotiations and agreements in corporate finance, where a transaction to raise investment funds will often involve months of efforts to reach understanding regarding secured and unsecured loans, exchanges of equity shares, confidence letters, and other credit instruments. Agreements of several hundred pages may be required to render the understanding in written form. That such a transaction is economic, instrumental, and mediated does not exempt the participants from reaching understandings in language. Nor does communication in integrative and solidary transactions preclude the use of media supplemented by linguistic clarification of the complexities surrounding the worth of media in particular transactions. In the case of power this point is even more clear. Habermas agrees that the use of power is not exempt from recourse to linguistic clarification. With bureaucratic office comes a certain measure of power defined by its scope of authority, but also limited by that scope. Questions of power quickly become questions of authority and legitimacy. Accordingly, the establishment of the power of office requires discussion and specification in language, and so does exercising that power in specific situations. In short, the need to communicate in ordinary language cannot distinguish money and power from influence.

If the need for supplementary discourse does not disqualify money or power from the family of media, why should it disqualify influence? If influence is defined as a medium that attaches credibility to a persuasive message, allowing the sender of the message to persuade by reference to a *symbol of credibility* rather than by *direct substantive argument*, then influence is properly conceived as a medium, even if the adequacy of the symbol is sometimes questioned and often requires additional amplification. For example, a lobbyist for a trade association might seek to influence a Congressperson by saying, "This proposed additional tax on our product will reduce sales and therefore reduce tax revenues; it will be counter productive. I've been in this industry for twenty-five years and I can tell you this will be the inevitable result." By way of additional demands for justification of the lobbyist's claimed expertise, the Congressperson might ask whether such a counterproductive outcome has happened before, but the ensuing conversation remains fundamentally in the realm of the validity of the lobbyist's tokens of prestige. It does not alter the character of the process of influence. In the New Public, the lobbyist might be asked whether an objective study has been conducted on the question and be told that a study by an independent accounting firm has confirmed this prediction. Again the Congressperson has asked for and been given *more influence*. Supplementary redemptive discourses remain in the arena of influence; it does not become a matter for substantive communicative action in Habermas' sense until the participants agree that the lobbyist lacks overriding qualifications and further persuasion must depend on substantive argument.

*A preliminary note on the inflation of influence.* The introduction of argument into influential communication does not negate its mediated character. On the contrary, argument is required to sustain the influential backing of the persuader's message. Persuaders redeem their prestige by providing convincing arguments. This brings us to the question of what is meant by the "inflation of influence." The substance of what is conveyed in influence is opinions and suggestions which, like commands backed by power, are normally expressed in words. Disagreements about the *validity of arguments* do not necessarily undermine *influence as a medium* any more than disagreement about the values of goods – that is, arguing about prices – undercuts the use of money as a medium of exchange. One can always refuse to "buy" an argument by saying in effect, your prestige does not provide adequate credibility to your assertions.[16]

Distinguishing the validity of arguments from trust in the media of influence entails a crucial implication. The more incredible my substantive argument – the more it is implausible, discordant with your experience and understandings, incomprehensible, illogical, and thinly supported my assertions – the more my persuasive rhetoric becomes dependent on my influence, and the less effective my influence becomes. A given amount of influence will then support less successful persuasion of the audience. The same amount of influence buys less agreement; its value has become *inflated.*

At the collective level, when the arguments, assertions, and suggestions of influential opinion leaders become incredible or implausible because they no longer comport with people's needs, experiences, and perceptions of their situations, influence as a medium becomes inflated. Influence may come to have too little value to provide resources for social integration. This is my reinterpretation, within a Parsonian mode, of the crux of Habermas' warnings about the failure of communicative action. Both schemes recognize that if integrative discourse bears no relation to the world as experienced, it may fail. This suggests that the two men's theoretical constructs are not entirely incommensurate.

*Criteria for the family of specialized media.* We are now in a position to define criteria for recognition of members of the family of media. Inappropriate objections to particular media based on the notion that each medium must be exactly like money have been forestalled, and with this straw argument put aside, it will be easier to defend the proposition that influence is a medium.

1. *Compressed symbolic codification.* A medium must provide a code that allows for compression of large amounts of information into relatively simple symbols, thus providing for abstraction from the open-ended detail of real situations and relieving interaction of the burden of complexity.

Money performs this function by representing values abstractly in a code that does not require reference to the grounds of valuation. It is enough that buyer and seller can agree on a price expressed in monetary terms, without the informational burden of barter. Barter requires traders to establish value equivalences between two separate properties without reference to any commensurate measure. Power allows giving commands by mere reference to a codified hierarchy of power, without explanation and debate, in each instance, of how compliance will achieve collective goals.

Influence meets this criterion. The use of influence substitutes codified symbols of prestige, reliability, or believability for massive amounts of direct information. If persuasion always required fully articulated expression of all pertinent facts through messages that convey adequate information to allow for independent verification, and were always subjected to testing by the person being persuaded, the process of persuasion would be too complex and time consuming. The communication of information is costly, and costs are reduced by substitutions of symbols of credibility. As we have previously seen, the substitution of "signals" for direct information is a necessary element in any market in which information is asymmetrically distributed; the market cannot work without them. In this sense, influence is a component of the economic system, and there is no reason to suppose that the asymmetrical distribution of information in other spheres of life can be overcome without comparable processes of signaling credibility.[17] On the contrary, because the division of labor creates experts in specialized areas of knowledge, it entails unequal distributions of information. Social integration therefore requires low-cost channels for distributing credible but compressed information.

2. *Quantification.* Media must be amenable to some form of measurement so that the participants in systems can calculate the sanctions at stake, making decisions as to whether the values or costs of the sanctions are adequate to the situation. The need for measurement is built into the symbolic removal of the media from direct access to things or to actual information. Money provides such a form, and there is no question as to its quantifiability. It provides a measurable, cardinal unit calculable to minute gradations, understandable to all as representing a quantity of usable value.

Forms of quantification differ according to the modes of abstraction appropriate to the functional systems they serve. Money, which serves to maximize the adaptability and flow of material resources, is suited to a high level of abstraction, independent of situations and particular social relations. Its acceptance can even extend beyond the political boundaries and solidarities of nations. Power, which serves the needs of systems that organize the use of controlled force to achieve collective goals, and influence, which serves the needs of systems that mobilize social solidarities to meet integrative needs within societies, employ different modes of measurement attendant to the way their codes abstract and simplify complexity.

Power cannot be as fully abstracted from its situation, so it is not as readily quantifiable as money. Nevertheless, it is measurable on an ordinal scale, as more power or less power, to a degree sufficient to allow calculation as to whether one can or cannot readily resist its use. An ordinal scale allows power to be expressed as a hierarchy, and this is exactly what bureaucratically organized power does – order power as a hierarchy of offices. Power cannot be universalized to the extent of money because of its functional use, which cannot be divorced from its need to be controlled. Whereas money operates through offers that can be rejected, power is exercised by threats that cannot be refused. If a given quantity of power could be transferred at will to anybody and used by its new owner to any purpose, everyone would be subject to direct and unexpected coercion.

In this respect, influence is somewhat like power. One need not (by definition) submit to persuasion, so its use can be allowed relatively free play, but the effectiveness of influence is still limited by its connections to the organization of society. The constraints on influence do not derive from needs to control its use, but from the structures of solidarity and prestige in which it is embedded. Everyone's money is money, but their influence is differentially accepted according to whether their prestige or credibility is recognized and valued in various social milieus. This is to be expected in a system that operates by invoking and mobilizing a structured set of social bonds. This does not mean that influence cannot be quantified within these networks of ties and bonded groups. Some have more influence than others within groups, or wider influence across a set of linked groups. Individuals can gain influence by building prestige, improving their credentials, or collecting the endorsements of larger numbers of individuals and groups. A petition of 5,000 signatures is assumed to have more influence than a petition of 500. Looking at the matter from the reciprocal perspective of those who accept influence, they can calculate, or at least gauge, the degree to which an appeal is so well backed by influence as to permit them to expend no more energy on looking further into its validity.

3. *Transfer, storage and deposit*. For media to flow, there must be means of transferring control of quantities of them from one social actor to another. Moreover, media must be transferable in a manner that does not dilute value, so that it can be stored for future use. In some situations the necessary transfer takes the form of a deposit, that is transferred to another on a revocable basis, to be returned at a later date.

Money transfers by the delivery of *property rights*, which are sufficiently differentiated to allow for varied and flexible forms of transfer and deposit. Habermas expresses some uncertainty about whether there are truly effective means of delivering power, arguing that it "cannot circulate in so unrestricted a manner as money," nor be "so reliably deposited as money in a bank." He seems not to recognize that the circulation of power can be put in proper perspective by positing *delegation* as a mechanism for transferring power that parallels the transfer of property rights in money. Viewing the circulation and deposit of power as a form of delegation immediately places the analysis of power as medium within the reach of current approaches to organizational theory in economics and other social sciences. Delegation involves a grant of agency, which in turn implies problems of monitoring and control, and these problems take on comparable coloration whether the delegations occur in economic or in political arenas. The concept of delegation highlights the connection of the medium of power to its particular functional imperative, the organization of control. This function is served by a medium that transfers defined powers within an organized collectivity rather than disbursing small bits of ultimate sovereignty.

*Endorsement* provides a parallel means of transferring influence. Using the term in this technical sense, endorsement occurs when people or organizations use their own influence to bestow influence on other people or organizations.[18] When a physician, relying on influence, persuades a patient to accept a dietary regimen, that is an exercise of primary influence. When that physician then introduces the patient to a nutritional guidance counselor, saying, "Here is the person who can help you to control your diet in a healthy and effective way; you should follow this counselor's advice," the physician is bestowing prestige by endorsement. This example suggests that endorsement is a close cousin of delegation, except that neither the doctor nor the counselor can issue orders backed by power. The doctor can only enhance the probability of cooperation by transferring prestige to someone who will need it in order to be effective when the patient asks for advice and support. Since influence is not legally binding in the sense that property rights bind money and delegation binds power, endorsement can be loosely controlled and more easily circulated to the nooks and crannies of everyday life where persuasion needs a boost. Again, the forms of a medium reflect its functional uses, and we would expect influence, which is used to exert integrative pressures, to reflect its adaptation to the situational variety of integrative problems.

There are many and varied forms of endorsement, too many to catalog here, but a few examples will suggest the pervasive sway of endorsement in social life. The most obvious example is the literal endorsement of candidates for office by persons or groups who seek to bestow their own prestige on the candidate. Signing a petition on behalf of a cause is a similar practice, as is acting as a sponsor of a speech or an honorary director of an organization. Credentials in the form of degrees and certificates are important sources of influence in everyday life. Indeed, some have argued that the value of the credential's prestige is more important than the actual learning it represents (Collins 1979). In any event, the credential transmits the prestige of the granting organization to the recipient, thus increasing the recipient's influence. The sponsorship implied by employment by a particular organization is an important category of endorsement, especially in the case of the mass media of communication. Being a network news anchorperson, for example, is not just a prestigious status its own right; the influence attached to the status derives in some measure from the endorsement implied by appointment to such a position by a prestigious news organization. This example illustrates the significance of embedding prestige within an organized institutional order. It is not just the personal prestige of individuals that makes influence so persuasive in social life; it is the credibility of institutions. Yet individuals and organizations, acting as prolocutors, can move out in front of the established institutional order, claiming to represent currently unrepresented interests and solidarities. If their claims are ratified, they gain prestige and influence as spokespeople for emerging movements. When people ratify the claims of prolocutors by supporting them, they are engaged in a process of endorsement, bestowing influence on those who bid for their support. Prestige flows not just from position in a status order, but from earned respect too. Individuals may have little prestige taken one by one, and little influence to grant, but there is influence in numbers. Decision makers who are acting in situations marked by uncertainty regarding other people's preferences and opinions take cues from the number of people who can be mobilized by someone who purports to represent their opinions. In the language of economic information theory, the number of active supporters becomes a "signal" of credibility; in media theory this signal is called influence.

### Does the medium of influence steer a functional system?

To concede that people do rely on prestige-based influence, both to persuade and to make judgments about the credibility of others, and to concede further that influence has the properties characteristic of the family of specialized media, would not require Habermas to abandon his central claim that no *medium* of influence can *steer* a self-regulating *system* capable of providing social integration to society. Habermas' position derives from his conception of how market mechanisms work through the "norm-free" regulation of conduct: "The market is one of those systemic mechanisms that stabilize nonintended interconnections of action by way of functionally intermeshing action *consequences*, whereas the mechanism of mutual understanding harmonizes the action *orientations* of participants" (TCA II, 150, emphasis in original). It is the impersonality of market forces, which regulate consequences without reference to their cultural and motivational grounding, leaving no one responsible for collective outcomes, which severs system integration from social integration.

Habermas' depiction of systems as regulated by unintended consequences is cogent. In an economic market founded on the division of labor, the individual gives up self sufficiency in return for freedom to choose from a wider array of options according to their individual preferences. Consumers decide what to buy and producers what to produce by calculation of their individual utilities, and they are largely free of responsibility for social outcomes. But there are outcomes nonetheless, for aggregate preferences create forces of supply and demand, which set prices, and prices limit both individual choice and collective results. Consumers cannot buy what they cannot afford and producers cannot make what people will not buy. Consumers cannot work unless the market will support their wage. Such a system may supply candy bars in adequate numbers, but it will not necessarily supply adequate health care at affordable prices. Yet this outcome is not the fault of particular physicians who have set their prices too high, for the prices are set by the market, which in turn is an expression of the consequential forces of supply and demand. Moreover, participants in the economy cannot fully understand the complex operations that subject them to its force, and in this sense the system is regulated by consequences that are outside their ken. Set in this very simple form, it is not hard to understand Habermas' contention that self-regulating markets are not a satisfactory means for "collective will formation." The collective will regarding health care, for example, can only find expression through discourse among responsible individuals, who tie questions of public health to culturally valid values, to ethical standards of justice, and to ideas of social responsibility.

We must, therefore, confront two questions: firstly, can social integration be steered by the medium of influence, flowing in market-like system; secondly, can influence systems be linked to socially responsible outcomes? The first of these questions should be addressed forthwith, for the answer will constitute the final step in meeting Habermas' objections to the formal properties that Parsons attributes to influence. The second question provides the framework for the next chapter, which uses a new influence paradigm to address the larger problem of whether influence in society contributes to social integration in modern, highly differentiated social orders, and to make an initial assessment of the conditions of integration in the New Public.

*Influence systems and the division of labor.* Influence systems arise when the division of labor extends to information; individuals give up their informational self sufficiency at the cost of becoming dependent on information provided by others, a bargain that they accept in order to be free to devote time and other resources to gathering the information most relevant to their personal, immediate, or pressing concerns. Since complex modern societies cannot provide clear normative guidance in uncertain situations, people are in particular need of information regarding how to coordinate their action and about means and opportunities for attaching themselves to others. Integrative experience takes the form of information about social facts, opinion, advice, suggestions, and reliable sources of solidarity. This information extends from the narrow, private, and everyday world to broad matters of public policy – from directions as to how to find an office where one has a health-care appointment, to getting advice and support regarding a course of rehabilitation that might make it possible to return to the work force, to suggestions as to what national heath care program to support, to recommendations regarding which candidates for office will bring about health care reform. The sources and targets of integrative information range from ordinary citizens to successful leaders. Just as most people are involved in both the production and consumption of goods, so are most people involved in both the production and consumption of integrative experience and information. We must conceive, then, a population of people who need assistance with their integrative problems and a population of people who are ready to supply information ranging from factual opinions to invitations to form bonds. Because the participants in this system have given up their informational self sufficiency, they need other people's information, and they must rely on the credibility of that information, not reproduce all the knowledge that went into producing and supplying it. They want abridged information and they secure this less than fully supported information by relying upon the influence of others, influence that they grant by accepting signals of reliability, including reputation and prestige. In broad terms, it is obvious that influence can operate in systems, that influence can steer such systems, that systems of influence do exist, and that these systems supply resources to people who look to them for help with their integrative needs.

It is less obvious that systems of influence are self-regulating and equilibrating, but this too can be derived from the general character of influence. The equilibrium "prices" of information are set by the system. They are a product of the unwillingness of economizing people to incur limitless costs in getting information for themselves. The *demand* for influence is a product of willingness to accept persuasion as a lower cost alternative to direct experience. The *supply* of influence is set by the actions of influence entre-preneurs, who from ideological or idealistic motivations, or for monetary reward, or because they want to settle integrative problems on advanta-geous terms, offer abridged information secured by their credibility. The equilibrium "price" of information backed by influence is the point at which the costs of gaining additional information through investing in direct study are too great in relation to the benefits accrued by relying on the provider's reputation.[19]

Since influence, as constructed here, steers a decentralized self-regulating system, regulated by the consequences of actions, rather than by commu-nicative action among all concerned, action oriented to the welfare of the whole collectivity, the process is still subject to Habermas' strictures. For most transactions in such systems, no one is responsible for developing a good and just informational foundation for the society as a whole. Nor does the process lend itself to fully elaborated and rational discussion, for it is too limited by the imperative of economizing the costs of information. Nevertheless, just because influence systems do not meet the criteria for communicative action, strictly construed, integrative systems based on influence do not necessarily lack capacity to balance meeting integrative needs with meeting the competing imperatives of economy, *modus vivendi,* and respect for plural lifeworlds. But can modern integrative systems tran-scend their apparent privatisation? According to Parsons, modern social systems include institutionalized roles governed by norms of collective responsibility rather than norms legitimizing self interest. He originally located such roles among the professions, such as medicine, where the inter-ests of the patient are normatively secured (Parsons 1954a). Professional constraints on the use of influence by the practitioners of the information-based "professions" of the New Public could conceivably enhance the inte-grative potential of influence by institutionalizing the social value of private advice, but these roles currently lack the social orientations that Parsons attributed to normatively regulated professions. In chapter 9, I will propose that only institutions requiring those who exercise public influence to enter forums wherein their token claims can be redeemed in information and argument could secure the integrative potential of influence.

### System and lifeworld: a Parsonian counter critique

*The integration of system and lifeworld.* So far I have put Parsons on the defensive, responding step by step to Habermas' claim that influence cannot be systematically organized to provide an integrative foundation for modern societies. Parsons could be placed in a more aggressive posture. He could, from his own standpoint, argue that Habermas' theoretical strategy is fundamentally misdirected. The radical disjunction of two social spheres, one founded on communicative action, secured by communicative competence, and manifest in the activities by which we transmit knowledge, enter into normatively guided personal relations, and socialize participants, the other founded on instrumental and strategic action, secured by functional rationality, and devoted to material reproduction and the organization of control, cannot be sustained, either in theory or in social life itself.

Unintended consequences, equilibrium states, moral neutrality, and self interest cannot be excluded from the lifeworld. The forces that impinge upon the communicative "intersubjective" world go well beyond events in economic and political systems. The material world is subject to change and uncertainty whether organized systematically into an economy or not. Well-formulated understandings and well-developed communicative competence cannot protect lifeworlds from disruptive conflict with other groups or from deviant conduct. The lifeworld process of socialization is always incomplete, and threats to the communicative order are ever present. Life is beset with uncertainty, and even understandings achieved by communication have unintended, unsettling consequences. Since the stability of social arrangements cannot be taken for granted but do tend to persist, it is reasonable to suppose that homeostatic mechanisms operate to restore stability in the face of actual or incipient breakdown. People resort to strategic action to restore the status quo; indeed normative orders often sanction non-communicative action on the part of keepers of the peace. Non-communicative action, founded on necessity and homeostatic restoration, has its place in the lifeworld.

The legitimation of strategic acts of domination goes well beyond punishment for destructive violations of the collective order. Lifeworlds, both premodern and modern, are generally predicated on stratification by gender and age, which provide ample opportunity for instrumental and strategic action. Gender in particular creates problems for Habermas' scheme. As Nancy Fraser (1989) has shown, gender roles reveal the inherent difficulty of assigning some activities to the lifeworld and others to systems. In the course of a feminist and critical (but sympathetic) extension of Habermas' scheme, Fraser points to child care as a problematic case. By a strict and simple application of the idea of internal colonization, child care qualifies as colonization for it transfers a communicative function of socialization to a commercial activity carried out within the cash nexus. But counting child care as an instance of internal colonization would be a rather embarrassing result for a theory that wants to be judged by its emancipatory potential. The situation can be saved by making refined distinctions that take social contexts and upgraded normative expectations within child-care institutions into account, but this theoretical move does not escape the Parsonian point: social arrangements involve blends of pragmatic freedom and normative constraints embedded in systems that inextricably link intersubjective social action and functional, equilibrating social forces.[20]

Just as the lifeworld involves functional systems, so do differentiated, media-steered systems involve normatively oriented communication. Economic relations mediated by money are not mere expressions of the forces of supply and demand. In the limiting case, pure markets exist, but the economy taken as a whole involves a nexus of long-term relationships whose participants have an interest in the continuity of their connections: the cooperation of their partners, the reliability of their creditors, the loyalty of their employees, and the dependability of their agents. These relations are often carefully negotiated and embodied in contracts reached by achieving mutual understanding and nurtured by communicative action.

Economic rationality must be achieved in the face of uncertainty, an uncertainty that is magnified by the very instrumental conduct that makes market organization possible. Accordingly, economic actors resort to contract and its institutional backing to stabilize their relations. But contract is not enough. Given uncertainty – i.e., imperfect information – economic actors must rely on indications of reliability, credibility, and sincerity. The economy is not solely based on information regarding the material world, but also on information indicating that the participants in economic relations set and respect limits on resort to strategic action. Establishing and assessing these limits requires communicative action. Functionally specialized systems increase flexibility through abstract, disposable media, but these systems remain normatively ordered by forms of regulation that differ from system to system. Economic systems allow a great deal of self-interested, affectively neutral conduct, political systems require more hierarchical monitoring of compliance, and integrative systems demand more demonstrations of commitment to the group, but all are constituted by combinations and arrangements of normative structures.

Habermas implicitly concedes that the lifeworld harbors what in Parsonian terms are systems of influence. According to Habermas, the lifeworld is transparent, not something that works behind people's backs and over their heads. How then can distorted and concealing ideologies influence people *within* the lifeworld? If ideology did not have influence,

Habermas would not need to be concerned about the need to rationalize the lifeworld itself by thematizing its distorted terms of discourse as a subject for communicative discussion. Habermas recognizes this problem in his explanation of the origins of ideology. The lifeworld is contaminated by dominated discourse, relatively immune from rational criticism, as a legacy of the separation of the sacred and the profane. The differentiated lifeworld order of religion, science, economic information, law, and the arts fails to reintegrate the grounds of validity for ontological, empirical, normative, and expressive claims. Matters that could be critically grasped "within the cognitive reach of everyday communication" escape critical discourse (TCA II, 189). Habermas attributes this unassailability "to systemic restrictions placed on communication," but these are certainly not restrictions operating through money or power as such, but through *linguistic communication* delivered within status-based systems of influence.

*The rhetoric of system and lifeworld.* Habermas' distinction between lifeworld and system gives him rhetorical leverage for a critical account of existing society. The ideal of communicative action is a standard by which the negative effects of differentiated systems can be evaluated, especially the anti-social, even anti-human, effects of the intrusion of systems on the lifeworld. Habermas refers to this intrusion rhetorically as a metaphorical "colonization." This term allows those sympathetic to the Marxian tradition to identify with the scheme and saves some face with those who, criticizing the theory from the left, are not happy with allowing any part to systems in sociological analysis. There are, to be sure, similarities between colonial regimes over indigenous peoples, and domination, on comparable terms, of distinct underclasses within a society, a similarity generally identified by the term "internal colonialism." There is even a formal similarity (at a high level of abstraction) between colonialism and intrusions in the lifeworld in the form, for example, of externally imposed requirements that workers acquire motivations suitable to bureaucratic work. The consequences of market organization and bureaucracy do intrude into people's lives. But the use of the term "colonization" to describe these effects is surely no less metaphorical than referring to influence as a medium that is in some ways like money. The term is a powerful rhetorical persuader that calls up a complex set of identifications and invokes the prestige of long-standing tradition of radical political analysis.

The very distinction between lifeworld and system, on which the notion of colonization of the lifeworld depends, is itself rhetorical. Its rhetorical force is apparent in the way its connotations are interpreted by its audience. One analyst, for example, takes the distinction to boil down to the "establishment" versus the "people" (Boyte 1992). And not without reason: lifeworld and system proceed from the long rhetorical tradition of sociological thought, which looks beyond the world of money and power for some more social phenomenon, some encompassing solidarity – society, community, public opinion, communicative understanding, the people – that provides, in Burke's dramatistic language, a *scene term* for a morality play of social life. The *agents* of communicative action in Habermas' drama are responsible moral actors but the agents of systems are not. Habermas' critique is embedded in a theoretical apparatus that employs a new version of the rhetoric of community and society – *Gesellschaft* and *Gemeinschaft* – which longs for a form of solidarity that might communalize the harsh forces of modern social life. "Rational communicative action" is an effective slogan, for it calls for community and modernity at the same time. Parsons on the other hand, whatever his own rhetorical ploys, attacked the rhetoric of *Gesellschaft* and *Gemeinschaft* from the beginning to the end of his career, starting with his famous note on Toennies in *The Structure of Social Action* (1937, 686–940) and continuing with a long series of insistent claims that the multiple, various dimensions of community and society are independent of each other and that all of them, in functionally appropriate combinations, are articulated in both modern and premodern societies. Modernity's own forms of community are coherently linked with the market order. These forms are already present in society, not utopian ideals that function primarily to provide a platform for attacking alleged social pathologies.

*Parsons' rhetoric of modernity: a final misstep.* Parsons cannot be allowed the last word in this exchange, for his own rhetoric also deserves scrutiny. He did not entirely escape the rhetoric of community, which uses "community" as a scene term, the source of ultimate values and ultimate direction for the players, or as Burke puts it, the "God term" that calls out their action. Parsons' scene term was his name for what he considered the core of the integrative system: *societal community*. He used this phrase to refer to "a patterned conception of membership which distinguishes between those individuals who do and do not belong." It is "constituted both by a normative system of order *and* by statuses, rights and obligations pertaining to membership which may vary for different sub-groups in the community" (Parsons 1966, 10). Although differences in the rights and obligations of membership may vary across groups, the long-term evolutionary trend toward modernity leads toward *inclusion* of all groups on equal terms (Parsons 1971, 86–94), and this process of inclusion is the principal guarantee of the integration of a diverse modern society (1961). Thus, Parsons' scene term functions rhetorically less as a utopian ideal than as an optimistic depiction of the ongoing social world and its developing modernity.

In modern societies, the mechanism of inclusion is citizenship, which, following Marshall, Parsons took to extend beyond purely civic rights to include political and social rights as well. It is by inclusion that the citizen comes to have access to the influence system by which participation in societal communication is assured. Parsons was not naively optimistic. He recognized that the full rights of citizenship are imperfectly extended and then only by struggle. His well-known paper on citizenship (1967e) amply documents his willingness to go beneath the abstractions of general theory to circumstantial accounts of historical variation, conflict, and failure, but he remained resolutely optimistic in affirming that the long-run trend of modern social evolution is toward the realization of democratic ideals. From a rhetorical standpoint, he invited his audience to go with the flow, not to see the system as corrupt but as in an inevitable process of positive transition. His scene term enters history as a driving force, describable in narrative terms and therefore comprehensible in moral terms. Habermas' communitarian scene term, rational democratic discourse, is set forth as a critical account of what contemporary society needs but fails to provide, while Parsons' comparable scene term purports to describe an ongoing, evolving reality. Parsons is less critical then, not because he uses such concepts as "system" and "equilibrium," which (*contra* Habermas) have no intrinsic conservative bias, but because he takes the direction of social development to be unproblematic and often seems even to pronounce that the future has arrived.

Parsons asserts that modern society must fully include all its citizens, but he does not ask whether it has evolved a workable communicative order for the fully included to join. He gives little attention to the institutions of communication, failing to ask whether they provide a stable foundation for an influence system or whether, on the contrary, their present organization makes them susceptible to chronic inflation, to the detriment of the citizen. The concepts of inflation and deflation of influence are critical concepts, but Parsons did not often use them as such to identify institutional pathologies. The New Public, as I have described it, is not something that he foresaw or recognized in incipient form, for his principal aim was to depict an idealized "model" for how an influence system would work. Habermas, on the other hand, working in the legacy of the Frankfurt School critics, saw the New Public emerging in embryo during the late fifties.

Parsons' theoretical writings, even his late works, often took influence to operate through tokens of prestige supplied by a background system of status stratification. He could have argued that modern differentiated influence is created by the influence system itself. The influence system bestows specialized, impermanent statuses upon its participants, statuses that depend on people's capacity to make others believe that they speak with endorsement and on behalf of larger collectivities. Instead, he continued to rely on his existing intellectual capital, calling on his earlier functional theory of stratification to supply an adequate account of the structural basis of influence. For all his rhetorical idealization of the life world, Habermas shows how misconceived such an approach can be. People cannot trust prestige alone. They want – at least at crucial junctures – to be able to test the claims of others, to ask questions, to get things straight, to be heard. A theory of the medium of influence must go beyond its backing in a status system to the backing of argument by persuasive reasons.

*Habermas' recent clarifications.* True to his commitment to discourse, Habermas regularly reconsiders his work in the light of criticisms, sometimes defending his positions, sometimes clarifying or adjusting his views in response to good reasons. *Between Facts and Norms* (1996), Habermas' most recent *magnum opus* places his criticism of the concept of influence in a new light. Disturbed by criticisms of an alleged "institutional deficit" in his scheme, Habermas begins by expressing the hope that this new work will "refute the objection that the theory of communicative action is blind to institutional reality" (xi). He then sets forth an integrated philosophy of sociology of law that places legal theory within the framework of the discourse principle. By viewing modern law as a practical institution whose norms and decisions must have both *de facto* effectiveness and achieved legitimacy, he is able to show that various legal institutions ultimately derive their legitimacy from discursive principles, even when they do not strictly follow discursive rules. This approach makes room, for example, for bargaining and for majority rule, even though those processes do not exactly conform to communicative standards for reaching consensus. Bargaining can be justified as long as its procedural rules give both sides equal voice and equal opportunity to prevail (177), and majority rule is acceptable if it is cast in a framework that takes outcomes as temporary conclusions subject to further discursive reassessment (179–80). Each discursive arena is governed by discourse rules adapted to its situational imperatives but also articulated with a legal system that is itself discursively legitimated and can thus lend its legitimacy to its constituent procedures. In this context, Habermas is able to claim that the ideal communicative situation, though "counterfactual" lies in the background of political and social action in constitutional regimes. This approach to the discursive background of less than fully rational discourse applies not only to such direct political phenomenon as legislation and elections, but to the life of the public itself, including the exercise of influence.

In *Between Facts and Norms,* Habermas (1996) takes influence to be important, but does not define exactly what he means by the term. He begins his account of public influence with a summary of Parsons' account of influence as a symbolically generalized form of communication based on trust in beliefs that have not yet been tested in discourse. Habermas does not decry this concept of influence. In fact, he treats it as an important means by which progressive ideas are brought to the agenda. He does, however, insist that its sway must *"ultimately* rest on the resonance and indeed the approval of a lay public whose composition is egalitarian" (364). In other words, influence must ultimately be ratified in the lifeworld. Nevertheless, in this and other passages, I see Habermas as rehabilitating influence, along with bargaining and majority rule, as potentially legitimate components of democratic deliberative orders, as long as they are connected to discursive procedures of legitimation. In my estimation, the necessary connection can be provided by institutionalized forums for testing claims in discourse. In the next chapter, I begin to lay the groundwork for this position and to argue that the lack of such forums undermines influence in the New Public.

# 5

## Public influence: a new paradigm

Habermas would describe the New Public as further "technicizing" of the means of domination. A new class of professional experts in the modes of mass rhetoric is seeking more sure control over what passes for public opinion. For Habermas, to speak of a public is to assert that there is a sphere of society in which discourse is free from domination by the state or any other organized system of power. To constitute a public sphere, such discourse must be open, accountable, and governed by good reasons. A loose, common sense notion of the "public" will not do. A true public sphere provides (and creates) *differentiated social space for public life*. Always fragile at best, the public sphere, has steadily eroded as the content of public discourse changed from debate about justifiable standards of integration to the manufacture of consent. The organs of power in society have learned to construct and present displays of their own legitimacy that support mere assent to their regime.

The division of sectors of society into either "spheres" or "systems" depends on where meaningful boundaries can be drawn. Are there boundaries defining the independence of the integrative system from the political system, establishing its *differentiation*? We must also ask whether integrative communication backed by prestige allows for voluntary compliance in the strict sense, and thus meets the criteria for persuasive communication, or whether it is fraudulent and therefore coercive. We again face the fundamental question of the nature of rhetoric and its place in social theory, a question that becomes all the more important with the rise of the rhetorical techniques purveyed by the new specialists in public communication.

In the light of these considerations, my account of the confrontation of Habermas with the concept of influence left crucial questions unanswered. Suppose that the concept of influence does describe a specialized medium of communication in the Parsonian sense, and suppose that in some modern societies there is even a self-regulating *system* of influence that contributes to social integration. Habermas can still argue that what Parsons called "influence" is part of the political system, not of a specialized integrative system. Influence is a species of power, for it relies on authoritative status rather than argument and therefore belongs in the realm of coercion, not persuasion.

In short, one might object that my arguments so far have been entirely formal and do not go to the real substantive issue: do modern democracies include a "public sphere" in the strong sense of that term? This question is best addressed in the context of a new approach to influence, one that follows the basic outlines of the Parsonian influence paradigm but departs from it in several respects: the influence paradigm should give proper weight to the role of affiliation in the rhetoric of influence, and having placed solidarity in a more central location in the scheme, must identify the respective roles of argument and appeals to solidarity in the process of social persuasion. Only a paradigm that sorts out these factors can avoid mere repetition of the longstanding debate that pits power and social stratification against collective reason as mutually exclusive sources of modern social order, with no middle ground.

### Influence: a new paradigm

Influence, as conceived in the following paradigm, is the capacity to speak on behalf of the solidarities of groups bound by common interests. Influence allows spokespersons to make statements and to urge actions that others take as accurate representations of the situation and interests of groups. Acquiring this capacity depends on engendering both trust in the sincerity and confidence in the efficacy of people who are viewed as speaking for groups, not just for themselves.

The Parsonian paradigm for influence started with the concept of persuasion, which he defined as a mode of "getting results from interaction" by using positive sanctions to affect others' views rather than by changing their situations. Persuasion is "positive" in the sense that it seeks to show others that what the persuader wants is, if properly understood, actually good for the person being persuaded. This definition appears to place persuasion in the realm of communicative action, in that it seeks understanding rather than relying on rewards or punishments. Indeed, it is precisely because persuasion seeks understanding that Habermas denies that influence can become the medium for a functional system. Persuasion lacks an intrinsic sanction that can be manipulated by an automatic system to affect the calculations of the costs and benefits of various possible decisions.

From Habermas' perspective, the influence paradigm, by starting from a distinction between altering actual situations and altering how situations are understood, has placed modes of "getting results" that are addressed to actors' attitudes forever outside the realm of systemic regulation. I will argue to the contrary, starting from the premise that persuasion implicitly involves a form of sanction – a type of inducement – because it offers *help*. An attempt to persuade implies that the persuader believes that the audience can benefit from the information and advice provided. A persuader's assertions are predicated on a claim that speaker and audience can make common cause.

*Warrants of solidarity.* Taking a page from Habermas' book, I argue that *persuasion involves a necessary presupposition, sometimes counterfactual, that the persuader and the audience share a common interest.* One who approaches another with a persuasive message affirms, whether implicitly or explicitly, that they share some common interest that lends credibility to the message. Without such an assumption there is no reason to suppose that persuasive efforts of another are compatible with one's own interests – that these efforts are not strategic.

According to Habermas, speakers oriented to communicative action warrant that their assertions are true, their normative evaluations right, their esthetic judgments grounded in standards, and their expressive statements sincere (TCA I, 10–23). "Sincerity" technically refers to honesty regarding the speaker's subjective state, but it implicitly refers to the entire range of the speaker's communicative good faith. Speakers may (and usually do) approach communicative action with less than truly communicative intent, including admixtures of ulterior instrumental and strategic motives. Nevertheless, listeners must assume that there is some communicative foundation – some level of warranty – or they cannot continue to communicate. These presuppositions are, as Habermas says, "counterfactual" idealizations, but they are necessary and unavoidable working assumptions at the outset of all attempts to achieve mutual understanding (1993 [1991] , 54–60).

I am suggesting here that when speakers attempt to change others opinions or to affect their conduct, there is another necessary presupposition: *speakers warrant that their arguments are predicated on identifiable shared interests.* Such warrants do not require a presupposition that speaker and audience are completely without differentiated or conflicting interests, only that with respect to the issue at hand there is some basis for common cause. In this sense, an offer of affiliation is a constitutive element of an act of persuasion. Employing Habermas' vocabulary and following the general line of his arguments (TCA I, 301–3), I will refer to offers of affiliation as *warrants of solidarity.* Like other warrants, a warrant of solidarity implies a *validity* claim and an implicit offer to *redeem* this claim through discourse. Successfully redeemed claims may be called *valid,* and it is offers to validate claims through discourse that provide *rationally motivated* force for accepting speakers' warrants.

*Habermas and the problem of sincerity.* Warrants of solidarity are akin to warrants of sincerity in that they purport to guarantee speaker's accurate representation of their subjective motivation. This raises a question of fundamental importance for influence theory, for it involves reappraisal of a crucial asymmetry in Habermas' paradigm for the discursive redemption of validity claims. Warrants of the truth of assertions, the rightness of evaluations, and the grounding of esthetic judgment can be redeemed through discourse, but according to Habermas, warrants of sincerity cannot. "That a speaker means what he says can be made credible only in the consistency of what he does and not through providing grounds" (TCA I, 303). If one does not believe that others' statements are sincere, then it does not increase confidence for them to affirm their sincerity and then to affirm that these affirmations of sincerity are truthful. Conversely, one cannot adduce evidence to controvert others' accounts of their subjective intentions.

The asymmetry between the warrant of sincerity and other warrants bears on the concept of influence, especially as regards the place of reputation in the dynamics of persuasion.[1] Habermas' claim that sincerity is grounded solely on deeds must be reassessed. To build a record of consistency of statements and acts is to build a *reputation* for sincerity. A reputation for sincerity makes one's statements credible, which is a prime requisite for communicative action, for it is credibility that allows assessment of another's motivation as communicative rather than strategic. Moreover, each communicative act in a continuing series implies a new affirmation of enduring sincerity, but the audience, without direct access to intentions, must still rely on the speaker's reputation to assess the likelihood of the speaker's sincerity. This assessment is easier and more reliable if the speaker has a validated reputation for honest statements of intention, but in the last analysis the hearer must take reputation, an indirect indicator, as a substitute for direct knowledge.

It is possible, then, to reconstruct the basic elements of the influence paradigm from Habermas' identification of the special place of sincerity in discourse. We must now apply the general logic of sincerity to the sincerity of persuasion, which warrants that the interests of persuader and audience are aligned, because both parties genuinely believes that a degree of true community of interest allows predication of the act of persuasion on common cause. The term "degree" suggests that a realistic concept of influence must recognize that the solidary interests embraced by persuaders and their audiences are not necessarily grounded in strong community. The relevant interests may be narrow or broad in scope, need not be generalized beyond the parties involved, and may derive from varied motives. The common interest presumed by persuasive acts need not include (and could not possibly include) every interest of the parties. It is enough that there be some aspect of their common situation that can be generalized in support of a common basis for a particular act of persuasion. For example, the interest of a physician in successful healing, which is built into the normative definition of the role, couples with the interest of the patient in being healed, and the fact that the physician is also paid for the service does not destroy their common interests in healing.

Habermas' discourse ethics require the participants to generalize their arguments in universal terms in order to achieve just results, but in actual discourse there is no inherent communicative presupposition requiring parties to ask whether their common interests extend to any others, let alone all others, and to seek, by generalizing their interests, an agreement that everyone would accept. On the contrary, persuasion often has a particularizing effect. One frequent foundation for persuasion is the common interest that some people share *against* others. As Kenneth Burke's rhetorical theory stresses, the dynamics of identification involve establishing that "we" are not "they." Nevertheless, it is important to recognize that as audiences become larger and more diverse, the demands on persuasive communication do become more universalistic. Accommodation of the interests of plural participants in persuasive discourse requires a higher level of value generalization, in order to construct common interests among diverse parties, and, in discussions involving the entire collectivity, to create a concept of the "public interest." It is not always possible, however, to achieve credible constructions of common interest sufficient to ground universally persuasive appeals. Consequently, the integration of modern societies creates both forces leading toward the universalization of claims to represent the public interest and also divisive claims based on the interests of various particular groups. Those who represent the claims of subgroups contest the claims of those who purport to speak for the whole. It is this tension between broad and narrow generalizations of interests that underlie pluralist politics. Some of the forces implicit in the New Public encourage the universalization of argument. Contemporary lobbying, for example, with its demands for analysis, research, and justification in terms of the public good, supports universalistic (though not necessarily sincere) discourse, while direct mail campaigns, based on geodemographic market research and aimed at segments of the public, have a particularizing effect.

*Plural sources of affiliation.* Human interests, whether weak and transitory preferences, the strong ties of primordial groups, or large stakes in financial investments, create a wealth of resources for finding common interests from which persuasion can be justified. Interests conjoined in solidarity may be instrumental and economic or strategic and political, but ideal and normative interests, social interests in human association, expressive, and esthetic interests also support affiliation. Normative interests in implementing what one thinks is right or ethically required may play a decisive role in providing the common grounds that justify persuasive communication and make it credible. Interests in personal identities that derive from group memberships are particularly important sources of social interests (McAdam and Paulsen 1993). The possibilities of interpersonal connection, persuasion, and influence are multiplied by modern social structures, which allow for disposability of both the investments on which interests are founded and the loyalties that people can claim or recognize. Any theory of influence in modern society must be sensitive to the multiplicity of possibilities for calling upon particular connections that do not require generalized appeals to public interests. The pluralism of modern society may or may not support equality, limit the state, and protect citizens from the power of elite groups, as some theories propose, but structural pluralism is an elementary feature of the organization of solidarity in modern society.

### From persuasion to influence: institutionalizing sincerity

*Strategic reputation: why are reputations credible?* That people do rely on the reputation of others and so come under their influence is undeniable. Nevertheless, reliance on another person's reputation as a basis for accepting persuasion is problematic, for according to the strictest criteria of rational choice, such reliance is ultimately groundless. A person may speak and act reliably for a long period, building a strong reputation, and then deliberately cash it in, revealing that the motive for building reputation had been strategic all along. This is what is meant by a "confidence game." Why, then, do people accept others' representations, despite the fact that to do so involves an element of trust that cannot be fully secured?

In the first place, there is no satisfactory alternative. Even if it were emotionally acceptable to eschew all trust, information is too costly to allow a Crusoe-like reliance on self sufficiency. There are means of securing expectations against confidence games, or at least of minimizing the risks of relying on the credibility of others. One can ask for precommitments, enforceable contracts for example, which link the social force of reputation to the political force of binding law. In the economy, prior commitments can take the form of legal warranties, security deposits, or non-refundable capital investments. This general principle also applies to influence: we can rely on others with greater security if they have a *stake* in their reputations and in the representations that they make. More generally stated, the credibility of others is enhanced if one knows the structure of their incentives.

*Signals.* The value of knowing the incentives of others is the starting place for signaling theory, which asserts that certain clues called "signals" explain how the recipients of messages can assess the credibility of the sender. The theory begins by positing that asymmetrical distributions of information make those who lack information dependent on those who have it. Signaling theory also assumes that people cannot be fully trusted to communicate honestly. In assessing credibility, rational actors look for "signals" that indicate that the providers of information have a stake or interest that supports the credibility of their assertions. A signal represents the *costs* that a speaker has incurred to send a message or might incur if the message proves false. If there were no costs associated with making a representation, then everyone would tend to send the same self-serving signals, so messages would become meaningless. For example, degrees from prestigious universities, with a good record of academic performance, are a form of endorsement that give some job candidates *influence*, in the sense that their claims to be well qualified are credible. Employers, who have relatively little direct information about job applicants, rely on credentials as signals because they can gauge how much such signals have cost applicants. An unlikely prospect would presumably not possess adequate resources of ability to pay the "cost," in effort, to complete the credential program (Spence 1973). If everyone could award themselves such academic degrees as might seem persuasive, degrees would cease to have value as signals. They would become what signaling theory refers to as "cheap talk," which is generally less reliable than costly signals, especially if there is good reason to suppose that the signaler might have strategic interests that the recipient does not share.

The presence of signaling in communication undercuts Habermas' contention that claims to sincerity cannot be redeemed by setting forth empirically valid assertions. In particular, the claims to common interest that underlie effective persuasion, and therefore influence, are subject to rational assessment of the credibility of the persuader's assertions of sincerity. For example, signaling theory has been applied to the activities of lobbyists, the persuaders *par excellence* in the New Public. Lobbyists must convince both clients and officials that their representations of group interests are accurate and trustworthy. According to Ainsworth and Sened

(1993), the very presence of a lobbyist as an ongoing intermediary is itself a signal, for the lobbyists' incentives as information brokers are known to both their principals and their audiences. Legislators and other officials know that lobbyists cannot afford to misrepresent either the available level of support for policies that they advocate or to advocate policies contrary to the interests of their clients.

*Signals of solidarity.* Signals and the stakes behind them need not be financial. Represented interests may be affiliative and idealistic, and affiliative interests provide particularly important signals in support of persuasion. In this respect so called "cheap talk" is not to be entirely dismissed. Students of signaling note that cheap talk can be effective when speakers and audiences share preferences (Crawford and Sobel 1982; Austin-Smith 1990). Cheap talk is economical for the information seeker as well as for the information sender. When looking for reliable information on which to make decisions that will implement one's interests, it is more economical to focus on sources that are perceived to share those interests than to sift through a broad array of contradictory information and contested perspectives.[2] People further assume that others who are like them – have similar experiences, group memberships, and social positions – will also share their preferences, and so assume the common interests on which persuasion depends. Trust in common interests are reinforced when these similarities are sources of personal identification. The sway of rhetoric depends on invoking identities that signal common cause, adding emotional punch to the merely economical advantages of accepting signals of similarity as rough and ready warrants of common interest. In consequence, people who are seen as trustworthy representatives of solidary groups, which provide sources of identification, possess generalized resources of persuasion, that is *influence*. Accordingly, the structure of influence in society parallels the structure of solidarity, which has a crucial consequence: *the independence of the system of influence, and hence the possibility of civil society, is grounded in a complex matrix of solidarities.* Whenever practitioners of the communicative techniques of the New Public succeed in bypassing this matrix, influence, cut off from its social base, becomes an inflated medium.

When influence is exercised successfully, its link to solidarity is reinforced by the satisfaction people feel when they have been well and honestly informed and advised. The common interests that persuasion must presuppose are then transformed into identifications with persons of influence. This paradigm for the analysis of persuasion, which began by examining the rational presuppositions of the process, and proceeded to ask what rational information-seekers would do to secure useful information at minimum cost, ultimately leads to recognition that the cues of credibility are not themselves rational. Audiences do, of course, employ rational standards to assess the plausibility of arguments presented to them, asking if they make sense and if they are in accord with what the audience takes to be the facts, but the process of influence is driven by powerful emotional forces, especially identification. The targets of influence have interests, both material and ideal, at stake, and they therefore seek spokespersons whom they can trust and with whom they can identify as bearers of their common concerns, people who stand for and represent their collective interests and identities. I refer to such persons as *prolocutors*, for they *speak on behalf of* groups. Prolocutors are the bearers of influence in society.

*Prolocutors, ratification, and the differentiation of influence.* Some prolocutors are appointed to positions that include responsibilities for speaking on behalf of groups, others do so through their independent advocacy. Such leaders, as Habermas puts it, "emerge from the public" rather than "appear before" it (1996, 375). In any event, high position in a modern status order does not ensure that a person will be accepted as a prolocutor. Generalized prestige, bestowed by a system of stratification can be employed to enhance one's claims, but it does not provide the differentiated, specialized legitimation that allows prolocutors to speak for particular solidary groups and alliances.

In modern societies, prolocutors use persuasion to capture free-floating, disposable loyalties. Their success depends on their rhetorical capacity to present, create, and adapt appeals to new situations and groups, but until these appeals have been ratified by audiences, claims to leadership remain mere bids, not validated influence. Institutions of prolocutorship arise from a process of differentiation of solidary leadership. The concept of *differentiated solidarity* is the key to understanding modern influence. In a traditional society, influence does tend to rest on general position in a well-defined status order – status in a caste hierarchy, or an aristocracy, or an order of wealthy, respected families. In modern society, influence becomes differentiated from the general status order as it comes to be based on resources that must be *created* by rhetorical bids to speak for particular, often new or emergent, groups and alliances of people who can be brought together under a banner of common interest.

### Becoming a prolocutor

*How is solidary leadership constructed?* Confidence in leadership is a generic concept that cuts across types of organizations. All sorts of groups, whether loosely or tightly organized, look to leaders for guidance. Groups may be founded on normative definitions of common membership or on actual ties of felt solidarity; some groups are motivated by mutual economic advantages, others band together to secure and exercise power, but there is one common requirement: leadership depends on trust. Claims to leadership are contested in every setting, from families to large-scale organizations, and the members of these groups look to signals of trustworthiness and credibility to make assessments as to which of those whom they love or fear, or report to, or cooperate with, can best be trusted and believed. The members of a solidary association, bound by a common interest, can trust a spokesperson because they believe that she shares their common interest, or because they like and identify with her, or because they know that she has a financial stake in properly representing them. If a financial stake is the prime signal available to the members, the association is nonetheless solidary for this mode of securing the trust of its members and the stabilization of its leadership.

*The concept of trust.* "Trust" refers to such a broad and diverse range of human relations that general definitions and theories are not easily applied to prolocutorship, which itself assumes varied forms ranging from paid lobbyists for economic interests to the leaders of nascent social movements. Nevertheless it will be useful to establish an initial definition of trust.

Diego Gambetta (1988), summarizing the contributions to a cross-disciplinary seminar on trust, noted convergence among the participants on a definition:

> trust . . . is a particular level of the subjective probability with which an agent will perform a particular action, both *before* he can monitor such action (or independently of his capacity ever to be able to monitor it) *and* in a context in which it affects *his own* action . . . When we say we trust someone or that someone is trustworthy, we implicitly mean that the probability that he will perform an action that is beneficial or at least not detrimental is high enough for us to consider engaging in some form of cooperation with him.    ( 217, emphasis in original)

This definition captures several aspects of current thinking about trust.[3] Current theories assert that trust is a precondition for cooperative undertakings and that the need for trust arises from people's unavoidable uncertainty about others' intentions with regard to their own plans. This line of thought presents an image of a person trying to decide whether to enter into relationships that will be successful only if other parties keep their promises, an image that lends itself to strictly economistic analysis based on assumptions of rational calculation of self interest. It slights the emotional investments that people have in each other and implies that trust is relevant only to deciding whether to enter into interpersonal relations, contracts for example, ignoring the trust that we place in sources of information to which we have no necessary lasting connection and, more generally, the trust we place in institutions rather than in specific others. It fails to recognize that uncertainty often runs two ways: the trustor is not certain that the trustee will act in the desired manner, but neither is the trustee sure what the trustor wants. Consider, for example, the problems that prolocutors for interest groups, private or public, experience in knowing what their constituencies would have them do, or even who, exactly, constitutes their constituency. In order to achieve a concept broad enough to encompass application to the special forms of trust that people place in influence, we need an initial definition that captures the essential notion that trust involves reliance in the face of uncertainty, but avoids several of the implications of the image evoked by Gambetta's terms.

I propose that *trust is the credit extended to sources that provide representations of information regarding states of affairs ( including the intentions and commitments of these sources ), when actors rely on such representations in the absence of fully adequate independent knowledge.* Sources of information may be personal or institutional; one can place trust in newspapers, political parties, associations, or other institutional aggregations, even when they are faceless constructs. I might, for example, believe representations regarding the prospects of health care legislation published in the newsletter of the American Association of Retired Persons in the absence of any information about who wrote it, or about who really runs the association and to what end, because for whatever reason I extend credit to the organization. Credit can be extended without calculation of benefits, costs, and risks when creditworthiness is assumed because of one's sense of identification with the source, or through strong emotional attractions, or simply because of taken-for-granted confidence in one's daily routines. Indeed, people may resist evidence that sources of information are not reliable (Festinger, Riecken, and Schacter 1956; Good 1988), responding to such information not by withdrawing credit but by extending more credit to cover the deficiency, just as investors, motivated by hope or desperation, sometimes cover the declining value of their stakes by investing additional funds to protect their positions. The foregoing analogy is instructive, for it points to the reason for defining trust as an extension of *credit* and prepares the way for understanding influence as sustained by creditors who extend their willingness to accept the views of others, beyond the available evidence. Would-be prolocutors, in order to garner influence, must achieve capacity to induce people to grant credit to them. Without this credit, they cannot sustain influence, for they would be asked to prove everything they say.

*The means of accumulating credit.* The principal paths to accumulating and sustaining credit are not fixed phases of an invariant process. In the daily world of seeking and using influence, leaders adapt to opportunities, circumstances, and challenges, but as an expository simplification, the elements of the creation of credit can be presented as if one could tell a chronological story about a typical sequence of steps. At each step, those who seek credit make two analytically separate types of statements melded into one coherent rhetorical plea: *factual statements* about the situation at hand, the effectiveness of proposed measures, and the common interests of the audience; and *statements of identification* – appeals to the audience to look to their solidarity, not as a matter of self interest but as a group obligation and a means for enhancing personal identity. It is appropriate to proceed as if a typical prolocutor is an individual, for there is mounting evidence that public interest organizations are usually started by individual entrepreneurs. Governmental, charitable, and private patrons often provide some financial backing, but for the most part entrepreneurial prolocutors rely first on their own resources and the solidary support of members of their networks (Salisbury 1969; Nownes and Neeley 1996).[4]

1. *Inaugural statements.* Building influence is an inherently creative process. It rests on the inventive powers of rhetoric. Each initial bid for influential status proclaims, in an inaugural statement, a solidarity that does not yet exist. A speaker says, "I speak for you, a solidary group, and I am included in your *we,* as your spokesperson; *our* aims will be advanced and *our* interests protected." The speaker's claim of solidarity with the audience is not entirely empirical; it can only represent a potential solidarity that must be realized in a successful process of representation and ratification. Even the internal solidarity of the audience is problematic, in that the speaker wants to strengthen and activate potential bonds that may be only dimly perceived at the time of the inaugural statement. In the first instance the would-be prolocutor must ask for a credit of influence, for the inaugural statement cannot correspond to an existing state of affairs. Since inaugural statements describe possibilities rather than current realities, offers of solidarity are optimistic affirmations of hope, tending to exaggeration, not necessarily because of motivation to deceive but because of their inherently inventive character. In the limiting but instructive instance, such statements may be "inaugural" in the strong sense that the literary critic J. Hillis Miller uses the term. Arguing along Nietzschean lines that the self is continually reconstructed by linguistic means, Miller (1992, 100–43) contends that to invoke past commitments is to hold people to a self that no longer exists! Promises truly grounded in the self emerge from dawning, possibly transitory, identities; hence, the grounding of inaugural statements cannot be realized in the present. They depend on the "power of language to posit fictitious identities that are then hypostatized" (268, n52).[5]

Further inaugural statements are made each time prolocutors ask for additional credit in the course of attempts to extend the limits of groups encompassed by their bids, to form new coalitions, to set more ambitious aims, to explain new circumstances, or be granted additional time to make good their promises of effective representation.[6]

2. *Initial signals: presenting bona fides.* Having made an inaugural statement that sets forth an invitation to affiliate, one who bids to represent solidarities must present evidence of sincere intent and plausible capacities. The bidder must present signals that go beyond cheap talk to a program with serious prospects, worthy of respect and consideration. In the first instance, such signals may be relatively weak, a mere presentation of *bona fides.* For example, suppose that a person decides to try to unite parents within a school district behind a program for improving their children's education by requiring more attention to mathematics. Her initial bid would include not only inaugural affirmations of solidarity and commitments to effective concerted action, but also enough information about her situation and biography to provide plausibility to her initial appeal. Her identification of herself as a resident of the district, a mother of school-age children, a former PTA chairperson, an erstwhile undergraduate mathematics major, and an active attorney with a local law firm would establish a set of solidary identities and indicators of competence in support of an initial credit of trust, adequate at least to command attention. Yet such signals, since they are only indicators of given statuses, are not expensive to send, and are in this sense relatively weak.

3. *Gathering endorsements.* Indicators of status cannot by themselves create adequate credit to endow a potential spokesperson with sufficient influence to create and mobilize effective solidary alliances. Any number of people could present plausible credentials of *structural* status, but only those who go beyond mere eligibility for becoming influential to a *process* of developing capacities for exercising influence in ongoing social relations can become prolocutors. Background statuses are transformed into effective influence by collecting endorsements, either naked endorsements that simply announce support, or elaborated endorsements that give reasons. Endorsement is the basic means by which influence is transferred, and collecting endorsements usually involves tapping or joining the existing structure of influence. Our hypothetical advocate of mathematics in the schools might, for example, seek endorsements from PTA chapters and educational support groups.

4. *Forming organizations and coalitions.* Our advocate may go beyond seeking support from the established influence structure as already organized into groups. She can start her own association, whose members, by

lending their names, serving on governing or advisory boards, or promoting the cause themselves – or just by adding the prestige inherent in providing countable numbers of adherents – create an identifiable symbolic structure of support for both the movement and its founder. She may enlist the support of other groups with congruent aims, forming coalitions to add to the weight of her movement.

Once an organization is founded, the situation of the founding prolocutor becomes complex and problematic. Who now speaks for the proclaimed solidarity of the represented group, the original leader or the organization that has, by their endorsement, created her legitimacy? In some cases, organizations come to be the primary symbolic repositories of influence, and individuals carry weight by speaking for the organization; in other cases, when organizations are led by particularly strong prolocutors, the leader's name carries its own weight. Ralph Nader is viewed as speaking for consumers, and few people know the name of the organization he created, whereas most people have no idea who lies behind Science in the Public Interest, a very influential consumer group, or Consumers Union. Some know the latter only by the name of its magazine, *Consumer Reports.*

The members and leaders of organizations bring multiple and varied interests under their overall banner of solidarity. Ulterior interests may cast a shadow over the participation of factions whose benefits attendant to participation in the larger organization may be secondary to their own interests and solidarities. Associations are often coalitions of disparate interests united in common loyalty to some more or less overriding, coalescent community. Coalition implies potential conflict, and the threat of conflict presents prolocutors with a challenge: they must sustain the relative importance of the coalition's goals and the larger solidarities on which the group is based. For example, our advocate for mathematics education, may, in an attempt to create a larger, more influential endorsing group, make common cause with a similar group with an interest in reemphasizing English composition, under a common aim of "Basics First." This in turn might attract supporters with rather different agenda; conservative opposition to mainstream educational trends, fueled perhaps by religious fundamentalism, or generalized opposition to the educational establishment, or elitist objection to multilingual educational programs. She may expand the range of her support at the expense of conflict within her group, threats to her leadership, and the displacement of her original aims. Successful representation of the overriding goals of a united, if diverse, larger community of concern requires strong leadership – leadership resistant to the pushes and pulls of division and disaggregation. Such leadership requires large stores of influence, and this in turn requires the capacity to send strong signals.

5. *Bold moves: sending strong signals.* In assessing the sincerity of leaders who proclaim solidarity with audiences and found their credibility upon these asserted bonds, audiences can gauge the strength and sincerity of speakers' commitments by the costliness of their signals. "Cheap talk" may be viewed as "rhetoric" in the pejorative sense of that term; all talk and no action. Costly talk provides a visible indication that speakers have invested in their words, have a stake in what they say, and are therefore less likely to be engaging in strategic action.

In building influence, two categories of strong signal are especially important, *success* and *sacrifice*. Success is a strong signal for it implies that leaders who are credited with bringing about successful results have invested effort in the project, costly effort that goes beyond mere repetition of claims of good intentions. As an indicator of effectiveness, success increases a group's confidence in its leaders' capacities. It redeems leaders' promises, even defines after the fact what these promises meant, and enhances leaders' claims to knowledge and to interpretive and diagnostic ability.

Sacrifice is a particularly strong indicator of costly effort. When leaders take actions that lead to visible losses, or risks of such losses, their signals of commitment are magnified. Risky confrontations, such as demonstrations or civil disobedience, can lead to physical retaliation or imprisonment. Fasts and vigils display willingness to bear costs on behalf of the cause. Leaders who carry out or lead such actions gain considerable stature, even if their efforts are unsuccessful in the short term, especially when their apparent failures to gain their stated aims on behalf of their constituents result in visible suffering. Gandhi and Nelson Mandela, for example, developed extraordinary stores of influence in the course of many years of dramatic sacrifice.

Sacrifice as a generic type of signal need not be so dramatic as the conduct displayed by Gandhi or Mandela, nor is sacrifice limited to social movements. Some prolocutors work outside the existing system to introduce change, but others use forms of strong signals to build influence within the established order. Ideological exaggeration allows insider politicians to signal their position on the political spectrum, leading some potential supporters to conclude that strong statements, made at the risk of alienating the cautious, provide good unambiguous indicators of where speakers really stand. Stronger display of risk with a more distinct aura of sacrifice send yet stronger signals of commitment (Hinich and Munger 1994; Iverson 1994). Actions that put one's entire political career at risk, or commitments to constituents that put one at odds with other influential political leaders, fall under the heading of sacrifice and exemplify the importance of "bold moves."

### Forms of backing: relational and system levels

Influence is created and sustained when prolocutors establish credibility as people (or organizations) who can be trusted to speak sincerely and effectively for the groups that they claim to represent. In Parsonian terms, this trust is the "security backing" of influence as a medium. Security backing operates at two levels. Firstly, people must feel secure in their trust that accepting media is not an irreversible surrender of items of value for mere symbols, that symbolic media can be redeemed in goods, in promises kept, and in convincing justifications for what they are told or asked to do. Secondly, trustees of the media can redeem its various "currencies" only if the organized systems that support them are solvent.

The two levels of backing are readily illustrated by the security of money. Money is backed by people's willingness to accept it in lieu of objects with intrinsic value. This level of backing rests on confidence that the monetary payments that people receive will be usable because currency, checks, and other credit instruments are widely accepted. This confidence provides the *relational* level of backing; it reflects the trust people have *in each others* tokens of value. But at a deeper systemic level, the long-term value of money, its resistance to inflation, is backed by the productive capacity of the economy. The economic system must have sufficient real capacity to turn credits that are extended to new investments – credits that create new money – into productive facilities. There must be sufficient productive capacity to increase the supply of goods and services in proportion to the supply of money. This underlying capacity may be referred to as *system* backing.

What, then, backs influence? In general terms, influence is backed by the willingness and capacity of prolocutors to fulfill their promises, but on closer examination it is clear that the backing of influence involves a duality that both parallels the two levels of backing for money and reflects the double imperatives facing those who attempt to perform the prolocutor's role. The rhetoric of establishing trust requires those who bid for affiliation to make both empirical statements about states of affairs and expressive appeals to solidarities and common identities. In subsequently employing their acquired trust to engage in influence, asking people to accept their diagnostic statements and their prescriptions for action without full presentations of evidence, influential people continue to make both forms of rhetorical statement.

In order to sustain confidence, bidders for influence present abridged, token arguments, implying that adequate factual and analytical details could be adduced, if necessary, to demonstrate that their statements are "good" – that their assertions are accurate and usable, that they can be "cashed in," so to speak, as checks can be taken to the bank. Token arguments and their redemption on demand constitute the rational side of influence, but prolocutors also refer to taken-for-granted social bonds rooted in systems of solidarity and common interest. Systemic solidarity provides backing for influential leaders' requests for the extensions of credit to them only if the mutual interests of the influential and the influenced are embodied in a solidary order of leaders and followers who, working together, can accomplish their aims. *Prolocutors affirm that the systemic resources of solidarity will be adequate to achieve common interests.* There are, then, both *relational* forms of backing that rest on the capacity of the targets of influence to demand (and influential people to provide) redemption of the token arguments on which the rhetoric of influence relies, and *systemic* forms that depend upon real (or realistically buildable) common interests and solidary ties that can be mobilized in support of collective projects.

*Linking Parsons and Habermas.* My use of the word "redemption" for explaining and defending token arguments calls attention to the convergence of my analysis of the backing of influence and Habermas' notion of a discourse ethic.[7] The idea of two levels of backing, relational and systemic, lends itself to partial syntheses of Habermas' and Parsons' contrasting approaches to influence. Habermas insists that authentic persuasion must rely on the rationality implied by open discourse, in which arguments must be redeemed when challenged. Redemption is not accomplished by repeated reference to one's influential status, but by substantive argument. The *relational* backing of influence requires a process of two-way communication through which audiences can test the assertions of those who would influence them and can demand that influential leaders take the audience's interests and their experienced needs into account. Habermas' depiction of a discourse ethic nicely captures this idea and grounds the very idea of rationality in just this sort of process. However, Habermas' standard for discourse requires that its participants generalize their thinking to the degree that the final product of discourse will both be just and seem just to everyone on universal, principled grounds. Give and take, compromise, and workable approximation are excluded as fully proper answers to disputes about just outcomes. To some critics, this high standard of rationality would ask people to approach social deliberations on such an abstract, depersonalized level as to deny them the human, identity sustaining, communally rooted motivation that makes such deliberation meaningful.[8] By denying the legitimacy of *rhetoric* as a communicative mode that social beings bring to their problem-solving action, Habermas in effect excludes rhetorical confrontation (including its rational component), the only socially and humanly possible procedural substitute for the direct use of power.

Parsons on the other hand, insisted on grounding influence in communal, or at least community-like, solidarities. Hence his work bears directly on the system backing of influence. Parsons' focus on the status order as the core of influence in the community failed to take being influential as a status *sui generis*, and neglected the necessary role of rational persuasion in supporting and sustaining influential status, but he did call attention to the essential place of community – a normatively defined "we" – in any process of influence capable of leading to social integration.

The synthesis proposed here goes beyond saying that the process of influence requires both communal connections and discourse, that it is both solidary and rational. It derives from a conception of influence systems as organized processes of rhetoric that cannot be stable unless the participants are given voice. Rhetorical approaches to problems of social integration imply that people can enter discussion that makes sense in relation to their personal experience in the groups that encompass daily, socially grounded life, but participation also requires opportunities to demand that speakers explain the grounds of their claims.

### The differentiation of solidarity

The influence paradigm allows reassessment of Habermas' assertion that modern democracies lack independent integrative systems that can establish processes for defining the normative terms of social coordination and policy-making and thereby provide for societal guidance. If the influence paradigm illuminates the organization of persuasion in modern societies, then it is possible to claim that the integrative challenges arising from the ubiquitous normative problems characteristic of modernity are addressed, if not fully resolved, through mutual persuasion among individuals and organizations endowed with influence. Influence, employing argument and organized around the coalescence of common interests and solidarities, provides systematic alternatives to coercive power and the marketplace as means of ordering human affairs.

The validity of applying the influence paradigm to modern social integration depends on whether there are societies with differentiated systems of solidarity. The preconditions for differentiated solidarity are: firstly, a population whose internal bonds extend beyond membership in primordial, traditionally defined groups to include elective affiliations and identifications with larger groups committed to defined interests and causes; secondly, effective spokespeople for these groups; and thirdly, organization of these groups and their leaders in an autonomous system. The first two of these conditions are relatively easy to define, and it is clear that modern democratic societies meet them to some extent. The third condition is more problematic.

*Autonomy and pluralism.* An autonomous integrative "system" of solidarity requires social organization that protects its boundaries, so that diverse groups and their leaders are not controlled solely by political and economic forces. On its political flank, independent systems of differentiated solidarity are protected by such institutions as freedom of speech and association. Nevertheless, power and wealth can penetrate systems of influence. Wealth, for example, provides a competitive advantage in campaigns for gaining and mobilizing influence, especially in the New Public, whose professional practitioners demand substantial payment for their services and a return on their investments in research and public relations.

The key to clarifying the differentiation among these institutional spheres is to stress the special character of the media they employ, especially the ultimate dependence of influence on persuasion. Persuasion allows for rhetorical appeals to solidary loyalties, but not the use of threats and bribes. The separation of the economy and the influence system is established in some measure whenever support for people and programs is not simply awarded to the highest bidder but is allocated consequent to some sort of deliberative process, however rudimentary. Hence, differentiated systems of solidarity are institutionalized not just by freedom of speech and association but by rules against bribery, by electoral systems, and by deliberative settings requiring participants to set forth persuasive reasons. A legislature in which each seat and each member's vote was literally for sale would not support an influence system, to be sure, but the fact that money is a resource for building and sustaining influence, and that influence-experts work for money does not make influence just a part of the economy. When an advocate engages in persuasive rhetoric to convince an audience, and cannot simply buy their agreement, success depends on addressing the concerns of the audience, including their culturally defined needs for convincing evidence. The sway of money on integrative systems may compromise their independence, but this does not demonstrate that no boundaries exist. Indeed, charges that the American Congress is "for sale" or that economic interests "determine" legislation and its enforcement, as well as what newspapers print, how people vote, and which causes associations support, are themselves arguments about how and where boundaries ought to be defined. Exaggerated charges of irredeemable corruption at the core of these institutions are indicators that their boundaries are contested, and such claims are to be expected in the course of rhetorical exchanges about whether particular measures designed to define and strengthen boundaries should be put in place. Campaign finance law, open-meeting regulations, disputes about ownership of the media, and investigative journalism designed to reveal lapses in independence or concealed dependence reflect normatively defined boundaries that exist but are not adequately protected.

To the degree that systems of associational solidarity maintain boundaries by protecting processes of influence from power and purchase, integrative systems come to have systematic properties, including equilibria within competitive *public* markets for influence. The concept of independence cannot be reconciled with the domination of society and its integrative processes by a close-knit economic and political elite. The assertion that autonomous, competitive systems of influence contribute to social integration implies that the interests and solidarities organized by these systems are multiple and varied, that is *pluralistic*. Theories of the independence and autonomy of integrative systems are therefore versions of pluralism, which claim that "the public" encompasses, aggregates, and gives *voice* to a range of competing interests.

### Conceptions of the public

*The general public.* In the traditions of democratic theory, "the public" refers in a broad sense to the people. The public is the electorate and the bearer of public opinion, the ultimate source of legitimate governing power. The state holds only delegated power as an agent of the people and is separate from and accountable to the differentiated public. This bare-bones concept of the public does not require that the bearers of public opinion be organized. Some form of franchise, together with a set of individual rights that protect public autonomy, is organization enough and, indeed, some theories of democratic sovereignty are hostile to organization within the public. Political parties or any other form of "self-created societies" come under the heading of faction, and factions prevent the people from direct sovereignty over their government and encourage the capture of that government by groups that represent special rather than truly public interests.[9]

*The public as aggregated opinion.* The legacy of the notion that the ideal public would be formed by individuals with personal preferences, unsullied by intermediate influences, is alive in the ideology of the practitioners of the New Public, who in their embrace of the theory and practice of marketing and their disdain for old-fashioned political parties, glorify the power of the new technology to achieve democracy through finding out what the people "really" want. As one advocate of political marketing states the case: "The marketing concept [proceeds by] first identifying consumer needs and then developing products and services to meet those needs . . . [The] marketing concept centers on a different philosophy than the party concept, the main difference being that the marketing concept centers on the consumer, in this case the voter, as the primary focus of the campaign" (Newman 1994, 33). Competition for political consumers' votes insures that the people's preferences will prevail: "In principle, a marketing orientation should lead candidates to better understand what voters want. Otherwise they won't stay in business." (Kotler, "Foreword" to Mauser 1983, vii.)

Richard Wirthlin, a leading campaign consultant, justifies his profession, polling, and television campaigning under the umbrella of consumer sovereignty:

In broad sense, then, the ultimate consequence of the rise of the campaign consulting industry is not found in the power of the consultant, nor even in the power of the candidate, but rather in the power of the voter. Through the medium of television a candidate now has more direct access to the voter's living room than ever before, and because of modern survey research the campaign and the candidate know more precisely what the hopes, fears and aspirations of the voters are.

("Foreword" to Luntz 1988, x)

Political advertising limited to evocative symbols is justified by practitioners on similar grounds. Tony Schwartz, a pioneer in the development of political advertising on television, lauded one of his own most famous creations as a model for political commercials on the grounds that it "conveys no information," asserting that the aim of such advertising is not to persuade or convince but to impel to action by striking a "responsive chord" among viewers who already have the requisite attitudes (Schwartz 1973, 92–7)[10]

Assuming the preferences of the public to be given, or, in the language of political science, "exogenous" to the political system, solves the problem of the autonomy of the public by begging the question.[11] A great deal of work in political science starts from the proposition that the democratic state and its legislators are and must be responsive to the demands of the public because of the constraints imposed by the imperatives of reelection. The autonomy of the public is simply assumed in a manner entirely consistent with the self-legitimating ideology of political practitioners. This is not surprising because both the academic and the practitioners' versions of the notion of independent public preferences derive from the same image of an economistic market for support.

On the academic side, the case for autonomy and effectiveness of the mass public is embodied in one or another variation on the theory that legislative policy tends toward the position of the median voter. Legislative compromises are designed to maximize the placement of candidates for legislative office close to the average views of their constituencies. The underlying assumption is that voters with a given array of preferences will follow a "spatial" model of two-party electoral competition: given a single issue and two competing parties, the equilibrium position that will attract the most votes will be the central tendency of the distribution of voter preferences, a position that minimizes the average distance between voters and legislative outcomes (Enelow and Hinich 1984).

The notion that electoral competition averages opinion has two important implications for the theory of pluralism. First, the spatial theory implicitly accepts the autonomy of the public (by accepting the preferences aggregated in party competition as given), and also assumes that the aggregation of these preferences is pluralistic. Each person's preference on any given issue has the same weight as every other person's preference. Accordingly, winning positions give some voice, however soft, to each opinion. Second, winning positions are compromises, reached not by deliberative discussion of the merits of the various policies but by sounding out the electoral consequences of supporting various points of view. Discourse is reduced to negotiation, and rhetoric is not a matter of persuasion but only a strategic means of maximizing voter support for the power one can muster at the ballot box. Integrative equilibria are produced by balancing aggregate views. Paradoxically the very theory that appears to assume the independence of the public, also reduces discussion among policy makers to strategic politics without integrative significance beyond the mere statistical aggregation of views. How this process of aggregation takes place is not of primary interest, for the results are presumed to be given by the underlying electoral power of the factions. It could hardly matter then if the practitioners of the New Public use all manner of manipulative techniques to ensure that preferences are turned into supportive votes, for both competitive parties will use the same techniques to purify the mobilization of their support. This model of the public presents an image of the boundary between politics and the public as a process enclosed in a black box. Citizen demand goes in the box, appropriate state action comes out. The model proffers an image of process without collective deliberation and pluralism without substance.

*Multiple publics, multiple contests.* A persistent line of criticism inaugurated by Herbert Blumer fifty years ago (1946; 1948) disputes the notion that public opinion is properly conceived as an array of preferences that can be measured by public opinion polls. Nor can the public be viewed as the entire citizenry in their roles as the bearers of public opinion. Public opinion cannot be abstracted from the process by which it is produced and brought to bear on public life, nor can it be understood apart from the groups that give voice to it. According to Blumer, public opinion is not the sum of the opinions of individuals, it cannot be adequately gauged in polls, and is not expressed solely at the ballot box. There is not one public, but as many as form around various issues that open, and are not resolvable by reference to established norms. Discussion of these issues is socially organized and connected to the political process at multiple social locations.

Answers to survey questions homogenize opinion by providing mere snapshots in standardized formats and avoiding attention to how respondents fit into an ongoing process of public discussion. In consequence, polls construct a public and purport to speak for it, but fail to represent the organized process by which opinion is brought to bear on decision makers, a process that includes some potential participants and excludes others. In this respect, opinion polls are illegitimate prolocutors who presume authority to speak for a public who, by the very design of the inquiry, cannot speak back to deny that they have been properly represented. Baldly summarized fifty years later, Blumer's account of public opinion polls appears to present a caricature of the current achievements of survey research. Practitioners in this field have developed very sophisticated methods to distinguish opinion from pseudo-opinion, to relate opinion to its social contexts, and, in recent work, to simulate the impact of subsequent discussion on first responses to survey questions (Sniderman, Brody, and Tetlock 1991; Zaller 1992, 29–39). Nevertheless, Blumer's underlying conception of publics remains challenge to the image of public opinion as the summed aggregate of the opinions of the citizenry.

In recent years, new versions of this critique have been associated with important continental thinkers (Beniger 1992). Pierre Bourdieu (1979; 1984 [1979], 397–465; 1990, 168–174) focuses on those who answer "don't know" to survey questions, on the efforts of survey researchers to minimize this response, and on respondents who choose among alternative responses provided by survey instruments, even though questions and their prefabricated answers do not map the world as they understand it (Herbst 1992). The problem presented by respondents who actually have no opinions within the frame assumed by surveys reveals the polls' part in creating their own results and the pollsters' role in shaping what they display as the opinion of the public, for whom they in effect assume the right to speak. The results of polls are biased precisely because respondents do *not* feel that they have the "right to speak" on the issues raised (Bourdieu 1984 [1979], 141–4). They cannot act as prolocutors for groups that they do not feel they represent. In a statement remarkably evocative of Blumer's earlier critique, Bourdieu distinguishes the "inclinations" that polls measure – vague tendencies that bear no necessary relation to the actual symbolic worlds of respondents – from "mobilized opinion, formulated opinion, pressure groups organized around a system of interests." The former is not opinion and the latter cannot be measured by polls, for public opinion is not the sum of individual inclinations: "Taking a position on a particular issue means choosing between real groups." (Bourdieu 1979, 126).

Habermas, too, has been placed among the severe critics of public opinion polling and the image of the public implied in the methodology of surveys (Beniger 1992; Goodnight 1992). Following earlier American writers (Blumer 1946; Mills 1956, 298–324), Habermas concluded *The Structural Transformation of the Public Sphere* by labeling public opinion a "fiction." The opinion of the atomized mass, manipulated to provide plebiscitary displays of consent to a regime, is not the opinion of a public, which can only be formed through public discussion of issues (Habermas 1989 [1962], 244–50).

Foucault is also counted among those continental critics who would include opinion polling in their inventory of the ills of modern society (Peer 1992). His attention to the means by which the public is constantly observed, both by organs of power and by social scientists as well, suggests that the apparatus of polling is one of the instruments by which the public is categorized, defined, and exposed to manipulation. Surveys are among the repressive instruments of the modern regime of power. Polling conducted on the supposed justification of democratic attention to the people's desires is in fact a part of the apparatus by which the population is systematically watched and disciplined.

These recent critical statements, though they add interesting theoretical dimensions to the debate, do not substantially alter the essential elements of Blumer's original critique. Placing public opinion in the general category of collective behavior, Blumer radically opposed any notion of the public that is not true to its organized character, including its links to the organization of society. "Collective behavior" refers to conduct that is not well defined by fixed conventional norms. Revolutions, social movements, the behavior of crowds, and mass behavior as manifest in fads and fashions are emergent responses to new situations and are necessarily structured collectively by interactive processes, not by preexisting rules. Public opinion is a type of collective behavior; though opinion is formed within relatively well-regulated institutions, the issues that give rise to public controversy are not decided in advance but negotiated in public discussion.

Placing the study of publics under the general rubric of collective behavior puts the organization of influence in the foreground. It becomes apparent that leaders speak for a variety of groups and movements, some that defend the established order from well-endowed positions, others that seek to redefine the normative regime. The latter can speak from a position of strength only if constituent elements of the population can be persuaded to redefine themselves. An approach that emphasizes the variety of public groups, the open character of public agenda, and the fluidity of the boundaries between the sectors of social life boundaries rejects facile presupposition about whether, *in a process of collective behavior*, expressed interests will be given weight or ignored. An organized public may establish its autonomy and, through its leaders, express effective demands. Or, attempts to alter the issues and terms of discourse may simply fail. Potentially active groups may lack the leverage to break free of political and economic domination to formulate more effective rhetoric backed by the solidarity of well represented groups. The reality of pluralism cannot be demonstrated by simply documenting varied views through opinion polls without asking what social conditions allow unrepresented demands to find voice.

*Civil society and the public sphere.* Habermas' concept of the public sphere is intended to elucidate the conditions that give rise to a public voice with roots in the lifeworld. Rather than emphasizing concrete groups or aggregates as "publics," Habermas avoids reification of the concept of the public by referring initially to the "public sphere," the public spaces wherein people can carry on open, rational discussion regarding the general interest.[12] The idea of public spaces directs attention beyond settings in which public discussion of immediate questions of state action take place, such as elections or lobbying lawmakers about proposed legislation, to spaces relatively distant from the boundaries of the political system. The early Habermas speaks of the "political public sphere" and the "literary public sphere," and credits the latter with preparing the way for a public sphere that directly impinges on the world of politics. "The process in which the state-governed public sphere was appropriated by the public of private people making use of their reason and was established as a sphere of criticism of public authority was one of functionally converting the public sphere in the world of letters already equipped with institutions of the public and with forums for discussion" (1989 [1962], 51). Habermas was thinking here of the public spaces created by eighteenth-century British journalism and the coffee houses to which men repaired to discuss the issues and writings of the day.

With the rise of media-based communication and politics in the twentieth century, a public sphere requires new spaces for egalitarian, open discussion within non-state organizations, and the publics formed within these organizations must be articulated, through the mass media, with another, "external" public sphere that connects them to state institutions. The question arises, then, as to what sorts of organizational publics, within what institutional realms outside the polity, might form within the organizations of society to establish a social base for a public sphere. In this view of public life, political organizations such as parties and politically oriented interest groups that have a direct hand in running the state are not the sort of organizations that Habermas has in mind; they are part of the political system, not "societal organizations."

Habermas' public spaces are relatively distant from the centers of political power. Their communicative practices must allow for open, public discussion, which implies rational discourse, that is, authentically free public discussion with special regard for giving reasons and honoring the sway of argument. I presume that these organizations and the institutional spheres that house them must enjoy a degree of autonomy, protected by normatively defined boundaries. One thinks of intellectuals within universities and research institutes and professionals within collegial organizations as examples of potential bases for the specifically modern public spheres that Habermas envisions. Such institutions as academic freedom, commitment to rational inquiry, and professional responsibility contain the seeds of the growth of public space. In this respect, Habermas' approach to the contemporary public sphere, and hence his approach to the autonomy of the public, is formally similar to pluralist theory in that it posits free discussion within a variety of autonomous social groups and the coalescence of this discussion in a politically active public sphere as the *sine qua non* for the existence of authentic publics. He is, though, skeptical about the current presence of a genuine public sphere and, at least in his early writings, rather pessimistic about its prospects.

A model public sphere emerged in the eighteenth century within the bourgeois class, and as long as discussion was limited to bourgeois men as presumed representatives of people generally, an effective public space was opened. But once the requirements of legitimacy opened that space to classes with interests fundamentally opposed to the bourgeoisie, authentic public discussion gave way to manipulation of plebiscitary consent through mere rhetorical displays of commitment to public welfare. For Habermas the roots of the New Public were sown in the nineteenth century with the extension of the franchise.

Habermas has been criticized for failing to provide adequate specification of what would now, in our age, provide for communication that could qualify as discourse. This species of criticism is animated by demands for realistic prescriptions for pragmatic improvements in public life rather than for counsels of perfection. Throughout the world, both activists and scholars are attempting to reformulate a political theory that would replace discredited Marxist orthodoxy, comprehend the situation of new democracies in formerly authoritarian regimes, or legitimize new radical movements in nations that, though formally democratic, exclude progressive voices (Cohen and Arato 1992). Definitions of authentic discourse are valuable, but the practical question goes to how and where potential public spaces for improved and effective discourse can be created or, perhaps, found and regenerated. Framing this question pragmatically leads to a shift in the master term of the project from "the public sphere" to "civil society," defined as the organization of plural interests within an independent social sphere outside the state.[13]

Cohen and Arato (1992, ix) begin their remarkable account of theories of civil society, both classic and contemporary, with a working definition. "We understand 'civil society' as a sphere of social interaction between economy and state, composed above all of the intimate sphere (especially the family), the sphere of associations (especially voluntary associations), social movements, and forms of public communication." This seemingly simple preliminary definition is by no means artless. It signals a number of the authors' carefully worked out positions regarding issues that divide proponents of civil society. They reject one classic liberal position that would locate civil society in a free economy. Civil society must also be independent of direct governance, for its mission is to "defend the lifeworld" wherein, by discursive communication, culture is reproduced, solidarity constructed, and identities formed. Only then can principled influence, which is created in the process of building solidarity through communicative action, be brought to bear on the political realm. Cohen and Arato propose a three-way differentiation between economy, state, and a sphere "between" them. Associational life is located in this middle sphere, a placement that links the authors to the pluralist position. Yet, unwilling to settle for degraded approximations of the democratic ideal of participation, they distance themselves from versions of pluralism that embrace a system of competitive plural elites who achieve a balance of forces within a political arena stabilized by manipulation of an apathetic public.[14] Valuing participation as a necessary condition for the representation of new claims, and rejecting the long-standing distrust of mobilized masses as unstable and prone to seduction by authoritarian forces, Cohen and Arato make room for social movements as a legitimate component of civil society.

Civil society as defined in this Habermas-inspired version is centered in the organization of solidarity and communication – the family, associational life, and solidary movements on behalf of causes. Public spaces for discursive communication among socially anchored participants allow for an independent social sphere, differentiated from both economy and state. Ideally, the discourse of civil society approaches the standards of the discourse ethic and, accordingly, the differentiation of a social sphere of pubic spaces parallels the differentiation of influence – the language of public discourse – from money and power.

*Habermas on civil society.* In his recent attempt to put his concepts of democratic discussion into an institutional context, Habermas himself (1996) has amplified his account of civil society. For Habermas, civil society is "composed of more or less spontaneously emergent associations, organizations, and movements that, attuned to how social problems resonate in the private life spheres, distill and transmit such reactions in amplified form to the public sphere" (367). When communication is not dominated by the politicized channels of the New Public, discourse can flourish and allow citizens' "influence" to be transformed into "communicative power" (371), Habermas' term for that collective moral force, which, in the extreme case, can allow unarmed citizens to stop tanks in the streets by the sheer potency of their social presence (148).

Civil society as such is weak. It is an arena for sorting issues, floating and testing ideas, and organizing "counterknowledge," but it cannot steer society. However, Habermas (1996) proposes, as an empirical hypotheses, that under certain conditions, civil society can acquire *influence* in the public sphere "through its own public opinions" and compel social and political change (373). As I understand Habermas' argument, these conditions arise when actors in civil society, working at the periphery of established institutions, develop and promote ideas that then make their way through the media and other centrally positioned carriers, transforming the public agenda and publicly available knowledge. The history of such public concerns as the nuclear arms race, ecological dangers, and feminist aims were not initially placed on the agenda by the state apparatus or by powerful organizations, but by intellectuals, radical professionals, and concerned citizens, and then moved from the periphery to the center through widely disbursed discursive channels (381). Habermas stresses that these processes of circulation rest on successful argument, which he refers to as "influence." It is clear, however, that partially discursive communication within these channels is supported by mobilizing solidary loyalties among advocates and their allies, by staging visible events for the media to garner public support, and by displaying expert opinion – a host of rhetorical techniques that resemble influential political communication more than communicative action.

From my perspective, Habermas' new conception of civil society depicts a *system of influence*. Pure market economies are also decentralized and not dominated by political power, their circulation of goods governed by equilibrating forces of supply and demand, which represent willingness to offer and to purchase goods. Ironically, the disbursed conversations in Habermas' civil society, for all their earnest truth-seeking, reach conclusions by processes parallel to systematic market forces. People either are or are not willing to "buy" arguments, pleas, and calls to action according to the balance of receptivity and resistance that affect their choices. Readiness and resistance are affected by argument and by influence in the larger sense, too – the prestige of prolocutors, solidary ties, and most important, forums that people can trust.

*Parsons on societal community.* The theory of civil society converges to some degree with Parsons' notion of an integrative system coordinated by influence. Cohen and Arato do not, to be sure, accept the Parsonian formulation. They treat Parsons in depth as an important contributor to the theory of civil society, but take his approach, with its weighty reliance on status hierarchies, to be a misguided neo-Hegelian theory reminiscent of Hegel's theory of estates (1992, 118–42). Generalized influence, which may even be a "quasi-medium," exists; it is involved in "the politics of influence" that are essential to the new identity-based movements, but it is backed by arguments, not prestige (486–7). Moreover, to use solidarity strategically as a mode of control, rather than relying on argumentative discourse, would damage the autonomy on which solidarity depends (377–80).

Parsons' defense of the independence of the integrative system was modified during his later years through a new conception of the integrative sector as a "societal community," a system organized around multiple resilient group solidarities that are relatively sheltered from the direct impact of economic markets and political manipulation. This treatment of the public was substantially reshaped by his final efforts to establish a macrofunctional theory of the social system. Parsonian macrofunctional theory was constructed around the notion that social systems must meet four functional requisites: adaptation, goal attainment, integration, and pattern maintenance. Differentiated subsystems emerge to address the four system needs: the economy adapts to changing needs by allocating resources in a flexible manner; the polity mobilizes power to achieve collective goals; systems of socialization organized around the family, education, and religion nurture attachment to values and motivation to conform to stable patterns of social structure. The institutional realm of social integration proved more difficult to define. At times Parsons had associated the integrative function with the normative order generally, viewing it as the locus for specifying general social values to the exigencies of action in concrete institutional spheres. Following that logic, he was inclined to identify the integrative system with law. In yet other contexts, especially when trying to trace the interchanges between the subsystems of society, he identified (in a rather casual way) the public as an integrative realm parallel to the economy and the polity. These lines of thought ultimately converged on the concept of "societal community."

Parsons came to the conclusion that the societal community is the integrative system of society in the course of working out the logic of social differentiation. As Durkheim insistently asserted, the division of labor implies a need for reintegrating newly differentiated roles. In the late 1950s Parsons set about developing a theory of social change directed specifically to Durkheim's problem, taking social differentiation and its concomitant processes of reintegration as the engines of social change. Examining integrative challenges that arise when new categories of units emerge from a previously undifferentiated, unified social system, he identified the *inclusion* of these new units in the larger community's overall system of solidarity as a problematic consequence of differentiation (Parsons 1961). How, he asked, can a specialized agricultural production unit, not a family farm, become anything other than a unit concerned *solely with its own self interest*, given its separation from the networks of kinship and status that have traditionally constituted the community? This is an instance of the generic problem of inclusion, which led Parsons to root the integrative system in the solidarity of a differentiated societal community that encompasses the whole of a society's population and defines the criteria, rights, and obligations of membership. Societal community organizes the bonding within and between constituent units into an overall system of associational solidarity that is normatively regulated by a legal system founded on the rights and obligations of citizenship.

Parsons' treatment of this problem became so bound up in the normative organization of community through the institutions of citizenship that it is easy to lose sight of what a societal community organizes. By the mid-seventies, Parsons had come to affirm clearly that societal community organizes solidary relations. In *The American University*, he squarely stated that "The societal community . . . is the relational matrix of solidarity; this relational matrix is differentiated into many subsolidarities" (Parsons and

Platt 1973, 203). He identified the adaptive component of the societal community as consisting in the "allocation of loyalties in manifold balancing capacities and opportunities" (428). In short, he came to see that modern societies achieve flexibility to mobilize human resources for diverse tasks by allowing allocation of disposable loyalties to varied groups and achieve integration of this array of "subsolidarities" by aligning them with loyalties to an overarching community. Nevertheless, the institutional core of societal community – the complex of institutional definitions that govern the rights and responsibilities of membership – are located in citizenship, which offers flexible opportunities for participation in the most inclusive levels of collective association.

Citizenship links the societal community, a system of solidarity, to the polity, a system for the organization of power to make and enforce binding collective decisions. Some forms of participation, voting for example, link citizens directly to the polity by the exercise of power, *but within the societal community the principle dynamic force is persuasion*. It is by persuasion that loyalties are mobilized, extended, and aligned. Alignment to larger coalitions, extending ultimately to the entire societal community, depends on setting forth appeals to broader identities and interests, and for this reason the rhetoric of societal community gravitates toward appeals to the public interest. As I read Parsons' various writings on influence, and societal community, he argued that the values governing societal community legitimize claims that forward individual and group interests *as long as they are couched in terms consistent with loyalty to the larger society and the public good*. In American society, with its emphasis on adaptive freedom, private initiatives enjoy a certain presumption of public value, but it is a rebuttable presumption and claims are contested through debates about the public interest. Recasting private claims in public terms enhances the value of universalistic forms of argument and moves public debate toward higher cognitive standards. Thus, from a different starting place and by a different route, Parsons arrived at a conception of public life parallel in some respects to Habermas' idea of a public sphere. The differentiation of arenas of argument leads to a rationalization of discourse driven by the intrinsic demands of communication among diverse parties. There is, however, a crucial difference between their approaches to the matter of the autonomy of the sphere of public discourse. For Parsons, the independence of the integrative system – the societal community – is grounded in the differentiation of a matrix of diverse group solidarities, and the participants in public debate enter the arena from their embedded positions in this matrix. For Habermas, with his high standards for authentic discourse, public life is not truly differentiated until a rational discourse ethic is in place.

*Rhetoric in civil society.* Following the lead of Cohen and Arato, I will classify both Parsons' account of societal community and my revised paradigm of public interest as versions of the theory of civil society. Like other theories of civil society, solidaristic versions seek to specify how public life can support a realm in which discussion and influence, rather than power or money, shape the normative order. Theories of civil society go beyond positing a public whose opinions determine or at least limit the actions of the state, its officials, and its legislators. Civil society is more then a public; it is an organized complex of institutions, groups, and communication that allow a public to form. Whether this organization makes civil society a "system" depends on how that rather touchy term is defined. One need not accept all the elaborate apparatus of Parsonian system theory, with its symmetrical, fixed, sometimes reified, scheme of subsystems and their interconnections, to recognize that differentiated sectors of social organization have boundaries and systematic properties.

Parsons' initial formulation of the differentiated location of the public and the systematic relations between public and polity borrowed substantially from the dominant model in political science. The public, acting as the bearer of public opinion, transmits messages to the polity in the form of demands and votes. Viewing the public as an integrative system, Parsons conceived the interchange between the public and the polity as composed of four categories of messages from system to system, two mediated by power and two by influence. *Voting* is an exercise of power, for its results are binding, as are the *legally binding decisions* of the state. Citizens casting their votes are affected by the *leadership* of political candidates, that is their capacity to set forth attractive programs in response to the *demands* of the public. Leadership and demands are categories of influence, for they are not guaranteed by binding force but are only as strong as they are persuasive (Parsons 1967d, 224–38). As long as the state does not control voting through domination of a single government party or by fraudulent elections, and as long as civic leaders are responsive to citizens' autonomous demands, the public is an independent force in society.

The stability of relations between the polity and the differentiated public is sustained by equilibrating (but not atomized) processes. When public demands exceed the capacity of the state to respond effectively, or when leadership is not responsive to public demands, the participants in public life have incentives to press harder or to retreat, incentives that are ultimately vested in competitive electoral processes. Empirical studies document varied equilibrating processes that sustain the boundary between the public and the state. Even conceptions of the public as weak and passive, such as Stimson's (1991) notion of a "zone of acquiescence," describe an equilibrium boundary. Stimson takes political leaders rather than the public to be the source of policy demands, and says the public accepts these demands if they fall within the range of the public's zone of consent. His studies suggest while leaders can move the public mood beyond its current position along its long term trajectory, leaders cannot normally go beyond the public's zone of acquiescence without encountering resistant counter forces of equilibration.

*Are equilibrating systems norm free?* The notion of equilibration is particularly objectionable to Habermas. He believes that equilibrium theory implies a conservative stance, a "norm-free" market, and actors who pursue private interests without regard for what would be valid for the whole of society, making expedient compromises rather than forging just solutions. His complaint that achieving an equilibrium allows, even encourages, compromise is accurate, and it is also clear that processes of adjustment do not necessarily guarantee rational discourse, but his overall argument is deeply flawed. To argue that market equilibria are inherently conservative and so, therefore, are sociological theories that make use of them is to rely on the connotations of words rather than on well-considered analysis of the concept of equilibrium. His critique conflates the ideologically conservative uses that free market economists often make of equilibrium theory and the generic concept of equilibrium, which can be employed to either conservative or radical ends. Equilibrium theory can point to pathological states of equilibrium by way of critique and to justify collective intervention, as in the case of Keynes' theory that economies can founder in an equilibrium state at less than full employment. Indeed, Lowi's (1979) critical claim that pluralist democracy in the United States reaches an equilibrium of balanced compromises without achieving the *public* interest is consistent with Habermas' own views.

Economic approaches to the study of markets, which posit rational individuals who instrumentally maximize their material self interest, have, to be sure, been copied by scholars looking for analogs to market behavior in political life, but however well such assumptions might fit economic markets, they do not apply to the achievement of balanced states of conflicting demands for public policies. Here the participants do not buy and sell material objects; they support policies, argue about rights and the public interest, and establish identities within the plural order. When Huckfeldt and Sprague (1990) show that the process of interpersonal social influence described in Berelson, Lazarsfeld, and McPhee's classic *Voting* (1954) can be described as a stable equilibrium, they are not depicting an impersonal, norm-free process. Individuals who have strayed into idiosyncratic positions between elections are brought back into alignment with their larger identities and loyalties when, during the heightened conflict of electioneering, they are thrust into new lifeworld conversations that bring new information and perspectives into their ken and require them to resituate themselves with respect to the matrix of their solidarities. The participants in these and similar systems have both material and ideal interests, and the latter include interests in realizing norms and in establishing solidarities. The process involves contesting a normative terrain, and individuals' decisions in this setting can hardly be called norm free. Nor does the evidence regarding how individuals form their private opinions about public issues (the "public" opinion that polls measure) support the idea that economic interests are an especially strong force. For the most part, ideological concerns and group identities are more significant (Sears and Funk 1990). The problems in Parsons' influence paradigm were not in the concepts of system and equilibrium as such, but in his failure to look more deeply into the social organization of civil society and its rhetorical forms.

*Rhetorical forms of contested influence.* In recent years, analysis of the communicative interchange between state and public has become more grounded in its institutional and organizational settings. Economistic accounts of political demand and responses of the state have become more institutionally specific as researchers became dissatisfied with positing a black box in which public opinion goes in and government action comes out. Students ask who are the participants, how is the process organized, and what role does influence play. In this vein, Page, Shapiro, and Dempsey (1987) found that among views that enter the public arena through the mass media, those of commentators have the most credibility and influence. Carmines and Kuklinsky (1990) show that elite congress members have an interest in becoming "policy entrepreneurs" who formulate and garner support for political ideas because it enhances their reputation as insiders and thus their influence as "people in the know." McKelvey and Ordeshook (1985) show that compressed information in the form of opinion polls and endorsements allow otherwise uninformed voters to replicate the behavior of well-informed voters. In a parallel demonstration of what might be called reverse influence, Lupia (1994) found that uninformed California voters used endorsements by groups viewed as opposed to their interests as negative symbols to clarify confusing array of ballot propositions and properly align their support. Baron (1994) presents a model showing how uninformed voters make it worthwhile for interest groups to invest in attempts to influence the electorate. In short, current research repeatedly shows that influence, which is based on asymmetrical distribution of information and employs a rhetoric of shortcuts – of informational tokens – plays a crucial role in the organization of public opinion. Moreover, the regularities demonstrated in repeated studies of the organization of public opinion (Page and Shapiro 1992) indicate that influence has a systematic character in the sense that I use the term "system." There are stabilities in the realm of influence that manifest the independence of organized spheres of persuasion from the political regime and from economic markets. The degree of autonomy creditable to civil society is debatable both as to its empirical strength and its normative validity, but it is not reasonable to deny that differentiated influence can be organized into a system.

*Universal and particular solidarites in systems of influence.* If integrative systems, whether called the public, civil society, or societal community, are conceived as formations of solidary ties, then it is crucial to ground this concept in accounts of organizational and institutional structure. Habermas' discourse theory founds social integration on solidarity, but not on the particular communal ties that we normally associate with institutionalized solidarity. Rather, Habermas' discursive solidarity would be universal, created by a union of everyone's common interest in justice, autonomy, and emancipation. It would be constructed by a community engaged in rational, unconstrained discussion, *without rhetoric*, of integrative norms for a just social order. It is not clear how this state of universal community would be achieved. It is not that the social process of achieving discursive community goes on within a black box that mixes inputs into outputs in a mysterious way, but that there is no box at all. As friendly critics of Habermas put it, there is an "institutional deficit" in his theory.[15] But when Habermasian proponents of civil society theory come to define how civil society would be achieved, failure to specify workable institutional arrangements becomes unacceptable, and when institutional means come under scrutiny, the limits of the concept of communicative discourse become apparent. Consider, for example, the matter of social movements.

Once social movements are posited as a component of civil society, especially the "new social movements" that emphasize issues of human identity, inclusion, autonomy, and universal interests – issues of peace, ecology, feminism, and citizen participation – we come face to face with the rhetoric actually employed in these movements. Habermasian civil society theory argues that it is necessary to create commitment both to the discourse ethic and to universalistic solidary community. Accordingly, social movements directed to universalistic issues of the common good, peace and justice, for example, support the development of a discourse community. Such movements are directed to establishing and recognizing identities and are "sources of new solidarities and the "further democratization of society." They create "defined social spaces in which collective identities can form"

(Cohen 1983, 101). What are we to make, then, of the use by these movements of such tactics as occupying strategic sites or physically blockading access with human chains? Is this rational discourse? Habermas treats this problem under the heading of civil disobedience (1985, 97–9), which he takes to be a "litmus test," indeed an essential condition for a mature democratic society, in which technically illegal actions taken do not necessarily undermine the constitutional state, because citizens recognize the legitimacy of performing "purely symbolic" acts directed at protesting the will of the majority as legal but unjust. Cohen and Arato continue this line of argument (1992), linking these symbolic gestures to discourse by asserting that such acts call attention to the need for discourse. Bold acts open discourse through "persuasive strategies aimed at forcing [*sic*] the majority to listen to counterarguments," and are therefore reckoned as *persuasive* and as belonging to the politics of *influence* rather than to the instrumental politics of power (584). Leaving aside the question of whether physical disruption is a special case of communicative discourse or whether influence can employ force, the authors have accepted rhetoric in the process of influence, for civil disobedience designed to disrupt by *presenting* powerful symbols of disaffection is a rhetorical act. It employs the rhetoric of presentation, which displays a message that is intrinsically irrebuttable. Rather than communicating a line of argument, it displays an undeniable presence.

The maturation of Parsons' concept of societal community led him to confront the same problems that challenge Habermas. Both thinkers equate modernity and universalistic modes of evaluation, so both must come to terms with the question of how citizens whose identities are grounded in narrow communities can be induced to take a broader view. Both ultimately recognize that rhetorical conflict over contested terrain is a necessary condition for achieving inclusion in large-scale, modern social structures. In the early 1960s, Parsons' political sociology appeared optimistic, even complacent. The capacities of the public to formulate demands for policies in pursuit of collective goals, of political leaders to forge effective programs, and of adequate solidary ties to make the system work were taken for granted.

When Parsons' mature concept of societal community emerged, in his (1967e), account of the integrative system, it took on a new coloration. Inclusion of ethnic and religious minorities in the same societal community was clearly seen to be neither an automatic, mechanical consequence of social forces released by differentiation nor an unproblematic application of fixed values to new social situations, but an achievement in the face of serious resistance. He repeatedly emphasized that inclusion is not assimilation, for inclusion brings groups into the larger society with intact identities as groups with positive values of their own. It entails negotiating contested new formulae for what it means to be a member of both society and a distinctive subgroup. It requires new programs designed to upgrade the capacities and effective rights of citizens, and new modes of withdrawing legitimacy from the forces of resistance. These outcomes are contingent, subject to failure, and likely to succeed only when the public can be persuaded to accept new views of the terms and conditions of social solidarity.

Communication within the public, or in civil society or the societal community, cannot escape rhetorical formulation. Even when public communication is predicated upon universalistic discourse and honors deliberation in search of the public interest, participants bring their particular interests to the table. Their interest in discourse is itself attributable to hopeful anticipation that their particular interests will be forwarded or at least clarified. The process of social integration entails *aligning* private and public interests. This is true even when, in ideal discourse, deliberation leads participants to learn that, properly understood, their own interests and the public good are already in alignment. Learning through mutual persuasion necessarily involves rhetorical appeals to reinterpret the meanings of situations so that identities and solidarities can be adjusted and reassigned.

Rhetorical exchanges by the assignment of negotiated meanings are cultural. Rhetoric furnishes cultural resources for the persuasive efforts of contending parties. These efforts can become a persuasive process of mutual influence only when cultural premises legitimate cultural disputation rather than suppress it as something destructive of a sacred, unchallengeable order. The following chapter examines, in historical perspective, fundamental questions about the cultural bases of the rhetoric of public life, old and new. What supports rhetorical appeals to the public good? What holds these appeals to rhetorical standards, and how are such standards derived from conceptions of good public discourse? What undermines such standards? These are tangled but crucial questions, for the same underlying forces that supported the original formation of a *modern public* based on influence – the legitimation of free speech and association, the rise of disposable loyalties, and trust in media – now support the growth of the *New Public*, whose practitioners are transforming the terms of public discussion and separating it from its social roots.

# 6

## The differentiation of rhetorical solidarity

Confidence in the integrating force of public discussion is a cultural product. Rhetorical contests are enacted within a cultural and institutional framework that legitimizes making and accepting arguments, including argument by appeals to solidarity. Cultural frameworks define what constitutes argument – what counts as persuasive. As a cultural artifact, rhetoric cannot be taken for granted as a natural and obvious realm that requires no explanation. Versions of rhetorical order emerge from historical circumstances as actors set forth explications in the form of ideals, narratives, and theories to justify and to make sense of the persuasive arenas in which they contest meanings and interpretations. The embedding of rhetoric in ideological frames has a profound effect on systems of influence, for these frames define the right to speak and affect the credibility of persuasive efforts.

The establishment of modern associational life required new ways of thinking about social relations, new modes of understanding that signal the arrival of cultural modernity in the social sphere. In modern social structures, connections between people no longer depend on the defining capacity and emotional security of traditional norms and statuses. Rather, normative definitions and obligations are created by conversations about ways of joining together and reaching collaborative understandings. The moral authority of associational arrangements, and their very comprehensibility as well, depend on the institutionalization of these world-making activities.

*Cultural differentiation.* The development of the modern discourse of association is an instance of cultural differentiation: conceptual elaboration of cultural materials around a special purpose or function. Strictly speaking, cultural differentiation is *sociocultural,* for its social consequences are carried by groups of specialized experts who, well versed in conceptual apparatus, form a community of discourse. When this community comes to monopolize the legitimate practice of their discourse, and that practice is generally seen to have valuable uses, then the cultural differentiation borne by the new discourse can have far-reaching social consequences, including concomitant social-structural differentiation. The differentiation of legal systems is an exemplary case that exhibits all the defining characteristics of sociocultural differentiation: conceptual elaboration, special purpose (the interpretation of binding rules), new discursive languages, monopoly of the use of these languages by a professionally organized group, and, consequentially, the differentiation of an autonomous legal system.

System-forming cultural differentiation and its dynamic potential for inducing internal differentiation in social systems are products of monopolies on specialized discourse. Such monopolies need not take legal and absolute form; a practical monopoly borne of the prestige of a particular new form of rhetoric that, within a community of discourse, gives this rhetoric a sway so strong as to require challenges to be answered in the new rhetoric, and not by recourse to older traditional forms of argument, is a strong indicator of system-forming capacity. Just as one confronted by a civil suit must engage legal representation, so one attacked in the public sphere must respond within the forms of public rhetoric, and with the rise of the New Public, may well need to employ experts in the new public discourse.[1]

*The cultural differentiation of rhetorical freedom.* Many strains of contemporary thought have lost track of the original cultural meaning of the right to speak, subsuming freedom of speech under an individualistic rather than a communal version of liberalism. Because modern solidarity emerged in the course of cultural contests about the meaning of community, it is important to try to recapture the early modern premises of group solidarity. The novel question of early modern debate about rhetoric and group life centered on the question of whether community can and should be purposefully willed or must be conceived as naturally inhering in primordial groups. Modern solidarity turns on this cultural hinge, for the differentiation of solidarity from its primordial roots in kin and clan, village and tribe, fixed status, and traditional religion depends on opening social spaces by allowing people to choose and forge their own affiliations. In a premodern setting, choosing solidary ties makes no sense and can only be interpreted as breakdown of a social order in which people are anchored in their social locations. Without cultural legitimation of a concept of voluntary association, willed solidarity seems a contradiction in terms, guaranteed to produce a social world with "all coherence gone."

The modern situation is confused by the prevalence of rhetorical chains of implication in discussions of liberal philosophy. Autonomy of the self is equated with selfishness and then opposed to supposedly antithetical terms, such as *republicanism, civic virtue*, and, of late, *communitarianism*, as if valuing personal autonomy were inherently at odds with social order, collective deliberation, and commitments to others. These dichotomies, whether fallacious or not, do organize people's thinking about their predicaments, including their concerns about the validity of their voluntary ties so these issues must be clarified in order to grasp how the differentiation of solidarity achieved legitimacy.

The raw materials for classical associational theory were handed down in several influential treatises, most notably Aristotle's *Politics*, which was extensively mined by the civic humanists of the Renaissance Italian republics.[2] The impact and legacy of civic humanism is significant and will be examined later in this chapter, but early civic humanism lacked a well-developed concept of a public organized around communication in print. A decisive resolution of the cultural contradiction between individual choice and community emerged from Protestant theology, beginning with the original sixteenth-century reformers and culminating in the theories of public life set forth by seventeenth-century English Puritan radicals. The embryonic notion that the public is a communicating solidary body generated a system-forming, cultural differentiation of the concept of community. The textual vehicle for early modern thinking about community was the ancient Christian doctrine of the Communion of the Saints.

### The Communion of the Saints

*Sharing the spirit.* Weber, in his account of sectarian Christianity, rightly emphasized the importance of the associational principle of solidarity in the early Protestant sects (Weber 1968 [1922], 1,204–10), but he did not provide an extensive account of the background of secular associational solidarity in Puritan theology. In his famous essay on the Protestant ethic, he identified the roots of the secular economic ethic in the doctrine of predestination (Weber 1930 [1904]). Had he accomplished a comparable study of the associational principle, he could have located the Protestant renewal of the doctrine of "Communion of the Saints" as equivalent in the solidary realm to predestination in economic life (Mayhew 1984b). From this doctrine there emerged a cultural ideal of community founded on free, persuasive communication among people who answered the call to membership.

"Communion of the Saints" is a pre-Reformation formula, professed in the Apostles' Creed, but in pre-Reformation Christianity it referred to the Eucharist and to intercessory prayers to and for the dead, rituals with other-worldly, sacramental, and passive meanings. By the sixteenth century, the Catholic version of the doctrine stressed communion between the living and the dead – the community of living saints militant on earth, beatified saints triumphant in heaven, and patient saints expectant in purgatory, who await good works on their behalf. The Protestant reformers, whose hatred of *Totenfresserei* (feeding off the dead) was a central element of their political appeal (Ozment 1992, 14) demanded a doctrine of Communion with active, this-worldly significance. The entire panoply of indulgences, masses for the dead, and intercessory prayers to the saints had other-wordly devotional implications, calling upon supplicants to unite with the dead rather than act within the community of the living.

Martin Luther, preached a this-worldly conception of communion, which, though it included a sacramental component, began to stress the shared experience of the living community, a community of fellowship that "consists in this, that all the spiritual possessions of Christ and his saints are shared with and become the common property of him who receive this sacrament" (Luther 1960 [1519], XXXV, 51–2). Calvin's parallel interpretation of the Communion of the Saints called for an obligation among the gathered saints, that is the living congregation, to share their varied spiritual gifts:

It is as if one said that the saints are gathered into the society of Christ in the principle that whatever benefits God confer upon them, they should in turn share with one another. This does not, however, rule out diversity of graces, inasmuch as we know the gifts of the Spirit are variously distributed.   (Calvin 1960 [1536], 1,014)

For Calvin, communion is more than mere common possession of one spirit; it is active sharing of this spirit among a group that, like a worldly community, is differentiated and requires exchange.

*Communion and communication.* The English Puritans worked out the organizational implications of the cultural concept of "sharing the spirit," defining appropriate social relations and forms of communication for people united in a body of common belief and forming a cultural template for the ideals of a willed solidary community. William Perkins (1595) made a clear statement of the Puritan concept of saintly communion. He defined the concrete obligations of communion as "separation from the ungodly," linkage of the godly in "society and togetherness," fellow-feeling and compassion, "labours of our callings to the common good," and redress of the "faults of our brethren." The instruments of these modes of communion are preaching, example, admonition, exhortation, consolation, and prayer.

Even in brief synopsis, the emphasis on communication as the means of community is apparent.

Active communion begins with preaching. Protestant faith in the word as generator and sustainer of the spirit entailed strong commitment to preaching, which was seen as the creator of the community. The idea of preaching was included in the very definition of a Puritan church: "a company of men professing the faith, assembled together by the preaching of the word" (Perkins 1595, 509). It is "a company called together by the voice of a preacher" (Seaver 1970, 244), an association of believers who profess and hear the Word, and by communicating the spirit achieve communion with each other.[3] From preaching it is a short step to the second dominant theme of Puritan organizational polemics: *discipline*. Discipline, said John Milton (1957 [1642], 682–4) is but preaching in particular. The spirit must be communicated not only in general principles but in applications to daily life in the community. Milton describes the ideal image of specific discipline as a series of gentle but persistent public and private exhortations to a wrongdoer, increasing in intensity, involving the culprit's friends and relatives, and ultimately (in cases of recalcitrance) excommunication: that is, *cutting off the wrongdoer from communication*. The entire course of discipline can be described as a mobilization of opinion through communication in the interest of restoring community.[4]

This concept of community through preaching, admonition, and discussion – of sharing of the spirit by communication – continued to inform the views of future generations of advocates of willed community. It is a system of intense and regular moral communication, guided by firmly grasped fundamental truths, and delivered, as far as possible, by persuasive words rather than by physical force.[5]

*"Quenching the spirit"; securing freedom to share.* If the spirit must be shared, by the same token there is an obligation not to quench the spirit by repression. The obligation to communicate extends to speaking the truths and insights revealed by the spirit, and from this obligation arose demands for freedom to express the spirit the better to share it. According to Simeon Ash (1647, 14), "a personal/experience is improved to a universal advantage . . . Be persuaded to impart your owne experiences for the more common use. Conceal not within your bosome, those things the communicating thereof may be for publique profit." Puritans of the left were willing to draw liberal conclusions from such premises. If some are morally obliged to communicate the spirit for the "publique" profit, then others, including the state, must not prevent that communication, an argument summarized in the subtitle of John Goodwin's (1644) influential pamphlet: *Theomachia: The grand imprudence of men running the hazard of fighting against God, in*

*suppressing any way, doctrine or practice, concerning which they know not certainly whether it be from God or no.*

The obligation to create community through communication enjoins both discipline *and* liberty. The preacher who calls the community together by his voice must be at liberty to preach, for to still that voice is to hinder the communion of the saints and thus to battle God.[6] In short, the Puritan doctrine of liberty derives from its doctrine of community. There must be liberty of communication, for it is the free flow of the Spirit through preaching, exhortation, and consolation that creates community.

*Extending the realm of free communication through print: the vocation of the publicist.* Puritan intellectuals were able to find a calling in pamphleteering, which seemed an exciting opportunity to people who believed that they were witnessing the birth of a free, rational, and responsive public. These early publicists did not think of themselves as salesmen of truth in the marketplace of ideas but as instruments of God's will, who knew truth and could disseminate it. They felt a sacred obligation to preach truth in order to enter into communion with their fellows. The idea of vocation legitimized individual activity in the world, but it also subordinated individual work in a calling to the common good. By Perkins' (1603, 903) definition, "A vocation or calling is a certaine kind of life, ordained and imposed on man for the common good." Each special calling is a specific obligation deriving from the communion of the saints.

Given their view that communion is created and sustained by the preaching of the word and that preaching is a vocation, it is not surprising that Puritan divines developed strong faith in the value of their communal contribution. The legitimation of the published word was not far behind. As John Foxe (1965 [1563] , V. 720) put it, "God hath opened the Press to preach." Demands for support and freedom for preaching were linked to similar demands on behalf of publication. Profound respect for the value of the printed word emerged early in Protestant England. The view that printing was God's instrument for spreading truth was a commonplace, fed by Foxe's claim in his popular *Book of Martyrs* that printing had been given to the world after the martyrdom of John Hus in order to ensure that never again would the Pope successfully suppress truth and reform (Foxe 1965 [1563], V. 718–22; VII. 252–3; Eisenstein 1979). The enthusiastic tone of Foxe's praise of the capacity of print to spread enlightenment and destroy "superstition" rivals Condorcet's (1933) [1793] paean to printing, which suggests that Puritan advocates of the spirit were no less confident of the power of print to create an enlightened public than were the eighteenth-century purveyors of secular reason. Condorcet explicitly identified printing as the ultimate source of the commerce in ideas that will create "a new kind of tribunal . . . a tribunal difficult to avoid and impossible to evade . . . independent of coercion and favoring reason and justice: the public" (116–19, 149).[7] As Voltaire put it, "Opinion is the Queen of the World, but the *philosophes* govern this queen" (Palmer 1953, 4). It is clear that this conception of public opinion was not an invention of the Enlightenment. The Puritan pamphleteers were well on their way to an optimistic conception of the public. Public space did not initially emerge in London's eighteenth-century coffee houses, as Habermas seems to suppose, but in the intellectual circles of radical seventeenth-century ministers whose writings exhibit self-conscious awareness of their public-creating roles. As educators of public opinion, this nascent group of intellectuals saw themselves as bringers of truth to a test in the marketplace of ideas and hence the creators of the moral forces that will dominate and guide the new society.

### The public spirit: from congregation to public

In the English Puritan movement, the new doctrine of Communion of the Saints was first institutionalized in the congregation. How then, did the doctrine of sharing the spirit come to be applied to the public questions of the nation? The logic of cultural creation proceeds by linguistic elaborations of root ideas, but rhetorical extensions of ideas from one situation to another, and from limited to broad applications, are made in the course of persuasive efforts by people engaged in socially located conflict. The original creators of the new doctrines of communion were sincerely concerned about the means of salvation, but they were certainly aware of the public appeal of arguments rooted in opposition to the unpopular institutions of *Totenfresserei* used by Rome and the established church to raise money.

For the English Puritans, the new communal concept resonated to issues of state policy from the beginning of the movement, for it bore directly on the independence of Puritan congregations from an established church controlled by an Episcopal hierarchy, and, in later battles over church organization, by Presbyterian organization, which also limits the autonomy of the individual congregation. It is not surprising then that the most radical applications of the Protestant doctrine of the Communion of the Saints were proposed by advocates of strictly congregational modes of church organization and, within the Congregationalist fold, by persons arguing for the rights of women or the untutored to preach.

On the eve of and during the Civil War, the rhetoric of free communication was further extended to general questions of public interest. Puritan interests, while not the only interests that framed the civic issues debated in the Civil War, came to enjoy a dominant position within the community of discourse created by the explosion of printing and preaching that accompanied the armed conflict.[8] The number of pamphlets published in England increased from twenty in 1640 to 1,916 in 1642 (Hill 1977, 65), many of them published sermons, and many of those preached to Parliament at their invitation. Within this community of discourse, Puritan pamphlets and sermons set the agenda, defined the issues, and supplied the terms of argument. Indeed, my examination of royalists counterattacks on revolutionary pamphlets show that apologists found it necessary to frame their own pamphlets within the new vocabularies, eschewing the divine right of kings in favor of creative adaptations of notions of communication and the public interest. This is an indication of the system-forming sway of the new rhetoric in creating a differentiated public that was presumed to be responsive to appeals to its new decisive role.

The germ of the idea that communication creates a public was already implicit in the idea that a congregation is created by the voice of a preacher, but during the 1640s, seventeenth-century Englishmen began to act on the parallel premise that a civil public is created by the voice of the press. Advocates began to take their causes to the tribunal of public opinion, often facing controversy over the propriety of such a radical approach to politics. The Grand Remonstrance of 1641 provides a first illustration. There was heated debate over a successful motion to publish the Remonstrance, ostensibly a petition directed from Parliament to the king. The traditional mode of parliamentary argument had invoked a claim to virtual representation of *all* the people to the king and hence to express the *public* interest as over against the necessarily partial (even wicked) advice of the king's *private* counselors. Sir Edward Dering, a participant in this debate, speaking in the idiom of this conception of Parliament as constituting the people, complained of the motion to publish the Grand Remonstrance, "I thought to represent unto the King the wicked counsels of pernicious counsellors . . . I did not dream that we should remonstrate downward, tell stories to the people, and talk of the King as of a third person" (Hill 1961, 125). But Parliament did remonstrate downward and the precedent was powerful. When Thomas Goodwin and his associates saw their national Assembly of Divines headed inexorably toward agreement on a presbyterian mode of ecclesiastical government in 1644, they took their case for congregationalism to the public in *An Apologeticall Narration* (Goodwin et al. 1664). When the Levellers debated the leaders of the army over the terms of settlement of the war, they also published their proposals for more democratic forms of representation (Woodhouse 1951). When Cromwell and his associates determined to execute the king, they took care to have a public trial reported in the nascent newspapers of the day (Wedgwood 1970). Petitions abounded during this era. Originally a medieval form of communication, private and often secret, petitions became public statements of grievance and were presented as indicators of public opinion (Zaret 1996).[9] One can find rather little explicit seventeenth-century theory about a new entity called "the public," but as civic consciousness developed, the course of practical political action came more and more to take the existence of such a body for granted.[10]

*The trade of truth.* Other, more secular interests and actors were conjoined in the anti-Royalist cause, most notably the commercial interests of a growing entrepreneurial class, so it is not surprising that economic elements entered into the dominant new rhetoric of community. Merchants and squires alike were quite ready to argue against taxes and monopolies, calling on the traditional rhetorical formula of the "ancient liberties of the English people." The opposition also employed the concept of "wicked counsellors," a formula that could be easily assimilated into the Puritan rhetoric. Unwise and partial counsel, like a bad idea that does not regard the good of the whole community, can be defeated by subjecting it to open, public competition. The pamphleteers proclaimed that reason and the printed word work together to propel the course of public discussion toward truth. Disputation is, after all, the very method of reason: "Reason works by elevating or vanquishing the grounds of doubt through discourse." This is so because reason, being the same in all people, allows us to prove things to each other. "Upon this supposition all Conferences, Disputes, and Debates whatsoever are grounded" (Hammond 1649). Print is particularly suited for rational debate; its open, public character ensures an impartial jury.[11]

One of the rhetorical vocabularies created to argue the anti-royalist cause is particularly interesting, for it wedded Puritan and mercantile arguments for liberty of public expression in a decidedly utilitarian manner, forming a bridge from sacred to secular modes of argument. The utilitarian case for freedom of expression asserts that the free play of ideas is an effective and efficient *means* of assuring that truth will prevail. This line of argument did not originate with eighteenth-century exponents of enlightened reason. It was well developed by the English Puritans in a form that drew upon both the Puritan conception of community and an emergent commercial defense of free trade. This melded approach is well summarized in one of its most striking images: the trade of truth.

Milton, writing as a Puritan revolutionary, asserted that books embody the labors of reasoning individuals. Those who are called to the vocation of publicist work to produce truth for the community, and the community should not be deprived of the gifts they exercise. Whatever evils are visited upon communities by monopolistic practices in the marketing of ordinary wares are all the more obnoxious obstacles to trading truth, which Milton called "our richest merchandise" (Milton 1957 [1644], 720, 736–7). The "trade of truth" became a common metaphor, and numerous commercial figures of speech were used to describe printing, debate, and the search for truth (Hill 1642). Truth was a "commodity" worth "purchase" at great "price," but one should beware of "hucksters" in the "market."

Free speech was said to allow the spirit to flow freely and the labors of the mind and spirit to find their way to the public for the common good (or utility), but freedom also allows a hearing to falsehood. Nevertheless, radical Puritans confidently supposed that in a free marketplace of ideas truth drives out falsehood. The method of public discussion was seen as a way to truth, not dissension, for truth is the one solid foundation of unity and peace. It is better to seek this truth through "trying each spirit" and communicating the results of one's striving to the public, than violently to force orthodoxy upon the unwilling. As John Goodwin (1644, 30) said (arguing for the congregational way):

and what manner of peace can reasonably be expected under the predominancy of such a way? That way which shall be able to *out-reason*, not that which shall *out clubbe*, all other wayes, will at last exalt unitie; and be it selfe exalted by gathering in all other ways unto it.

Truth, the embodied collective labor of vocationally directed, active seekers, is a public good. The products of strivers for truth must freely flow to the public, who should freely test this merchandise. A free public, endowed with reason, will not purchase shoddy wares.[12] On the contrary, free discussion, especially in print, *creates* a public whose members are infused with a public spirit, and collectively constitute a moral order. These advocates of the trade of truth suppose that reason in individuals is the foundation of order in society, but reasonable individuals create order through a collective process of communication. The image of trade was intended to be an account of how a community can forge a rational consensus through a socially organized process that engages a public oriented to organs of communication and intellectuals whose special role was to educate public opinion.

*Discussion and the common good.* In the public space of seventeenth-century England, communication came to be seen as effective in producing truth generally, not just spiritual truth for members of congregations, but truth about the public interest as well. The public is not merely a body to which competing politicians appeal; it is also the bearer of the public interest.

The idea of the common good or common weal is deeply rooted in medieval and early modern political and social thought and was one of the elements of the Puritan conception of communion. There is an equally long history behind the notion that the ruler comes to know the common good through a process of advice (Ferguson, 1965). The general idea of public interest does not necessarily imply participatory discussion, but the concept moved decisively in this direction when theorists began to assert that a free public is the best judge of its own interest, a notion that emerged as a by-product of the distinction between *private* and *public* advice to the king.[13] A maxim of regal and feudal polities had held that the advice given a king or lord ought not to be a mere reflection of the private interests of the counselor. By the same token, if an advisee wants sound advice, it is not prudent to interfere with the free speech of the advisor. We see here an early source of the idea that free discussion produces truth, in the case of parliamentary counsel, a true account of the public interest. Parliament gives a true account of the public weal, while private advisers – "flatterers" or otherwise evil counsellors – do not. Once one accepts the premise that the best judge of the public interest is the public itself, or a parliament that represents the public, it is a small step to the idea that in matters affecting the common good, the king must act solely on the advice of Parliament. Indeed, according to Henry Parker, the advice of Parliament to the king constitutes an *infallible* statement of the public interest, for the people, who are all virtually represented in parliament, cannot be mistaken about their own best public interests any more than individuals can be mistaken about their best private interests. By the same token, private advice to the king is wrong because partial and *necessarily* founded on the personal private interest of the adviser. Henry Parker's pious formulation (1640, 45–60) manifests a particularly strong faith in the public spirit as embodied in representative assemblies:

That an inconsiderable number of Privadoes should see or know more than whole Kingdomes, is incredible . . . Parliaments are infallible, and their acts indisputable to all but Parliaments. It is a just law, that no private man must bee wiser then law publickly made . . . Secondly, no advice can be so faithfull, so loyall, so religious and sincere, as that which proceeds from Parliaments, where so many are gathered together for Gods service in such a devout manner, we cannot but expect that God should be amongst them . . . so their ends cannot be so sinister: private men may thrive by alterations . . . and common calamities, but the common body can affect nothing but the common good, because nothing else can be commodious for them.

The doctrine that representative bodies necessarily express the common good became a central dogma for Harrington, one of the principal builders of seventeenth-century political thought, who explicitly attributed the true expression of public will to a collective process of communication (Zagorin

1954, 137–8; Macpherson 1962, 184). His view has been aptly restated by Pocock (1977, 87): "For Harrington, rationality was a civic process in which two partners discovered their interconnectedness." In short, discussion produces truth in representative public deliberative bodies just as it does in printed public discussion. Public reason is dialogical, a collective product embodied in a process of communication. It cannot be a mere instrument of individual will, for it expresses the solidarity of the community.

*Public spirit in liberal theory.* The doctrine of sharing the spirit provided system-forming cultural premises for the differentiation of the solidary public. If prolocutors are to mobilize novel solidary combinations by speaking for new groups, they must have the right to bid for support. Prolocutorship cannot be institutionalized without the legitimation of free speech and publication, for a differentiated public allows would-be spokespeople to ask for support without evoking a presumption that such bids are *per se* disloyal to the larger society. In Anglo-American thought, the legitimation of free communication, and with it the right to speak to the public interest, emerged in the wake of the differentiation of the grounds of cultural authority away from official spokespersons for established doctrines and toward the individual. In this sense, "individualism" is deeply implicated in liberal philosophy, but liberalism cannot be simply construed as a philosophy of freedom from collective constraints. Rather, it is a philosophy of freedom of individual thought and commitment from constraints of force, not from constraints generally. The individual must be freed not *from* community but freed *to form* community, for the deepest communal ties come from individual commitment driven by reason and choice. As such, liberalism constitutes a celebration of persuasion as much as a plea for individualism. Community must flow, say the advocates of liberal thought, from the free play of processes of persuasion. Initially, in the doctrine of Communion of the Saints, arguments for freedom of expression were based on the notion that community must rest on free communication – freedom to preach and receive the Word. An attuned spirit was the test of truth. With the merger of spirit and reason, the Puritan formula for communion forged a justification for freedom of speech and publication. This complex, which above all valorizes persuasive communication, constitutes a significant strand in the complex thread of cultural differentiations that legitimized the modern public.

### The formation of the rhetoric of civil society

*Polarities and bridging terms in the discourse of civil society.* The Protestant rhetoric of the English Puritans, as employed in civil and political struggles before and during the English Civil War, initiated the characteristic polarities of the Anglo-American rhetoric of civil society. The rhetoric of liberty, communion, and public spirit is constructed on binary distinctions that reveal dichotomies cognate with the discourse of American civil society as described by Alexander and Smith (1993). The primary dichotomy opposed the public and the private, and, surrounding this polarity, several related oppositions formed a complex of terms that allowed intelligible argument among parties engaged in mutual persuasion: the secret and the open, selfishness and sharing, the special and the common, wickedness and virtue. The parallel sides of each of these pairs resonate with each other in what might, after Kenneth Burke, be called "logological" chains of implication, which, whether valid or not, formed a vision of good civil life and of its inverse image of civic corruption. Virtuous citizens, animated by public spirit, value the common good and share their conceptions of this good in public forums. Conversely, civic life is corrupted when citizens pervert their civic judgment by subordinating it to private interests. Wicked counsel in secret replaces open discourse in public, and cabals of special interests impose their will on the whole, avoiding the persuasive arena to rely instead on their illegitimate access to the force of the state.

*Polarities and social tensions.* The idea that discourse forms around polarities derives from a structuralist approach to culture that locates the independence of the cultural in the binary logic of its codes. The binary logic of culture rests on the postulate that we understand concepts in terms of differences (Alexander and Smith 1993). Yet the binary pairs of rhetorical discourse do not stand alone as irreconcilable opposites. The human experience that enters into rhetorical communication includes perceptions of the inescapable reality of both sides of each pair, and cultural codes also include an amplifying discourse of connection that refers to how the gulf between opposing terms is bridged. Much of the implicit theory behind complex systems of dichotomies is found in these bridging terms – terms of overcoming, transcending, reconciling, balancing, or muting opposites. These terms correspond to our daily experience of the integration of phenomena that are separated by logical opposition in our codes of communication.

Bridging terms often refer to experiences of overcoming oppositions. For example, the terms "knowledge" and "ignorance" are in binary opposition, but are linked by the the term "education," which refers to how ignorance is overcome. Bridging terms such as "education" have a special rhetorical force of their own, for they appeal to audiences' desires to transcend the disturbing tensions inherent in the terms of their discourse. In the seventeenth-century discourse of public versus private, the principal bridging term is "communication," a term that accounts for how the conflict between personal ends and the common good can be resolved. The vocabulary of the communicative ideal includes a number of related words. Seventeenth-century writers frequently use the term "communication," but they also refer to debate, deliberation, discourse, consultation, and of course, the underlying term "communion."

I do not posit an immanent dialectical movement of bridging terms, as if specific dichotomous oppositions and bridging relations were universally inherent in the structure of thought. Rather, I see the common abstractions that underlie varied rhetorical conceptions of the social world as referring to inherent tensions in social life itself. These tensions, which are universally experienced by social actors, can be conceptualized at a higher level of abstraction than the various substantive issues that animate disagreement and conflict, such as inequality, social divisions, powers of control, possessions and statuses. Some tensions are inherent in the conditions of social organization. For example, adequate *personal autonomy* allows adaptive responses on the part of people who are in touch with the scenes of action and are able to see what rules must be bent or broken to allow successful effort in the face of particular contingencies, but autonomy can undermine adequate *social regulation* to coordinate conduct among actors who might utilize freedom strategically to undermine group efforts. In the cognitive arena, orientations may be so particularized and short-term as to imprison actors in the pursuit of immediate, at-hand gratifications, or cognitive frames may be so abstract and generalized as to fail to accommodate knowledge of practical means of obtaining short-term results.

These sorts of problems were the grist for Parsons' development of his scheme of "pattern variables" for classifying social norms according to dichotomous polarities that define the socially relevant orientations that actors bring to social situations (Parsons 1951). Later, Parsons sought to connect the pattern variables to his fourfold functional scheme by demonstrating the functional importance of each polar term to particular problems in interaction (Parsons 1967a, 192–219). Many find his proffered translation forced and unpersuasive, but the success or failure of his technical efforts are less important than his underlying insight: polarities are embedded in the very structure of social conduct and the organization of this conduct into systems. This insight is generally overlooked by those who would make of Parsons a static theorist of stable structures, insensitive to the conflicts that animate social life. On the contrary, his later structural-functional system of analysis was predicated on the notion that the functional requisites of social systems are fundamentally in tension with each other. Social systems cannot simultaneously maximize social integration,

stable structure, adaptation to changing environments, and the achievement of collective goals. Systems achieve a measure of working integration,
but deep-seated dynamic tensions continue to give rise to forces of change,
particularly forces that promote structural differentiation as one mode of
resolving the conflicts inherent in asking a single system to solve several
functional problems at once. Civil society is one such differentiated sphere.

In Parsonian terms, the primary functions of civil society are integration
and adaptation. The incompatibility between these functions derives from
the dependence of integration on social control and the dependence of
adaptation on freedom to respond to contingencies that cannot be foreseen
in normative schemes of coordination. Balancing these conflicting functions is accomplished in various ways – by normative generalization, by
setting aside special spheres of autonomy, and by contractual institutions,
which allow for mutual negotiation of terms that are responsive to current
circumstance within a regulative framework. In civil society, tensions
between autonomy and regulation are accommodated through communication. Hence communication and the terms for its various forms become
bridging concepts in rhetoric describing how communication is supposed
to work: deliberation, persuasion, and influence. The polarities of
seventeenth-century liberal rhetoric and its variations on the bridging
theme of communication presuppose the differentiation of a civil sphere
within which people can freely join with others through discussion that
clarifies their common cause without resort to force, and that ensures
taking account of the special knowledge and interests of individual participants by giving them an opportunity to speak.

### Civic virtue

*Civic virtue in classical and Renaissance thought.* Puritan theology was
neither the sole cause of the differentiation of solidarity nor the sole source
of its intellectual justifications. The impact of the Protestant notion of the
Communion of the Saints is interwoven with developments in the concept
of civic virtue, which arose in secular philosophical and political thought.
Of classical, rather than Judeo-Christian provenance, the ideal of civic
virtue was deeply embedded in the culture of the Greek *polis* and was
carried forward in Aristotelian political philosophy, which captured
ancient Greek allegiance to an intense and all-embracing communal political life. By "all embracing," I refer to Aristotle's view that the self can be
fully expressed only through participation in the *polis*, through ruling and
being ruled as citizens in politically organized communities. This exclusive
assignment of meaningful collective life to the political realm is the start-

ing point for contemporary notions that liberal rights and *civic virtue*, comfortably conjoined in early liberalism, are inherently opposed, even mutually exclusive.

By the late middle ages, Greek ideas had merged with Christian philosophy, in large measure through Aquinas' embrace of both Aristotle's *Politics* and his *Nicomachean Ethics*. For both Aristotle and Aquinas, contemplation was the highest good, and worldly action was relegated to subordinate status as a realm of mere means. The organizing polar dichotomy became the active versus the *contemplative* life, and civic affairs fell within the devalued category of the active. Legitimizing active life in civic communities became a project of the so-called "civic humanists" of the fifteenth- and sixteenth-century Italian cities, whose justifications of the *vivere civile* constituted another road, outside of the Protestant reformation, to the legitimization of worldly values. The story of the civic humanists, their motives and their significance has been well told in a number of classic and influential works (Baron 1955, Garin 1965; Gilbert 1965; Seigel 1968), but the most comprehensive and paradigm-forming account of humanist political thought and its continuing reception in the Anglo-American tradition is set forth in Pocock's *The Machiavellian Moment* (1975) and other works (1977; 1987).

Pocock's interpretation of civic humanism begins by observing that the neoclassical Renaissance mind had difficulty understanding and accepting historical particularity. Classical philosophy accorded general categories a privileged epistemological status, a status that can be readily accommodated within Christian theology and the City of God, but not easily adapted to the hurly-burly particularity of secular affairs and the conflicts of political life. In the late medieval and Renaissance world view, particularity could only be understood in terms of chance and accident – *fortune*, whose revolving wheel favors now one group, now another. Only a social order guaranteed by timeless universal truths can generate a stable regime imbued with value – a comprehensible and dependable moral community. Renaissance humanists were, faced with the challenge of resolving the conflict between universalism and particularism in a secular normative order. The heritage of classical thought provided a resource for coping with this problem. Aristotle's notion of *politeia*, a political order organized around the virtue of citizens, provided an account of an ordered and stable regime founded on the intrinsic nature of the human being as a political animal. A proper *politeia* gives all citizens an opportunity to exercise their particular civic virtues and to benefit from the reciprocal contributions of the virtues of others. Each group can contribute to decisions in a way for which they are best fitted, and all individuals can participate both through their particular group memberships and their membership in the *polis* as a whole. If properly constituted in this balanced manner, a civic order can be both autonomous and stable, and thus express the ultimate values of sentient social beings (Pocock 1975, 63–77).

In a broad way, the Aristotelian idea of the *polis* constitutes a theory of communication as the source of social order. It is, according to Pocock (1975, 64) an affirmation that the particular is made intelligible in conversation and that the universal is "immanent in the web of life," so that the highest values are realizable only in association. But political theory must still explain how all this occurs in *particular* conversations. The theory of *politeia* seeks to account for how constitutions can give proper voice to particularly constituted and located groups. It is not difficult to see how Aristotle's approach lends itself to theories of mixed constitution in which the voices of "the one, the few, and the many" are assigned their proper function, separated, and balanced. Constitutional analysis along these lines was the strongest legacy of Renaissance humanism in what Pocock calls "the Atlantic republican tradition."

Communication may, as Pocock claims, lie at the heart of Aristotelian political thought, but the republican tradition evolved as a structural account of the organization of power, not as a theory of the process of communication; it is an extension of Aristotle's *Politics*, not his *Rhetoric*. Public opinion was not a key concept in civic humanism, nor did influencing the public through mediated appeals in print play a significant role in the humanist concept of a civic order. The larger public came under the heading of "the many," and capacity for deliberation was not the virtue of this group. Something on the order of public opinion, but perhaps more akin to the modern notion of national character or civic culture, entered into the background of republican thought in the idea that a given populace is more or less governable by one or another form of constitution. Florentines, for example, were long accustomed to freedom and hence not governable except through some form of republican state. From Machiavelli forward, the virtue of the many was identified as their collective military prowess, and the guarantee of the sustained power of the many in a balanced republic was the citizen army, which protects the autonomy of the city from both external aggressors and internal tyrants. This particular Machiavellian concept has continued to play a major role in Anglo-American republican thought through centuries of changing issues, from attempts to justify the rule of Cromwell's army after the execution of King Charles, through objection to the rise of a standing royal army during and after the restoration, to advocacy of the right to bear arms in support of a "well ordered militia," an idea that continues to reverberate in contemporary American discussions of gun control. Interpretation of the virtue and strength of the many as ultimately military underscores the focus of the republican tradition on power within the organization of government, not on the organization of the civic sector.

*Changing conceptions of virtue.* The concept of civic virtue had originally referred to those particular worthy capacities that given individuals or groups could bring to civic life in order to secure the stability of secular government. So conceived, virtue was capable of rescuing life in the worldly community from incomprehensible and valueless chaos. Gradually, this conception of virtue, in which virtue is opposed to fortune, gave rise to a new polarity that set virtue in opposition to *corruption.* Illegitimate power, not incomprehensible flux, became the dreaded consequence of the breakdown of virtue.

Corruption arises when the part is elevated above the whole, faction above the common good, private interests above the public interests of the commonwealth. Virtue is therefore a species of public-spirited selflessness. Since this conception of corruption was already in place in the early seventeenth century, particularly in the notion of wicked royal counselors whose advice is based on their own interests rather than the good of the kingdom, I cannot entirely credit Pocock's emphasis on the rise of the idea of corruption as a later development.[14] Nevertheless, the ancient idea of virtue as capacities that qualify citizens for effective political participation did gradually give way to the use of "virtue" as a rhetorical term for contrasting the public interest and selfish private interests.

*Liberalism and civic virtue.* When civic virtue came to be defined as subordinating individual interests to the public good, the compatibility of the republican tradition and liberalism became problematic. If liberalism is defined as a political philosophy that locates the rights of individuals outside of and prior to society, and insists that the state is merely an instrument for protecting these rights from infringement by others, then the notion that the state promotes collective aims and goods on behalf of citizens, who should virtuously sacrifice their own interests for the greater good of the political community, comes to be regarded as a competing, rival philosophy (Pocock 1975, 424; Sinopoli 1992,19–38). Accordingly, "Lockean" or "rights liberalism" is now generally regarded as an adversary of the Atlantic republican tradition that Pocock describes, as if liberalism and republican virtue were logically incompatible polar opposites. If rights liberalism is viewed as the only authentically liberal philosophy, and Locke as its original author, then the earlier protoliberalism of the English Civil War cannot be regarded as liberal, and my assertion of a social component in liberal thinking from its very outset seems to combine incompatible ideas. On the other hand, when liberalism is seen as a social philosophy that supplies a rhetorical base for the *differentiation* of solidarity, not its *devaluation*, the continuity between the original liberal defense of free communication and subsequent movements of liberal thought is easy to trace. The merger of ideas about *rights* with ideas about the *moral framework of rights* in the working rhetoric of the founders of associational democracy, underscores the difficulty of separating republican and liberal views. The continuing rhetorical force of the republican notion of civic virtue well after the introduction of Locke's more individualistic liberalism cannot be disregarded.

Ongoing controversies among interpreters of the late colonial, revolutionary, and federal periods of American history regarding the relative strength of liberal and republican theory in that era illustrate this problem. Bernard Bailyn (1967) broke ground for the debate by tracing a continuous and consistent history of pamphlet literature from the English Civil Wars, through the tracts of late seventeenth-and early eighteenth-century radical "country" groups in England, to the revolutionary literature of the American colonies. My reading of Bailyn's account suggests that American pamphleteers simply did not distinguish rights-based from virtue-based defenses of the colonists' liberties. They constructed a broad ranging rhetorical vocabulary of polemical terms from sources ranging from philosophical works by Locke to less sophisticated topical pamphlets, all shaped by a master dichotomy of power versus liberty. Colonial pamphleteers certainly knew their Locke and spoke the language of natural rights and contractarian theories of government, but the most important English sources for libertarian ideas among the colonists were the republican writings of John Trenchard and Thomas Gordon (Bailyn 1967, 35–7).

Trenchard and Gordon, working together during the early 1720s, produced *Cato's Letters* and the *Independent Whig*, collections of newspaper articles that were widely circulated in England and in the American colonies throughout the eighteenth century. Their writings were directed against the corruption that surrounded the South Sea Bubble episode, an early speculative fiasco, and the rise of patronage and administrative control in parliament. Trenchard and Gordon were convinced that power is controlled by virtue, that virtue is grounded in independence, and that corruption and tyranny follow dislocations of social supports of constitutional separations of powers. Liberty cannot be squared with the pernicious influence of finance and patronage on the body politic. When free and independent voices are overcome by conspiracies, the public good is sacrificed to the interests of conspirators, whether they be venal financiers or

174

their co-conspirators in Parliament. Pocock rightly places Trenchard and Gordon squarely in the republican tradition (1975, 467–77). Issues changed and some specific rhetorical terms changed, but the underlying logic of virtue and selfishness, communication among free citizens, power and corruption, and wicked counsel remained. Public debt joined standing armies as enemies of the commonwealth, but the faith of the old "country" party remained in place in the writings of Trenchard and Gordon and their successors, and this tradition crossed the Atlantic in *Cato's Letters*.

Trenchard and Gordon's affection for republican virtue is apparent throughout *Cato's Letters*. They speak of the "Publick Spirit" as "the highest virtue," and define it as "a Passion for the Universal Good, with Personal Pain, Loss and Peril" (Jacobson 1965, 89).[15] Yet the authors of *Cato's Letters* were clearly heirs to the ideas of Locke as well. They confidently asserted that "All Men are born free: Liberty is a Gift which they receive from God himself" (108). Their theory of government is clearly contractarian in the sense that they viewed the state as created by the people through a process of consent in order to secure their liberties and the public good. Far from seeing any contradiction between the primacy of rights and the necessity of virtue, they say of the "Passion for Liberty" that it is "the Parent of all the Virtues (131). Nor did the colonists think to question whether the republicanism of Cato's Letters was entirely consistent with either Locke's theories of natural rights or Cato's own rather muddled views of natural liberties. They knew they had liberties and they wanted to know how these liberties could be preserved and defended and how to recognize the signs of danger.

*The virtue of communication.* In republican thought, preserving liberty requires exercising freedom to speak. Trenchard and Gordon present their defense of free speech as if the prototypical act of free communication is one that unmasks corruption, subordinating the role of free speech in validating truth to its instrumental effect in establishing public virtue. They argue that the public depends on publicity, on opening the deed of the magistrate to examination by the people, which in turn implies freedom to criticize all acts that would sacrifice the public interest to the wicked designs of selfish magistrates and their evil advisors.

Liberal thought, too, has always linked freedom to concerns about creating moral community. That this birthmark has remained on a great deal of liberal thought throughout its long history is attested by the strong connections between virtue and rights in liberal defenses of free communication. From Milton, through Madison, to Habermas' current pleas for open discourse, the value of personal autonomy is a decisive premise. For Milton, as for his Puritan colleagues, persuasive communication is an inherent element of virtuous relations among humankind, for conduct can be virtuous only if it is autonomous. "If every action which is good or evil in a man of ripe years were to be under pittance [i.e. rationed] and prescription and compulsion, what were virtue but a name?" His argument goes well beyond the alleged efficiency of free speech in sorting truth from falsehood; it rests in the first instance on the *valuation of personal autonomy*. We do not esteem, Milton observes, "obedience, or love, or gift, which is of force" and concludes that this is why God gave us freedom. Freedom, for Milton, derives from the making of humans in the image of God, and this concept is the theological ancestor of the secular ideal of respect for every person's autonomy. It is the reason that persuasion is the only virtuous means of affecting the conduct of others. Moreover, the passions are not the opposite of the virtues, but the only possible motivating source of virtuous conduct. "Reason is but choosing," and virtue is a matter of harnessing passions in the service of good choices.[16] By a parallel argument, personal autonomy implies opposition to authoritarian regimes and support for self governance within a community that has willingly contracted to live under communally formed laws of association.

To argue for personal autonomy as a moral imperative is not to defend ignoring other moral claims, including the claims of the public interest. Habermas' program of "emancipation," with its reliance on uncoerced agreement – the force of the better argument – and its valuation of autonomy, is clearly liberal in its fundamental premises and aspirations. Its immediate roots are not found, of course, in either Puritanism or English "country" thought, but in an enlightened philosophical tradition stemming from Kant. Nevertheless, Habermas' recommended blend of autonomy, discussion, and public justice illustrates in our own day the tight connections between these concepts in any ideological scheme that understands individual rights to have a moral dimension.

*Liberal and republican ideas.* Current disputes over republicanism and virtue turn on establishing analytical distinctions that would make the two ideologies mutually exclusive and allow judgment of which is the proper label for a writer or an era. Advocates of establishing definitive criteria for two distinct and rival modes of thought seek to go behind rhetorical uses of concepts of freedom and virtue to the underlying analytic logic of political conceptions (Sinopoli 1992, 8–12). We can then ask whether, say, Madison or Jefferson were really republican thinkers, or whether colonial radicals are better described as liberals. The latter argument usually proceeds by asserting that the substance of American ideology is primarily attributable to the influence of Locke, whom Pocock placed "among the adversaries" of the republican tradition (Pocock 1975, 424), rather than to the more eclectic writings of Trenchard and Gordon, or others who stressed virtue and other elements of the British oppositional tradition. Locke's assertion of natural rights and the contractual basis of the state makes government a means of securing individual rights that exist prior to the state. This view of the state is inconsistent with the Aristotelian cast of civic republican thought, because republicans view government as valuable in its own right. It provides citizens opportunities for realizing, through civic participation, the highest potential of humankind: association in self government. For liberals, virtue is merely part of the political psychology of a liberal regime; it helps explain why governments founded on interests and consent can avoid difficulties consequent to excessive calculated conduct on the part of free riders (Sinopoli 1992, 33–7).[17]

This line of argument presents an important analytic distinction, one that identifies significant differences in political philosophies that make for decisive differences in approaches to particular problems of government policy. On the other hand, emphasizing these distinctions can obscure the course of cultural history by drawing lines that do not correspond to the way advocates make use of rhetorical opportunities provided by political vocabularies and the lasting influence of vocabularies of discourse on people's common understanding of their public life. Lance Banning (1986, 12) has succinctly summarized the empirical confluence of analytically distinct ideologies of revolution: "Liberal and classical ideas were both available to America's Revolutionary generation . . . Logically it may be inconsistent to be simultaneously liberal and classical. Historically, it was not . . . Eighteenth-century opposition thought was always a complex blend of liberal and classical ideas."

Republican virtue and liberal rights are not necessarily incompatible rivals. The root traditions behind these two ideas occupied common ground for centuries. Pocock (1981), following Quentin Skinner (1978), notes that the language of virtue and the language of rights had been aligned on the same side since the twelfth century. In one language, virtue is displayed by citizens who follow a civic ideal; in the other, rights are recognized in the law of a sovereign (or a sovereign people). The republican citizens of the Italian cities asserted the autonomy of their self-governing communities as a matter of both equal and active citizenship and of the sovereign's protection of the citizens' authority. Citizenship implied both rights and duties, both law and community, both freedom and participation. Lockean theory did not establish these pairs of terms as polar opposites. Theoretical recognition of conflicts between the obligations of citizenship and the right to protect one's own individual interests became problematic in later generations, when the growing dominance of market-driven economies brought problems of selfishness to the fore.

In any event, the two traditions are on the same side of the ledger with respect to the theme of this chapter. Locke's liberal ideas had important consequences for the legitimation of differentiated solidarity. When America's constitution makers, referring to themselves as "we the people" and to their task as forming "a more perfect union," undertook to write a new compact between the people of the states, they were engaged in creating associational solidarity. The people through their representative institutions could decide whether to ratify the document and join the United States, thus willing a new nation into being. Making the new constitution presented a variation on Locke's state of nature. The citizens of the confederated states were not creating a state *de novo* from a state of nature, but they were creating a new agreement among themselves to recognize a new state. The parallel to Locke's liberal conception of the social contract was not lost on the participants, and in arguing for and against adopting this new agreement the debaters often appealed to the contractual logic of the situation, asking how the proposed arrangement would secure the benefits of government without sacrificing the rights of liberty. The republican tradition was also useful, for its traditional theory of *politeia* – mixed and balanced government – was reinvented in a new version, in which each office, whether executive, legislative, or judicial, was itself constituted as a form of representation, *but none were traditional social estates* (Wood 1969, 162–73). This new form of differentiated representation raised fundamentally new questions. Without a fixed locus for sovereign power in any traditional institution, whether royal or parliamentary, and with the people themselves taken as the sovereign, it became necessary to reconsider the nature of representation. Virtual representation (a conception of republican provenance) held that representatives constitute the whole in institutional form and therefore cannot fail to *represent* the whole. The new constitution invalidated virtual representation and made officers agents of constituencies, whose varied interests became the legitimate stuff of political life and established a new model for liberal polity .

The idea of popular sovereignty within a polity created to preserve individual rights rather than to create a good state as such – an instrumental state that was not conceived to be the very source and locus of the virtuous life – owes much to the Lockean legacy. Nevertheless, the problem of virtue remained, for the ancient question of stability is not resolved by the creation of a social contract. How is the legitimacy of the democratic state established? What is to prevent factional disputes from destroying the state's capacity to sustain the whole? Locke's conceptions of civil government were a ready source of basic ideas about how to write social contracts, but it is misleading to view his social contract as a mere means of establishing property rights, or of subordinating the state to the private interests created by individual preferences. To do so is to read nineteenth-century ideologies of economic liberalism and the *laissez faire* state backwards into Locke's version of Puritan ideals. His promotion of the individual, like that of his Protestant forbears, rested on moral respect for individuals as autonomous agents whose understandings must derive from personal experience and therefore cannot be established by coercion. His view of civil society cannot be understood apart from his valuation of communication and persuasion as the only proper foundation of social order. Viewed from this perspective, *the social contract is a willed agreement to associate, a compact that creates associational solidarity.*

### Liberalism and modernity

Liberal redefinition of representation as acting as an agent of constituencies and their interests does not necessarily imply a parallel transformation of politics to a mere play of interests within a purely procedural political system that lacks collective political values. Several contemporary liberal theorists continue to affirm that liberalism is not entirely neutral with respect to conceptions of good community life. For example, Galston (1991, 43), who asserts that "Liberalism does not undermine community; it is a form of community," affirms that liberalism asks citizens to practice several participatory virtues, including restraint, civility, respect for both the arguments as well as the rights of others, and above all, commitment to resolve disputes through public discourse (213–37; see also Selznick 1992). Nevertheless, early communitarian liberalism did have to come to grips with the forces of commercial modernity. However important the civic idea had been in the development of early modern concepts of associational solidarity, the ever increasing spread of markets and of market mentalities, which legitimated self-interested economic life, led to a more rights-oriented conception of the democratic state. Early modern liberalism, despite its commitments to individual rights, encountered strains in its grounding of the differentiation of solidarity, because the republican components of protoliberal thought included strong affinities for conservative, traditional visions of society.

Conceptions of republican virtue require an institutional locus for sentiments and motives to induce participation in free self government. Machiavelli found such virtue in citizen armies, Harrington in widespread ownership of freehold property. The rise of commercial enterprise and other modern institutions challenged advocates of republican virtue either to defend new sources of civic stability or to attack modernity as a threat to public life. Trade, especially international trade that could build the home nation into a republican empire, giving citizens a stake in national prosperity, found its way into republican rhetoric, but two other modernizing institutions were not easily absorbed into the traditional ideological scheme: parliamentary government and public debt. The former turned representatives of the people into rulers and, in its early development in England, operated through systems of patronage, which create dependence, the enemy of virtue. Subordinate bureaucrats are not free to represent the public and become the functional equivalent of wicked counselors. Financial institutions were problematic to eighteenth-century republicans for reasons even more crucial to the differentiation of solidarity, reasons grounded on antimodern fundamentalism.

*Fundamentalism and community.* Modern and antimodern ideologies divide on issues of trust. Fundamentalist rejection of modernity on issues of community stems from this division. I use the term "fundamentalism," as Parsons did, to refer to attitudes that prefer the real to the symbolic, the literal to the interpretive, self sufficiency to dependency on the division of labor. A fundamentalist prefers money based on precious metals, productive work over speculation, and a militia of citizens over a professional standing army, preferences that illustrate the fundamentalist streak in the civic republican tradition. Parsons used the term to refer to conservative, antimodern attitudes toward the media of exchange, views that cannot wholeheartedly embrace symbolic media, demanding gold standards or their equivalent in each of the markets that equilibrate the division of labor. The least common denominator of various fundamentalist attitudes is suspicion of modernity – resentment of the burden of trust that modern institutions require in lieu of providing direct connections to real things that stay put. Entrenched social stratification and local community were among the sources of stable connections valued by republican thinkers for their putative contributions to civic virtue. The idea of civic virtue had always distinguished the different virtues of "the one the few and the many." Its proponents feared assignment of too much power to the unpredictable many, and trusted the few with responsibilities appropriate to their station. Accordingly, civic republicanism, even in its democratic versions, readily gravitated to aristocratic conceptions of society, as the status-based flavor of the debates between Federalists and Antifederalists clearly reveal. Civic virtue was also attributed to local community. In the debates over constitutional ratification, the size of the proposed consolidated nation was a matter of deep concern. Antifederalists claimed that the attachments and affections on which trustworthy political relations depend decline with increasing size of the state and the corresponding distance between participants (Sinopoli 1992, 144–6). Notwithstanding the common view that Madison inaugurated the legitimation of representation of special interests, his celebrated Federalist o was not a defense of faction as a proper part of political life; it was an attempt to defend the proposed new republican nation against the charge that the new government would be too far removed from the governed by arguing that a larger state would contain and incorporate a larger number and variety of interests. Factions, inevitable but not legitimate, would be less likely to gain a dominant majority against the interest of the people. His argument is only intelligible against the background of popular fear that the new government would no longer be attached to natural communities.

*Fundamentalism and the public debt.* The issues of fundamentalism revolve around the question of what sort of surrounding society could provide sustenance to a stable and moral state. A supportive civil society would be based on solid, dependable knowledge and on social relations that carried similar guarantees. Antimodern sentiments expressed distrust of the new significance of mere opinion and interests; fancy, appetite, and fantastic imagination cannot provide sober grounds for responsible social conduct. This battle was waged in the first instance over speculative investment.

During the eighteenth century, the British state developed a modern and successful system for funding public debt. Largely generated by military expenditures, the national debt increased fifteenfold between 1697 and 1783 (Brewer 1989, 114–22) and was to grow after the Napoleonic wars to levels high even by twentieth-century standards, reaching in 1820 a figure equal to two-thirds of the entire reproducible assets of England (Clark 1994). The rise of public debt and the establishment of institutions of public borrowing created a new property interest in competition with land.[18] Competition between land and debt as forms of property was not merely economic; it led to social, political, and cultural conflict, for land was the fundamentalist preference. Land is real and directly productive, and to hold land was to participate in a system of rights and responsibilities, including responsibility for shouldering the burden of taxes that financed interest payments on the debt. Landholding was at the center of an entrenched system of solidarity, deference, and power that conveyed status and status-based influence to the gentry class, offering them opportunities to control both local and parliamentary politics. Freehold property was the putative source of virtue for republican theoreticians seeking sources of stability in the precarious seas of a politics that, if not strictly democratic, allowed for distribution of power beyond a regal establishment. Debt, on the contrary, is divorced from the real world of productive property and separated from the web of traditional social relations. It is merely backed by the public trust.

The collapse of the South Sea Bubble in 1720 gave opponents of public debt and of property in debt instruments grounds for attack.[19] They saw investment in debt as speculative rather than productive. The value of a debt instrument is based on mere *opinion* – fancy, imagination, and fantasies fed by mere cupidity. The ideologists of the country opposition, including Trenchard and Gordon for example, made the South Sea fiasco a prime exhibit in their bill of particulars against governmental schemes contrary to the public interest, and more sophisticated writers eloquently derided the dependence of credit on fantasy and its vulnerability to manipulation by the hated "stockjobbers" (Pocock 1975, 436–61). Yet the financiers learned the lessons of the South Sea experience, stabilized the debt, and created a system of debt that gained the confidence of the public.

The fundamentalist defenders of property in land were right on one count: the stability of property in debt is based on public opinion. The development of public opinion as a political force is closely connected to the rise of public debt, which put governments in jeopardy of losing public confidence. While this point has been noted by several scholars, its implications have not been fully recognized.[20] Confidence in the credit instruments of the public debt institutionalized public opinion as a new form of solidarity. The fundamentalist attitudes that were overcome in the economic sphere by stable monetary systems continued to distrust solidarities not based on close-knit communities, but this social fundamentalism was undermined by the emergence of confidence that opinion can function as a stabilizing force, rather than a source of disarray.

*Public opinion and information.* In modern society, public opinion replaces deference as the prime organizing principle for influence. Even though prestige continues to support influence over opinions, in the modern social order the ultimate backing of influence becomes information. While property in land had supported a system of *deference*, investors in government securities came to have an insatiable appetite for *information*. The rise of public debt in eighteenth-century Britain introduced an information revolution wherein investors demanded information from the state, and the state, driven by the needs of taxing authorities and regulative bureaucracies, demanded information from the private economy. The consequent interchange of information was brokered through a sophisticated lobbying process not unlike lobbying in our day. Newly legitimate associations of interested parties used information as counters in a complicated exchange of information in support of practical adjustments and compromises in the details of statutes and regulative schemes (Brewer 1989, 221–49). Private and public interests remained in tension but were no longer strictly antithetical and irresolvable; they could be negotiated through rhetorical exchanges that were controlled by the norm of accountability and conducted on the principle that demands must be justified by reference to the public interest.

Our new understanding of the development of associational lobbying in the late eighteenth century casts doubt on the orthodox picture of this period as conservative and politically organized entirely around established personal connections. Bradley's (1990) studies of English radicalism during this period are also apposite. He marshals evidence of the continuing strength of the legacy of the congregational tradition. Strongly opposed to the principle of deference and committed to the idea of individual autonomy in voting and in expressing opinion, English radicals, largely religious dissenters, engaged in participatory politics, including movements to express popular opinion through petitions. Bradley concludes that the "idea of consent in church matters becomes the basis for the idea of consent in civil matters. Ecclesiastical polity was the primary ground for political radicalism among orthodox and heterodox alike" (139).

*Party and secondary association.* At the dawn of the nineteenth century, the legitimation of associational solidarity remained on less than fully secure ground. Elements of an ideology of association were well established in public rhetoric: the whole of society could be referred to as an association and a larger associational solidarity abstracted from the concrete institutions of family and religion; the solidarity of individually chosen subgroups could be protected in the religious realm by the rhetoric of tolerance; and at the center of this rhetorical field lay a concept of free deliberation that called for mutual consultation as a means of finding common grounds for the public good. Still, neither republican fondness for civic virtue nor Locke's liberalism could stomach interests united into factions without blanching at the thought of the inherent evil of partial community. The public interest was indivisible, whether conceived as republican consensus or the plenary authority of the people, who, however private their individual interests, form governments to protect the public good.

The first amendment fell short of endorsing freedom of association as such. Not until the twentieth century did the Supreme Court strengthen the constitutional protection of the associational and organizational means of "speaking and assembling," but even the Court's late and oblique endorsement of interest-group liberalism must be seen as an extension of an earlier discussion-centered liberalism, which started from the concept of autonomous public deliberation regarding the common good.[21] Public deliberation is the social end protected by such means as free speech, assembly, and petition – means that imply the differentiation of solidarity in a body of citizens rather than in an order of ascribed statuses. "Discussion" has retained its rhetorical sway as a bridging term between social integration and adaptive diversity.

Despite liberal recognition of the practical and moral value of *freedom* within a deliberative *community*, concern for the *public* interest taken together with the notion that *individuals* are the bearers of rights creates tensions that complicate legitimation for the representation of social groups with special, differentiated interests. This problem was nowhere more evident than in the theoretical embarrassment of the creators of the first political parties, who established *de facto* parties even while denying that they were supporting such heresy. Studies of the early American Congresses indicate that divisions occurred from the outset, but none dared call the nascent groups who shared ideological commitments and tended to vote together "parties" (Hoadley 1986). "Party" and "faction" were synonymous and both stood for less than the whole public interest, as the root word "part" suggests. The participants were trapped in a rhetorical system that knew only one language for legitimizing opposition to a regime. The regime must be charged with failure to represent the public interest of the whole people. The strength of the lingering republican tradition is apparent in struggles of Madison and Jefferson to create justifications for organizing opposition to the policies of the administration. Even when Madison first attempted to move to the explicit language of party in 1792, he resorted to the notion that legitimate parties must stand for the whole people against the bad advice of advocates of special interests (Elkins and McKitrick 1993, 263–70). This was, of course, another version of the seventeenth- and eighteenth-century English oppositional rhetoric of court and country.

Eventually, with the rise of a party system, full-scale legitimation of party competition emerged, and parties were accepted as coalitions of interests. Nevertheless, the heritage of court and country remained, and yet remains, in that even groups representing their own best interests must enter into a rhetorical arena in which they are required to show that their proposals for public policy meet the test of public interest. The echoes of eighteenth-century rhetoric can be heard today in accusatory references to "special interests," in references to people "inside the beltway" as a contemporary metaphorical equivalent of a court out of touch with the country, and in justification of political proposals in the name of what the "people of America" want.

*The elements of modern solidarity.* By the early nineteenth century, the principal elements of modern solidarity were in place in the Anglo-American republics. Some were still contested, and their genealogy remains contested among those who wish to create historical rhetorics to raise questions as to how well society lives up to its associational ideals. The means were in place to define the state as the creation of an association of citizens and governmental bodies as agents of this association. The ancient idea of the public good was reborn as the very purpose of government and public opinion its ultimate governing voice. Public opinion was understood to be the opposite of deference, for it is properly formed through the open deliberation of free citizens. The associational means of deliberation were instituted and legitimized in the form of freedoms of speech, assembly, and petitions which were clearly conceived as participatory means of associating persons of like interests and views. Political parties and interest groups formed. Lobbying in the name of associated groups was legitimized by a framework of rhetorical norms requiring justification of private interests in the service of the public good. The complex of associative solidarity was not conceived as a purely instrumental means of freeing individuals from all social constraints. The pivotal role of deliberation in creating associational ties and collectively created policies implies, as an end in its own right, the emergence of societies that can make themselves.

Liberal thought conceives self-creating, self-regulating societies as founded on persuasion, but persuasion need not always start from scratch, renouncing the mobilization and coalescence of existing solidarities. On the contrary, it is presumed that this is precisely how larger associational solidarities are forged. Indeed, it is the growing separation of persuasion from the social organization of solidarity that makes problematic the methods of persuasion utilized in the New Public, techniques designed to appeal to manipulable individual attitudes rather than to attach citizens to likely allies and to collective support for programs of public action.

Neither Parsons nor Habermas sees an unbridgeable gap between liberal rights and civic virtue. Parsons did not confront this issue as such, but his whole system of thought is constructed to avoid such false dichotomies. For Parsons, all social systems are normatively regulated. Systems of norms create rights, and the same system that creates rights also regulates their meaning and use. Freedom can only exist within a system of institutionalized norms that socialize individuals to adhere to social values and obligations – to be virtuous, as it were. Habermas directly confronts the current conflict between liberal and republican conceptions of democracy and "reconciles the two sides by taking elements of both" and, through discourse theory, "putting them together in a new way" (Habermas 1994).

Discourse plays a role in Habermas' work comparable to the role of norms in Parsonian thought. If liberal rights are created by a discursively legitimated legal system, and civic commitment is played out in discursive conversations, then the discourse ethic both justifies and integrates the civic activities of democracy.

Neither Parsons nor Habermas provide fully adequate tools for comprehending the New Public and its problems. Neither could countenance the domination of public communication by professional experts who seek instrumental ends unconstrained by civic virtue or liberal communicative ideals, but neither employs an adequate concept of influence. Parsons' optimistic faith in the normative force of status-based influence understates the chronic inflation of influence by professional persuaders who are not truly professional in Parsons' sense. On the other hand, Habermas' standards for discourse are so high as to make fully discursive influence an unattainable goal, even in the procedural democracy he now advocates. Borrowing Habermas' phrase, perhaps it is possible to "reconcile the two sides by taking elements of both and putting them together in a new way." Parsons' emphasis on signals of credibility leads me to the notion of tokens, and Habermas' emphasis on interpersonal understanding leads to the notion of the *redemption* of tokens. The following chapters on the institutions of the New Public attribute the weak integrative capacity of influence in the New Public to inadequate forums for discursive redemption of rhetorical tokens.

# PART III

## The New Public

# 7

# The emergence of the New Public: advertising, market research, and public relations

The rise of the New Public could be recounted as a tale of Enlightenment betrayed and rationality perverted by good intentions gone awry. There is some merit in this ironic interpretation. Public opinion polling can be traced to late nineteenth-century British surveys of poverty by researchers motivated by hopes for reform (Abrams 1951). Market research was promoted by people who sincerely believed that increasing consumption was an essential means for ensuring prosperity in a late capitalist economy. Some of the earliest lobbying in pre-revolutionary America was conducted on behalf of the religious liberties of American left-wing Protestants through friendly, mutually beneficial exchanges between parliamentarians and British dissenters representing their American brethren who, in a colonial situation, were without representation of their own. Later, in the nineteenth century, mass lobbying began in the United States in the name of legislating general rights for groups of people – initially veterans – who had until then been required to pursue redress individually, seeking the personal patronage of legislators powerful enough to secure private bills for them. The electoral reforms of the progressive movement, including the direct primary, were directed against the party bosses. Reforms were designed to promote democratic aims, but they helped undermine political parties and thus contributed to creating the vacuum that was ultimately filled by political consultants.

### The rationalization of persuasion

Whatever the immediate aims of the creators of the New Public, the dominant principle governing their means was the rationalization of persuasion. The pioneers of the movement sought effective means of persuasion based on research on audiences and the organization of systematic campaigns. The rationalization of persuasion transforms influence by altering the character of its tokens. When persuasion becomes entirely instrumental, its techniques governed by the criterion of effectiveness, the warrants of sincerity that allow audiences to extend credit to their persuaders are undermined. There is no longer a presumption that persuaders' tokens will be redeemed on demand. On the contrary, the strategies employed by the new breed of expert communicators are designed to avoid confrontations that would require serious elaboration of their claims. In consequence, influence becomes inflated in the sense that it lacks what I have called "relational backing." Influence comes to be based not on conversation but on token appeals to the general predispositions of the audience, which does not build commitment to common cause. Accordingly, the "system backing" of influence is also neglected.

*The prehistory of the New Public.* Expert communication is not an invention of recent decades, nor is concern over the distorting effects of communication for hire a modern phenomenon. Socrates' critique of the teachers of rhetoric is the prototype of attacks on instrumental approaches to communication that aim to win, not to seek enlightenment through deliberation. Primitive versions of virtually every element of the New Public preceded the full-blown domination of expert communication that burgeoned and matured in the 1970s. For example, in 1903, Rowntree Chocolate began placing sample packets of their Elect brand cocoa in British homes. Influenced by social surveys begun in England by Charles Booth and others in the last decades of the nineteenth century, Joseph Rowntree authorized the deliverers of the samples to administer survey questionnaires to the recipients (Goodall 1986).[1] Market research is the principal historical root and the current core of instrumentally rationalized public communication, but Rowntree's early entree into the genre is an isolated harbinger, not a paradigmatic beginning. Modern market research reached Britain in the 1930s as an import from the United States after new methods for assessing markets and marketing had became prominent on the American scene in the 1920s. Despite Rowntree's early experiments, *systematic* use of marketing strategies guided by *rational research* programs did not follow in the wake of his efforts. Rationalized market research did not begin to take hold until valid sampling techniques for surveys were established, and this development was stimulated less by trends internal to marketing than by pressures to improve the accuracy of public opinion polling following the famous debacle of the Literary Digest poll predicting that Roosevelt would lose the election of 1936 (Abrams, 1951; Lockley, 1974). These events belong to the prehistory of a complex that did not become the New Public as we now know it until marketing research moved beyond selling consumer goods and came to dominate the management of persuasive communication across a broad range of public spheres. Even the export, by professional experts, of rationalized persuasive techniques to political communication, a development that began in California in 1933, when Clem Whitaker and Leone Smith successfully defended the Central Valley Project against a destructive voter initiative sponsored by the Pacific Gas and Electric Company, presaged rather than established the New Public. The employment of political consultants by a limited number of candidates and causes was an important innovation, but it was not until after the 1970s that political consultants were regularly employed in American elections at national, state, and local levels, and later spread to the international scene.

### Advertising: the roots of the New Public

The New Public did not emerge full blown. It grew in increments as each component built upon and reshaped practices already in place to create the system of rationalized, specialized, and professionalized, public communication that defines and dominates the New Public. Advertising was the first component, the root from which the complex grew.

The early professionals in the advertising business did not need Marxist or postmodernist interpreters of late capitalism to tell them that their function within the economy was to create markets for mass consumption equal to the capacities of industry for mass production. They knew their role and welcomed it, and, indeed, used this theory of the historical necessity of advertising to legitimize their enterprise, including the role of advertising in *creating* rather than merely responding to human wants. Earnest Elmo Calkins, in his popular *Business the Civilizer* (1928), justified advertising as a means of educating the public about wants that they did not know they had. Advertising, he claimed, overcomes resistance to progressive change and sells products that have a civilizing effect. This is the mode of thinking that Roland Marchand (1985) has in mind in referring to the founding leaders of advertising in the interwar years as "apostles of modernity," who encouraged the public to believe that "new" means "better" and to accept ceaseless change as the new order of life (Jameson 1991). Yet, as Marchand astutely notes, advertising professionals' assumption of the mission of advocating modern attitudes did not lead advertising consistently along a path predictable from the logic of modernization. The imperatives of success led advertising campaigns to do whatever might increase sales, whether the thematics of the effort were modern or not. If nostalgia sells, use it too.

No simple logic of modernization can account for the development of advertising. The transformation of advertising in the nineteenth century from the circulation of information about products to visual display is better explained by the logic of advertising than the logic of modernity as such. The new advertising that appeared in the first three decades of the twentieth century used appeals to status striving and status fear, employing a rhetoric of association and insinuation (Wouldn't you like to acquire the status of the person displayed in this advertisement?) and a rhetoric of pictorial display that implies rather than argues. Arguments were presented implicitly, which if baldly stated in words would be rejected, even angrily dismissed as offensive. A complicated interplay of technological development of the mass media, the rise of national media in tandem with the rise of national markets, and discoveries in the rhetoric of market persuasion altered conceptions of what counts as legitimate persuasion in the arena of consumption.

These transformations cannot be taken for granted as natural concomitants of economic and technological change, without normative significance, for again and again novel practices were initially opposed in the name of constraints grounded in the ideals of *civic* modernity, ideals more consistent with a civic conception of advertising as providing information for the public rather than stimulating consumers' desires. Before the 1850s, newspaper advertising was sold (in both Great Britain and the United States) first by the year at a common price to all advertisers and later by the "agate square" system. Agate squares were of equal size, enclosing ten to sixteen lines of type depending on the size of the font, and were sold by the number of squares and the number of appearances. Although the new pricing scheme no longer enforced absolute equality among advertisers, it did envision an informational approach to advertising. It constrained the use of illustration and spacious, attention-grabbing displays. When in response to pleas from larger advertisers, editors tried to sell larger spaces, smaller advertisers complained that they were not treated equally. The agate square system did not break down until 1853, when American advertisers, imitating novelties they had observed in British newspapers, achieved extraordinary public attention by merely bending the rules, repeating identical messages over a whole page, or spelling out longer messages down columns of contiguous squares (Boorstin 1973, 138–45). The success of this tactic sealed the fate of the agate square, but the long tenure of schemes of enforced equality among advertisers should be well noted, for it suggests the early strength of concepts of public communication deriving from ideals of information-based persuasion and level playing fields for competition among ideas.

Eighty years later the emergence of broadcasting again challenged historic conceptions of public communication, this time the appropriate boundary between the public and the private spheres. Radio seemed an intrusive media that would bring commercial advertisement uninvited into the home. Some argued that radio should be commercial free and devoted to cultural enrichment and public information. In the early years of radio a compromise developed around the institution of sponsorship. Businesses paid for and lent their names to cultural programs for public relations rather than directly advertising their products, a practice with visible if vestigial remains in the form of the Texaco opera broadcasts and the Hallmark Hall of Fame (Marchand 1985). Although this mode of sponsorship quickly turned away from exclusive attention to cultural programs and allowed hard-sell commercials, the regime of sponsorship required corporations to take responsibility for the quality and acceptability of programming in a way that the sale of advertising time by the second does not.

Paid testimonials – celebrity endorsements that we now take for granted – provide a third example of an innovation initially opposed as contrary to the norms of public discourse. Originally opposed by a substantial fraction of the industry, including influential trade publications and several major agencies, paid endorsements became even more controversial following the appearance of a cigarette commercial in which a celebrated sea captain, whose courageous actions had recently saved many lives, attributed his coolness in a dangerous situation to smoking Lucky Strikes. Outraged opponents of paid endorsement claimed that such tactics undermine the credibility of advertising, presumably because monetary payment for endorsement is obviously inconsistent with the premises of public influence. Walter Resor of J. Walter Thompson, the agency responsible for the offending advertisement, defended it by insisting that advertising must be true to its own logic, the logic of mass persuasion. If the mass audience can only relate to the larger social scene through personal identification with celebrities, then celebrity endorsement is a necessary part of modern advertising (Pease 1958). Resor's view ultimately prevailed. Without permanent damage to the institutional status of advertising, audiences accepted endorsements as another informational short cut.

Throughout the period of its maturation, the advertising business struggled for legitimacy and social status, trying to shake off the legacy of the inflated claims of early patent medicine advertising with its connotations of selling snake oil. The rapid growth of advertising in the 1920s raised the specter of a public drowning in deception and misinformation and diverted from attention to matters of civic concern by the saturation of public space by commercial promotion. Again, novel practices of mass persuasion were resisted in the name of norms of a civic order founded on the ideals of modernity. The domination of public space by commercial selling, unconstrained by regulative norms that, in the name of rational discussion, would prevent misrepresentation and demand two-sided presentations of controversial issues, does not conform to the ideals of influence and persuasion as envisioned by the original enlightened champions of a modern realm of public discourse.

The first wave of the critique of advertising reached a peak in the writings of Stuart Chase and F. J. Schlink (1927), whose work led to the formation of the American consumer movement and to the founding of such groups as Consumer Research and Consumer's Union, whose programs included independent testing and publishing information from a noncommercial perspective – *forums*, as it were, for two-sided discourse. The advertising business defended itself by adopting its habitual posture as a progressive provider of information with its own niche in the legitimate marketplace of public persuasion, but this line of argument did not achieve sophisticated, rational expression until economists (and the research departments of advertising agencies) discovered the apologetic power of the new economics of information.

*Justifying advertising.* In the fall of 1971, the Federal Trade Commission held hearings on then current American advertising practices. Twenty six witnesses, primarily advertising executives and publishers, testified on behalf of the Association of National Advertisers and the American Association of Advertising Agencies. Harold Demsetz, a noted economist, was also among the witnesses, and he contributed an apologetic statement that can be considered paradigmatic for the defense of advertising in the era of the New Public.[2]

Demsetz framed advertising as an instance of economic specialization and argued that an intensive division of labor requires a great deal of communication. Both producers and consumers must communicate information about products and prices, but information is not a free good. Information is not free to consumers, for they must expend time, attention, and effort to gather it. Since they cannot afford excessive efforts to become well informed, consumers must satisfice rather than maximize information. Mass communication provides efficient, relatively low-cost channels for providing information to consumers. Advertising provides just the sort of abbreviated, easily digested information that consumers need. Moreover, advertising encourages consumers to put their trust in brand and company names, which economizes information and, in turn, requires producers to sustain the quality of their goods in order to maintain that trust.

At the same hearing, A. A. Achenbaum, then Vice President of the

J. Walter Thomson Agency, defending against charges that advertising does not fulfill its communicative function because it is deceptive and misleading, restated the case for advertising on linguistic and philosophic grounds. Complementing Demsetz' positivist approach, Achenbaum presented an implicitly antipositivist argument to the effect that persuasive advertising practice is not necessarily deceptive because facts and values are not separable. Information is not necessarily cognitive. The presentation of facts has an inescapable rhetorical dimension and facts come to have communicable meaning only when set in an attitudinal context (Nicosia 1974, 256–62). In the arena of persuasive communication, it is difficult to demonstrate that advertising messages misrepresent or mislead any more than rhetorical discourse generally. We can properly say that the New Public has matured, its prehistory at an end, when advertising, the model for rationalized, instrumental persuasion, has appropriated a variety of modes of social science not only to construct successful sales messages but to justify its own project as well. Along the way, professional ideologists managed to create legitimating frames consistent with the informational ideals of civic culture.

Legitimating advertising requires the professionals who produce it to clothe their vocation as service in the public interest. In 1925, President Herbert Hoover spoke to advertising professionals in terms entirely consistent with Calkins' estimate of the civilizing nobility of his profession. Addressing the Associated Advertising Clubs of the World, Hoover congratulated his audience:

> You have devised an artful ingenuity in forms and mediums of advertising . . . In the past, wish, want and desire were the motive forces in economic progress. Now you have taken over the job of creating desire. In economics . . . desire in turn creates demand, and from demand we create production, and thence around the cycle we land with increased standards of living.          (Quoted in Leach 1993, 375.)

Lest we imagine that Hoover's words were distinctively Republican, spoken by a former secretary of commerce known for his activist, governmental promotion of commercial activity, Franklin Roosevelt said that a high standard of living is impossible without "the spreading of the knowledge of higher standards by means of advertising," and across the Atlantic, Winston Churchill proclaimed that "advertising nourishes the consuming powers of men" (Ogilvy 1963, 150).

Public homage to advertising marked the emergent establishment of a system of public persuasion in which professional experts in influence dominate public channels of communication in civil society. Advertising (along with the rise of the mass media) was the first institutional realm to display this process of differentiation. When Hoover and others publicly recognized the existence of professional advertisers as a new force in society, they were acknowledging the significance of recently formed institutions. Specialized advertising agencies were no longer limited to an intermediary role in placing merchants' copy in media outlets, but themselves organized persuasive campaigns of influence, employing professional copywriters, artists, designers, and researchers. "Account executives" coordinated campaigns and articulated the efforts of the agencies with the aims of their clients. Participants in the enterprise formed professional associations and supported trade magazines, and American universities began to include courses in advertising in their curricula. The collective efforts of this array of specialized occupations and groups played a part in both promoting and defending the use of advertising, accelerating the growth and importance of the institution. As advertising grew, it gradually gave rise to a new force in the world of rationalized persuasion: market research.

### Market research

*Rationalized advertising campaigns and market research.* In 1879, the advertising firm of Ayer and Son undertook a systematic, if hurried, market survey on behalf of a manufacturer of threshing equipment. Working feverishly over three days and nights, Ayer documented the quantity of threshable grain produced in the US on a county-by-county basis (Hower, 1949). While this survey, the first accomplished by an advertising agency, might not at first glance seem a remarkable achievement, it signaled the beginning of fundamental changes in the advertising business. Agencies had been primarily responsible for placing copy supplied by advertisers in newspapers and magazines. The economic rationale of the enterprise was based on either obtaining space for their clients at minimum cost to the client or at maximum profit for media outlets. The Ayer agency defined their role as assisting the advertiser, not the media, and began to identify their mission as not just placing advertisements but mounting *planned campaigns.* Once this became the aim of the agency and the means by which they demonstrated the value of their services, "rational" advertising meant planned advertising, and planning must start with systematic knowledge about customers, beginning with information about who and where they are.

Market research had roots in academia as well as in commercial life. Academic studies of marketing and advertising began at the turn of the century, with courses in marketing (usually called "distribution") offered at ten American universities by 1910. Academic books on marketing research began to appear in 1916, led by Percival White's *Marketing Analysis* in 1921 which insisted that markets were measurable (Bartels 1976). Commercial advertising and the academic teaching of marketing formed a mutually supportive relationship from the beginning, each deriving prestige from the other. Commercial advertising was attracted to the scientific claims of the new academic field as well as the prestige of the universities that sponsored it. On the academic side, involvement in the commercial world buttressed business professors' claims to practical knowledge.

By the late nineteenth century, science and engineering had acquired great prestige, and institutions sought status prestige by associating themselves with the progressive forces of applied scientific reason. Market research was to distribution what scientific management was to production. Drawing on the methods of science and engineering to further the rationalization of business activity could not stop with improving the efficiency of the productive process. Marketing, too, must be placed on sound rational principles. Broadly considered, marketing includes several components that appear well adapted for rational management: the location of customers and distribution points, transportation, management of sales forces, policies regarding customer credit, and the design of products with utility for consumers lent themselves to applications of the ideas of Frederick Taylor, the chief apostle of "scientific management," a rationalizing movement that was soon extended to the process of persuasion. Advertising agencies promoted themselves by appeals to the rationality of science, some advocates going so far as to call advertising "consumption engineering." By the late 1930s, agencies sold their capacities to prospective clients by boasting of the excellence of their research departments.

On the academic side, both the prestige and the utility of positive science and engineering were easily applied to the study of production, but distribution and marketing also drew on a different form of positivism, the scientific, putatively objective, German approach to historical study that lay in the background of institutional economics as advocated by John R. Commons and Richard T. Ely. Only detailed studies of the actual practices of distributors and consumers and their complex institutional arrangements could comprehend the modes of distribution in vast and powerful modern economies. It was in this spirit that Paul Cherington (a disciple of Taylor) formed the Harvard Bureau of Business Research in 1911 and undertook exhaustive studies of the shoe industry in New England. Henry C. Taylor (a student of Ely) led a similar research team at the University of Wisconsin in 1913 in extensive studies of the distribution of cheese (Jones and Monieson 1990).

In the meantime, advertising practice began to move well beyond Ayer's early market survey, employing demographic techniques to obtain more refined knowledge of customers. Later, purely demographic information about potential customers was supplemented by audience research, which was first directed to learning which particular media reached which customers, then to research regarding which advertisements caught people's attention, and then to studies of motives for buying and the effects of various sorts of appeals. When the virtues of random sampling were recognized, more refined survey research began to play a larger role. Specialized research companies were formed, enterprises dedicated to objectivity and unburdened by loyalties to particular products. Academic values – faith in facts and in objective research – filtered into the advertising profession as academicians moved into important positions in commercial market research, beginning with the hiring of John Watson, the father of behavioral psychology, by J. Walter Thomson in 1921 and Cherington's appointment as director of research at the same agency in 1922. The appointment in 1932 of George Gallup, then a young faculty member at Northwestern, by Young and Rubicam had a more important long-term influence, for he led the way to more careful and serious use of polling techniques and other research devices designed to reveal the minds and habits of consumers. The impetus behind all these developments was predicated on faith in the value of rational planning in marketing – on *the rationalization of instrumental persuasion.*

*The differentiation of market research.* Demand for objectivity was a driving organizational force in the differentiation of market research. Objectivity was highly valued in the early years of market research, both for its presumed effectiveness and because of the prestige of science, but advertisers did not fully trust the purveyors of market data. For a time, the media played the leading role in market research. Magazine publishers, beginning with the appointment of Charles Coolidge Parlin by Curtis Publishing in 1911, established research departments early in the century. This movement was particularly strong among the publishers of women's magazines, who wanted to know more about their audiences and how to reach them. Publishers, though, had an interest in conducting studies that would convince advertisers of the relative merits of their own magazines as effective vehicles for advertisement. Advertisers did not find publishers' own studies entirely credible and so turned increasingly to research performed by advertising agencies, whose interests were more aligned with their own, and who could make strong selling points of their professionalism and objectivity. Yet even advertising agencies were not entirely independent, for they had an interest in demonstrating the effectiveness of their campaigns. The problem of reliable objectivity opened a niche for independent market research organizations (Waller-Zuckerman 1989). The formation, in 1914, of the Audit Bureau of Circulation to establish reliable information on the distribution of magazines, whose circulation had been puffed by publishers, represents a first order prototype for the large-scale independent studies that began to dominate market research in the 1930s. By the mid 1930s, market research became dominated by permanently established projects for continuous measurement of carefully drawn samples of consumers or distributors, with emphases on actual behavior wherever possible. A. C. Nielsen's panel studies established this new genre. His Food-Drug Index compiled and audited actual sales figures for a large sample of retailers, and his later Radio Index recorded actual radio listening by installing electronic equipment in the receivers of a sample of households (Nielson 1951). Nielson's approach to objectivity through audited behavioral measures and disciplined sampling methods was expensive. Such studies were beyond the reach of any one firm's marketing budget or any advertising agency's account for a single client, but multiple clients could subscribe to a research project to gain access to the putatively reliable data and trustworthy expertise of such specialized research companies as A. C. Nielson, Crossley, Inc., Cherington, Roper and Wood, and Market Research Corporation of America. Advertising agencies began to purchase much of their research, both standardized data available from permanent projects and special purpose studies by independent, specialized firms. Because advertising agencies used the promise of rigorous, effective, and objective research to promote both the legitimacy of the profession and the prowess of their firms, their claims were often exaggerated. Were their public relations efforts taken at face value, the actual role of market research during the formative years of modern advertising would be overestimated.[3] Nevertheless, as imaginative and effective research techniques improved, so did the practical effects of market research.

*George Gallup as prototype.* The impact of George Gallup is a particularly telling illustration. Gallup, who is now remembered as an influential survey researcher and founder of the Gallup Polls, began his career in market research and worked for fifteen years with Young and Rubicam. His career provides a remarkable example of Converse's (1987) thesis that market research was the immediate forebear of public opinion research and also demonstrates the important practical consequences of market research in its mature phase.[4] His 1928 doctoral dissertation in psychology on "A New Technique for Measuring Reader Interest in Newspapers" preceded stints of academic employment, including a year at Northwestern

University before Raymond Rubicam, himself a strong advocate of market research, brought him to Young and Rubicam in 1932 (Wood 1962b). Rubicam became interested in Gallup's potential for advertising research on the basis of two studies that Gallup had begun while still employed in academic institutions. The first of these studies was based on work undertaken during his tenure at Drake University. He reported that adult readers of the Des Moines Register preferred reading the comic strips over even the main news stories of the day and that interest in the comics extended across social classes. This widely circulated finding had a powerful affect on advertisers, who concluded that the public taste should not be overestimated (Marchand 1985, 110–11). Gallup's next studies showed that while advertisers tried to appeal primarily to the economy and efficiency of their wares and that sex and vanity tied for ninth and last place as bases for advertiser's appeals, female readers most frequently remembered ads appealing to sex and vanity and male readers best remembered appeals to sex and to the quality of products. The apparent power of sex appeal did not go unnoticed among Gallup's professional readers, nor did his continuing research under the aegis of Young and Rubicam have the relatively weak impact of much of the work of research departments in other mainline agencies. Agency officials regularly huddled around his latest findings, debating their implications for advertising practice and developing specific plans to exploit his insights (Fox 1984, 138–9).

Gallup's successful challenge to the Literary Digest poll in 1936 further enhanced his reputation. His analysis of the Digest's plans for gathering straw votes to predict the Roosevelt-Landon election, led Gallup to announce, before it was even taken, that the digest poll would be incorrect. He predicted, contra the Digest, that Roosevelt would win. When Gallup's predictions proved correct, his achievement became paradigmatic in the Kuhnian sense; his techniques for questioning survey participants and his sampling methods were viewed as exemplary for all who would claim to assess the public temper.[5] He did not hesitate to use his new prestige to promote his market research, including his entry into audience research for the film industry in 1938, a project that dramatically prefigured the shape of the New Public (Ohmer 1991).

Organized as Audience Research Inc. (ARI), a firm loosely affiliated with Young and Rubicam, Gallup and his associates applied techniques that he had developed over the previous decade to the study of film audiences. He devised a means of drawing samples that mirrored the movie-going population and began to gather basic data on the relative draw of titles, storylines, and stars. Soon after, he started pretesting ongoing film productions, giving clients advice on particular titles, stories, and promotional plans.

During the decade of the forties, ARI conducted over 5,000 such surveys, much to the discomfiture of directors, screen writers, actors, and other film creators, who saw their artistic authority diminish as their work became subject to review and revision on the authority of outsiders who claimed scientific capacities to decide what the public wanted. This conflict intensified when, beginning in 1944, ARI added preview screening to their methods of audience research.

Preview screening had long been a fixture on the Hollywood scene, but ARI set out to replace *ad hoc*, multipurpose screenings, whose audiences often included friends and allies of the film makers, or people selected on no particular planned basis. Gallup presented screenings to groups chosen by the same sampling techniques he had developed to draw samples of typical moviegoers. Audiences were not only questioned about their responses but were provided with Hopkins Televoting Machines and asked to register their reactions continuously. Moment-by-moment graphs of average viewer interest were then used to recut and edit films. We see here a full-blown prototype of the institutions of communication in the New Public. Communicators, in this case film makers, were not permitted to display their product directly to the public and then allow ordinary processes of audience formation and reaction to determine the public verdict. Rather, in the name of rationalizing the process of assessing public acceptance, authoritative experts used supposedly scientific techniques to predict acceptability in advance and to adjust messages to secure positive responses and avoid unwelcome surprises. Gallup's techniques and the institutions that developed around them place the New Public in perspective. The public I designate as "new" is not just new in the formal sense that communicative expertise is more differentiated.[6] A fundamental question of social organization advances to the foreground: in these new differentiated institutions of market studies and pretesting, who speaks for the public? Who are its prolocutors?

### Public relations

Early in the century, specialists in publicity began to establish themselves as members of the new profession of public relations, the third institutional complex, together with advertising and market research, through which the institutions of the New Public became differentiated from traditional politics and journalism. In 1900, a trio of journalists established the Publicity Bureau, an agency devoted to producing and placing newspaper stories favorable to their clients, including Harvard University, which provided a source of considerable prestige for their fledgling business. The firm's primary clients were utilities and railroads, sectors of the economy under critical attack in the progressive era. The Publicity Bureau lasted only a decade, but by 1904 Ivy Lee, the renowned and controversial leader of the early public relations industry, formed the first of his several partnerships devoted to what was still referred to as "publicity" work. By 1926, ten public relations firms were in active practice on behalf of major American corporations (Cutlip 1994).

The ambiguous term "publicity" is indicative of the incomplete, amorphous differentiation of specialized persuasive roles during the prehistory of the New Public. Even today, specialized roles within the New Public overlap, but in the first three decades of the century, the very term "publicity" was so ambiguous as to create difficulties for the entrepreneurs who were trying to define their new role as links between business and the public. The terms "publicity" and "advertising" were used interchangeably as synonyms for dissemination of information to the public, and both terms were used to describe activites that would now be called public relations (Raucher 1968). Moreover "publicity" could have positive or negative connotations. "Publicity stunts" seek only to make some organization, person, or product more well known, yet "publicity" also refers to disclosure to the open public view that stems corruption, a usage that reflects the classic ideals of the civic public. The term "publicity agent" implicitly draws an ironic contrast between the agent's actual devotion to advertising and the increasingly degraded ideals of honest public debate, yet publicity agents could also claim to serve these very ideals by honest disclosures in the public interest. The new developing specialists in the field of publicity sought a new, unambiguously positive name for their work and began to promote the term "public relations" and to refer to their role as "public relations counsel."

In seeking professional status for their work, the early advocates of public relations proposed six principles to guide practice in the new field: the use of *specialized knowledge* about the public; *honest representations* to the public; *two-way communication* between the public and the client, so that clients know what the public wants as well as how to speak to it; *status as counselor to the client* rather than as a mere conduit for whatever the client proclaims; *commitment to the public interest;* and *professional organization* to establish basic requirements for training and accreditation and to create and enforce professional codes of conduct. These were, of course, idealized images of what professional public relations should be rather than accounts of what it was, and to this day the vision of the founders has not been realized.

The professionalization of public relations practice, including the establishment of national associations to set standards and codes, has been slow and deficient. After false starts and a long period of endemic internal conflict, the Public Relations Society of America (PRSA), was finally created in 1948. PRSA has created a code of ethics for practitioners and established an accreditation program, but the code has proven difficult to enforce, and accreditation remains voluntary. Realizing the ideals of the founders has proven difficult in part because the early leaders did not always take their own advice. Ivy Lee was an early advocate of honesty and full disclosure, ideals that derive from the civic concept of publicity as bringing matters to the public for judgment, but the conduct that earned for Lee the epithet "paid liar" from Carl Sandburg (Raucher 1968, 28) did not promote the cause of professionalization.[7] Current professional and academic journals regularly include comment and debate on the question of truth in public relations, and consensus seem to have crystallized on the idea that truthfulness requires only avoiding blatant and knowing misrepresentation. Public relations professionals are not responsible for balanced, objective presentations, or even for scrupulous avoidance of misleading implications, for their role is advocacy before the "court" of public opinion. They are no more bound by detached, disinterested approaches to the facts than attorneys who argue on behalf of clients in courts of law. Providing selected truths in support of clients is entirely appropriate; it is up to the other side to present its own truths. Public relations advocacy conducted in accord with this concept of honesty implies a framework for a species of objectivity, one that does establish broad boundaries for appropriate argument, but it does not meet the standard of *disclosure* as contemplated in the civic ideal of bringing the public's business to the public's view.

The idea of two-way communication is a pivotal element of the ideology of public relations. As espoused by Ivy Lee and Edward Bernays early in the century and advocated in professional models of public relations ever since, two-way communication requires public relations professionals to represent the public to their client as well as transmitting the client's message to the public. Several elements of the founders' agenda for professional status turn on this idea. It gives the professional an area of expertise – the public, its organization and perspectives, and the means for assessing its opinion. Obligation to represent the public would give practitioners a degree of insulation from complete domination by the client, a measure of independence grounded on the notion that professional public relations experts are bound to work in the public interest. Independence, in turn, supports professional capacity to communicate accurately and honestly. Yet the ideal of two-way communication, for all its centrality and impact, has never been fully institutionalized, as least in anything approximating a symmetrical version in which both directions of communication would assume equal importance. Public relations experts, whether working in independent agencies or within public relations departments of organizations, are employed to affect public opinion on behalf of the interest of their employers, not to be independent brokers of the public interest, standing between the constituent organizations of society and the interests of the general public.

The fate of the idea that the "public relations counselor" should in some sense represent the public to clients and thus, in this limited sense, represent the public interest effectively summarizes the dilemma and the limitations of professionalization of the field. The Code of Professional Standards for the Practice of Public Relations as promulgated by the PRSA in 1954 states that "A member shall conduct his or her professional life in accord with the public interest." What, then, is the public interest? Does the public interest in health require a member of the PRSA to urge full disclosure by tobacco manufacturers of all the evidence in their possession regarding the dangers of smoking? This question immediately reveals the rocky terrain of the public sphere in which responsible public advocacy on behalf of private interests is supposed to take place. It is hardly surprising that the PRSA came to define the public interest quite narrowly, ruling that the term "public interest" as used in the code means "respect for and enforcement of the rights guaranteed by the Constitution of the United States of America." In short, the public interest to which public relations professionals are committed is an interest in rights liberalism, including freedom of speech. Tobacco manufacturers can say whatever they want, so long as it is not downright illegal. By contrast, public accountants have a more meaningful and definable relation to the public interest, and disclosure is at the heart of it. The public has an interest in accurate information regarding the investments they are invited to make, and public accountants cannot participate in misrepresentation or certify financial statements that fail to meet approved standards. In this sense, accountants are not advocates. It is difficult to see how public relations, avowedly engaged in public advocacy to change public opinion, could develop a strong standard of commitment to a comparably broad conception of the public interest.

*The institutionalization and growth of public relations.* Despite the failure of public relations specialists to achieve professional status in the strong sense implied by their preferred model, we cannot conclude that the model has been without effect. Public relations has become institutionalized in American society, and its establishment is manifest in the pervasive influence of its basic conceptions and techniques. Originally animated by concerns within American business that an aroused public might lead to hostile governmental regulation, even public ownership of some types of business, the early public relations movement reflected the growing importance of public opinion. Public relations advocates sought to establish programs for influencing public opinion in order to affect governmental action through garnering public support, but having turned down that road there was no turning back. One can no longer imagine a business tycoon following William Henry Vanderbilt's lead by telling a newspaper reporter, "The public be damned." Having conceded respect for the public and a need to seek public support, experts in public relations were inevitably accorded authoritative status within their special sphere, even if their aspirations to become true counselors rather than paid publicists were not fully accepted by their employers. As practitioners gained knowledge and experience of the means necessary to exercise public influence, professional ideology came to affect their practice, despite their employers' and clients' interests in private gain. They could press for policies of honesty and exposure as necessary means of maintaining the trust on which effective public communication depends. Moreover, when influence moves to the public sphere, its rhetoric, however insincere, requires appeals to universalistic grounds. Public relations specialists cannot argue that pollution is good because it is profitable for the polluter; arguments must be made that the public will not be harmed. Public interests beyond the protection of constitutional rights slip into the rhetorical equation despite the limitations of the PRSA code.

In its simplest sense, "institutionalization" refers to the *establishment* of widespread social practices. Practices become fixed when supported by norms, attached to interests, and embodied in expectations, conventions, and social roles. There is no doubt that public relations are now established in the New Public. Virtually every major corporation in the United States has and is expected to have a public relations department. As the "new institutionalists" shrewdly note, the establishment of new practices does not always depend on their instrumental success (DiMaggio and Powell 1983; Powell and DiMaggio 1991), so we should not assume that public relations units always implement their presumed aims. In some cases, public relations serve purposes internal to organizations – instilling pride among employees or reinforcing the authority of the central core of the organization (Marchand 1987, 1991). Public relations spread by diffusion and imitation, and once widespread, public relations departments became necessary in order to articulate corporate voices in a manner that other organizations can locate and understand. Major trade associations and public interest groups also employ public relations specialists or engage independent agencies, as do public interest organizations that advocate social, civil, and environmental causes. Public relations is, indeed, one of the principal purposes of such groups.

With the growth of corporate public relations departments and independent agencies, the profession has grown in numbers. The PRSA, which had 6,000 members in 1970 had 16,000 in 1995.[8] As independent agencies increase in number, many of them begin to engage in specialized practices. A recent (1994) Service Directory of the PRSA listed firms under eighty-seven specialized headings, some substantive (e.g. health care), some functional (e.g. direct mail, issue management, and crisis management), some both. For example, of forty-two agencies that advertise themselves as specialists in the health care sector, fifteen claim expertise in "governmental relations," that is, political work.

*Rational techniques for public relations.* The use of specialized knowledge about the public is the most fully realized of the five elements in the professional model of public relations. Drawing on methods developed in market research and the study of public opinion, practitioners now claim and use expert knowledge based on research, but even before current methods were fully developed, the first cadre of public relations specialists had learned a great deal about the means of public influence and had articulated their practical knowledge within a theoretical framework that both explained and justified their work.

In 1928, Edward Bernays summarized his views in the *American Journal of Sociology* in an article entitled "Manipulating Public Opinion: the Why and the How." Bernays thought he was using the term "manipulating" in a constructive sense. Someone must take responsibility for integrating and aggregating the diversity of opinion in modern mass societies. Drawing on a long tradition of fear of the tyranny of an unanchored majority, and exploiting liberal optimism about the capacity of truth to prevail in well ordered debate, Bernays proclaimed that "Every man who teaches the public how to ask for what it wants is at the same time teaching the public how to safeguard itself against its own possible tyrannous aggressiveness" (Bernays 1928, 960). Experts in public opinion can provide these lessons for they understand this basic principle: "Public opinion is the power of the group to sway the larger public." In an argument that both reflects his actual practice and remarkably anticipates the social-influence theory of opinion, Bernays describes public opinion as embedded in social groups and transmitted to members of such groups by sources with which they can identify: prestigious leaders and groups that are seen as representing the views of larger categories of people. Public relations practitioners affect public opinion by working with groups and their leaders, creating events where leaders can be seen and heard endorsing desirable views, and even by creating "fronts" from scratch, artificial groups that purport to represent the interests of similarly situated or like-minded people. The latter practice is sometimes said to have originated with Bernays and, whatever its origins, remains a prominent rhetorical strategy in the New Public – a technique sometimes called "astroturf politics" to distinguish it from grassroots efforts. Bernays' vision of public opinion, tainted as it is by questionable practices that he introduced, is still manifest in the aspirations of current practitioners. At the 1993 conference of the PRSA, the chair of the event remarked, "By the year 2250 minorities in the United States will be in the majority. Coordinating pluralism will be the public relations role" (*Public Relations Journal*, January, 1994, 1).

The socially anchored methods introduced in the early days of the craft remain at the base of current practice, but contemporary public relations also appropriates methods of social research brought into the public sphere through marketing studies. As in the case of advertising, this movement has been driven by the rationalization of practice around the concept of planned campaigns. Current texts describe the ideal campaign as highly rationalized and research-driven at every stage (Nolte 1979; Simmons 1990). Nolte presents a sequential model of public relations as proceeding in four stages: first, *inbound communications* are assessed through research on the opinion of relevant publics; second, *campaign planning* addresses how opinion can be affected in beneficial ways; third, *outbound communication* is created in accordance with the plan, pretested as necessary to ensure effectiveness; finally the results of campaigns are appraised through *evaluation research*. It is difficult to gauge how faithfully the costly models found in textbooks are followed in practice, but practitioners must justify their budgets to those who are paying the bills, and this requires indicators of professional quality and measurable results. Systematic evidence is not easily compiled, but there is evidence that rationalization of public relations through research has become the norm. For example, of eighty projects completed by Ketchum Public Relations in 1993, 57 percent included evaluation research, and among a recent survey sample of 725 practitioners, about three quarters reported using survey research and the same proportion reported using focus groups (*Public Relations Journal*, January 1994, 25).

Public relations departments of corporations also undertake continuous behavioral research comparable to the studies that became prominent in market research fifty years ago. Wal-Mart, a company with well known public relations problems, especially in communities that perceive Wal-Mart stores as destructive to traditional downtown districts, has contracted with a research firm to collect all mentions of Wal-Mart in the media and to compile them by sales districts, congressional districts, and the combined districts of key congressional committees. In turn, the management of

Wal-Mart engages in continuous adjustment of their public relations activities in response to changes revealed by their research (Shinkle 1994).[9]

Wal-Mart's systematic, research-based public relations program illustrates rational methods of communication in the New Public. It is to public relations what Gallup's audience research and its contemporary descendants are to advertising and market research. Such methodical, research-based systems of communication are often referred to as "manipulative," especially by their critics, but practitioners modestly deny that they have such awesome capacities. Both are right, depending on what "manipulation" means. The term has connotations of consistent success, and those who try but sometimes fail can deny that they really manipulate; they merely try to persuade. We can avoid this terminological morass by recognizing that professional experts may or may not be able to manipulate, but they can pull communication away from its mooring in and among solidary groups. In the New Public, instrumental influence is dominated by professional practitioners who largely control the channels, forms, and messages of public communication and can therefore set the agenda and terms of public discussion. Chapter 8 continues to outline these features of the New Public, moving on from their origin and development in commercial advertising and corporate public relations to their subsequent application to new professional roles located at the intersection of civil society and the political system – the point at which civil society influences public policy or is dominated by the polity and its allies.

# 8

# Political communication in the New Public

Contemporary political consulting is a direct outgrowth of public relations and the methods of influence developed in advertising and market research. Political advising is as old as politics, and advising about electoral strategies and tactics began with the first mass elections. Andrew Jackson's friend and political associate John Eaton helped shape Jackson's image in 1824 with a campaign biography that "turned a conservative planter and slave holder into the idol of the common man" (Melba Hay in Schlesinger 1994, 94). Eaton promoted Jackson as a man of the people who would restore to public life the virtue implicit in his military leadership (Remini 1981, 75–8). The tradition of republican virtue and its binary oppositions to corruption and loss of liberty was not dead. In 1828, Jackson's campaign operatives mobilized support by organizing public endorsements at staged events by methods not unlike those used in twentieth-century public relations, but Jackson's managers were party loyalists, embedded in the newly emerging party organization of that era, not professional consultants working directly for the candidate and employing the science as well as the lore of campaign management. Full-time professional consultants originally appeared on the political scene a century later to direct a 1933 campaign against a non-party California ballot initiative.

### The rise of political consulting

*The origins of independent campaign management.* The firm of Whitaker and Baxter was the first player in the new political game that transformed so-called "advisers" into authoritative managers of political campaigns. Their story displays in microcosm the dynamics of professional political management. Clem Whitaker was a former newspaper reporter and sometime lobbyist who had established an independent news bureau that supplied political news to eighty California newspapers; his partner Leone Smith, a former newspaper reporter, was the manager of the Chamber of Commerce in a small city in California's Central Valley when she met Baxter in 1933. They began their partnership by leading a successful campaign to defeat a Pacific Gas and Electric (PG&E) sponsored voter initiative that would have crippled the state-managed Central Valley Project, whereupon PG&E, recognizing the talents of their adversaries, offered them a $100,000 retainer to change sides. Whitaker and Baxter accepted and soon after began to offer their services as independent campaign directors to candidates for public office. In California, party organization was in disarray, largely because of the progressive reforms of Governor Hiram Johnson, whose electoral innovations, including open primaries and voter initiatives, opened the door for more direct appeal to the mass populace. Whitaker and Baxter managed the 1934 campaign of George Hatfield for Lieutenant Governor of California but initially kept their distance from the parallel race of Robert Merriam for Governor, which was being managed by the West Coast office of Lord & Thomas, a prominent advertising agency. Engaging Lord & Thomas to run the campaign, rather than leaving it in the hands of the Republican Party, was itself unprecedented, but in the eyes of some participants the situation called for yet more novel measures, not only because of the weakness of the party, but because of their fear of the Democratic candidate (Mitchell 1992).

Merriam's opponent, the noted "muckraking" novelist Upton Sinclair, earned his candidacy by sweeping an open primary. Sinclair's views seemed dangerously extreme to the California establishment, and when the efforts of Lord & Thomas to stop him faltered, Whitaker and Baxter were called to the rescue and entered the campaign as publicists for the California League Against Sinclairism, a nonpartisan front for the Merriam campaign, and began by undertaking a rigorous issue analysis, which is still the starting point for most campaign consultants. Consultants first identify issues that might favorably situate their clients and opponents in relation to public attitudes and opinion. Sinclair, as a prolific author, had committed himself to a large number of positions on social and political issues, often in colorful and hyperbolic terms. Whitaker and Baxter had no difficulty in assembling a large array of statements and quotations that could be used (and in many cases distorted) to discredit Sinclair as a pink-hued radical whose views were far removed from the mainstream of opinion. They commenced a campaign of hard-hitting attack politics, typical of their lifelong aggressive, give-no-quarter style. The film industry entered the fray by producing and distributing short anti-Sinclair films which in retrospect are said to be the earliest models for the television attack commercials that now play a formidable role in elections in America and around the world (Cutlip 1994, 600–1). Sinclair was defeated, and Whitaker and Baxter went on to manage the campaigns of scores of candidates and ballot issues over the next two decades, winning 71 of 75 contests between 1933 and 1955 (Nimmo 1970, 36).

Whitaker and Baxter insisted on complete control of every campaign they managed and invented a device to give the firm leverage to enforce their dominion. The firm established a carefully constructed campaign budget, and in return for a promise to stay within that budget, received a commitment that only Whitaker and Baxter would have authority to spend the funds allocated to them (Nimmo 1970, 61–2). This contractual device was copied by other firms that followed Whitaker and Baxter into this new business arena. The authority of consultants over political discourse is a crucial feature of the contemporary political arena, and that this authority was achieved through stabilizing a budgetary process is a telling indication of the significance of organizational rationalization in creating the New Public. The firm's approach to political consulting also established precedents for other campaign-management tools that are still employed by professional management firms: systematic issue research to position the candidate, media saturation, direct mail, opinion surveys), and grassroots organization from above.

*The growth of political consulting.* Whitaker and Baxter's early successes may have been facilitated by a lack of serious competition in the business of independent campaign management. The new niche did not fill quickly, but with the rise of television and technical improvement in opinion polling, professional campaign management began to expand very rapidly. Only a few firms entered the arena before 1950, but by 1957 Heard (1960, 417) counted forty-one public relations firms offering full campaign services. By 1972 about sixty firms identified themselves as in the business of campaign management, and another 200 agencies offered some services to political campaigns as a part of their business (Rosenbloom 1973, 50). Rosenbloom has also traced the growth of political consulting as measured by the number of campaigns using professional management services rather than the number of firms engaged in this business. The rapid growth of professional management between the 1950s and the late 1960s is apparent in his data. Comparing the period 1952–1957, the beginning of the age of televised campaigns, with 1964–1969, the period when poll-based management fully matured, the number of campaigns employing full-service management increased greatly at every level of elected government: in presidential campaigns, including primaries, by 622 percent; in US Senate campaigns, by 722 percent; in campaigns for the House of Representatives, by

842 percent; in statewide races by 626 percent: in local contests, by 298 percent. The raw numbers for 1964 and 1968 are particularly striking. In 1964, professional services were provided to 280 campaigns; in 1968 the number rose to 658 (Rosenbloom 1973, 51–4).

In the last decade, political consulting has flourished, expanding on the base established in the 1960s, as professional political management became the prevailing norm. *Political Resource Directory* listed approximately 900 firms in 1989; by 1994, the number had increased to 2,787 (*Political Resource Directory* 1994). The *Directory* also lists firms by the various specialized services they provide. A summary overview of these services and the number of providers of each type provides impressive evidence of the range, differentiation, and availability of professional political assistance. The *Directory* lists 698 "general consultants," who offer advice across a broad range of problems, but do not provide full-service management of campaigns; another 332 agencies do offer hands-on management of the full range of activities involved in modern campaigns. Many firms offer services in one or more of several specialties: media consulting, 391; advertising, public relations, and press relations, 358; research, targeting, and analysis, 292; fund raising, 284; production video, 249; polling, 241; direct mail, 240; petition and campaign issue management, 220; bumper stickers and yard signs, 202; computing, 174; telephone voter contact, 174; media placement, 146. Smaller numbers of firms offer newsletters and directories, financial reporting services, legal services, campaign photography, graphics, news clipping and TV monitoring, speech writing and consulting on public speaking, databases, campaign software, voter list brokerage and rental, and logistic services.[1]

*The role of polling in managed campaigns.* I take 1968, the last year for which Rosenbloom compiled data on the large and rapidly increasing number of campaigns employing professional management, to be an important turning point. The Nixon–Humphrey presidential contest of that year was chronicled in Joe McGinniss' (1969) well known *The Selling of the President.* McGinniss portrayed Nixon's campaign as a successful commercial marketing job on the part of Nixon's managers. Most observers believe that McGinniss' account somewhat exaggerates the capacity of advertising alone to turn elections. Moreover political marketing through extensive advertising was established long before 1968. In any event, the campaign of 1968 was a watershed in another crucial respect: the unprecedented importance of public opinion polling.

In the early days of professional campaign management, firms like Whitaker and Baxter lacked capacity to undertake reliable polls and to use them strategically and tactically to guide campaigns. By 1968 polling fully occupied center stage in the drama of campaign management. Shortly after the election, Mendelsohn and Crespi (1970, 164) succinctly summarized the place of opinion polling in that year's presidential contest:

In the 1968 Presidential election poll data undoubtedly comprised the single type of information used by political leaders to evaluate candidate strength and weakness within different sectors of the public to determine the effectiveness of alternative campaign issues, and to assess the progress (or lack thereof) being made in campaigns. Decisions about over-all strategies and specific techniques (from the type of image to be projected to the selection of advertising media) were all conditioned by information obtained from surveys of public opinion.

The rise of contemporary campaign management is commonly attributed to the influence of television and the large sums of money now required to saturate the airwaves with visual appeals. The impact of television on the current format and dynamic of campaigns – the new electoral public as we know it – cannot be denied. Nevertheless, if we are to hold to the dictum that causes must precede their effects, the core features of late twentieth-century electronic campaign practice cannot be attributed to television *per se*, or to the powerful effects of visual broadcast images. All of the essential features of a modern media campaign were employed in Lyndon Johnson's successful campaign for the Democratic nomination for the US Senate in 1948, with radio playing the role that now features television. Spending unprecedented amounts of money, Johnson employed attack politics, radio messages, and an early equivalent of the photo opportunity – swooping around Texas in a helicopter, which virtually required extensive and robust reporting in the media. Johnson employed his ample funding on repeated opinion polls as a means of managing issues, discarding themes that did not work and pressing appeals that seemed to garner support (Caro 1990). The modernity of Johnson's efforts provide an instructive contrast to another senatorial campaign in the same year. Jon L. Jonkel, a Chicago public relations' expert, managed John Butler's successful campaign to unseat Senator Millard Tydings, a campaign that Kelley (1956) took to be a significant and ominous chapter in the (then relatively modest) intrusion of public relations professionals into politics. Jonkel, like current political managers, started by taking a poll. He queried patrons as they left movie theaters, a technique so crude as to be unimaginable in today's world of political consulting (Kelley 1956, 113).

Every presidential campaign after 1948, starting with George Gallup's work for Eisenhower in 1952, has employed sophisticated polling techniques to gauge the public mind and to sort out the effects of various campaign issues and strategies. Important as television has become as a means of political communication, the late twentieth-century electoral campaign and the attendant changes in the social organization of the influence system are products of new means of managing political marketing, not television alone. Poll results can be used to persuade potential donors that investment in a candidate has a good probability of success or to encourage the efforts of campaign workers. Polls are used to guide the planning of systematic campaign strategy. Strategic planning typically begins by assessing the climate of opinion within which the campaign must proceed, gauging the views of various subgroups within the electorate on a variety of relevant issues and topics as well as the popularity and images of candidates and their opponents. Using this information, planners can forge strategies for exploiting combinations of issues and target groups that promise possibilities of victory. Tracking polls inform managers regarding the changing intentions of the electorate and its constituent groups, sometimes on a daily basis, allowing tactical adjustments by way of counter attacks, spin control, or new lines of appeal.

The primary purpose of political polls is to provide research-based information for planning and managing the *messages* of the campaign. A recent (1994) successful campaign to defeat an anti gay-rights initiative in Oregon illustrates poll-based message planning and also underscores that this technology now pervades the electoral arena, reaching beyond national presidential contests and high-stakes elections in the larger states. The opponents of the initiative, known as Proposition 13, hired a professional manager who in turn engaged a polling and research firm, a media consultant, and a direct mail firm to integrate the effort (Meadow et al. 1995). The campaign began with an opinion survey to assess the opportunities and constraints that would ground the design of their persuasive efforts. The survey established that the majority of the electorate did not, in an abstract sense, want to discriminate, but did not see Proposition 13 as discriminatory. It also revealed that some voters were troubled by the extreme rhetoric embedded in the text of Proposition 13 and its similarity to a comparable initiative that had failed to gain voter approval in 1992. Demographic analysis of the survey convinced the campaign planners that parents of school-age children comprised the group whose votes would be decisive. Armed with this data, the team decided that an appeal to mainstream values promised the best probability of success. Any intimation that advocates of No on Proposition 13 were promoting a gay life style must be assiduously avoided and, instead, the campaign must appeal to the electorate's underlying belief in fundamental rights.

The team designed advertising that would persuasively set forth promising themes. Two television spots proved effective. One stressed similarities to the earlier failed initiative, and the other, deemed by the team their most effective ad, featured "Mom," a teacher and mother (played by a professional actress) who told the audience that she always tried to teach her children not to discriminate. Television spots were paid for by funds raised primarily by the team's professional direct mail operation, whose work depended on demographic research designed to provide information regarding the location of potential donors. All the team's campaign materials were used to pursue those target populations most likely to affect the outcome. Focus groups and tracking polls helped the experts to adjust and hone their tactics as the campaign progressed. In short, the entire effort was planned and managed through research on public attitudes.

*Pretesting.* Important as polling has become in the design of political campaigns, the pretesting of themes and messages has equally significant implications for the New Public, for it is pretesting that removes the shaping of public debate from the public arena and locates it instead in the research designs of professional political experts. Just as George Gallup and his Audience Research Incorporated could pretest titles, themes, players, and pre-release versions of films, avoiding the unpredictable judgments of moviegoers whose reactions emerge in processes of socially mediated evaluation *in situ*, so political market researchers can test themes, messages, and penultimate versions of commercials without waiting for the political marketplace to make its judgments within a public political process.

Pretesting was well established by the 1960s. Campaign managers learned that pretesting could allow designing campaigns that turn on a single issue that favors their side, effectively avoiding balanced public consideration of the full range matters at stake. In the course of an effort to defeat a 1960s' California initiative calling for higher state pensions, the campaign's managers found that the theme "Don't vote an increase in taxes" was not working because of public sympathy for elderly pensioners. Pretesting of alternative attack points revealed that the specter of seniors coming from other states to take advantage of higher pensions in California struck a responsive chord. Existing campaign communications were junked and replaced with a new pretested theme: "Unfair to you . . . Don't pay for pensions for migrants from other states." The tide turned and the initiative's opponents won by more than two to one (Baus and Ross 1968, 197–8).

*Focus groups in pretesting.* Once focus groups had proven their value in commercial marketing research, political marketers were quick to adapt the technique to their purposes, including pretesting campaign themes. Focus group research is unlike survey research in two important respects. Firstly, in selecting focus groups, no attempt is made to secure broadly representative samples. The technique relies on selecting particular segments of the public whose views and responses can enlighten researchers regarding strategically important groups, most notably swing voters. Secondly, focus groups do not put queries to individual respondents in isolation from their peers. As I interpret focus group research, one of its main instrumental values is that it allows observers to see how well ideas play *in discussion among like-minded people*, simulating in advance, as it were, the sorts of discussion that sociologists attribute to the second stage of the two-step flow of communication. Some ideas are cast out, some reinforced, others reinterpreted. To the extent that this technique works, market research can bypass the two-step flow and avoid unanticipated negative responses or reinterpretations of carefully planned campaign messages.

The well-known Willie Horton spot, which proved remarkably effective in the Bush campaign of 1988, illustrates the use of focus groups in identifying and pretesting campaign themes. A research director within the Bush campaign organization first spotted the issue in a transcript of a local primary debate and suspected that prison furlough policy would provide an opening for attacking Dukakis. Willie Horton, a black prisoner committed rape while on leave from a Massachusetts prison, and Dukakis, as Governor of Massachusetts, had supported a furlough policy for his state. The matter was brought to the attention of senior campaign officials, who then formed a focus group to pretest this and other issues. Paramus, New Jersey was chosen as the site of the research, and the group was selected from among nominal democrats who had voted for Reagan but were leaning to Dukakis – swing voters on the very edge of the cusp. Dukakis' veto of a bill requiring the pledge of allegiance in schools was also tested, and both issues played so well that they were promoted to a central role in the national media campaign (Germond and Witcover 1989, 11–12). The themes were so effective that a post-election poll by the Gallup organization showed that these two hot buttons, together with the idea that Dukakis was simply "too liberal" were the three leading campaign issues in the minds of Bush voters (Gallup 1989, 226–30).

The issue of prison furlough policy did not make its way up through a social filter of organizations that made demands on the national polity, nor was the Republican party mobilized on behalf of reform of prison release policies, either before or after the election. The prison furlough matter was strictly a campaign issue, manufactured in isolation from the actual process of governance. It was identified and constructed by a differentiated group of communication and campaign experts. In this regard it is interesting to note that some public opinion polls distinguish between "campaign issues" and "political issues," tabulating voter responses in these two categories separately. Dukakis and Bush voters differed in their views on *campaign* issues, but in the *political* category, profiles of the relative importance of various issues to the two groups of voters did not differ appreciably. I take this anomaly to be further evidence of the differentiation of campaigning from the larger political process.

Focus group research has accelerated the disjunction of electoral politics and the politics of governance. The new public persuasion, honed in modern advertising and public relations, and reinforced by the ever widening scope of the new electronic media, centers on techniques of translating data on the public and its views into televised messages. The election of 1968, identified by Mendelsohn and Crespi (1970) as a turning point in the emergence of the overriding influence of research-based campaigns, was also marked by Richard Nixon's unprecedented reliance on television and his avoidance of direct forums of discussion. James David Barber (1980, 303) has remarked that Nixon's campaign displayed a new level of separation of the themes of public persuasion from the substance of political action: "In 1968, as never before, the link between reality and rhetoric in political discourse was broken – consciously, even proudly." The New Public had come of age.

### Lobbying

*Lobbying and the exchange of information.* "Lobbying" in its most general sense – using influence to affect the actions of people with power – is as ancient as power and influence themselves, but modern lobbying has distinctive markers. It draws upon generalized resources of influence, especially information and prolocutors' capacity to speak for groups, rather than relying entirely on exchanges of favors.

Information-based lobbying emerged early in the modern era as an integral part of the public sphere. The modern public was originally borne by political movements that proclaimed their legitimacy through appeals to ideals of free association and open communication, but its fully developed form was shaped by the rise of public debt. Financing state debt through individual financiers or great families rests on very different social foundations than borrowing money from the public. Lending capital requires an act of trust, and trust must be secured by information. Information, in turn, implies disclosure – *publicity*. When the public is asked to participate in a state venture as stake-holders, the footing for an information society must be established, and as the public debt accelerated in eighteenth-century England, so also did public information. Brewer (1989), examining the concomitants of the rise of public debt in eighteenth-century England, documents the extraordinary growth of public information that accompanied the rationalized administrative practices of the expanded state. The state came to require knowledge of how much revenue a new tax would raise in relation to the revenue required to back a new issue of bonds. At the same time, public access to information regarding the state's business also grew as citizens, now participants in the collective financial affairs of the nation, demanded to know more about government affairs. Citizens demanded information not just about the general state of the government's solvency, but about details of many facets of the administration of state finances, including a complicated array of taxes, fees, franchises, and associated regulations of trade. Arguments justifying access to information proceeded with a new application of the polarity of public and private: state papers were not to be viewed as the private property of those who wrote them, but of the public at large. In the first instance this claim was successfully brought by parliamentarians who insisted that financial measures could not be adequately deliberated without access to all available information, but once this principle was established, lobbyists were able to use it to secure information on behalf of segments of the public that they claimed to represent.

Ironically, even as fundamentalist advocates of civic virtue railed against the growth of public debt, seeing only greed, instability, and a society based on paper rather than on real social ties, they failed to recognize what was written on this paper: unprecedented quantities of public information about the affairs of state, information that would open new opportunities for citizens to participate in the public sphere. In the new climate of rationalized, information-based public administration, a form of interest representation that recent historians do not hesitate to term "lobbying," emerged in the first half of the eighteenth century (Brewer 1989; Olson 1991; 1992a, b; 1993).[2] The successful efforts of the Anti-Corn Law League (1838–46) are generally regarded as the first example of a modern lobbying effort because of the League's highly organized, centrally directed strategies and their effective use of propaganda (Schonhardt-Bailey 1991), but the underlying methods of eighteenth-century lobbying were already modern in their reliance on information. Lobbying is a process of influence that travels along routes sustained by exchanges of information. Legislative and administrative regulators need information about the targets of regulation and their practices; regulatees need information about the intentions of regulators. In the course of this exchange, both parties have an opportunity to make their messages influential as well as informative. Current theories vary in their characterization of the types of information exchanged in lobbying, some emphasizing substantive and technical information, others stressing political information regarding the location and strength of support and opposition to various policies. Nevertheless, sophisticated social science models of lobbying, detailed journalistic accounts of lobbyists' daily efforts, and practical manuals designed to help lobbyists do their work all agree that information is at the heart of the process.

Recent academic models of lobbying employ economistic concepts of exchange, assuming that lobbyists and their targets calculate the cost and benefits of lobbying efforts, of accepting lobbyists' influence, of compiling information, and of checking lobbyists' information against independent sources. The economistic style does not imply that benefits are always material. Information-based lobbying in seventeenth-century Britain served economic interests to be sure, but dissenting religious groups lobbied on behalf of religious freedom. In a move that anticipated the professionalization of lobbying, dissenters hired an attorney to monitor events in parliament and give notice regarding events that might threaten their interests (Brewer 1989, 240).

Alison Olson's (1991;1992a, b) accounts of the representation by London lobbies of the mercantile and religious interests of American colonists in the mid seventeeth-century is instructive. The concerns of dissenting English sects were represented by a London based lobby known as The Three Denominations, whose leaders also took it upon themselves to speak for the claims of their co-religionists in the colonies when religious liberties were jeopardized by colonial overseers. London ministers were willing to listen because they were eager to secure detailed information about colonial conditions and affairs, information that representatives of The Three Denominations acquired at the coffee houses where dissenters gathered to hear and discuss the daily news, including news borne by the latest batch of mail from relatives, friends, and associates in the colonies.

Eighteenth-century, information-based lobbying led to rhetorical practices requiring advocates to justify their cases in terms of the public interest (Brewer 1989). The rhetoric of public interest became particularly important when lobbyists failed to achieve their objectives by direct lobbying with parliament or officials and chose to move on to what is now called "the outside strategy" or "going public" (Kernell 1986). Appealing to the public implies that the public interest is at stake and must therefore be addressed. Moreover, arguments based on substantive premises and delivered in the public sphere imply a normative presupposition that the public has a stake in the quality of dialogue as such and that procedural standards of rational argument apply.

The proto-lobbying of the seventeenth century should not be idealized. It operated within the framework of a political system based on patronage, wherein bribery and corruption were not uncommon.[3] Early modern lobbying was not precisely like present-day lobbying, but modern interest group representation, based on the logic of publicity, was present in embryonic form. A permanent, elected, body of representative legislators is subject to the varied demands of citizens. As participants in this arena develop a taste for information and to demand it, discourse comes to employ arguments as to the merits of competing claims. Arguments are put to the test of publicity and subjected to the universalistic standards implied by the concept of public judgment.

*The character and growth of modern lobbying.* After the Revolution, American lobbying necessarily became an indigenous institution shaped by its own modes of influence. With the rise of party government, influence became deeply embedded in patronage, and lobbying followed a path consistent with this development in the larger political system. Before the 1870s, lobbying activity was largely undertaken on behalf of particular individual claims. Individual congressmen, acting as patrons engaged in a favor-based influence system, introduced private bills to secure these claims. Beginning in the Grant administration, a new mode of lobbying began to take shape: interest groups rather than individuals or small *ad hoc* groups became the units of representation, and group interests were advanced through general legislation. Although railroads are often regarded as the preeminent lobbying group of the era, the alleged power of the railroad lobby has been exaggerated. Interest-group lobbying by representative organizations first developed among veterans, whose situation clearly displays *democratic reform* as the original animating principle of group lobbying. Veterans had been required to seek redress as individuals by finding sympathetic congressmen and, if successful in this search, by entering into an arena of patronage and political payoffs that easily shaded over into downright corruption. Organized by the efforts of such prolocutors as George E. Lemon of the Pensioners Committee, whose leadership techniques anticipated the methods of present day grassroots, propaganda-based lobbying, veterans were able to achieve legislative reforms that removed implementation of awards from the legislative arena and placed the process in universalistic, bureaucratic channels (Thompson 1985, 256–62). Because of its reformist, modernizing aims, the early interpreters of interest group politics were often advocates of this new politics, which they saw as a democratic movement.

These reforms did not fully differentiate lobbying from the realms of power, money, and favored-based influence, but the logic of publicity, which links information, rational discussion, universalistic standards and the public interest dominates the *theory* of lobbying to this day. Academic theory, which posits that lobbying rests on exchanges of information, is consistent with the ideology of the practitioners I have interviewed. Current views converge on the idea that lobbying, however imperfectly insulated from power and money, operates in the realm of influence through the sway of information and argument. Yet we must now ask whether the impact of the New Public has altered the practice of lobbying even in the specialized arena of information and influence.

The expansion of interest-group lobbying in the United States in recent decades has been fed by striking growth in the number of organized associations. By 1995, the *Encyclopedia of Organizations* listed approximately 22,000 groups, up four-fold since 1955 and 50 percent since 1980 (Loomis and Cigler 1995). Gross totals of this sort include large numbers of small and politically dormant groups, yet by merging these figures with Schlozman's (1984) count of the number of organizations with representation in Washington (*c.* 6,600), I estimate that approximately 20 percent of American associations participate in national political life to some degree and that about 15 percent have Washington offices. Between 1960 and 1983, public interest groups grew disproportionally in relation to private groups, increasing to about 2,500 groups representing 40 million members and collecting $40 billion annually (Shaiko 1985). More lobbying means more professional lobbyists. It is difficult to estimate the number of active lobbyists in the United States, for the boundaries of the category are not clear. Attorneys, staff members of interest group organizations, public relations experts, and other political professionals sometimes lobby, but may not be picked up in counts of lobbyists. Casting a broad net to include such *de facto* lobbyists, produced an estimate that, in 1989, 90,000 lobbyists worked in Washington DC alone, and, of course, many more were active in state and local politics.[4]

The proliferation of lobbying by organized groups is driven by expansion of the realm of governmental regulation within a highly differentiated democratic order. Interests are not given; they emerge in the course of social and political interaction (Salisbury 1991). Each real or potential act of state regulation creates interests among those who are positively or negatively affected. In a highly differentiated and complex society, the implementation of state action requires flows of information regarding the conditions and consequences of effective regulation. Though contentious, rhetorical, and partisan, lobbying is the process by which politically colored information is exchanged.

There can be little doubt that information is at the center of modern lobbying. Favor-based influence continues to play a role in the process, especially in gaining the access that is prerequisite to sending messages. Since the realm of campaign finance is implicated in networks of access, "favors" are involved in the process of group representation. Nevertheless, there is virtual unanimity among both participants and observers that "it is not whom you know but what you know" that makes for successful lobbying (Rosenthal 1993, 190).[5]

Schlozman and Tierny (1983) asked representatives of interest groups to identify the means of lobbying they employed and the resources committed to these means. Among their respondents, 98% reported testifying at hearings and 92% reported presenting research results and technical information, while 58% reported making political contributions and 56% doing favors for officials. Asked which three activities (among twenty-seven general categories) consumed the most time and resources, the largest numbers of respondents said "contacting officials directly" (36%), "testifying at hearings" (27%), "presenting research and technical information" (27%), and "mounting grassroots efforts" (26%). Only 8% included making contributions to campaigns and 2% listed doing favors. In sum, substantially less resources were allocated to favors and contributions than to informational activities and to political activities designed to affect and mobilize public opinion.

*Grassroots lobbying.* Lobbying by mobilizing opinion is the arena most affected by developments in the New Public. Despite the central place of information exchange in modern lobbying (and, indeed, despite the growing importance of information-based lobbying right up to the 1980s), there are strong indications that new practices among political professionals are putting serious strain on the informational base of the lobbying system.[6] In the last decade "grassroots lobbying," has become a specialized practice among political consultants and their clients. It is a version of the "outside" strategy, an approach to lobbying that relies more on creating a climate of pressure-packed public opinion than on invoking direct personal connections with legislators. In this mode, lobbyists *make* rather than merely *report* political information for exchange. Through grassroots effort, public opinion is mobilized and directed at decision makers by going beyond making representations about what interest groups or the public at large wants, and beyond faceless mass letter-writing or phone campaigns. Instead, the leaders of organizations, often working through consultants, identify (by polling techniques), cultivate, and organize activists to create a cadre of people who can be called upon to exert pressure on legislators and officials. Grassroots lobbyists put their chosen activists on display in personal but well-organized persuasive efforts. For example, some sizable interest groups organize activist members into lobbying committees for every congressional district in the United States and insist on personal meetings with congresspersons whenever important issues arise. Faucheux (1995) cites several examples of particularly well-developed grassroots lobbies established by trade associations. The National Association of Life Underwriters has established a network of 10,000 members who serve on over 500 congressional liaison committees covering more than 95% of the congressional districts in the United States. Local coordinators, who themselves meet with congresspersons three or four times a year, organized over 900 such face-to-face meetings for local constituents in 1994. Core activists in grassroots organizations are supplied with newsletters, videos tapes, and instruction manuals. With the aid of computerized information systems, they can be rapidly mobilized and supplied with persuasive materials when important issues appear on legislative calendars.

More than 1,000 trade associations engage in this form of grassroots lobbying, which make such groups the largest pool of potential clients for the growing number of political consulting firms that either offer advice about methods or actually perform this service for hire. As of 1995, at least 117 firms offered consulting in grassroots organizational techniques of which 71 engaged in field operations. Although professional grassroots lobbying was well established by 1985, the practice grew rapidly in the early 1990s. By 1993–4, grassroots lobbying had become an 800 million dollar a year business, with 340 million of this sum going to outside consultants and vendors, twice the comparable expenditure for 1991–2. Faucheux reports that the field's top consultants say "We're entering the golden age of grassroots lobbying. Only a decade ago, it was the exception rather than the rule. But now both sides of most major issues have a grassroots component. Interest groups that don't play the game risk becoming political eunuchs" (1995, 20).

The rapid growth of grassroots lobbying is made possible by technological innovations in the means of communication: electronic mail, fax machines, video conferencing, and cable television are the channels by which core activists can be quickly informed and mobilized by expert masters of the current rhetoric of political discourse. Yet despite the label "grassroots," these are channels for narrowcasting, largely devoid of opportunities for two-sided discussion, exposure to alternative information, or testing ideas in a public arena.

*Grassroots techniques and political parties.* The rise of professional political consultants and managers is generally attributed to the decline of political parties. Waning parties left a vacuum that new forms of political organization filled. While the success of new professional modes of management seems to make the parties all the more dispensable, the continuing importance of parties should not be overlooked. Elections and representative bodies are still organized around party labels, and party identification remains a central locus of political loyalty which cannot be ignored in bidding for support in legislative bodies or in activating the allegiances of voters. Parties continue to play an important role in fund raising, canvassing and other political tasks that require mass participation. Both the Republican and Democratic national parties now try to improve their political effectiveness by using the new technologies and professional techniques developed by the makers of the New Public.

The application of contemporary grassroots organizing techniques could substantially strengthen the position of the national political parties. Were the managers of grassroots efforts to use their specialized skills to identify activists, to organize and train them, and to mobilize them of behalf of party aims and strategies, local party organizations could become a formidable source of influence on national politics. This development, which is already underway, would indeed strengthen political parties, but were the practices of professional grassroots organizers taken as the model – and there are strong indications that this is precisely what is now occurring – the consequences would be to extend the influence of the parties' highest levels of elite national leadership, not to empower local party organizations to send their autonomously created grassroots messages forward.[7] The purpose of professionally managed grassroots organization is not to encourage discussion of alternative points of view but to focus support for consistent and unified positions.

*Hyperpluralism.* Cigler and Loomis (1995, 393–406) have labeled current interest group politics in the United States "hyperpluralism." In 1983, Schlozman and Tierny could refer to the rapid growth of lobbying in the previous decade as "more of the same," but with the rise of new electronic technologies in support of grassroots lobbying, with scores of professional consultants and managers spending enormous sums on behalf of thousands of interest groups, the game has changed. The new system became evident in the great conflict over health care in 1993–4, when over 700 interest groups spent over 100 million dollars on lobbying and public relations, employing the "outside" strategy to mobilize the public for or against the Clinton health plan.[8] The television advertisements of the Health Insurance Association of America, which displayed "Harry and Louise" worrying about the proposed system, wondering what would happen to their freedom of choice, probably had some influence on the outcome, but the new overall information environment was decisive. Lobbying was no longer a matter of purchasing access in order to establish systems of information exchange. Battles for public support, carried on with the new weapons of media-based, managed campaigning have been superimposed on the old modes of lobbying. The old fault line of pluralism – the gridlock of competing elites *canceling* each other out – has been replaced by a new dialogue of many loud but inarticulate public voices *drowning* each other out.

*Technical and political information.* I use the figure of "drowning" as metaphor for the *inflation of influence* in lobbying. In grassroots lobbying, political information drives out technical information. *Technical* information supports arguments regarding the substantive consequences and instrumental means of public policy. The lobbyist relies on knowledge of the theory and practice of the domain that he or she represents, citing, for example, current economic and social conditions, tax incidence studies, applications of the economic theory of regulation, or inside knowledge of how things are really done. *Political* information apprises legislators or officials of the political consequences of various courses of action – where support is to be expected and when political prices must be paid. Information about public opinion is political in this sense. This distinction is parallel to the contrast between direct and outside strategies of lobbying. *Direct* strategies rely primarily on lobbyists' capacity to give advice or warning about the state of affairs in the domain under discussion. *Outside* strategies mobilize statements of support or opposition in order to persuade decision makers that the political costs and benefits of action support compliance with lobbyists' recommendations. In concrete situations technical and the political information are easily distinguished, for calculations of political and practical consequences are inextricably joined in both the rhetoric and the reality of politics, but the "outside" component still points to the consequences of professional grassroots lobbying as an outside strategy.

Political scientists with a taste for mathematical models of political processes recognize that the informational aspect of lobbying makes it amenable to treatment within the conceptual apparatus of modern information theory. Their models may treat information as a generic category, not distinguishing technical and political information, but recent models have stressed the primacy of the question of whether political information is sincere. Austen-Smith (1993) argues that specialist information is most valuable early in the agenda-setting phase of debate. He suggests that clues indicating that the target and the lobbyist share preferences as to outcomes – a species of political solidarity – allow an assumption of credibility, for under this condition signaling theory allows for the credibility of "cheap talk" about information which the informer has acquired at low cost. Rasmussen (1993) assumes that the common aim of legislators is to be reelected, so they set great store by political information. They want to know whether lobbyists are honest in their statements about political support for proposed positions. Lobbyists must know that there is a chance that their audiences will independently check information, and Rasmussen constructs a model showing that there is an equilibrium level of checking in any stable lobbying system. Ainsworth and Sened (1993) also present a politically oriented model based on the notion that legislators and interest groups need information about the viability of the interests proclaimed by lobbyist entrepreneurs who make a business of representing groups. Caught in the middle of this structure, lobbyists must always attend to their credibility, but they can successfully negotiate their position between two audiences because the situation is structured so that both sides can infer the motivation of lobbyists from their knowledge of the structure of interests created by the system of representation. These varied models, despite their differing emphases on particular aspects of information, have a common theme: lobbying takes place under conditions of uncertainty. Because it is a political process of instrumental confrontation, the sincerity of information providers cannot be assumed. Accordingly, the logic of asymmetric information and signals applies, especially warrants of sincerity. Trust and sincerity drive the influence system and support its stability.

The growing use of professionally managed grassroots lobbying as a means of attempting to signal political support has profound implications for the stability of lobbying as an institution for linking information and influence. Ron Faucheux (1995, 20), an advocate and apologist for professional political consulting, has remarked that the new "technology has made building voluntary organizations as simple as writing a check." Though offered in an enthusiastic spirit, his apt summary suggests the fundamental problem of manufactured grassroots support. Large numbers of varied interest group organizations, each pursuing an outside strategy and implementing it with organized grassroots support, create inflationary pressure on influence. How does the decision maker distinguish astroturf from the real roots of growing grass? If grassroots can be created by a professional hired hand, how does the audience distinguish signals from noise? The concept of *signaling*, as developed by students of the problem of asymmetric information, requires means of distinguishing authentic communication from messages that anyone can send – in this case anyone with a checkbook. Once again we see that the professionalization of communication in the New Public generates chronic inflation of influence and threatens the historic normative order of modern lobbying, which calls for exchanges of factual information in conversations directed to the public interest.

### Certifying facts

The growing business of certifying facts is another source of the inflation of influence, another opportunity to create information by writing checks. One means of warranting the sincerity of a message is to call upon an expert and disinterested third party to substantiate its factual content. Third-party verification transfers some of the burden of trustworthiness from advocates to agencies that base their credibility on knowledge and the professional norms of objectivity. Professional certification of facts is a form of signaling that would be more reliable were it not for the widespread belief in the maxim, "For every Ph.D. there is an equal and opposite Ph.D." to the extent that audiences assume that anyone can purchase an expert, experts lose their capacity to communicate signals. Influence becomes inflated when it is perceived to be backed by money rather than by trustworthy argument. The cynicism expressed in adages about equal and opposite experts derives from the battles of experts that the public witnesses in adversarial legal proceedings, legislative hearings, and disputes about issues of applied science as reported in the media. Still, science, expertise, and professionalism have not altogether lost their prestige. It is the very strength of such influence that leads advocates to stage battles of experts. Most people still believe their physicians and follow the advice of their attorneys and their mechanics, too. Indeed, it is impossible to imagine a social world in which every statement by every expert is put to independent investigation – a social world without influence based on the prestige of credentials.

*Public accounting as a prototype for certifying facts.* The professional role of the public accountant is an informative prototype of social organization for the certification of facts. Traditional auditing practice provides an ideal type of the certification of facts, and recent expansion of the range of certification work done by accounting firms illustrates yet another transformation of the public sphere along the trajectory toward the New Public. When performing the traditional audit function, public accountants mediate between economic enterprises, whose managers know a great deal about the financial condition of their organizations, and creditors and investors, who lack the necessary access and time to be fully informed about crucial matters that bear on their stakes in these enterprises. Asymmetrical access to financial information, like other categories of informational asymmetry, raises questions of trust and threatens the viability of market exchange. Investors and creditors require reliable signals that summary information provided to them by accounting statements is trustworthy. Public accountants are given access to the detailed information behind the summary statements and, following professionally sanctioned practices of verification, attest to the accuracy of their clients' statements.[9] Since clients pay for this certification, there would appear to be an incentive for collusion, or at least weak resistance to clients who insist that misleading statements or procedures should be certified, especially if there are competitive accounting firms ready to be more flexible. Public accounting must therefore rely on signals of professional probity to override the message implied by the private character of the parties' economic incentives. These overriding signals are provided by expertise and professionalism, which create public confidence that accountants will be constrained by their expert knowledge of accounting rules and their professional obligations to follow them. Individuals and firms with strong reputations for professional performance garner prestige and come to stake this prestige each time they confer a certification and, as signaling theory posits, make an *investment* in their signals. This system of institutionalized probity is supported by a panoply of rules and organizational apparatus, including educational requirements and examinations for entry into the profession, procedures for licensing and discipline, and professional committees with authority to establish rules for acceptable procedures.[10] In the United States, professional accounting has come to be dominated by five giant firms with great prestige. These firms, of which Price Waterhouse is perhaps the most well known to the general public, perform the audits for nearly all the largest corporations in the nation, and their representatives occupy strategic positions on the most important professional committees. A major corporation cannot engage a small, minor firm to audit them lest it be seen as hiring a kept auditor without adequate size and influence to sustain independence.

Price Waterhouse has such prestige that the firm may be relied upon to count the ballots for the annual Academy Awards of The Academy of Motion Picture Arts and Sciences. This might seem a trivial example of "certifying facts," but it illustrates an important principle: once accounting firms have developed a reputation for skill, honesty, and objectivity, that reputation may be mobilized to warrant facts and figures unrelated to financial statements. Beginning in mid-century, accounting firms added management consulting to their range of practices, a movement that accelerated rapidly in the 1980s (Carver and King 1990). This work readily edged over into practices with political overtones, such as testifying on behalf of trade associations on economic conditions in particular industries. Certifying facts to political ends reached new levels of importance within the accounting profession with the rise, in the 1980s, of tax-revenue and tax incidence studies. Price Waterhouse played a major role in this development. Between 1983 and 1990, the firm built a national tax practice in Washington DC that mirrored the range of expertise of the staff of the

Congressional Joint Tax Committee. Price Waterhouse's Washington team of accountants, economists, and attorneys – a professional staff of 123 persons in 1990 – outnumbered the parallel staff of the Joint Tax Committee by nearly three to one, and could produce studies (based in part on data supplied by clients) more rapidly than the congressional staff agency. They began, in effect, to engage in a form of informational lobbying (Birnbaum 1992, 217–19). Accounting firms with the prestige of Price Waterhouse can employ their professional status to certify facts rather than merely advocating positions, bringing an aura of objectivity to the process and "present[ing] themselves not so much as corporate hired hands, but rather as senior statesman of a sort" (218).

*Other certifying agents.* Public accounting provides a strong example of a rhetorical mode based on signals of credibility that derive from locating speakers in an institutional structure that enhances their claims to expert, objective knowledge. Scientists, including social scientists in such relatively prestigious disciplines as economics, also rely upon signals of expertise and objectivity, though not always so successfully as public accountants, for some scientists are too visibly engaged in disputes among themselves to sustain an illusion of objective and reliable knowledge. According to one adage, "Economics is the only discipline in which two people can be awarded the Nobel prize for saying exactly the opposite thing." Disputes are visible in natural science too, especially in controversial applied arenas of health and environmental science, but the expertise of science is regularly mobilized as a signal of credibility in public debate. For example, the battles over regulation of airlines, trucking, and communications during the 1970s were won by advocates of deregulation in large measure because of the influence of free-market economists on the staffs of both regulatory agencies and congressional committees. These economists repeatedly asserted that deregulation was technically correct economics (Derthick and Quirk 1985; Quirk 1990).

Public interest groups also rely upon an institutionally supported rhetoric of objectivity, but the structural underpinning of this implicit claim to objectivity takes a different and interesting form. It is not founded on independent expertise, but on such groups' claimed position in the terrain of public controversy. A group claiming to represent the public interest implicitly asserts that it advocates the good of the whole, not partial, *private* interests. The very existence of a proclaimed public interest group implies advocacy of the general good: everyone benefits from a clean environment and good nutrition; we are all consumers; we would all benefit from a more democratic political life, peace, and a just society. Groups advocating variations on these themes claim to transcend conflicts between merely private interests and declare that they assert policies for the benefit of the whole public, identifying, as it were, with public virtue in the solidary community. In so doing they reaffirm the liberal tradition by educing a dichotomy between the public and the private. Commitment to public virtue does not, however, prevent public interest groups from employing professional public relations firms to advance their causes by the methods of the New Public, as when, in 1988–9, the Natural Resources Defense Council secured the services of Fenton Communications to run a publicity campaign against the use of the pesticide Alar on apple crops. Fenton persuaded "Sixty Minutes" to broadcast two segments that set off a national alarm by featuring frightening but questionable research findings (Schulz 1996).[11]

Establishing a claim to speak for the public buttresses the credibility of an interest group's factual statements, but the presumptive impartiality of its position can be magnified by employing a rhetorical strategy that relies upon the imprimatur of research. The order of magnification depends on the prestige of the source of an advocate's research. Private research organizations known for the quality, professionalism, and impartiality of their work offer stronger support than research by an organization's own staff. Published research from the academic sector and published government reports provide their own special brands of facticity, and even research by agencies known to be partisan or strongly ideological carry a certain weight, for the very concept of research implies some measure of commitment to factual standards that do not necessarily apply to the rhetoric employed in more frankly partisan arenas, where hyperbole and misrepresentation are accepted as part of the game. The credentials of economists, nutritionists, medical researchers, and environmental scientists bring a presumed trustworthy objectivity to their certification of such facts as political advocates would have us believe, especially when the advocate can successfully lay claim to the mantle of the public interest or claim a protected, independent status. When, on the other hand, the interest at stake is obviously special and private, paid-for science loses its prestige. Witness the low esteem of the Tobacco Institute, whose obvious loyalty to and dependence upon the tobacco industry thoroughly undercuts the public credibility of their research.

Faith in third-party certification of facts by research studies is not necessarily well placed, even when carried out by reputable professionals on behalf of public interest organizations. The "public interest" is not value free. Because there is no single objective public interest, the process of certifying facts is a rhetorical strategy in a political arena. Varied views of the public interest compete for public attention and support, each based on different philosophies and priorities and each unavoidably benefiting some part of the public at the expense of others. The public is regularly exposed to these dilemmas in the form of conflicts about the proper weights to be assigned to such problems of priority as a clean environment versus jobs, welfare versus the alleged dead weight of welfare programs on the economy, and the relative benefits of regulation and competition. The value stances taken by advocates of particular priorities inevitably influence how research is conducted and what are reported to be facts. Research is also affected by deep philosophical assumptions, a principle best illustrated by Proctor's (1995) conclusion that the attitudes of scientists to assessing environmental hazards is strongly influenced by their preconceptions as to whether nature is benign until disturbed by human intervention or is already fraught with risk in its undisturbed state. Media accounts of research pay little attention to the biases of research or its problematic objectivity, especially when a research study is merely cited by one or another party to an ongoing conflict. It suffices to report that an advocacy group claims that "studies show . . ." often not even mentioning who did the study, thus relying on the intrinsic prestige of research rather than the prestige of the research agency.[12]

Public interest advocates are often spared the burden of defending their objectivity before the general public, a phenomenon I attribute to the common presumption that private money is a uniquely corrupting force. This assumption is a byproduct of the dichotomy between public and private that permeates our conceptions about deliberations regarding the common good. Other forms of interests certainly affect the way researchers investigate and report facts, interests that affect omissions and inclusions of data, particular interpretive slants, and the rhetorical exaggeration of results: organizations' interests in research that supports their clients' positions, competition among scientists for attention and grants; motivation to sustain the success of research enterprises and thus sustain their capacity to support groups of professional colleagues; and, of course, ideological commitments that can affect the objectivity of research just as much as the profit motive in the private sector. Scientists also have an interest in speaking autonomously, as scientists, to their social values (Moore 1996). Yet these organizational and ideological sources of bias, even if recognized in a general way, are seldom subject to public scrutiny in daily journalistic discourse. Occasionally, an enterprising journalist will track down the panoply of interests involved in organizing and reporting science, collating it for public use, and disseminating summary collations to shape public opinion. In *Heart Failure*, T. Moore (1989) traces the development of professional opinion regarding the medical risk of elevated serum cholesterol, means of treatment, guidelines for public education on diet, periodic serum testing, medical care. Moore's report presents a convincing case that consensus among professionals was not so overwhelming as generally reported in the media, at least at the time national policy was first set in place. He points out that over and above the financial interests of drug companies in creating huge markets for anticholesterol drugs, the dominant cholesterol research establishment, led by the National Heart, Lung, and Blood Institute of the National Institutes of Health, had interests of its own and a controlling agenda. The Institute and associated research laboratories and projects came to have a vested interest in demonstrating the dangers of high levels of serum cholesterol, the reversibility of this undesirable condition by diet and drugs, and a stake in their avowed policy preferences for both public education and standard medical practice. Spurred by these interests, research directors and other responsible officials made questionable decisions regarding statistical procedures and logical inferences, exaggerated their findings, and at their worst, organized a "consensus conference" to establish scientific orthodoxy on the matter, at which, according to minority participants, consensus was declared in a report prepared in advance, despite the complaints of scientists who found the conclusions of the organizers premature (Moore 1989, 57–64). In consequence the public was presented with findings and recommendations without any publicly visible debate, and the media presented the orthodox view as founded upon unquestionable scientific research, acting as if reporting dissenting views would be a violation of the public interest.[13]

### Think tanks: advocating and certifying policy

The array of agencies engaged in research oriented toward crafting public policy and influencing public opinion has become quite large and differentiated. The certification of facts to the public has not yet become the mission of general purpose research firms willing to contract to study issues on demand. Political consulting firms sometimes represent themselves as ready to do "issues research," but this refers more to the political dimensions of issues than to substantive matters. Polling firms include questions in their surveys at the behest of paying clients, and the presence of these clients lurking in the background is often apparent in poll results as reported in the media. There are, though, any number of research agencies that can be called upon to undertake specialized research designed to certify facts, ranging from academic laboratories and research groups, to teams assembled as research wings of interest-group organizations.[14] The boundaries between research organizations and organizations formed for advocacy range from fluid to invisible. One feature of the New Public is the extraordinary growth of small-scale interest organizations with shadowy purposes and ambiguous names.

The proliferation of advocacy groups led by policy entrepreneurs with frankly partisan aims has blurred the criteria by which organizations can be clearly identified as policy research institutes or "think tanks," that is, organizations that undertake large-scale, professional studies of policy alternatives.[15] It has become difficult to distinguish research institutes from groups of like-minded policy advocates, especially now that many think tanks take a politicized tack both in their ideological coloration and in their enthusiastic participation in the political methods of the New Public: marketing ideas, lobbying policies, and advancing causes through programs of public relations.

Think tanks, like other institutions of the New Public, originated in the early years of the twentieth century in a spirit of progressive, reformist rationalism. The original animus of the movement was in a sense anti-political: rational policy should be based on factual research and objective analysis rather than political maneuvering for power and payoffs. The movement began in 1907 with the establishment of the Russell Sage Foundation and immediately began to grow: the Carnegie Endowment (1910), Twentieth Century Fund (1911), the Institute for Government Research (1916 – later the Brookings Institution), and the Hoover Institution (1919) were founded in the next ten years. By 1970, after sixty years of growth, the count stood at thirty-two. Then, as is typical of the institutions shaping the New Public as we now know it, the pace accelerated during the 1970s. Fifty-six new think tanks were founded in the next twenty years (Ricci 1993, 162). The story of this rapid expansion can only be read as an account of the politicization, within the framework of the new politics of public relations, of what had once been conceived as institutes for objective policy studies carried out above the fray.

The seeds of politicization of policy research institutes – the capture of this institutional form by predetermined ideologies, promotional aims, and partisan loyalties – were sown by their success as trusted, and therefore influential, purveyors of policy studies. When the fellows of the most prestigious institutes became connected to and identified with the governing elite, they came to be viewed as sources of that elite's underlying political aims. Many years of Democratic and moderate presidencies and congresses made the principal think tanks seem part of an establishment that conservatives viewed as ideologically liberal and radicals as ideologically conservative. By the end of the Johnson administration, conservatives saw the think tank establishment, particularly the Brookings Institution, as presenting an obstacle to a full hearing for conservative ideas within the governmental elite.[16] President Nixon and John Haldeman came to fear that Brookings would house a shadow government in exile and contemplated outright political warfare with the Institute, "to blast the hell out of them and scare the hell out of them," by investigations of their tax status and accusations of radical, stigmatizing ties (Smith 1991, 197).

During this period, Edwin Feulner imagined a new sort of think tank that would bring frankly conservative ideas and advice to elite political actors and employ more effective, action-oriented methods. It would also serve as a training ground for a new, respected conservative political elite to replace the elite of the entrenched liberal establishment. In 1973, he organized the Heritage Foundation, which has had a major impact on the administration of think tanks, establishing a public relations model that measures successful performance not in weighty books but in the placement of editorials, op-ed pieces, and magazine articles, in distributing brief and timely bulletins to a well-placed audience, and in media appearances. The Heritage Foundation devotes as much as 40 percent of its budget to public relations, retailing ideas that had their origins in larger scale research projects (Smith 1991, 201). Heritage did not originate all the practices that have blurred the distinction between policy research institutes and lobbying organizations. The trend toward strategic public marketing of the ideas embedded in the scholarly books that had always been the principal product of think tanks was underway before the Heritage Foundation was created, but Heritage perfected the techniques of think-tank public relations. Many new, smaller think tanks established in the last two decades – not all conservative in political orientation – tend to focus on narrowly defined agenda, practical aims, and organized marketing efforts.

Ricci's (1993, 182–207) perceptive treatment of the new "politics of ideas," suggests a convincing schema for placing the contemporary research institute in the New Public. In the new battle for public opinion, many new voices crowd the national public arena, and "the result is a political system overflowing with forces." In such a multivocal situation, the first battle is over the agenda, and in contests over forming agenda, ideas – especially ideas about policy alternatives – are potent resources. Accordingly, those who are in the business of constructing and certifying facts and ideas now employ the contemporary instruments of organized public persuasion, public relations, marketing, and lobbying to promote their ideas. This movement parallels current shifts to the outside strategy in lobbying. Rather than bringing expertise directly but discretely to decision makers, the new think tank affects the climate of opinion surrounding decision makers by shaping the views of strategic public groups, especially the elite "policy communities" of organizations that define public issues.[17] In sum, the think tanks have been assimilated by the New Public.

# 9

## Forums for the redemption of influence

The dominance of professional institutions of public communication has a crucial effect on rhetoric and influence in contemporary public life. Rhetoric takes linguistic and social forms that lead to the inflation of influence, not just the overstatement typically connoted today by the very word "rhetoric," but a chronic, socially structured inflation produced by the *dissociation* of public discussion and underlying issues of public concern. The issues discussed in debates readily accessible to the public at large – campaign debates, for example – often fail to evoke and to aggregate the solidarities of groups whose socially grounded backing could bring about new, realistic, problem-oriented policies.

### Contemporary rhetoric and the inflation of influence

*Sources of the inflation of influence.* Four rhetorical practices dissociate public deliberation from the structure of social life: lack of meaningful policy issues on the public agenda; appeals to attitudes that do not tap structures of solidarity that could support effective responses to social problems; one-sided communication that fails to provide opportunities for demands that claims be redeemed in discourse; evasive, strategic responses that attempt to spin rhetorical descriptions rather than to supply straightforward answers to queries and objections.

The first type of dissociation occurs when broad symbols of generalized attitudes are merely displayed rather than explicated. Dissociated symbols have only weak ties to authentic issues of public policy, as in the case of the famous Bush television spot of 1988 showing a black prisoner moving around a revolving door. The generic issue was crime and the treatment of criminals, which was an authentic popular issue, but the specific issue of prison furlough policy, made notorious by the case of Willie Horton, was not on the public policy agenda then or since. Voters were asked to respond to displays of attitudinal symbols, not to participate in, or even to hear, discussion about effective or proper treatment of criminal offenders. The second form of dissociation follows when rhetorical strategies sever the ties between discourse and social structure by avoiding appeals to solidary social groups and coalitions and instead appeal to vague themes and undercurrents of sentiment in the public. This form of dissociation is magnified by political market research that pretests possible campaign themes simply to see what works, without reference to building loyal constituencies of support. Just as candidate Bush's researchers had used focus groups in 1988 to see whether the Willie Horton issue would strike a resonant chord, so candidate Clinton's chief pollster used focus groups in 1992 to discover that Clinton's humble beginnings was a potential theme to convert voters initially hostile to him (Maltese 1994, 225).

Dissociation can also be created by the organization of discourse itself. When messages are sent through channels and by techniques that avoid public response or opportunities for rebuttal, then arguments are not tested in the public realm. "Narrowcasting" in all its forms illustrates this form of dissociation. Direct mail is a strong example. When ideological appeals and requests for funds are sent to narrowly formed lists of people known in advance to be sympathetic supporters of a cause, particular solidarities are invoked and reinforced, but the larger public is not invited to participate in dialogue or to evaluate the appeals or their grounds. Avoiding public debate invites inflated rhetoric, a phenomenon that purveyors of direct mail understand well. When, after the Oklahoma City bombing of 1995, a senior representative of the National Rifle Association was confronted with a recent illustration of that organization's exaggerated and inflammatory rhetoric, he responded that, after all, the offending statement came from an item of direct mail, as if this obviously excused it from the ordinary standards of public discourse.[1] Sometimes debate may appear to be two-sided but fails to meet a strict standard of authenticity because one or both sides refuse to join the issue, substituting spin for rejoinder. By "spin," a term popularized by the current and apt expression "spin control" (a feat accomplished by "spin doctors"), I mean the use of strategic rhetorical devices to avoid answering questions or objections directly. Instead, the issue is restated in different terms, changing the subject without abandoning the argument. Spinning is frequently accomplished by changing the frame of discourse. For example, in 1995, Republican plans for balancing the American budget included proposals to reduce Medicare spending. When challenged by Democrats, who saw a good opportunity to discredit Republicans by charging that the plan would pay for a tax cut for the rich by reducing health care for retired persons, Republicans tried to spin the issue by changing the frame and terms of the argument; they began to claim that the cut in Medicare was not intended to balance the budget but to ensure the long-term solvency of Medicare. In short, advocates may avoid redeeming arguments in public discussion either by positioning themselves so as to foreclose opportunities for objections to be voiced or by refusing to provide direct answers. There is, of course nothing intrinsically insincere or logically invalid about attempting to frame issues in protective language that forestalls objection. On the contrary, by proposing new frames, new perspectives are brought to bear, and incorporating multiple points of view is one of the defining aims of democratic deliberation. Dissociation occurs when frames are altered in a strategic effort to avoid issues *instead* of discussing them.

*A note on money in the New Public.* The most prevalent current criticism of the New Public attacks the role of money in contemporary politics, an issue already very extensively treated in academic literature, journalism and, for that matter, in everyday popular discussion (Alexander 1992; Kubiak 1994; Morris and Gamache 1994; Regens and Gaddie 1995). I have focused instead on the rationalized communicative practices that lie behind the high cost of contemporary persuasion, rather than issues of corruption, important as they are. Advertising and polling are costly and so are the fees of the professionals who manage political communication. Accordingly, campaign expenses have risen substantially, and this makes candidates beholden to contributors.[2] In consequence, incumbent legislators must redirect their efforts to raising money and keeping track of political action committees and other donors, whose contributions have earned favor-based influence redeemable in access at the very least.

This critique asserts that what appears to be a process of influence has become a disguised process of drawing upon wealth. Exchanges of money for favor-based influence, which avoid persuasion in open discussion, undermine what should be a discursive arena and, by assimilating influence to money, erode civil society. The ideology of the operatives in the New Public makes room for the influence of money under the broad tent of democratic values. Public relations practitioners have claimed that the very right to speak is and should be contingent on capacity to raise money. Herbert Schmertz of the Mobil Corporation remarked that opposition groups' "ability to raise money to support a point of view is also indication of whether they have a constituency to support them. Otherwise they are just self-appointed keepers of the public morals." He went on to complain that while Mobil was responsible to 200,000 shareholders who have invested money in the corporation and the directors are elected by these shareholders, opposition groups are responsible to no one, and in that sense are not a real constituency (Sethi 1978, 19). Schmertz's view hearkens to a narrow view of liberalism that privileges economic liberties and obliquely inflates influence by devaluing influence as such in relation to the money that buys it.

*How dissociation inflates influence.* In order to clarify the effect of rhetorical practices on the stability of influence, it will be useful at this point to review the concept of influence as a medium and the sense in which influence can be "inflated." Influence occurs whenever one person persuades another by argument, but if a person comes to have a generalized capacity to persuade others, that person has a store of influence, and influence can then be seen as a medium. When one person accepts another's influence, the influencer gains support in return for providing guidance, and influence has mediated this exchange. When the target of an attempt to persuade refuses to accept generalized influence, but instead insists on a fully developed argument, then the exchange becomes like the barter that takes place when participants in trade do not use or accept money as a medium. Accepting influence is a matter of degree. Readiness to accept a medium reflects one's level of confidence in its value. When confidence in the value of a medium declines, we speak of inflation, and control of inflation depends on adequate backing of a medium with real capacity to redeem its tokens – to exchange money for goods, or influence for explanations and proofs as necessary.

Redemption is not always necessary. Systems of media are overextended in principle, for their purposes are accomplished by extending credit in order to allow people to rely on symbols instead of insisting on constant access to the things those symbols represent. In the case of influence, extending credit means accepting representations without fully developed evidence in order to overcome the potentially paralyzing constraints of time and resources were discussion given over to endless argument. Nevertheless, it must be possible to redeem tokens of influence so that people can get information when they need it, or else confidence in the system of influence will not be sustained. Hence, systems of influence like other media systems, require backing – capacities to redeem symbolic tokens.

In chapter 5, I suggested that influence is backed at two levels. *Relational* backing rests on the capacity of the targets of influence to demand (and influential people to provide) redemption of the token arguments on which the rhetoric of influence relies. Avoiding debate and spinning responses are direct threats to the relational underpinning of webs of influence. *Systemic* backing depends upon the real existence of common interests and solidary ties that can be mobilized in support of collective projects. The substitution of symbols for policy issues and failure to engage solidary groups deplete systemic backing for influence at the institutional level. The institutions and practices of the New Public are implicated in all four categories of dissociation and account for the chronic inflation of influence in the contemporary public sphere.

*Inflation in the New Public.* Political consultants, working with pollsters and media experts to design and implement electoral, public relations, and opinion-based lobbying campaigns, attempt to identify issues that will work in their favor, without regard to underlying political and social problems and concerns. They create a differentiated category of issues called "campaign issues." The differentiation of campaign issues has stimulated the growth of a subspecialty among political consultants known as "issue research," which focuses on issues as potential tools for campaigns rather than for their substance. Polling and pretesting are employed to determine what messages will appeal to which constituencies (or demographic categories) and what packaging of these messages will be most persuasive. The methods of political consultants are intended to discover winning strategies, and it is apparent that this mode of issue selection and campaign design tends toward public discussion on manufactured, dissociated issues.

George Gallup's audience research for film studios is the prototype of polling and pretesting designed to reduce the risk of unexpected reception of messages. Showing versions of films to audiences representative of moviegoers and then adjusting the final product to avoid negative responses predicted by these pretests reduces the risk of mistakes attributable to lack of understanding of the public's measurable tastes. But the objections of writers, directors, and actors to these procedures contained the germ of a larger critique of audience research generally. When audience research is used to tailor political messages fashioned to accord with public attitudes and tastes, the primary communicators who purchase research and consulting services are cut off from their socially organized audience. Real audiences, by word-of-mouth social interaction, can define messages, adjust their views, and respond collectively in ways not predictable by extrapolation of the initial responses of sample audiences.

The studies of social influence launched by the Columbia school half a century ago seemed to give reassurance that mass media do not create mass society because of the so called "two-step flow" of communication whereby media messages do not flow directly to the public but are instead defined, interpreted, and evaluated in a process of socially organized daily discussion within the constituent units of communities. But what about the flow of opinion back to the producers of the media – the would-be influencers?

Is that also mediated, aggregated, and defined through organized social groups? Modern market research attempts to skip that step and allow campaign managers to gauge the public temper from direct and atomized individual opinions (Mayhew 1992).

*Focus groups.* Focus group discussions have provided pretesters with another strong technique for identifying issues, reducing risks, and avoiding direct responses from the public at large. The members of focus groups are not as atomized as poll respondents, but gauging opinion through focussed discussion bears its own risks of distortion. Observing social interaction in microcosm, in advance of the uncontrolled process of response and redefinition that occurs when messages are subjected to discussion within the complex groups, networks, and institutions of the larger society, allows those who fashion public communication to anticipate the reception of persuasive appeals as they will be constructed in their audiences. The process of communication in natural settings is bypassed during the initial phases of shaping programs of public persuasion in order to avoid the risk of choosing themes (or spins) that will fall flat in the give and take of discussion. Focus group research can also discover stimulating themes that are actually amplified as group members influence each other. Some themes may appear to lack support in public opinion polls, but when brought up in group settings, command surprising levels of assent. In 1985, focus groups of Democratic Party defectors spontaneously expressed outspoken opposition to affirmative action programs, which surprised the polling firm that conducted the discussion sessions, because at that time such sentiments were not apparent in opinion surveys (Kolbert 1992). Standard procedures for focus-group studies of political issues readily explain this sort of discrepancy. Focus groups are formed by assembling homogeneous groups of people with similar locations on the political spectrum. The aim of this research is often to explore in depth the views and responses of strategic swing voters. The power of the Willie Horton theme was validated in a focus group made up of nominal Democrats who had voted for Reagan but were leaning toward Dukakis. Similarly, the groups that manifest a reservoir of resentment against affirmative action programs were comprised of Democratic Party defectors. Participants in these groups soon discover that they are among like-minded people, and when the first racist remark gives no one pause, constraints on expression fall away. People feel encouraged to state opinions that they would not share with an anonymous poll taker who is presumed to hold to opinions legitimated in the dominant forums of public discussion.

Once a promising line of appeal has been identified, the impetus to use it is strong, even if the prevailing norms of correctness have inhibited the use of this appeal in the past. Once articulated by a respectable candidate, a questionable line of rhetoric becomes legitimized by its very use. Given the first premise of campaign design – try to appeal to themes that market research identifies as potentially effective – the extensive use of focus groups as a means of finding and testing themes has predictable consequences: it changes the terms of public discussion and magnifies the importance of themes that appeal to swing voters.

Appeals to swing voters are not designed to further the process of coalition formation, either by reinforcing existing coalitions or by establishing new ones. Campaign designers are either satisfied with transitory appeals that might capture sufficient support at the margin to win an election or, if they are so fortunate as to discover a so called "wedge issue," they can draw off votes that would normally go to the opposition in accord with the ties of solidarity that constitute the opposition's normal base of support. Even wedge issues are not ordinarily used to create new groupings of solidary constituencies, but merely to capitalize on dissatisfaction, hot-button stimuli, and negative appeals.

*Avoiding debate.* Influence, like other media, depends on trust. Sustaining its value requires opportunities to test the promises on which it rests. In the case of money and its various token forms, such tests are conducted continuously as people experience the acceptance of their money, checks, and credit. Influence, too, is continuously tested, at least in daily life, as people ask each other to back their claims. It is entirely legitimate to ask a trusted person, whether a friend or a professional adviser, for explanations and evidence. In the political sphere, where the citizenry has meager access to public leaders, there is little opportunity to test the trustworthiness and reliability of their information and arguments or to demand redemption of their claims. Most people must rely on public forums within which advocates and counter advocates debate issues, allowing the public at large to judge the presentations of leaders who are acting as surrogates for those who cannot themselves join directly in the discussion. If such forums do not exist, then the public cannot engage in redeeming debate, even vicariously. The standard practices of professional advocates schooled in public relations and advertising often lead to just such avoidance of two-sided debate.

Public relations experts advise their clients to "get their story out." If a client is charged with polluting the air, the accused firm is advised to provide an alternative narrative about their conservation programs. The client is told to avoid debating the charge, to change the subject, to spin the issue by telling a new story. The public lacks institutions to sustain attention to issues and to demand answers from responsible organs of information. There are sometimes voices in the wilderness, but not regular procedures to test the backing of the stories that professional influence experts place in the media. When public relations experts and lobbyists tell their clients' stories, they appeal to facts certified by faceless experts, whose independence is compromised by financial, political, and ideological interests that preordain their expert conclusions.

In the current political environment in Washington DC (and in some of the American states), lobbying the public in order to bring tokens of public opinion to bear on legislators and officials has become a prominent mode of exercising influence. Accordingly, public relations techniques have become more pervasive. The public at large has little knowledge of what grassroots groups organize in Washington, for expert organizers narrowcast their pleas for participation. Moreover, the targets of their influence often have difficulty distinguishing grassroots opinion from the astroturf that specialists can create by sheer technique. Mobilizing public opinion to get things done is a democratic instrument of influence, and influence is held by prolocutors who build their rights to speak for constituencies. This is a normal part of the influence system, but the influence it creates is ultimately inflated if it is constructed by illusion and not tested in processes of open public deliberation.

### Signs of inflation

A variety of evidence, much of it indirect, suggests that the proliferation of persuasive techniques in the New Public has led to spiraling inflation of influence. Indicators that display waning faith in a system of influence that makes trustworthy information increasingly hard to acquire and that fails to provide venues for explication and verification of leaders' token messages are signs that these leaders' influence has become inflated. As persuasion loses its backing, leaders' influence buys less support. Three categories of data are suggestive: declining rates of political participation, diminishing confidence in social institutions, and specific studies of the sources of citizens' feelings of alienation and disconnection.

*Participation.* Participation is often cited as an indicator of public cynicism, but voter turnout is an ambiguous measure. American elections as measured by voter turnout has fallen over the course of the twentieth century, from a little over 75 percent in 1900 to 50 percent in 1920. After a modest rise during the New Deal era, voter turnout has again fallen to the level of the 1920s (McGerr 1986). The decline of participation clearly corresponds to long-term replacement of party-based mobilization of mass participation with what McGerr calls "the politics of education," a product of the progressive era, and "the politics of advertising," a core element of the New Public. The data from 1960 to 1990 indicate continuing and substantial declines in voter participation during the period of the efflorescence of the New Public (Rosenstone and Hansen 1993). Voter turnout is not however a direct measure of voter cynicism and the inflation of influence. Indeed, failures of mobilization (attributable to the underlying decline of civic participation) and voter cynicism are sometimes treated as competing explanations of low voter turnout. The effects of the interrelated complex of waning civic organization, public disillusionment, elite management of communication, and low voter turnout cannot be readily disentangled.[3]

*Confidence.* A number of polls have traced declining public confidence in governmental institutions over the last few decades. Few institutions have escaped the downward trend in approval ratings, but the US Congress has fared especially poorly. During the two decades before the 1990s, only a third to a half of those polled approved of "the way the US Congress is handling its job," but in the 1990s this approval rating has dropped, sinking below 20 percent on several occasions (Patterson and Magleby 1992; Magleby and Patterson 1994). Such measures fluctuate in response to political tides and the latest scandal, but one query that is regularly included in the American National Election Study (ANES) has shown a relatively consistent trend over the last thirty years: "Would you say that government is pretty much run by a few big interests or that it is run for the benefit of all the people?" Since most political leaders claim that they speak and act for all the people, I take this question to be a rough surrogate measure of public confidence in the claims of leaders to be national prolocutors who exercise their influence on behalf of the public. In 1964, 65 percent of ANES respondents said that government was run for the benefit of all. By 1972, only 38 percent could agree that government runs for everyone's benefit and in 1988 agreement dropped to 31 percent. In 1992, 75 percent said that government was run for a few big interests, and belief that it is run for the benefit of all dropped to an all time low of 20 percent.

*Why citizens feel alienated.* Beginning in 1989, the Kettering Foundation sponsored a series of studies of citizens' views of the political process. The Harwood Group, a Virginia research company, used focus groups to go behind the general measures of dissatisfaction supplied by public opinion polls. The most widely publicized of these studies, *Citizens and Politics* (Harwood Group 1991), was based on discussions in ten focus groups in ten different American cities. The 120 people who participated in these groups cannot be considered a random sample that would allow generalizations, but their discussions suggest the bill of particulars that brought 75 percent of the respondents in the 1992 ANES poll to express the view that government is no longer run for the benefit of the public. As one focus group member put it, "The original concept was for elected representatives to represent your interests. That is no longer true. It is now whoever has the most money can hire the most lobbyists to influence representatives" (Harwood Group 1991, 20). Much of what people had to say about their rejection of the contemporary political process reflected dissatisfaction with the dominant institutions of the New Public. David Mathews' summary of the Harwood study includes a succinct summary: "These Americans felt that they had been pushed out of the political system by a *professional class* of powerful lobbyists, incumbent politicians, campaign managers – and a media elite" (Mathews 1994, 12, emphasis supplied).

The Harwood discussants expressed particular resentment against the influence of special interests and lobbyists. As one participant concisely stated, "Citizens don't have a voice; lobbyists, special interests – *they* have a voice" (Harwood Group 1991, 19). The rhetorical dichotomies of public and private, part and whole, so important in the discourse of seventeenth-century English liberalism, live on. "Citizens" correspond to the "good counsellors" of seventeenth-century tracts, those counselors who advise the king as to the needs of the whole public, and "special interests" correspond to the tracts' references to evil counselors, "bands of mere privadoes." The current cultural form for rhetorical expression of unjust exclusion from the public has survived. Only the names of the players have changed to reflect new structures of interest and representation. Our evil counselors are PACs, and lobbies, and influence peddlers.

Although exclusion from meaningful participation is the overarching theme of dissatisfaction among Harwood's discussants, many of their particular complaints are directed against specific practices of the professional communicators. Several of these citizens' statements demonstrate their rejection of contemporary political debate: "I want fair campaigns – no more mudslinging. I want to hear more about the issues." "You can get into and out of office on a single negative issue . . . case in point: Willie Horton." "The whole idea of sound bites – getting a message across in 20 seconds – is absurd." "[Sound bites] have distanced every one of us from what's really going on, and has distanced our leaders from what's really going on with us, to a tremendous degree."[4]

Inflated influence and its relation to the unavailability of forums from which citizens can get answers to their questions was most directly addressed in the groups' discussions of "straight talk" and evasion: "[You can ask a public official] What's your stand on an issue? You ask them and you never get a straight answer." "People have lost their faith in their policy makers because they always tell what they're going to do, and they never follow through. Or they stand up there and tell blatant lies . . . " One citizen's comment deserves special emphasis, for it goes to the heart of the public's desire for a forum that would not accept evasive answers: "In a recent debate, I hoped that the candidates would say something that would be really clear. But it turned out to be mudslinging about the other candidate. Sometimes I feel like *making* them answer the question."[5]

*Can professionalism temper the New Public?* In his later years, Parsons employed a concept of collegial organization to amplify the connection between professional conduct and the normative integrity of society (Parsons 1954a; Parsons and Platt 1973). David Sciulli (1985; 1990; 1992) has proposed a revised collegial model in his work on what he calls "societal constitutionalism," a scheme intended to synthesize Parsons and Habermas by grounding Parsons' concepts of collegial organization and procedural legality on Habermas' standards for communicative action. Well-grounded concepts of proper procedure would allow participants in society and its constituent organizations to know whether they are treated fairly as associated equals or as mere objects of manipulation by organizations that feign social commitments to gain their private instrumental ends.

Given the aims of Sciulli's articulation of Parsons and Habermas – establishing concepts for recognizing manipulative influence – he appears to offer a promising vantage point for viewing the problems treated in this book, but in my estimation the collegial model offers little hope for amelioration of the problems of the New Public. Sciulli supposes that professionals in organizations will, out of self-interest in sustaining their autonomy, insist on sustaining the integrity of the professional norms that support their fiduciary status, and, in so doing, will resist the corrosive drift toward domination of the social order by instrumental uses of rational techniques. Despite his theoretical optimism, in his critical moments Sciulli (1990, 389) concedes that "The leadership of professional organizations have become incapable of establishing and maintaining even the most minimal standards of professional duty among their membership."

Professional norms do constrain instrumental conduct in several roles within the New Public. Professional pollsters certainly resist pressure to make polls to order. I have interviewed representatives of polling firms who proudly narrated accounts of refusing to accept engagements that would require them to produce the results that clients want. (Prospective clients do ask for such services and sometimes shop around for firms that will comply.) Nevertheless, polling firms have little control over how their product is used and even collaborate in planning for its instrumental use. This example defines the limitations of the collegial model. Professional

norms have limited scope, even when leveraged by the authority of professionals within their collegial settings. Attorneys are officers of the court
and are bound to standards of legality and probity, but they are paid to and
*expected* to assist clients to achieve their instrumental ends. Public relations
groups, polling firms, and campaign consultants, whatever the ethical constraints on their conduct, lack even the quasi-official status of attorneys
and are hardly in a position to restrain clients merely by insisting on professional autonomy, not while the the encompassing system is predicated
on advancing the plural ends of actors exercising their rights of advocacy.
As Sciulli suggests, the principal impact of the professional advocate's role
in a market oriented, bureaucratic society is to encourage setting forth
causes in reasonable presentations (1992, 254–7). Important as this is in
establishing a prerequisite for rational discussion, discourse cannot become
institutionalized until it provides forums for citizens to engage in public discussion.

### Forums and the mass media

Citizens who participate in civic dialogue largely through surrogates are
dependent on mediated communication. Public communication is not
direct, but transmitted between citizens and public figures by third parties.
Public opinion and collective action is led by people with influence, and the
most important channels for transmitting influence and information to the
larger public are the mass media. Television, radio, and the press are the
principal sources of public information in the New Public, and their crucial
role in presenting surrogate debate raises the critical question as to whether
they do so effectively – whether the mass media support or impede public
discussion.

   *Modern communications.* The modernization of communications was an
essential component of the modern public and paved the way for the arrival
the New Public. From print to television, technological innovation has
made communication cheaper and easier and has transformed the relation
of the audience to the speaker. Print and its contemporary rivals share a
crucial social capacity: they free communication from ascription to face-to-
face interaction and thus allow the larger and geographically extended
audiences that enable "imagined communities" (Anderson 1983) to become
units in the networks of modern solidarity. Television is the most dominant
medium in the New Public, not because of any special powers of the visual
as such, but because it is so easy to use. Once in place, television affects the
nature of mass appeals. It lends itself to broad-based appeals that undermine the older solidarities of class-based politics that cohere in the work

place and in neighborhoods; communicators look instead for messages that appeal to new arrays of consumers, demographically similar people, and cultural groups (Negrine and Papathanassopoulos 1996). Television is not unique in this respect. The cultural logic of mass appeal applies to all the media, and the other modes of mass communication, including print, are still alive and influential.

As we saw in chapter 6, advocates of public life once saw print as the foundation and guarantor of public discussion precisely because its emancipation from personal life allowed insulation from institutional control. It was seen as the means *par excellence* for the objective, discursive search for public truth. Are the media still well adapted for effective, redeemable public discourse? I have delayed discussion of the new mass media as a component of the New Public in order to juxtapose contemporary journalism and the problem of the redemption of influence.

*Criticizing the mass media.* Many critics think that the media obviously fail to enhance democratic discussion or to provide the necessary information for public debate. They argue that the press is dominated by an increasingly small number of big corporations whose only responsibilities are to their financial bottom line and to the sustaining values of capitalism (Bagdikian 1990). The media is biased in favor of government and the business interests of the elite; the media suppresses news that conflicts with these interests and manipulates coverage in order to lull the public into consenting to their governance (Herman and Chomsky 1988). The White House press corps kneels to the President, relying primarily on press releases rather than independent reporting, which is exactly what their profit-seeking employers want them to do (Hertsgaard 1988). In any event, the public cannot be well informed, for they are exposed only to sound bites, paid political advertisements, and entertainment thinly disguised as news.

These perspectives view the media as rather sinister, the more fearfully so to the degree that the media are actually effective in influencing the attitudes and actions of the public. To recognize the role of the new practitioners in public life today is not to assert that their rationalized techniques allow manipulation of the public at will. There is still a two-step flow of communication. Messages are interpreted by opinion leaders and leaders pass their views on to others who themselves interpret their experience through a cultural prism. As some observers put it, all interpretation is local, and this maxim is nowhere more apparent than in studies of the reception of American television programming around the world. Cultural presuppositions affect how viewers interpret the soap opera *Dallas*. Their reactions range from seeing J. R. as a moral hero in some traditional cultural settings through rejecting the program altogether in Japan, whose citizens cannot accept the program as real, for it corresponds to no reality in their experience (Liebes and Katz 1990). The New Publicists cannot wholly manipulate their audiences. But they can try, and their efforts affect the social structure of communication itself, especially when audience research is employed in an effort to bypass the influence of local settings.

For a time, orthodox opinion among social scientists tended to the view that the effects of the mass media are minimal (Klapper 1960). Opinions are anchored in networks of people whose views and social influence often run counter to media messages. Ordinary citizens are capable of discounting claims, reinterpreting ideas, filtering out discordant information, or just not paying attention. Today, the dominant view among media scholars accords a more influential role to the mass media, especially in defining the public agenda, controlling the stores of readily available information, and establishing the frames within which information is interpreted (Ansolabehere, Behr, and Inyegar 1993). Yet a strong countercurrent of recent scholarship, sometimes called "active audience theory," continues to insist that audiences may not take messages as their senders intend them. According to Stuart Hall (1981), all messages are encoded and must be interpreted through a process of decoding. The sender's preferred decoding is but one of several readings, including oppositional readings contrary to the sender's intent.

Those who follow Hall are also influenced by the political animus of British critical "cultural studies." Perhaps the mass media are not so dominant after all; there is room for oppositional cultures within the public, cultures that provide resources for groups to resist mainstream, elite influence by shaping the messages and information of the mass media in new molds and thus injecting new voices into public discourse.

In a related American line of research, Gamson (1992) has studied discussion groups of ordinary people, the sort of folks who are often said to be incapable of holding and expressing well-considered opinions on complicated issues. Gamson found, on the contrary, that his groups were "not so dumb" and "not so passive" as much commentary makes them out to be. They do not simply take information from the media uncritically, but negotiate its meaning and use it selectively in the construction of their views. In short, both British and American research suggest that citizens are capable of civic discussion and we need not dismiss projects of improvement as intrinsically unrealistic and naive. The question is whether the mass media on which people must depend for access to the raw materials for forming opinion helps them to engage in public dialogue and the formation of public judgments.

*Professional practice in the media; the problem of objectivity.* The most useful insights into the effects of journalism on public deliberation come not from studies of media monopolies or of alleged biases of the press toward the left or the right, but from sociological investigations of the practice of producing news. Beginning in the 1950s with classic studies by the Langs (1953) on the logic of television coverage and Warren Breed (1955) on the impact of organizational routines in the newsroom, and flourishing in the 1970s with influential studies by Tuchman (1972; 1978), Molotch and Lester (1974; 1975); Sigal (1973); Epstein (1973); Schudson (1978), and Gans (1979), American sociologists and students of organization created an enduring contribution to the sociology of culture. These investigators demonstrated that news as reported is not a simple mirror of a real social world but a socially constructed cultural product, affected by the world it purports to represent and shaped by its own rules of production. Professional journalists, whether working in print or electronic industries, take pride in their work and value the respect of their colleagues and therefore experience pressures to meet conventional standards of workmanship. Stories written by competent journalists must be understandable to their target audiences and entertaining enough to capture their understanding. An economical and plain style of writing is highly valued, and stories are told within the "inverted pyramid" format, which starts with a catchy lead and proceeds with the most newsworthy bits of the story, including examples of how the story is played out in individuals' personal experiences, leaving other details and background materials at the end in order to facilitate easy cutting by an editor economizing on time or space. Standard professional practices encourage reporting discrete interesting events – so-called "news pegs" – and discourage reporting contexts and connections. The professional journalist's concept of good writing as telling stories with a human face in a few accessible words links the journalists' craft with the media's commercial drive for large audiences and low costs of production.

The role of the media in the influence system is profoundly affected by a production rule calling for professional objectivity: a rule that has, ironically, gone awry and produces less rather than more of the information required for public debate. Objectivity cannot be taken for granted as an obvious and natural feature of good journalism. Newspapers originated as organs of opinion, indeed partisan opinion, and the idea of objectivity did not emerge until after the First World War (Schudson 1978). Non-partisan journalism supported the rise of the mass media by establishing a claim to serve the entire public, but the ideal of objectivity as such arose as an element of journalists' aspirations for professional status. Professional journalists' commitment to unbiased objective reporting buttresses their claim to a measure of autonomy and insulation from managerial interference in their work. The idea of objectivity holds that journalists serve the public by following universalistic standards, but the institutionalization of the idea in journalistic practice has rendered the universalistic character of objectivity ambiguous.

In the journalistic setting, objectivity is supposedly achieved by following two principles: stick to the *facts* and maintain *balance*. Facts, which are presumed to be true for everybody, are counterpoised to opinions, which are personal. Reporters should only observe, corroborate, and report the facts, without allowing their personal opinions to intrude on the process. The scheme of objectivity starts, then, with a polar dichotomy of fact and opinion, but the dichotomy is not self contained; it quickly eludes its boundaries because the existence of other people's opinions are themselves facts. If a public leader expresses an opinion, that is a newsworthy fact. Yet it would not be objective to report an opinion without comment, for the audience may suppose the opinion to be factually true. Reporters' arms-length objectivity precludes them from offering their own critical counter opinions, so they must find others whose contrary views can be reported. Thus balance arises as the second pillar of objectivity and, in consequence, reporting becomes a matter of recounting conflicting views. Achieving balance by merely reporting statements of opposing sides facilitates presenting interesting tales of conflict, without assuming responsibility for providing independent information about the actual issues at stake, social contexts of the struggle, or links between dramatic episodes. The press narrates disembodied conflict, with issues of public policy treated as secondary to tales about who is winning and by what strategies. A standard that reduces objectivity to the presentation of facts, and defines facts as accurate accounts of what participants in conflict say, may well protect news workers and their employers from angry complaints of bias by public figures and angry citizens, but such a concept of objectivity conflates objectivity and *neutrality*, very different concepts of a universalistic stance.

Freedom from intrusive personal biases and instrumental partisan interests may allow some messages to be trustworthy and useful to audiences interested in coming to judgments regarding the public interest, but mere neutrality is a weak standard; it fails to call for placing information in context, explaining the substance of issues, and evaluating the reliability and biases of sources. Objectivity in reporting cannot be justified by reference to a factual and neutral style of rhetoric any more than universalism in science can be grounded in an empiricism that claims that the facts speak for themselves. Moreover, recognition that journalistic "facts" are derived from the statements of third parties leads to yet more questions about the claimed objectivity of factual journalism.

*The problem of sources.* Given constraints on time and on access to the vast array of events in the world, journalists are dependent on sources. Access to sources is, indeed, the mark of a good reporter. As one of Gaye Tuchman's informants said of a fellow reporter, "He's the best political reporter in the city. He has more sources than anyone else" (Tuchman 1978, 68). Reliance on the economical use of sources, taken together with the notion that objectivity means reporting what sources say, makes news coverage a conduit for transmitting prestige-based influence, not a vehicle for presenting objective analysis of the issues and events of public life. This generalization derives from studies of how workers in the news industry decide who should be granted the status of a source. There are two categories of sources: *routine* sources that provide press releases and similar forms of packaged information and *enterprise* sources that are generated by reporters' independent efforts to find people who can supply or corroborate stories (Epstein 1973). Epstein's study of 2,850 news stories published in the *New York Times* and *Washington Post* over a fourteen-year period documented that only about a quarter of these stories were based on enterprise sources. The rest were based on ready made information. More than half were supplied by officials of the federal government, including the legislative branch (Epstein 1973, 119–30). Many other sources are also bureaucratic officials, in state and local government, business, or public interest organizations. Choosing officials as principal sources flows directly from the two main criteria for choosing sources: credible knowledge and capacity to represent constituencies. Officials are presumed responsible and close to the scenes of action, which makes them what Fishman (1980) has called "people entitled to know what they say" and thus "authorized knowers." Networks of authorized knowers upon whom journalists routinely depend constitute a "web of facticity" (Tuchman 1978, 82–103) that bestows credibility on news workers.

The web of facticity is clearly a system of influence, supported by group solidarities and the prestige attendant to status in these groups. The influence of the media rests on the prestige accorded to sources, more than on rigorous, independent investigation, and such elements of independent inquiry as do enter the typical news story are known to the journalists who produce them but are opaque to the viewers and readers. The audiences of the mass media are located at the end of two stages of influence, the influence of sources and the influence of news organs that transmit the knowledge and opinions of sources to the public.

Newsmaking is regulated at the source by a process of negotiated exchange between two bureaucracies, the bureaucratic leadership of the political sector and the hierarchy within the mass media (Sigal 1973; Fishman 1980). As in the case of lobbying, the subject of this exchange is information. Bureaucrats, both governmental and private, provide information to the press in exchange for opportunities to promote their views and enhance their public relations (Molotch and Lester 1974). The press receives inexpensive and routine access to interesting stories and ready made materials to use in meeting their obligation to balanced coverage of matters of opinion. The term "negotiation" is not metaphorical. The parties must decide how much sources will reveal and how much the media will print or broadcast. Terms like "off the record," and "deep background" are unintelligible except in the context of negotiation about telling more in return for printing less. To negotiate how much must be disclosed or held back in order to sustain the parties' integrity and trustworthiness is to negotiate the very terms of their relationships – the trust and solidarity on which their networks rest.

The public is not generally aware of the negotiations that bring them the news, does not know how much news is taken from press releases written by interested parties. The public does not know that news is contructed by a proccess that is the reciprocal of the technique of public relations – *placing stories*. The public is unable to engage news makers or their sources. Accordingly, news messages can be resisted but not redeemed.

*Citizenship and information.* Do the faults of the media matter? Recent research suggests that traditional ideals for journalistic presentation and coverage of civic life, ideals centered on the notion of an informed citizenry, may not be relevant to the way citizens actually gather and process information. In the course of defending the rationality of the general public, investigators have been influenced by Downs' (1957) contention that people economize information just as they do other resources, gathering enough to allow a measure of confidence rather than absolute assurance, which in a world of uncertainty is not possible anyway. Members of the public exercise a "bounded rationality," limited by realistic constraints on time and resources and, in their civic roles, use informational shortcuts such as applying rules of thumb, noting suggestive clues, and *accepting the influence of others.* Voters can often use radically simplified strategies for making decisions and come to the same conclusion they would have reached if they had studied the issue in much greater detail (Lupia 1994). By this round-about route, investigators have rediscovered reason in a supposedly ignorant and apathetic public. Influence is the principal means by which bounded rationality works, so it not meaningful to criticize the mass media as an institution based on influence. Assistance in economizing the search for information is precisely what people expect of the media. Nor is it realistic to bemoan the superficiality of the media in relation to the notion of an informed citizenry, for creating a highly informed public is not the way the process of public information is played out.

A recent study by Lodge, Steenbergen, and Brau (1995) makes a case for abandoning the traditional concept of civic knowledge as a remembered store of facts about public affairs. The authors present evidence that people store information in the form of summary evaluations that are amended each time new information is perceived to be important enough to alter an overall opinion. The new information is promptly forgotten, but the new summary evaluation remains in the memory until another opportunity for a responsive change comes along. Survey respondents seem politically ignorant when asked to recall specific facts, but their apparent ignorance may only reflect how poorly current methods of testing civic awareness capture citizens' strategies for gaining and using information in an economical manner. By implication, the time-honored notion of an informed public must be replaced with a process-oriented concept of a public engaged in learning.

Recognition that members of the public trust influence in order to economize information and that in relying on influence the public accepts rhetorical tokens in lieu of fully presented facts and well developed arguments does not mean that intelligible public discourse is unimportant. Granting the importance of influence brings us back to the crucial question: what backs influence? Public discourse cannot function without the use of influence, but influence ultimately fails if it cannot be redeemed. The question is not whether all public discourse can be made to conform to Habermas' high standards for communicative action, an ideal that could be realized only if all public voices were willing to forswear the rhetorical mode and all public ears became deaf to appeals based on influence. A public sphere without influence would be like a political realm without government – a species of anarchy, without solidarity and without leadership. Rather the question is whether there are readily available means for people who wish, from time to time, clarification, explanation, and factual support for the statements of those who seek to exercise influence. Public forums are means of stabilizing systems of influence and protecting them from inflationary pressure by linking groups to their leaders through grounded dialogues.

*Inflation and media events.* Inflation is a relative term. Influence is always inflated to some degree, for its usefulness depends on the extension of credit that makes communication possible. In this respect, bypassing intermediary organization through communicating directly to citizens is not necessarily destructive of social organization. Indeed, this process, called "disintermediation" by Dayan and Katz (1992), lies at the heart of modern solidarity, which promotes new, more inclusive solidarities among audiences. Dayan and Katz point out, disintermediation is not a product of electronic communication; print played this role in the Protestant movement. In our own day, "media events," by drawing audiences together to experience national events, can provide moments of mechanical solidarity with powerfully integrative effects. Special media events, such as Anwar el Sadat's address to Israel, a species of inaugural statement delivered over the heads of Israel's leaders, may transform the balance of public opinion in an adaptive direction. Nevertheless, inflation becomes problematic when it is not possible for audiences to test, on appropriate occasions, the contestable claims and proposals of leaders.

### Deliberative forums for communicative redemption

Several strands of thought have contributed to recent interest in the concept of deliberation. Not all advocates of deliberative discourse insist on Habermas' demanding ideals, but most converge on definitions that both capture Habermas' principal concerns and presume the idea of a public sphere. They agree that deliberation requires a voice for all who have a stake in its outcome, for without fully representative discussion, collective decisions neither incorporate the range of pertinent information on which workable decisions must be taken nor garner the support of those who must live with them (Dillon 1994). Strong models of democracy require public participation (Barber 1984). Deliberative public discourse should produce reflective public judgments that assume responsibility for consequences rather than merely collate ill considered attitudes and demands (Yankelovitch 1991). Aggregating individual opinions, whether by voting, or by averaging preferences, or by bargaining, is the antithesis of deliberative decision making. Hence the theory of deliberation is hostile to concepts of democracy that would resolve pluralistic tensions by resort to procedures to implement preference models of collective choice, as if preferences were fixed and external to the process of aggregation, unaffected by the dynamic and dialogical processes of deliberation itself. Bargaining implies the use of threats and promises backed by the parties' capacity to employ power and money; it belongs to the political and economic realms. Deliberation requires principled argument within an arena of discourse not dominated by political and economic resources, an arena that advocates of civil society call a public space. It limits participants to influential appeals to persuasive facts and arguments (Bessette 1994).

The mass media are too bound up in systems of prestige-based influence to provide opportunities for people to test prolocutors' claims to speak sincerely for their groups, or to require justification of leaders' claims to speak for the general public interest. Where, then, can the public turn in search of validating information? What forums might permit citizens to engage in deliberations that would allow them to ask for and to receive answers to questions regarding what lies behind the rhetorical tokens that dominate public discourse?

*Platforms and forums.* A person who attains the capacity to speak as a prolocutor on behalf of a group and who, in that role, achieves access to the public through the mass media gains a *platform* for advocating agenda and for offering accounts and diagnoses of states of affairs, policies, and proposed actions. The groups represented from platforms range from concrete communities of similarly situated segments of a population – neighborhoods, ethnic groups, professions, social classes – to the imagined communities that form around categories of people whose solidarity is created by the acts of the prolocutors whose rhetorical appeals call attention to their common aims and interests as consumers, taxpayers, or citizens. Assertions delivered from public platforms do not enter into public discourse unless the public can question and challenge them, and such inquiries are without force unless the challenger also has access to a platform from which public audiences can be addressed. Only when issues are addressed from opposing platforms, can we speak of public *forums*.

Forums vary considerably in their structure and in their capacity to facilitate joining issues directly, ranging from diffuse multicentered arrangements that allow many voices to be heard, but do not lead to direct, platform-to-platform confrontation, to well focused, face-to-face debate.

*Diffuse* forums are the most common loci of public discussion. They are characterized by multiple platforms and types of presentation and minimal normative regulation of format. People and organizations with access to platforms express their messages directly, or as press releases, or as paid advertisements. Their messages may be substantive or may steer away from issues and attack the character of their opponents. Others may or may not respond from their own platforms and, if they do respond, their statements may occur at any time. Responses may be placed in the same organs of communications as the message to which they are responding or may be placed in different organs directed to more or less different audiences. Responses may address the issues or may try to change the subject. Diffuse public discussion is well adapted to encouraging open participation and to delivering messages to many audiences. It allows multiple questions to be addressed to public platforms but does not provide strong constraints requiring those who speak from these platforms to reply. Demands to redeem the tokens of rhetoric can be relatively easily evaded. From the perspective of the general public, attempting to confirm the claims of leaders and advocates in this chaotic informational climate is very costly.

*Third-party forums* are organized by independent, presumably neutral groups, usually media outlets, that take it upon themselves to present, from their own platform, both sides of an issue at one time and place, so that readers or listeners can evaluate juxtaposed arguments. Standard newspaper articles that present accounts of speeches or press releases and, by way of balance, include comments from others, exemplify third-party forums framed as efforts to make a contested issue their prime subject and to present an even-handed, critical account of both sides. In recent years, in response to media and public concerns about attack politics (and its attendant inflation of influence), newspaper critiques of spot political advertisements have become an important variant of the third-party forum. The contents of the spot are allowed to speak for themselves, and the newspaper provides factual background and evaluates what appears to be true, false, or misleading. There is, however, evidence that such "ad watches" are not effective and may even be counter productive (Ansolabehere and Inyegar 1996).

*Citizen* forums invite ordinary citizens to query candidates and other public figures directly from a media platform. This type of forum has proliferated in recent years with the rise of talk shows and audience participation in public appearances and political debates. Many talk shows are not forums because they are narrowcast to particular constituencies with a clear aim to build support for particular points of view, but when open-mike or open-call programs (without intrusive prescreening of questions) are broadcast to general audiences, they provide citizen forums. Since the participants are not known to the audience and display no obvious credentials, listeners and viewers cannot rely on prestige as a signal of credibility or of authorized prolocutorship. Nevertheless, citizen forums do draw upon rhetorical solidarity, for audiences identify with particular participants, view them as like themselves, and hear their questions as their own.

*Moderated, indirect debate* is a common form of nearly face-to-face discussion from opposing platforms. It falls short of traditional direct debate by protecting the opposing sides from direct confrontation. Instead, third parties (usually virtual representatives of the public) put questions, either the same or different questions, to the debaters, who answer from the relatively insulated position of not having to answer persistent questions from their actual antagonists. This format is well known to us as the usual arrangement for American presidential campaign debates.

*Direct debate*, in which people argue face to face from opposing platforms, are rare in the New Public. Although most of the American public would prefer to see electoral debates in this form, candidates consistently reject formats that are not carefully structured to allow them to pursue their own agenda and to avoid direct demands to respond to particular questions and attacks as formulated by their opponents.

In summary, contemporary American social structure provides many platforms for many voices, and conflicting views can be presented from these platforms. Access to platforms requires financial resources, social connections, and capacity to persuade the media of the importance and newsworthiness of one's cause. In the present context, I am approaching the problem of equal access from a different angle of vision. Rather than looking at the problem of equal access generally, I ask whether the public has access to authentic debate through two-sided (or several-sided) presentations of public issues from equally prestigious platforms on the same occasion. At present there are few such opportunities for people to participate in or to witness deliberative debate that nurtures demands to redeem the tokens of public rhetoric. It is appropriate and necessary that leaders employ rhetoric in order to signal current and potential supporters as to what they stand for, to establish solidarities, and to mobilize their supporters, but sustaining the value of influence also requires deliberative occasions on which positions are not just set forth but defended in public arenas.

*Improving forums by reforming the mass media.* Given the importance of the mass media as channels for transmitting both rhetorical tokens and demands for redemption, it is important to ask whether inflationary pressures on influence could be relieved by innovative reforms of journalistic practice. There are signs that journalists are concerned about the inflation of rhetoric and are ready to experiment with new formats that call public leaders to account. The most obvious example of an attempt to provide the public with rebuttal of overblown claims is the appearance of the ad-watch genre in the wake of the extraordinary outbreak of negative, issueless advertising in the electoral campaigns of 1988. Nevertheless, some journalistic voices express skepticism about whether campaign watchers can provide objective critique of political advertisements and insist the public would be better served by allowing the candidates to slug it out, letting the people ask the questions through talk shows, and asking journalists to do their part by focusing on issues rather than the dramatic suspense of political horse races (Lichter and Noyes 1995). The participation of a number of elite journalists in the Twentieth Century Fund's Task Force on

Television and the Campaign of 1992 provides additional evidence of uneasiness engendered by the excesses of the campaign of 1988, but the tenderness of this critique is not encouraging to advocates of aggressive reform. Little can be expected of critics who take heart in the fact that sound bites in the 1992 campaign were marginally longer than the sound bites of 1988. Nor did this group take particular note of one of their member's report that when CBS attempted to introduce longer sound bites of thirty seconds, the enterprise was not successful because program executives found such "long" excerpts "unwieldy."[6]

Other observers see promise in stronger pragmatic changes in the practices of the news media. Schudson (1995a, 211–23), for example, examines practices that have been repeatedly documented as biased and ineffective. He argues that journalists should go beyond providing citizens with better information in support of democratic electoral politics to report on forces in the larger society that impinge upon the political order. He emphasizes the need for journalistic attention to the larger contexts of political affairs, including the workings of political parties, the influence of big business on legislation and government, and the process of lobbying. He particularly stresses the need "to report more fully and on a regular basis about decision making in the private sphere that directly affects public policy" (219), reporting, for example, the positions of pressure groups and the nuanced variations of views among socially defined constituencies. Schudson also believes that more stories on how well leaders have remained accountable for their statements and promises would provide (what I call) forums for redemption, albeit forums in which the public accepts journalists as representative surrogates for their own concerns. I interpret Schudson's recommendations as a plea for more extensive and deeper coverage of civil society. Publicizing the activities that constitute civil society strengthens the civic sphere. His recommendations are grounded in careful analysis of recognized weaknesses in the civic performance of mass media and are consistent with longstanding conceptions of the proper role of socially responsible media. He calls for modest and realistic reforms, yet some observers might well remain skeptical on the grounds that corporate journalism is hopelessly mired in its conviction that only sound bites, quick-cut images, dramatized horse races, and sensational tidbits can draw and hold sufficient audience attention to sustain high profits. Moreover, his suggestions rely on journalists to be virtual representatives of the public interest rather than ensuring that public constituencies acquire platforms for their own views.

Curran's (1991) essay on broadcast journalism in Europe, where public networks play a central role in providing civic information, asserts that democratic communication must go beyond reliance on journalistic norms of public service. Even in settings that insulate influential broadcasters from the distortions of profit oriented practices, commitment to public service among journalists does not ensure that the interests and perspectives of broad ranges of social groups will find voice. Curran's recommended "third route," beyond either private or collectivist control, would rely on grants of radio frequencies, video channels, and financial subsidies to allow under-rep-resented groups to enter media markets within institutional arrangements that give them control over their own voices and thereby create a public sphere with adequate ideological and cultural diversity. But neither Schudson's nor Curran's approaches to improving the media's contribution to civic dialogue confront the problem of creating forums for direct challenge to the purveyors of rhetorical tokens, forums that would provide citizens opportunities to demand that speakers back their prestige-based, token argu-ments by setting forth evidence and explanation in defense of their claims.

### Civic dialogue

Champions of improved civic discourse to achieve the mutual influence that sustains civil society look beyond reforms in the media, and insist on more face-to-face, unmediated discussion, and participatory democracy – more of the genuine dialogue that allows public citizens to transform ill considered public opinions into deliberated public judgments (Yankelovitch 1991). The challenge is not to restore public confidence in government or faith in the pronouncements of public leaders. Rather, the challenge is to restore the public's confidence in itself. We must abandon our presumption that public discourse takes place between government and cit-izens and relocate this discourse within the public. It is this discourse that creates and constitutes the citizenry as a public (Mathews 1994). Although some of the partisans of this position have been inspired by Habermasian ideals and influenced by the concept of a public space, domestic American political traditions – Jeffersonian ideas of democracy and such institutions as the town meeting, for example – stand in the background of the projects of contemporary advocates of participatory democracy. These ideas are consistent with the historic conception of civil society, which exists to the degree that citizens are organized to discuss questions of public relevance, to form public judgments on issues of public policy, and to express these judgments in politically effective forums.

The convergence between American exponents of public dialogue and advocates of the version of critical theory set forth by Habermas is espe-cially apparent in American critics' attack on expertise as the basis for public persuasion. Officials who see the public as uninterested and uninformed, and themselves as educators whose responsibility is to *tell* the public what should be done, take their own technical knowledge to be definitive. They do not listen to the public and therefore fail to understand that people rightly bring their values and experience to their perceptions of public problems and their evaluations of proposals for collective action (Yankelovitch 1991; Mathews 1994). Forums are doomed to failure unless participants come to discussion with mutual respect for each other as persons, not as objects of rational administration.

*Projects for civic dialogue.* Many activist supporters of civic dialogue do not organize citizens for partisan causes. They see themselves as facilitators who help people join in discussion of their common problems, advising discussants on methods for ensuring that they listen to each other and include all relevant voices. They are, ironically, *experts* on process, who employ their influence to encourage realistic discussion that transforms a congeries of wishful opinion into responsible public judgment. They advise public officials who become engaged in public dialogue to listen to citizens and to avoid the educational mode that comes so naturally to officials who assume that their expertise and experience provides right answers that need only be explained to the public.

Public forums are not necessarily designed to allow citizens to confront powerful and influential leaders and demand answers to their questions. Projects for civic education allow citizens to engage in productive discussion and thereby reconnect with each other and with public concerns. Such projects can be judged on their effectiveness in collective problem solving in particular local contexts, but their worth is measured by their contribution to the revitalization of civic culture. In the terms introduced in chapter 5, these projects are directed not to the relational backing of influence but to its system backing – the underlying solidarities that support mutual faith in people's representations and promises.

Some students of public discussion are optimistic that properly organized dialogue can unite people in problem-solving civic communities. The Harwood Group (1993) conducted focus group sessions designed to tap citizens' views on current opportunities for public discussion and their hopes for what such discussion would give to them if good forums were available. According to Harwood's research, people are hungry to connect themselves with public issues, ready to draw upon these connections to discover areas of common concern and opportunities to work together, and eager to find community with others through such work. People believe that public dialogue could serve these ends if it provided opportunities to relate issues to their personal experience, placed issues in larger contexts, employed ordinary, non-technical language, and offered authentic sources of information – sources that can be trusted to speak plainly and without ulterior motive. The Harwood Group does not use Habermas' terms, but they seem to assert that public dialogue can succeed were it approached as an extension of the participants' "lifeworld."

The Harwood Group is closely connected to the National Issues Forum (NIF), the largest project in the genre of civic dialogue. The Kettering Foundation commissioned Harwood's most influential studies, including *Citizens and Politics* (1991). In *Politics for People* (1994 ), David Mathews, the President of Kettering, drew on *Citizens and Politics* for his own diagnosis of the civic ills of the body politic. Together, these two works spell out the *raison d'etre* of NIF: improving the effectiveness of the citizenry by helping people to engage in public discussion, to learn deliberative skills, and to reconnect themselves to civic life. Since 1981, The Kettering Foundation, together with the Public Agenda Foundation, have assisted groups that are interested in sponsoring their own forums. Three public issues are chosen each year, and three issue books are prepared to help guide open and equal discussion by presenting alternative perspectives and frames while avoiding any suggestion that the right ideological formula or technical information would readily resolve the issue at hand. "Public Policy Institutes" are held at several locations to provide the conveners of issue forums with advice on guiding deliberative discussion (O'Connell and McKenzie (1995). According to Mathews (1994, 108–90), "thousands" of organizations have now made use of the issue books and other support services to sponsor deliberative forums. Many sponsoring organizations are educational institutions, which is consistent with the program's greater emphasis on teaching deliberative skills rather than resolving substantive problems. Nevertheless, some advocates of egalitarian forums see the program as a model for "democratic leadership" (Gastil 1994).

*Aggregating diverse forums.* Most promoters and practitioners of democratic deliberations work in local settings. Whether their aims are largely educational, as in the case of the National Issues Forums, or immediately practical, as in projects to democratize the workplace, to promote deliberative discussion and decision making on community issues, or to ensure democratic self government within associations and social movements, most deliberative forums take place within local groups engaged in face-to-face discourse. Less energy is applied to bringing the results of localized deliberations to larger forums within metropolitan, state, and national political systems, and even less to how the outcomes of local forums could be communicated to larger, encompassing communities by means consistent with the deliberative principles by which these outcomes were achieved. When the leaders of local efforts encounter problems of large scale communication and the resistances embodied in entrenched political institutions, their approach to communications often becomes strategic and instrumental. Social movements that operate on strong democratic principles within their own ranks may even resort to the means of the New Public, employing public relations firms and using the same rhetorical techniques as their adversaries.

The efforts of National Issues Forums and like enterprises cannot be altogether dismissed, for they seek to encourage the serious, organized, and independent discussion that creates the public and nourishes civil society, but efforts to connect deliberative discussions to governmental officials and public institutions have had little impact to date. One NIF informational statement, printed in their 1995 Issue Books, claims, "Generally a public voice emerges, which sends a clear message to officeholders about the direction citizens want their government to take. Each year, the results are shared with people in public office and, in this way, forum participants help set the government's compass." My conversations with leaders of the movement and my perusal of their literature suggest that this is more a statement of aspiration than of reality.

It is not surprising that the initial efforts of the Kettering Foundation to make legislators aware of products of deliberations were not effective. How could we expect gentle quasi-lobbying about local discussion groups to compete with well organized and financed mobilization of constituency pressure brought to bear by the professional practitioners of grassroots lobbying? On the other hand, a recent inventory by the Harwood Group (1993) of efforts to reconnect citizens and public life lists several promising enterprises. In projects of "public journalism" in Wichita, Charlotte, and Minneapolis, newspapers attempt to bridge the gap between the deliberative forums of civil society and the communicative channels of the mass media by sponsoring, organizing, and *reporting* civic discussion. Some critics complain that these programs breach journalistic objectivity by involving reporters in making the news they report, but these critics also confess that public journalism can be seen as a response to waning confidence in the media's contribution to deliberative civic life (Jurkowitz 1996; Kurtz 1996). Projects in Oregon, Dallas, Dayton, and North Dakota seek to communicate citizens' concerns and views, as formulated in deliberative forums to legislators and public officials. These programs are not designed to provide citizens opportunities to insist on further amplification of the low-information bites and bits, slogans, and summary statements – the tokens of argument – that are the carriers of influence in the real world of communication. Deliberative forums quite properly aspire to give voice to citizens, not to test the claims of leaders. But if leadership is the principal means by which diverse claims can be aggregated through accepting leaders claims to speak on behalf of large-scale solidarities, then forums for the redemption of these claims would play a crucial role in the democratic establishment of social solidarity.

Failure to aggregate discursively formed opinion is not necessarily tantamount to complete failure of civil society. As we have seen, some advocates of civil society locate its functions at the periphery in serious and reflexive discussion among interested citizens who produce and test new ideas that gradually make their way to the center where they become attached to groups with social power (Cohen and Arato 1992; Habermas 1996). A case can be made that civil society and social influence are most healthy in myriad local special-purpose associations, informal and formal, in all the rich diversity of their forms and aims. Despite Putnam's (1995 a, b) well-known "bowling-alone" thesis, a warning of the incipient decline of civic organization, other observers have mustered considerable evidence to the contrary. The June, 1996 issue of The Roper Center's journal, *The Public Perspective*, reports on what editor Everett Ladd (1996b, 1) calls "a huge volume" of data on rates of participation in school affairs and social services, number of organizational memberships, volunteerism, and political activity *outside parties and elections*, all of which refute Putnam's theory of declining civic engagement.[7] Nevertheless, inflation of influence in political civil society, at the border of the polity and the public, undermines the capacity of civic organization to press for adaptive change for the whole society.

### Deliberative polls

James Fishkin's (1991) proposal for the establishment of "deliberative polls" takes one further step toward an aggregated public voice and redemptive discussion of the claims of public leaders. Fishkin envisions a forum in which randomly sampled citizens engage in dialogue that leads them to informed and exemplary public judgments. Yankelovitch (1991) distinguishes public opinion and public judgment. Opinion is off the cuff and unenlightened by serious discussion; public opinion as measured in polls merely aggregates individual opinions. Public judgment, by contrast, is achieved through deliberative processes. It is considered and responsible, for deliberating citizens weigh the arguments of others, become aware of the value choices involved in public decisions, and take responsibility for the consequences of the positions that they advocate. Fishkin has serious reservations about plebiscitary democracy in which ill-considered public opinion, whether measured by polls or by other manipulation of the appearance of support, all but governs public policy in the name of direct democracy. Yet direct democracy embodies important values, especially if it is truly deliberative. The problem is that deliberative processes, which presuppose direct, face-to-face give and take, cannot be readily adapted to huge populations in mass societies.

Fishkin proposes an ingenious device for establishing an institution for face-to-face democratic deliberation in an influential position at the center of public life. "Deliberative Opinion Polls" would combine the democracy of sampling procedures with the virtues of deliberatively achieved opinions. A national sample of citizens is brought to a single venue for a series of meetings on important issues. This randomly selected panel watches debates, questions candidates or other public figures, and discusses issues with each other. These proceedings would be televised to the public at large. Panelists would be polled both before and after their discussions, and because the opinions of the panel are reached after public discussion, their views could have greater influence than the results of a normal poll. The results of deliberative polling can be considered a tally of the opinions of representatives of the general public *after they have seriously considered the matters at stake.* As Fishkin said to one reporter, "This is meant to measure what the public would think if it were thinking."[8] It is not too fanciful to view the results of a deliberative poll as the verdict of a non-binding jury, a form of virtual representation through which panels represent citizens' *civic* process of deliberation rather than a *political* process of binding public choice. It would be, then, one means of building differentiated civil society.[9]

In January of 1996, Fishkin achieved his ambition of producing a national deliberative poll. With support from foundations and the University of Texas, 450 Americans, chosen by rigorous sampling methods, were brought to Austin to discuss three clusters of issues in small groups and, in plenary sessions, to ask questions of both experts and political candidates. Six hours of the proceedings were broadcast on the Public Broadcasting System. As of this writing it is too early to assess the results, although it is clear that the event was not extensively publicized and had little effect on public consciousness. It is interesting to note, however, that several defenders of conventional polling view the Fishkin enterprise as subversive. Allowing the members of a sample to influence each other violates the assumptions on which we are allowed to generalize from polls (Ladd 1996a: Newport 1996; Mitofsky 1996). If the results of discussion lead to changes in opinions it is because some participants have been influenced by others, which, say the critics, is actually undemocratic. This critique is particularly popular among practitioners, some of whom believe that authentic opinion is how people respond to surveys, and ignorant opinions must, as a matter of democratic right, count for as much as informed opinions. These practitioners make a virtue of what others see as the unfortunate practical limitations of costly civic education. By implication, paid professionals in the employ of political apparatus are the only legitimate sources for the public's influence on itself.

#### "Sometimes I feel like *making* them answer the question"

One of Harwood's focus group members expressed her frustration with the evasive strategies of public leaders by saying she wished she could make them answer. At present this seems a mere wishful hope, for political leaders, advised by their communications specialists, set great store by controlling the agenda and terms of discussion in order to allow space for spinning, imposing frame-defining catch phrases, avoiding defensive postures, and fixing consistent messages. As Newt Gingrich is reported to have said, no amount of time spent on controlling communications is wasted (Bruck, 1995). In short, public leaders avoid direct public demands for the redemption of rhetorical tokens as carefully as financiers avoid runs on their banks. Can one imagine, then, institutional forums that would effectively require public figures to give straightforward responses to questions the public wants to ask? Let us try.

*A national forum for citizens.* Let us call this imagined institution the National Citizens' Forum (NCF) and suppose that it would be founded and sponsored by a new national association named Citizens for Democratic Deliberation (CDD). CDD would choose a panel of public representatives to put carefully selected questions to important policy makers, opinion leaders, or candidates. The questioning would take place on a very public stage, and while leaders under examination would be allotted time enough to give substantial answers, panelists would be given ample time for repeated follow-up queries designed to insist on adequate, direct responses. This scenario may or may not be achievable, but simply imagining what it would entail will clarify what is meant by the notion of a "redemptive forum." Such a forum, were it institutionalized, would not only provide for authentic national debate at critical junctures in policy making, including national elections, but would put public leaders on notice that they might be held accountable, before a national audience, for public defense of their diagnoses and prescriptions, in a forum that will not accept spinning the questions, evasion, or yet more tokens.

The success of a National Citizens Forum would depend on achieving four necessary conditions: *impartiality, publicity, representation*, and *access to leaders.*

1. *Achieving legitimacy: Universalistic grounds for impartiality.* The legitimacy of NCF would require that both the forums and their parent organization be perceived as completely impartial – intellectually neutral as to ideology and politically neutral as to party. Caveats regarding the possibility of complete neutrality would be set aside in order to support public perception that the forums were not pressing ulterior agenda items of their own. Although the sponsoring agency might bear some resemblance to contemporary political reform groups, it must avoid becoming involved in procedural causes of the sort espoused by Common Cause or the League of Women Voters, let alone going so far as Common Cause once did by taking sides on nuclear issues (Rothenberg 1992). To the extent that tough questions will be perceived by some as partisan, some queries brought to the forums by panelists may be suspect, but a fair balance of questions should help correct that impression. Moreover, the best defense of the panelists is the universalistic premise behind all their questions: "What we are asking reflects what the public wants to know about your genuine commitment to the public interest. Are your policy positions for the public good? Do your arguments for your positions meet the test of honest, persuasive argument?" In short, *panelists achieve their legitimacy by taking the role of prolucutors for the public.*

2. *Publicity and effectiveness.* Through this national forum, audiences of citizens participate (albeit through identification with surrogates) in a process of exploration of what lies behind the token statements of influential leaders. Without national publicity through the mass media, sessions of the NCF could not achieve their purpose. Ideally, each session would be considered an important national event worthy of simultaneous broadcast on all the major television networks. This level of publicity would encourage exposure of the public to national political discourse.

3. *Representation and integrated participation.* Deliberative forums require that a wide range of voices representing diverse perspectives, interests, and experiences are included. An adequate level of diversity cannot be achieved by simply selecting elite panel members to ask such questions as seem important to them. On the other hand, at least some members of the panel must possess their own stores of influence in order to give weight to their presence, so that the audience does not believe that the panel is overmatched or lacks capacity to carry forward aggressive lines of follow-up query. Yet it is equally essential that the audience be assured that the panel's questions reflect the actual concerns of the public at large. At this point the

work of the National Issues Forum might well lead the way, for this institution has generated considerable knowledge and experience of the means of conducting public deliberation at the local level.

One can imagine the formation of a number of local deliberative groups in each of the principal regions of the country and asking them to discuss the meta-issue of which among the many issues facing the nation most deserve serious discussion in the NCF. Selected conveners of these local groups could be invited to join the national panel to ensure that groups asking questions at the final events – nationally televised forums – include a mix of elite leaders and local citizens. Reports of local deliberations would be forwarded to the governing board of CDD for selection of a limited number of issues for treatment by an NCF panel, whose members would then develop an agenda of questions to address to public leaders. Care must be taken to ensure that the array of local groups is ethnically and socially diverse to ensure representation of a variety of socially based perspectives in the discussions that produce the raw material for the selection of issues and the formulation of questions.

4. *Access to leaders.* All social institutions require a means of securing the compliance of the people whose actions are to be regulated. Before cooperative compliance with group norms can be established there is a yet more elementary condition to meet: physical access to those whom the institution purports to control. How do we get national leaders – presidential candidates, for example – to come to the forum and answer the panel's questions? An NCF panel could not compel leaders to appear and to answer questions by power of subpoena and would, therefore, rely on normative force of public opinion. NCF would rely on their capacity to create social pressure to cooperate, which in turn would depend on public ratification of the Forum's claim to be acting as prolocutors on behalf of the public. Ratification grants *influence* to the NCF. The public itself would be the source of sanctions against unwillingness to participate, for the public can in turn withdraw their willingness to accept the influence of those who refuse to enact their accountability. Publicity is the channel for transmitting these sanctions and, accordingly, the mass media are the brokers for the transactions in influence that could establish the normative jurisdiction of the NCF. Broadcast of the forums by major networks would establish the proceedings as national events. Refusal on the part of an invited leader to participate would then become news in its own right – news of refusal to face the nation.

# 10

## The rhetoric of presentation

Influence is a social phenomenon. It works through appeals to solidarity and is therefore grounded in solidary groups and networks. Accordingly, the structure of influence is a component of the structure of society. On the other hand, rhetoric, the means of creating and activating influence, is cultural; it employs systems of linguistic and visual meaning to evoke solidary attachments. Since the sociocultural contexts of rhetorical practice vary across societies and eras, understanding the rhetoric of a given time and place requires understanding of the cultural assumptions of those who create and consume it, the *rhetorical cultures* that allow people to make sense of rhetorical appeals and to evaluate their persuasive sway. The variability of rhetorical cultures leads us to a final question about the New Public. Does public communication now operate within the framework of a new rhetoric defined by new norms of persuasion? I argue that it does and I call this new rhetorical culture *the rhetoric of presentation*, a mode of persuasion that instead of relying on facts and arguments that purport to *represent* the world, employs direct *presentations* of stimuli that stand on their own as effective persuaders.

The defining marker of a given type of rhetorical culture is what its participants take to count as legitimately persuasive. In the new *rhetoric of presentation*, minimal informational content is taken as ideal rhetoric. There has always been a rhetoric of presentation, in which the display of symbols outweighs discursive argument, but the new rhetoric of presentation, developed by media specialists, has produced profoundly anti-discursive techniques that devalue high levels of information as confusing and dangerous.

### Types and stages of rhetorical culture

*The classical means of persuasion.* Aristotle classified the "artistic" means of persuasion as reliance on the character of the speaker (*ethos*), argument (*logos*), and appeal to the emotions of the audience (*pathos*). Argument is an artistic means because, though logical, its *rhetorical* use employs syllogisms that are truncated and artfully arranged.[1] Premises are suppressed and audiences must supply missing stages of the argument for themselves, which not only moistens dry expositions but also draws the listener into the argument as an active, if silent, participant. Aristotle's emphasis on this technique, known as *enthymeme*, suggests that even the most rational category of rhetoric makes use of tokens. Some premises are denoted in the argument and others connoted by suggestion, and by implication the speaker warrants that omitted premises could be supplied if necessary. *Logos* from the mouth of an orator is not strictly rational. It is a special form of connotative argument that operates by suggestion, with all its pitfalls, including innuendo and evasion. Argument by enthymeme is standard practice in advertising and political persuasion, especially in the presentation of brief token arguments that implicitly suggest that a product or policy will have positive consequences, but do not specify how or why these promised benefits will be achieved.

*From types to stages.* Aristotle's three means of persuasion can be restated as accounts of three types of the social organization of influence. In sociological terms, a rhetorical system founded on *ethos* or character corresponds to a status order wherein credibility is awarded to those accorded status by traditional norms. In societies with well established institutions of debate, those who demonstrate command of the *logos* of argument build stores of capacity to persuade and so achieve respect and influential status. When the platforms of debate are used to appeal to attachments to groups by evoking loyalty, fear, envy, anger, and like emotions, the rhetoric of *pathos* offers a route to influential status to those who are able to to use this means to acquire prolocutors' roles, especially the right to speak on behalf of status groups.

It is always tempting to transform analytical typologies into theories of phases in the movement of history, and Aristotle's typology is no exception. The history of influence could be narrated, though not very persuasively, as a series of stages marked by the successive dominance of character, argument, and emotion. Traditional societies allocate prestige according to a hierarchy of social status, and the influence of character adheres to status-based prestige. Institutions of public debate are a hallmark of modernity and, with the appearance of the ideals of enlightened philosophy, persuasion by rational argument became the privileged mode of rhetoric. However imperfect and brief its institutionalization, rational discourse was the preferred means of persuasion in modern civic culture. Now mass democracy and institutions of mass, impersonal communications have led to demagogic appeals to popular sentiments, and the rhetoric of *pathos* has risen to a dominant position. The civic history of the United States could be given a similar reading. Influence in early colonial America was overwhelmingly interpersonal, face-to-face, and status based. Even when important messages were conveyed by correspondence, letters were often delivered in person by representatives with status appropriate to the occasion (Brown, 1989). The sway of personal influence and local community elites was somewhat attenuated by the national democratic movements of the revolutionary and federalist eras, but American civic life and politics remained tied to the prestige of notables until after the Jacksonian revolution, when the rise of political parties established an alternative base for the exercise of influence. Party competition for the loyalty of a larger electorate and regular efforts to mobilize these loyalties supposedly introduced the golden age of political oratory, most commonly illustrated by the Lincoln–Douglas debates or the careers of any number of famous nineteenth-century American orators. The public space created during this era of oratory has now contracted, it is said, in consequence of the rise of advertising and television, which put an end to authentic debate and substituted brief appeals to emotion for serious argument about issues. This sequence (or parts of it) are stated explicitly or taken for granted in a great deal of writing about the history of American politics, but positing a grand historical movement from systems of status and character to civic arenas for political parties and argument, and then to mass societies and appeals to emotion is too simplistic to suggest telling insights into the nature and genesis of the New Public (Schudson 1992).

In the first place, the distinctions between *ethos*, *logos*, and *pathos* are analytical; concrete rhetorical appeals make use of all three means in many compound forms. Second, every historical era supplies social contexts in which multiple types of compound appeals will be appropriate and effective. The study of particular historical eras and transitions reveals not just a dominant rhetorical mode, but currents and cross-currents of rhetorical culture that reflect the social conflicts and institutional upheavals of the times. Finally, because of this historical particularity, useful typologies of rhetorical cultures must often include modes of rhetorical communication that Aristotle's general categories do not encompass. To understand the rhetoric of the New Public, we must define and distinguish two such rhetorical modes, the rhetoric of *spectacle* and the rhetoric of *presentation*.

## The rhetoric of spectacle

The notion that spectacle is a pervasive means of persuasion is widely accepted among students of communication, including Habermas, whose historical account of public life is centered on the idea of "refeudalization," the notion that medieval spectacle was reborn in late capitalist electioneering.[2] For Habermas, the modern politics of advertising and contrived publicity is comparable to the medieval practice of dramatizing the hierarchical social order in spectacles: processions, ceremonies, tournaments, insignia, and elaborate dress and manners. All this derives from a concept of representation in which the manorial lord "displayed himself as an embodiment of some sort of higher power." Such "representation pretended to make the invisible visible through the public presence of the person of the lord." In this sense the prince and the lords represented themselves to *be* the country, not just its representative, and hence can be said to have "represented their lordship not for but 'before' the people" (Habermas 1991 [1962], 7–8).

In current parlance, spectacle *enacts* the social order, persuading the viewer to consent to hierarchy by presenting it as real and grounded in the nature of things. For Habermas, displaying forms of democratic social order through apparently contested elections, but without authentic public discussion, is a mere enactment on the part of the dominant elite who "stage" this spectacle. The democratic show of the liberal bourgeois state is enough like the show of nobility to justify labeling the decline of true public space "refeudalization" (Habermas 1991 [1962] , 231–2). Of course the two shows are also so different that it is difficult to resist noting that using this label was a rhetorical gesture on Habermas' part. Nevertheless, enacted spectacle does have powerful rhetorical sway, and control over opportunities for public enactments provided a base for social influence.

The rhetoric of spectacle should not be so broadly defined as to include every rhetorical appeal that employs images or visual displays. A subcategory of rhetoric should not be so all encompassing as to include virtually all rhetoric. It is more useful to reserve the use of "spectacle" for reference to occasions and displays that rely upon persuasive enactments of social relations. The gleam of a new car in a glossy advertisement, or the play of search lights in the sky attracting people to a dealer's showroom, has tangential connections to social relations in that commercial relations are social and automobiles are perceived as status symbols, but such displays are far removed from medieval processions, fraternal regalia, and party conventions. The rhetoric of spectacle is not, however, limited to enactments of status hierarchies that symbolize and reinforce the established order. Spectacles may enact lateral conflicts, as in the case of party conventions and rallies. Nineteenth-century American elections employed more spectacular enactment than contemporary elections in the age of the New Public. Spectacle may also enact attacks on hierarchy through protests and demonstrations. The 1995 Million Man March, on the Washington Mall, designed to promote solidarity among Black males was as much a spectacular enactment as any medieval procession.[3]

*Rhetorical stages in American politics.* McGerr's (1986) account of the transformation of American politics between 1865 and 1928, a movement he describes as "the decline of popular politics," demonstrates both the importance of the rhetoric of spectacle in nineteenth-century party politics and the vulnerability of overgeneralized theories of stages in the grand (or tragic) course of rhetorical culture. Nineteenth-century party politics was less a matter of persuasion by oratory than of mobilization of the faithful, and the technique of mobilization was, above all, the staging of spectacular events to dramatize the solidarity of the party. Solidarity was enacted in a spirit of exuberant celebration and featured mass rallies, marches, parades, bands, uniforms, and banners (McGerr, 22–41). Party-based spectacle also included reference to the status order. Notables were honored during the course of these events, even to the point of stopping in front of homes to serenade important community figures. Nor were verbal appeals neglected. Mass rallies included vigorous oratory, and the attitudes and loyalties mobilized by spectacular events were learned and sustained by strenuously partisan newspapers, but the system was capped by spectacular displays designed to get party adherents to the polls. The effectiveness of this partisan system in mobilizing voters is manifest; in the last quarter of the century, voter turnout for presidential elections exceeded 75 percent.

Voter turnout began to decline at the turn of the century in the wake of criticism and reform of the rhetoric of spectacle by progressive leaders who wanted educated voters to make informed decisions on the issues. In the late nineteenth century, Samuel Tilden and Abram Hewitt forged new methods of campaigning that emphasized rationally organized, systematic canvassing and the distribution of campaign literature that addressed the issues of the day. They eschewed messy and partisan spectacles and (perhaps because they saw the need to appeal to non-partisan "swing" voters) instead developed information agencies, originally dubbed "literary bureaus," that operated outside the control of the party machines. This move, undertaken in the name of rational campaigning and rational voters, ironically signaled the birth of the propaganda apparatus of contemporary political campaigns in the New Public.

At first glance, the reform politics of Tilden's supporters and successors appears to have introduced a rhetoric of *logos* that featured rational discussion, but the movement did not envision a form of politics in which the people's own experience and concerns set the public agenda and animated forums for discursive contests about public policy. McGerr rightly calls Tilden's movement "educational politics." The ideal rhetoric proclaimed by the advocates of educational politics includes a strong preference for rationality, to be sure, but it also presumes that the citizenry must be educated by an elite that already knows the rational answers. Educational politics is driven by a *rhetoric of expertise*.

*The coming of advertised politics.* The waning of partisan spectacle, which by the turn of the century was moribund, and the rise of elite reform politics led to declining political participation, and as political leaders looked for new means of mobilizing voters, advertising began a slow rise to its dominant place in American political rhetoric. Like the educational mode, advertising relies on elites to inform the public, but unlike the political educators, who produced reams of pamphlets that treated policy issues in great depth, political advertisers used slogans and posters to present tokens of their arguments. The old Literary Bureaus became Publicity Bureaus. According to McGerr, the election of 1896 marks the historical moment when the rapidly fading politics of spectacle, the stalled politics of education, and the ascending politics of advertising were bound together in a balanced mix. By 1896, Theodore Roosevelt could already say of Mark Hanna, McKinley's campaign manager, "He has advertised McKinley as if he were were a patent medicine" (McGerr 1986, 145). By the election of 1912, the old spectacular politics was dead, and advertised politics assumed unprecedented importance. Publicity bureaus, operating from national headquarters, busily cultivated the press, and advertisements were placed in magazines and newspapers (McGerr 1986,164). But only in the last decades of the twentieth century, when advertising became conjoined to market research, did a new rhetoric of presentation come to dominate the production of political messages.

### The rhetoric of presentation

The rhetoric of presentation takes the rhetorical token to be self contained, sufficient in itself, and needing no redemption. Images speak for themselves and slogans do not require explication. They are like jokes, which are also self contained; if a joke requires explanation it is not funny, and it is pointless to defend the proposition that it is. In the rhetoric of presentation, tokens are, in a sense, still tokens; they still stand for larger chains of argument and bodies of evidence, and they still carry an implied warranty that they could be redeemed if necessary, but it is not necessary. If a token carries its message and evokes a responsive chord in the underlying values and sympathies of the audience, it has done its job. If a token fails, it is better to find a new one than to try to explain it.

When Tony Schwartz (1973, 92–7) says that the best advertising contains no information and that "truth is a print ethic," he is espousing the rhetoric of presentation, but his reference to print manifests his bias toward the image. The presentational mode subsumes spectacle as well as other visual rhetorical means that aim for self-contained messages, but important as images are in the rhetoric of presentation, words remain the principal vehicle of persuasion by presentation. Phrases can be just as self-contained as images. Searching for the most persuasive words is, of course, as old as rhetoric itself; it is called eloquence. But in traditional rhetoric, eloquence was an integral component of oratory, not a search for catch phrases to serve as self-contained substitutes for fully developed rhetorical pleas. In the rhetoric crafted in the New Public, professional specialists devote substantial resources to finding just the right words, slogans for use as sound bites or constantly repeated refrains for longer arguments. Such refrains serve not to strengthen particular whole speeches, but to etch defining phrases on the public mind.

Newt Gingrich's search for the right words to defend the Republican position in the Medicare debates of 1995 is a case in point (Weisskopf and Maranass 1995). Early in 1995, Republican leaders decided to cover the costs of a tax cut by reducing the rate of growth of the Medicare program, but realized at the outset that they would encounter political risks. Medicare is a popular program, and the Republican plan was vulnerable to the charge that benefits for the elderly were to be cut to finance a tax cut for the wealthy. Gingrich and his associates began a "relentless search for the right words" (6). An initial meeting of Republican leaders and consultants established that words like "cut," "cap," and "freeze" should be avoided. The plan, what the consultants called the "product," should be sold as *saving* Medicare. Linda DiVall, Gingrich's personal pollster and a consultant to the Republican National Committee, reported that her extensive focus group work with seniors suggested that "preserve" would be a more effective word that "save."[4] Over the next six months, several groups worked together to refine the language. A team of party and congressional press secretaries known as CommStrat lead the way. Aided by further focus group research, including decisive work by consultant Frank Luntz, "preserve" was expanded to "preserve, protect and improve," and then, to avoid the implicit promise of the term "improve," to "preserve, protect, and *strengthen*." Finally, on the strength of Luntz's advice, the phrase "for future generations" was added in order to capture the most effective argument identified by polling techniques, appeals to intergenerational solidarity – what we must do for our children. The aim of this enterprise was to forge a summary phrase that could be used constantly and consistently by all Republicans. As Haley Barbour, Chairman of the Republican National Committee, put it, once you find a theme, "the biggest thing is to get everyone saying the same thing." A staff member at the committee described the idea more colorfully: "Repeat it until you vomit" (Weisskopf and Maraniss 1995, 7). This process does not lead to embedding civic messages in situationally relevant, eloquent discourse. It is designed to create eloquent tokens that will stand on their own to frame and to crystallize public opinion. When this tactic succeeds, discourse is undermined, for critical rebuttal of crystallized phrases is answered by claims that the token words uniquely state the only correct descriptive *connotations*. A good joke cannot be rephrased. Dialogue becomes frozen in repetition, and the rhetoric of presentation becomes beyond redemption in deliberative forums. Its tokens present too little information to invite dialogue, or even to allow it. As Cmiel (1990, 261) has noted, such statements as "Coke is it," or the parallel political slogan "Nixon's the one," make no discernible truth claims.

Brief token arguments are not necessarily "presentational" in the sense I have used that term. If brief arguments lend themselves to amplification and defense and are presented in contexts that allows for requests for explication, they are legitimate, indeed necessary, components of civic discourse, but thirty-second spots presented on television do not generally provide any opportunity for two-way communication. Their authors presumably intend them to be self sufficient. Hence such spots fall under the rubric of the rhetoric of presentation. Yet defenders of brief spots do not concede that public dialogue is in any way cheapened by brevity. The culture of presentation takes its modes of communication to count as legitimately persuasive.

Political consultant Richard Deardourff once complained to a Harvard conference that he was sick of the charge that brief spot commercials undercut civic discussion and proceeded to read a twenty-four second statement on abortion to demonstrate how much content can be packed into such a short message. Paraphrased, this straightforward statement indicated that the (hypothetical) candidate supported a woman's right to choose and, by extension of this right, the legitimacy of paying for abortions with public funds. Deardourff then asserted, "I don't know how much more one needs to know about that subject in order to form an opinion" (Diamond and Bates 1992, 377–8). I suspect that many listeners would want to know a great deal more. Voters could easily recognize this as a prochoice statement and apply an appropriate litmus test, but in any serious discussion, many listeners would want additional information. Do you support abortion at any stage of pregnancy? If the prospective mother is a minor, should parents be notified? What would you do to make your preferred policy a reality in this jurisdiction? How are we to know whether your statement professes your true belief? Diamond and Bates, who present this example in a serious book about political advertising, do not take issue with Deardourff's claim that this statement presents all that anyone would need to know. I attribute Dearourff's claim and the authors' consent not to lack of imagination regarding the many concealed issues in this or any other twenty-four second spot, but to a fundamental failure to distinguish between a *cue* that provides adequate information to allow voters, given their general preferences, to approximate the rational decision that they would make if they were truly well informed, and the information that especially interested voters would need to redeem the candidate's tokens. Not to make this distinction is to honor low information and to mistake models of how the electoral process works in practice – through cues and signals – for the way it should work were influence to be protected from inflation. Long-term faith in the process requires redemptive forums that approximate civic discourse, not mere summations of general attitudes. To dismiss the need for such forums is to accept, as many do, the rhetoric of presentation.

### Postmodern communication

Advocates of postmodern perspectives might claim that my account of modern communication and influence is fatally flawed by its stubborn grounding in the premises of modernity. Insistence on the necessity of forums for the redemption of tokens assumes that symbols refer to some form of discoverable reality, but even apart from postmodern rejection of the correspondence theory of truth, many postmodernists claim that the symbols we use to communicate no longer have referents. There is nothing behind symbolic tokens that could be used to redeem them. In the world of images, the inflation of symbols is already infinite. Jean Baudrillard, the most extreme exponent of this view, goes so far as to say that Americans are so ensnared in a media-created world of interlocking images, which have lost all reference to objects and refer only to each other, that it has become necessary to create frankly fantastic spectacles in order to draw people's attention away from the unreality of their every-day world.

Disneyland exists in order to hide that it is the "real" country, all of "real" America that *is* Disneyland. . . . Disneyland is presented as imaginary in order to make us believe that the rest is real, whereas all of Los Angeles and the America that surrounds it are no longer real but belong to the hyperreal order and to the order of simulation.                        (Baudrillard 1994 [1981], 12)

The "hyperreal" comes about when images become so strong that they "implode" with the objects that they once represented and, becoming indistinguishable from each other, create a simulated world of simulacra that seem more real than the humdrum objects of earlier eras.

Baudrillard is known for his indulgence in hyperbole. His work is sometimes referred to as "totalizing," as attributing the entire social world to the systematic impact of a single overwhelming, dynamic force. Just as Enlightened Philosophers thought they saw the eve of a world transformed by unleashed reason, and Marx proclaimed that the economic order, in his day capitalism, drives and determines all society, Baudrillard asserts we are in the age of the image and the simulacrum, which have in effect *become* society. In this respect, Baudrillard loses track of the mainstream of postmodern thought, which starts from the premise that there are no longer any convincing metanarratives for human history that allow us to locate our personal provenance, venue, and identity within a larger framework of defined meaning. Hence our schemes and lives become fragmented (Lyotard 1984 [1979]). Baudrillard retains a master narrative – the loss of reference and the rise of simulated life – but nevertheless remains in the postmodern camp, for he locates fragmentation in the loss of even short-term narrative, in the instantaneous character of media images, presented as pastiche or collage, or at best as self-contained mini-narratives, that offer occasions for enjoyment but not sustained stories linked to a larger world with an ongoing history (Baudrillard 1983). This, too, is hyperbole, but Baudrillard's challenge should not be lightly dismissed, for he is referring, however colorfully (even recklessly) to features of the modern media and to forms of social consciousness that these media promote, including *the legitimation of the rhetoric of presentation.*

When the media present staged events as news, it becomes difficult to demarcate a border between events in the world and the symbolic presentation of the world to the public. When the public identifies with celebrities, even celebrities primarily famous for their celebrity, it does not require a great leap of inference to conclude that these constructed figures (many of them defined by the fictional roles that they play) have taken on a powerful species of reality. The public cannot distinguish between images of public figures as presented in the media from these figures' off-stage selves. In the mass society, communication about the larger society and its public figures is mediated, and we cannot get behind the media's symbolic presentations as linked in a web of films, videos, advertisements, printed displays, radio and television programs, and logos. These images are connected by cross references to each other, and consumers of products and services, entertainment, sports, and public affairs are drawn into the web and led from one image to another by a chain of symbol-rich advertising and promotion. These are the social realities on which Baudrillard draws to construct his image-centered account of the postmodern age.

In a crystalline passage about media language, Poster (1990, 46), reconstructs Baudrillard's premises without recourse to the heady language of "implosion," "simulacrum," and "hyperreality." Poster contends that "Speech constitutes subjects as members of a community." while "print constitutes subjects as rational autonomous egos . . . who, in isolation, make logical connections from linear symbols." In contrast, media language, which provides no contexts, allows communication in only *one direction* and is *self-referential*. It dispenses with the community of speakers and, lacking clear reference to an outside world, undermines the discourse of rational subjects. Media language, then, "invites the recipient to play with the process of self-constitution, continuously to remake the self in 'conversation.'" In consequence, the self comes to have no stable meaning, and without anchorage in an external world, lacks criteria for stable evaluations.

I find Poster's exposition plausible but unconvincing. Insofar as he is describing the rise of the rhetoric of presentation, his schematic exposition correctly depicts the loss of referentiality in a great deal of contemporary communication, but he overstates the case by strongly linking referential communication to speech and print and locating non-referential communication squarely in contemporary "media language." This theoretical move adopts a stage theory of phases of communication – traditional, modern, and postmodern – and in so doing loses sight of the analytical independence of the dimensions of rhetoric. He conflates mass and media, as if mass communication were inherently tied to a particular mode of persuasion.

Analysts of postmodern communication are eager to claim that contemporary modes of persuasion are entirely new, unprecedented in speech or print, and created by their electronic character. In fact, speech, print, and television can all present messages that do or do not erase context, allow response, or refer only to themselves. Print also mediates communication in mass societies, and can certainly be employed in the service of monological, non referential communication. Poster stresses the use of "floating signifiers" in television, signifiers that have no referents within the presented message, but implicitly invite recipients to connect symbols to advertised products. The message is thus both self referential yet potentially linked to objects in the world. For example, Poster cites one ad in which an attractive man inexplicably appears in a kitchen wherein a woman ineffectively scrubs away with the "wrong" wax. The man represents a Prince Charming who rescues the woman from her drudgery. The ad does not specifically identify Johnson's floor wax as the cause of romance. The man's presence remains a floating signifier until the viewer concludes that using the sponsor's floor wax is somehow a romantic act. But this is an old advertising technique that does not depend on electronic communication; it originated in magazine layouts. Ironically, practitioners refer to messages constructed by this technique as *referential ads*, because they aim to refer, by indirection, a product (or candidate) to a desire or value already present in the recipient. The underlying concept of "referential" advertising is psychological. It is a product of learning theory, not of the linguistic turn. The floating signifier is not special to either electronic communication in general or to advertising in particular. It is a literary device, a special case of the ancient category of enthymeme. The premises, "floor wax will warm the hearts of all husbands" and "your spouse is a husband" are suppressed and must be supplied by the audience. In short, advertising is a type of rhetoric and can be understood in terms of the varied means of rhetorical presentation, without recourse to any unique features of electronic communication.

*Are media messages subject to critique?* Prominent postmodern theoreticians are prone to exaggerate both the novelty of contemporary rhetoric and its capacity to generate an unreal world. Nevertheless, the pervasiveness of electronic communication, television's capacity to deliver the rhetoric of presentation, and the exploitation of this capacity by political consultants are central features of the New Public. Taken together, these points require serious consideration of the postmodern claim that media persuasion has become beyond criticism. If so, discussion of redemptive forums is obsolete.

Baudrillard's assertion that postmodern language lacks reference to a world of objects is coupled to the corollary view that statements in nonreferential form cannot be subjected to rational criticism. The public's only defense is silence. Claims that texts do not refer to objects in a real world, have no stable meanings, and are reinterpreted by each reader are common among postmodern thinkers, some of whom extend this critique beyond electronic "image-speak" to language generally (Derrida 1976). Postmodern criticism generally concedes that referential communication is possible and effective in everyday life, especially in instrumental transactions. People can make arrangements to meet at a certain time and place and can understand directions as to how to get to the meeting place. But critics insist that this sort of communication is trivial. In a famous exchange between Derrida and John Searle, Searle's obvious, common-sense examples of clearly effective referential speech in the service of coordinated interaction failed to win any explicit concessions from Derrida, who refused to join the issue, responding instead in an evasive, playful manner. His response can be read as stating in effect, "Well, of course, but so what. What does this have to do with important philosophical questions."[5]

Why should what happens continuously in everyday life be considered trivial? To the critics, the billions of counter examples that take place every day are trivial because they do not bear on ultimate questions of guaranty: global questions of social meaning, interpretive questions of literary meaning, questions about the meaning of our selves. Ordinary speech cannot settle these questions with understandable, once-and-for-all answers. As Poster (1994, 82) puts the matter of triviality, granting everyday efficacy of instrumental communication, even in a hyperreal world, does not resolve the problems created by the non-referential images that dominate the airwaves, for "what is in doubt is that this sort of thinking [about walking from here to there] enables a historically informed grasp of the present in general." Nevertheless, the bulk of contemporary communication is referential and coordinative, and to dismiss this vast body of messages as trivial, uninteresting, and instrumental is a serious theoretical mistake. What we find interesting is a consequence of what we want to understand, and if we want to understand influence in the New Public, it is necessary to recognize that influence involves factual claims, at the very least a claim of sincerity.

Limiting the scope of referential communication to "instrumental" messages is misleading, for the term is packed with connotations of self interest, individualistic economic motivation, and the use of power. In the first place, means and ends cannot be conceived as concrete categories of action, for ends are also means to other ends in a means-end chain. Secondly, instrumental communication can be oriented to collective ends, as when a neighborhood group arranges a time and place for a meeting to establish, through mutual influence, agenda, plans, and priorities for a neighborhood watch or a clean up project. Priorities constitute an especially interesting category, for they are inherently normative and yet they are objects of reference, "things" to be talked about. Priorities and agenda are implied even in the rhetoric of presentation, and for this reason it is a mistake to reason from the non-referential character of "hyperreality" to its alleged immunity from criticism. Even a statement that makes no truth claims as to objects implicitly proclaims an agenda that is subject to criticism and can be called to account. In summary, useful as the idea of postmodern communications might be in some contexts of inquiry, it does not imply that social influence is moribund and, being already hyperinflated, is no longer redeemable in communicative forums.

## Postmodern self and society

Postmodern thought exaggerates the fragmentation of contemporary society, treating an imagined future as if it were a current reality. We have seen such overstatement in the idea that communication has lost its moorings in representation and become wholly engulfed in a world of images and simulations. While this view stretches the current reach of self-contained communication, the new rhetoric of presentation, featuring hyperinflated rhetorical tokens, is rather like the communicated hyperreality identified by Baudrillard. Nor can exaggerated postmodern portrayals of a new era in which fragmented selves, unable to construct meaningful narratives of their own lives, inhabit disintegrating social worlds that lack compelling narratives to define their origins and destinations, be accepted as a sober account of self, society, and culture in our time. Life goes on, and people continue to define themselves and their daily histories, and in so doing, draw upon meanings embodied in cultural materials. Yet the insights of postmodern thought can inform our understanding of new possibilities for willed solidarity.

We have already encountered (in chapter 5) an example of the usefulness of postmodern insights in Hillis Miller's concept of "inaugural" statements, which affirm solidarities that are initially groundless and take on substance only when reciprocated. Although Miller used this idea to interpret works of literature, the concept has a broader reach, and can be employed to construct the first step in a model of the formation of new social solidarities. Miller's glimpse of the potential of groundless assertion suggests the capacity of postmodern thought, in its denial of fixed social worlds and stable cultural definitions, to embrace the liberating possibilities in what others might see as merely fragmenting. In this respect, I find the writings of several relatively moderate postmodernists, including Gianni Vattimo, and Zygmunt Bauman, to be particularly suggestive. Habermas too, though not literally a postmodernist, shares some of the perspectives embraced by the postmodern movement.

*Habermas and the postconventional.* Habermas' assertion (1981) that modernity is an "incomplete project" and will remain so until the promises of the Enlightenment are realized seems to place him among modernists who have retained faith in reason and progress. Yet several of his working premises are congruent with postmodern thinking. In rejecting a purely referential theory of language, a correspondence theory of truth, and any attempt to ground epistemology in the experience of the individual subject, he enters the territory of postmodernist thought. For Habermas, truth is what emerges as consensus through dialogue conducted in accordance with the principles of discourse. His faith in reason stems from his faith in a collective process in which giving and accepting the best *reasons* is the controlling force. Appropriate discursive dialogue is now possible because we are in a *postconventional* age. Traditional, conventional norms can no longer ground public dialogue and, accordingly, successful dialogue now depends on starting to resolve public issues by achieving understanding through discourse freed from the residues of power and based, instead, on presentations and critiques of reasons. Habermas' reference to the end of convention runs parallel to the idea of the collapse of anchoring narratives, a loss that can fragment our social worlds but, at the same time, presents openings for renewal of the normative order and the construction of new forms of social solidarity.

*Vattimo: weak grounding and the place of rhetoric.* Gianni Vattimo starts his analysis from a position closer to the center of postmodern concerns. He draws on Gehlen's notion that we have reached the "end of history" (i.e., historical consciousness) and can, therefore, no longer ground our narratives. Then, in a typical postmodern move, he attributes this change in consciousness to changes in the media of communication (Vattimo 1988, 10):

Living in history and feeling oneself as a moment that has been conditioned and sustained by a unitary process of events is an experience that is possible only for modern man: reading the newspapers is, in this sense, the morning prayer of the truly *modern* man . . . contemporary history is . . . the history of that era in which, thanks to the use of new means of communication (especially television), everything tends to flatten out at the level of contemporaneity and simultaneity, thus producing a de-historicization of experience.

Vattimo refuses to take the new transformed consciousness as utterly fragmenting and destructive, for it may help us to see positive opportunities in a new world of possibilities. If the postmodern condition makes it impossible to locate ourselves and to understand our experience using a positivistic model of truth as scientific knowledge, it allows new interpretive understandings on different models – "on the basis of either an experience of art *or the model of rhetoric instead*" (Vattimo 1988,12, emphasis supplied).

Vattimo's inclusion of rhetoric in his employment of the esthetic turn (another typical theoretical move among postmodernists) is significant; he not only accepts rhetoric as a means of communicative understanding but, given his particular conception of art and rhetoric, he simultaneously takes a linguistic turn. Following (albeit critically) Hans Gadamer's hermeneutic approach, Vattimo argues that interpretation requires membership in a linguistic community and the cultural tradition that it contains. Accordingly, he can say (1988, 134) that our encounter with a work of art is an "experience of belonging."

Vattimo concedes that the postmodern esthetic anchorage of our experience of truth is a relatively "weak grounding of being," but by locating this experience in art, including rhetoric among the arts, and attaching artistic understanding to communal feelings, he posits a role for persuasion and influence in the construction of postmodern social integration and solidarity.

*Bauman and tokens of identity.* Zygmunt Bauman's (1987) version of the demise of the modern speaks less of the end of history than of the collapse of a fundamental binary opposition between reason and unreason in Western culture. Modern consciousness confidently placed the modern, conceived as the embodiment of evolving reason, in opposition to the premodern, which in either Western or non-Western forms represents unreason. The triumph of reason was viewed by apostles of modernity as an incomplete, ongoing process led by educated elites whose work accomplished the constant rationalization of the world. Once intellectuals come to see this opposition as false, to see the world as inherently uncertain, and to accept diverse cultures as grounded on nothing but their own competing and historically contingent conventions, their capacity to act as society's legislators came to an end. Modernity was then no longer incomplete; it was over and passed. With the passing of modern positivism, the language of sociology can no longer pretend to scientific status. The deterministic language of science should be replaced by a new vocabulary that connotes human freedom and creativity. We should not speak of society but of "sociality," not of normative groups but of "habitats." People are not socialized, they constitute themselves by "self assembly." The latter phrase is the key to Bauman's concept of the postmodern condition. People "assemble" themselves from symbolic tokens of belonging. "Normative groups" may have become "habitats," but we are not to infer from this change in vocabulary that identities are assembled comfortably and without contest.

Habitats are scenes of political struggle, and access to the tokens of belonging from which the self is assembled becomes the principal dimension of inequality and the subject of political struggle (Bauman 1992). In these struggles, success is judged by the amount of regard accorded to offers of identity. Freedom of self-constitution creates strong needs for reassurance of the validity of the assembled self, reassurance by experts, by authority, and by mass followings. In Bauman's words, "Postmodern politics are mostly about the reallocation of attention" (201). From insecurity regarding assurance arise forms of tribal politics, politics of fear and desire, and politics of uncertainty, in which experts claim their place as brokers of information that can ground reassurance. But absent any means of checking the experts' expertise, trust and the betrayal of trust become the core issues of the politics of uncertainty. Trustworthiness, credibility, and perceived sincerity are the criteria by which offers of information regarding identities are judged. Ethical matters, including the evaluation of life purposes, require parallel processes of dialogue, in this case discourses that include "reference to principles wide enough to command authority of the sort that belongs solely to ethical values" (202).

In some respects, Bauman seems to be describing the politics of identity in mass society – the sorts of politics that generate the techniques of persuasion endemic in the New Public – yet he approaches his subject with a note of optimism. The freedom accorded subjects under postmodern conditions may allow for realizing ideals born in the modern era but left unfinished by the failed project of modernity.

*Influence, solidarity, and the postmodern world.* Habermas, Vattimo, and Bauman present three interpretations of the postmodern world. Their accounts are not entirely consistent with each other, but is possible to use them to construct a composite portrait of postmodern self and society. Their combined views suggest a rapprochement between modern visions of social integration based on associational solidarity and postmodern images of social fragmentation.

Many important students of the modern had themselves complained of social disintegration attributable to such modernizing forces as markets and instrumental rationality. Such was the moral animus of Toennies' conception of *Gesellschaft*. Postmodernists see a new and deeper source of fragmentation in the disintegration of modern society at the cultural level. Modernism had at least harbored one strongly integrative conception: the idea of progress. History could be seen as an achievement of culturally valued ends, envisioned as a triumphant technological order, a free democratic society, or a just socialist regime. As long as such visions define historical development, people can anchor their own lives in a larger historical reality. When intellectuals lose faith in historical metanarratives and the public finds them unconvincing, intellectuals, whether pure theorists or practical leaders, lose their influence and can no longer legitimize their interpretations and prescriptions. People lose their moorings because they can no longer locate themselves or attach motives to their aims: conventional norms lose their force. How, then, can a moral order be reconstructed? The answer can no longer be found in positive science. Solidarity – experiences of belonging – must now be at the core of social integration, and solidarity is created by communities of discourse. Fragmentation has two faces. What from one perspective is a loss of stable traditional identities is, from another perspective, a gain of freedom to construct new identities and hence new solidarities. Individuals can now assemble and disassemble identities, which, though weak, are flexible.

All this looks familiar to observers who see solidarity as created through processes of influence. When leaders who command trust and exercise influence are willing to commit their trust to advocacy in public forums, there can be hope that participants in public discourse will reassemble their identities, willingly commit themselves to new solidary attachments, and forge postconventional norms. They will, that is, create postmodern *community* through public discourse. Such, at least, is the updated vision of the potential of public discourse, but this promise cannot be fulfilled without reordering the New Public, so that people in search of new selves and new values can find serious rhetorical forums not entirely given over to commerce in rhetorical tokens.

# Notes

## 1 Public influence in modern society

1 I refer to the *American Heritage Dictionary* . The reference to wealth in this definition is ambiguous. I take it that the lexicographers are referring to the aura of wealth and would not include, for instance, bribery as a type of influence, or for that matter the purchase of commodities for money.

2 Durkheim's choice of "organic" and "mechanical" as terms for types of solidarity and his designation of modern solidarity as organic was an oblique attack on Toennies, who, following romantic usage, had refered to traditional society as organic (Lukes 1973, 143–4). Earlier, the young Durkheim had made a more direct attack on Toennies' nomenclature in a review of *Gemeinschaft und Gesellschaft*. This interesting review, which anticipated Durkheim's claim that modernity has its own forms of solidarity order, is reprinted in Loomis' translation of Toennies' classic work (1940 [1887]).

3 Or, put the matter rhetorically, what sort of stable legal environment would be provided by a system in which cases were always won by the rich and the powerful, or by the state? In such a situation there would be no *law* as we usually understand that word.

4 That social systems cannot, *by definition*, provide for social integration is most explicitly stated in Habermas' response to a critical paper by Held (Habermas 1982, 281).

## 2 Rhetoric and reason

1 My use of the term "knack" here follows Hamilton's translation of passages in Plato's *Gorgias* (1960). The famous phrase "make the worse appear the better cause" originated as a paraphrase of a satirical comment on the Sophists in Aristophanes' *The Clouds*, but it fairly summarizes much of the substance of *Gorgias*, which includes even stronger language of condemnation. "Oratory" (rhetoric) is referred to as "pandering" and is defined as "a spurious counterfeit

of a branch of the art of government." "Rhetoric is to justice as cookery to medicine" (43–4, 46–7).

2 Though Burke is not himself a sociologist, his work has influenced sociologists and has been prized for its significant insights into the connections between rhetoric, human conduct, and the social order (Duncan 1962; Gusfield 1989). In the case of Parsons, who knew Burke well and considered him a personal intellectual companion, Burke's influence is most evident in Parsons' use of his logology of religious language (1978, 213–322).

3 In *The Structure of Social Action*, Parsons' sole reference to the term "persuasion" is to rational persuasion as a utilitarian option. He refers to "rational persuasion of advantage to be gained by entering into relations of exchange" (1937, 101).

4 Burke's dramatism includes a logological element. Cycles of implication apply to the concept of action as well as to linguistic terms. Gusfield (1989, 33) has succinctly summarized the cycle of dramatistic terms for order: "If there is drama there is conflict. If conflict then hierarchy. If hierarchy then guilt. If guilt, then redemption. If redemption then victimage . . ."

5 This remark appears in Habermas' Frankfurt inaugural lecture, delivered in 1965 and included as an appendix to *Knowledge and Human Interests* (Habermas, 1971). It is a rhetorical simplification of the line of thought developed in his "universal pragmatics" (McCarthy 1978, 272–89; Habermas 1979, 1–68), an attempt to ground social philosophy on the *a priori* social conditions of human knowledge. Since communication is such a condition, establishing the possibility of rational communication is a necessary part of any argument claiming that knowledge of social life is possible.

6 These remarks of Habermas occur in the context of a critique of the role of rhetoric in Hans Gadamer's hermeneutic critique. Gadamer replies: ". . . an assertion such as Habermas' to the effect that rhetoric contains a coercive character and must be circumvented in the interest of coercion-free rational dialogue seems to me to be shockingly unrealistic. If it is the case that rhetoric contains a coercive moment then it is nonetheless certain that social *praxis* – and in truth revolutionary *praxis* – would not even be conceivable without this coercive moment" (Gadamer 1990, 292). For Gadamer there is a moment of consent in rhetoric, even in the technical forms of shaping opinion in which our society has come to excel. His general line of argument is consistent with the view that I develop herein. Gadamer is among those contemporary critics who insist that rhetoric is an inextricable component of communication. He claims that consensual interpretation of language requires an element of persuasion which in turn places all who understand a text in a *community* of interpreters.

7 The rhetorical side of bookkeeping was first explored in the literature of rhetorical scholarship. See Aho 1985.

8 I refer here to Lukacs (1971 [1922]) on the "reification of consciousness in the commodity form," Gramsci (1971) on "cultural hegemony," Bourdieu (1987

[1971]) on "cultural capital," Foucault on "discourses of power" (1978), and Horkheimer and Adorno (1972 [1947]) on the "culture industry." Horkheimer and Adorno pointed to the penetration of culture by commercial interests through the mass media, an approach that influenced others in the Frankfurt School. It was from this starting point that Habermas began to develop his central idea of "distorted communication."

9 Westbrook (1991) and Shalin (1992) have examined the relation between pragmatism and Habermasian rationalism. Westbrook notes Habermas' admission that when he wants to reflect upon aspects of democracy that the Marxian tradition overlooks, he turns to Dewey.

### 3 Influence

1 In calling this formal scheme "the influence paradigm," Parsons used "influence" both as the general term for all the ways of securing compliance and also as the term for the generalization of one of the four ways, i.e., persuasion.

2 The influence paradigm emerged in the 1960s in a series of articles on power, influence, and political processes. Most of these articles, including "On the Concept of Political Power," "On the Concept of Influence," and "Voting and the Equilibrium of the American Political System" are reprinted in *Sociological Theory and Modern Society* (1967). "On the Concept of Value Commitment" (1968) appeared a year later.

3 See Gouldner's (1960) classic treatment of the norm of reciprocity and its capacity to create an unsettled and unsettleable set of reciprocal accounts that motivate continuing cooperative mutual interaction.

4 At his most utilitarian moment, Parsons appears to reduce the motivating commitment for stable relationships to interests in securing relationships as sources of future gratification: "Attachment" means "that the relation to alter is the source, not merely of discrete, unorganized, *ad hoc* gratifications for ego, but of an organized *system* of gratifications which include expectations for the future continuance and development of alter's gratificatory significance" (1951, 77).

5 For a well-developed and persuasive argument that Parsons consistently loses his grip on his avowed multidimensional perspective by reducing phenomena, including influence, to their normative elements, see J. Alexander (1983), especially at pp. 254–9, regarding the normative reduction of the media.

6 Parsons' conception of power reflects the traditional utilitarian version of democratic political theory: personal enforcement is surrendered to government in return for the benefits of an organized state, but the rights of citizens to govern the use of state power in the public interest are retained in the form of suffrage. See, for example, his comments on relinquishing self sufficiency and one's "strong right arm" for the advantages of participation in a "power system" (1967b, 366–7).

7 Consider, for example this statement: "attempting to influence is to a degree an attempt to establish a common bond of solidarity, on occasion even to bring the

object of influence into a common membership in a collectivity" (Parsons 1967b, 370).

8 Parsons' sociology of knowledge uses the concept of ideology in this way. He noted that societies institutionalize patterns of meaning that help societal values "make sense." The social functions of ideology include facilitating social acceptance of scientific professionals and of the empirical knowledge they produce (1959, 47–8; 1970). It seems to me that Parsons here suggests that influence derives its force from value-laden cognitive frames.

9 In signal theory, "cheap talk" is a term designating signals that are not costly to send and are therefore unreliable in that anyone can easily send the same signal. In recent years, a substantial body of work by students of politics has predicated the credibility of signals on the receiver's knowledge of the incentives, costs, and risks of the sender. Illustrative examples of applications include Lohmann (1993) on assessing information and manipulation on the part of political leaders, Austen-Smith (1993) on signaling among lobbyists, Ainsworth and Sened (1993) on lobbyists as political entrepreneurs, and Lupia (1994) on voting on referenda.

10 In chapter 5, I will argue that this alteration in the Parsonian influence paradigm counters one of Habermas' principal objections. If affiliation is treated as a sanction that supports attempts to change definitions of the situation, it is easier to see that influence is systematically organized around sanctions with *intrinsic motivating force* and thus to rebut Habermas' assertion that influence lacks the sanctions that would allow it to be organized as a self-regulating system.

11 The original paradigm for personal influence has been attacked from several perspectives. The Michigan School argued that partisanship in the individual voter remains the primary force in voting (Weimann 1994, 159–63). Gitlin (1978) charged that the "dominant paradigm of two-step flow" is the product of a conservative cast of mind that would minimize the direct effects of powerful media institutions. But the personal influence paradigm is not moribund. Weatherford (1982) pioneered the articulation of social influence and network theory, an approach put to good use in recent studies by Huckfeldt and Sprague (1995). C. Brown (1995) has shed a distinctly contemporary light on the significance of the "social milieu" in which political processes are embedded by showing that milieu, treated statistically as a context effect, can have profound nonlinear consequences ranging from electoral landslides to political collapse. Writers now speak, after Nimmo (Nimmo and Combs 1983), of "intermediation" between direct political experience and the second-hand information normally available to citizens, treating the mass media and personal influence as two types of intermediation. See Beck (1991) for a study of intermediation in the 1988 presidential election. For a recent account of the continuing strength of the theory of personal influence, based on 3,900 studies of influentials and opinion leaders, see Weimann (1994).

12 Page and Shapiro (1992), citing a chain of research going back to Cantril and Research Associates (1947), summarized in Citrin and Green (1990), and

culminating in their own research on trends in public opinion over last fifty years, report that citizens form policy preferences not just in relation to self interests, but rather "draw upon group and societal-wide values and information and take account of the perceived interests of the larger community" (286). They conclude that "people of all sorts, in all walks of life tend to form their policy preferences . . . in terms of group interests and – especially – the public good or perceived national interest" (318).

### 4 Habermas and Parsons

1 For an insightful summary of Habermas' absorption of Parsonian ideas, see J. Alexander (1991, 51ff). Alexander stresses Habermas' use of Parsons' notions of system, of the centrality of socialization and normative integration, of the sociology of universalism in the rise of modernity, and of the differentiation of cultural systems that embody rationality in the world today.

2 Arnason (1991), for example, believes that Habermas' analysis of Parsons makes a premature capitulation. In accepting the idea that money and power do coordinate the functionally differentiated spheres of economy and polity, "both spheres are entrusted to the theory of media," and Habermas' "critique of Parsons thus remains within a conceptual framework which is largely indebted to him" (1991, 194–6). Other critics concede that while some functional systems may be necesary to the operation of modern society, we should not prematurely draw arbitrary boundaries around the polity, for we may thereby implicitly foreclose radical visions of democracy (McCarthy, 1991).

3 Earlier, in *The Social System*, Parsons had specifically distinguished these two concepts of integration (1951, 114ff).

4 Habermas does not consider the possibility that agreement and disagreement are sanctions.

5 On Habermas' tendency to turn analytical distinctions into concrete types, the better to use them as ethical concepts, see J. Alexander (1991).

6 Habermas displays a curious and telling blind spot in the course of his remarks on structure-forming effects. He notes that physical strength can become a resource for the generalization of power, but that reliability, good looks, or sexual attractiveness do not have similar generalizing potential. This seems a rather off-hand dismissal of the importance of reliability in institutionalized social life. He precludes, as if it were obviously absurd, this intuitive analogy: *strength* is to force/power as *reliability* is to reputation/influence.

7 On Parsons' critique of "fundamentalist" criticism as immature, see Mayhew (1982, 52–62).

8 Habermas' criticism of Parsons' thought as lacking critical purchase is closely akin to his criticism of Hans Gadamer's hermeneutics, which according to Habermas, fails to allow for critical interpretation against the grain of tradition (Habermas 1977 [1970]; Ricoeur 1981a, b; Gadamer 1989 [1960]). Any theory of communication, whether rooted in humanistic esthetic philosophy, as in the case

of Gadamer, or in positivistic social science, as in the case of Parsons, must meet the test of providing a critical standpoint from which to diagnose the existing social order.

9 On this count, Habermas excoriates Luhmann in more severe tones, for Luhmann's strategy more completely severs the system and the person. According to Luhmann, if we know the system's need for simplification we know enough to understand its imperatives; we need not bring the individual's needs into the picture. Parsons, on the other hand, "unlike Luhmann," is at least able to "*translate* the increase in system complexity grasped from the outside … into the internal perspective of the lifeworld-bound understanding of system members. He can connect the growing system autonomy with the developing autonomy of moral-practical understanding and can interpret the increasing inclusion and value generalization as a progressive approximation to universalistic ideals of justice." (*TCA* II, 284, emphasis in original.) Habermas understands the difference between Luhmann's severe macrofunctionalism and Parsons' refusal to take human motivation as given.

10 My assertion that Habermas' project presents an ethical philosophy is controversial. McCarthy claims Habermas seeks " to identify empirically the actually existing possibilities for embodying rationality structures in concrete forms of life" (translator's Introduction, *TCA* I, 405–6). White (1988) claims that Habermas' work since *Knowledge and Human Interests* has moved away from attempts to ground ethical critique and towards construction of a valid research program for the study of modern life. Nevertheless, despite the empirical turn of his recent volume on law (1996), his continuing philosophical defense of critical/rational communicative action (1991) indicates that he has by no means set aside the quasi-transcendental project set forth in his inaugural lecture.

11 Camic (1992) provides an account of Parsons' early intellectual development and the effect of his striving for legitimacy on his intellectual strategies. For a critique of Camic's interpretation, see J. Alexander and Sciortino (1996).

12 Baum's (1976 a, b, c) amplification and revision of the Parsonian media schema suggests that media are mechanisms of specification, an idea that helps clarify the application of the terms "inflation" and "deflation" to the generalized media. A medium is inflated when it fails to supply enough situational specification to provide usable guidance, and deflated when it provides so much specification as to fail to perform the economizing and simplifying functions of mediated communication. Restated in terms of a balance of trust, media become inflated when senders lose the trust of receivers because mediated messages are inadequately specified, and deflated when, in response to lack of adequate trust, messages are withdrawn from their mediated form and presented in specific detail.

13 Cf. Turner (1968, 132) on the mediating functions of traditional ritual processes.

14 Buying votes rather than influencing voters illustrates substitution. The cost of both means can be calculated in dollars, but the transaction cannot be called buying influence, which would be a contradiction in terms, like the common oxymoron "influence peddling."

15 Karpoff and Lott (1993) have shown that charges and convictions for business fraud lead to reputational losses that far exceed monetary losses from fines, perhaps by a magnitude of twenty to one.

16 Parsons does not define influence as a right to state opinions that *must* be believed, only a "right to state them without alter's need to verify them . . . to expect to be taken seriously, over and above the intrinsic cogency of what he says." To demand more than this degree of compliance would be to confuse influence with power (Parsons 1967b, 369–70).

17 In this sense economists ironically point out that *ignorance* is sometimes "rational ," for it avoids investments in information that are excessive in relation to potential returns.

18 While Parsons did not elaborate the concept of "endorsement" as the means by which influence is transferred and deposited, the idea is implied in a passage referring to "lending names." "The 'joiners' of . . . associations are analogous to depositors." They have . . . " 'lent their names' to the association and its leadership" (1967b, 381).

19 Fraser (1989) examines a number of points at which women's subordinate and constrained roles remain implicated in modern institutions, especially the welfare state, and proposes an extension of the communicative model to allow treatment of these issues in a more refined and sensitive manner. (See also Braaten 1991 , 92–4, 147–50.)

## 5  Public influence

1 Economic theories of credibility parallel the general premises of both Habermas' notion of sincerity and add the concept of reputation: reliability can only be communicated through actions; consecutive acts that consistently provide accurate information and useful services build reputation; reputation is a valuable indicator of reliability both for those who possess it as a form of capital and to those who rely on it in order to make judgments in the absence of personal information (Sobel 1985; Root, Greenbaum, and Thakor 1993). It is interesting to note that Sobel defines the maximally effective condition for credibility – when the utility functions of the sender and receiver of a message are identical – as in "friendship," i.e. a form of solidarity.

2 Downs (1957, 87) noted that spokespeople "influence voters to adopt certain views as expressing their own." In order to reduce informational costs, citizens seek biased sources of information, looking for sources that share their own biases, influentials with them they can *identify* (219).

3 For parallel treatments of trust, see Coleman (1990) and Elster (1989). Coleman calls trust a form of bet: one "places" trust according to one's calculations of possible payoffs and losses, together with the estimated probability that alter will make good on commitments. Elster views trust and credibility as so closely related that both can be treated in the same terms.

4 On entrepreneurial support versus patronage, see also Walker (1991) and Cigler and Nownes (1995).

5 Miller presents his analysis in the context of a feminist argument. Women in particular have been held to linguistically constructed identities and accordingly their commitments are not well grounded. Women's movements seek to reallocate influence in accord with emergent, proclaimed identities not yet "hypostatized" in the real world, a phenomenon that may be paradigmatic for social movements generally.

6 Habermas is aware of the phenomenon of the extension of initial credits and their role in the generalization of influence: "When a prestigious or influential person takes the initiative, he can count on receiving a certain "advance" of trust or confidence, which may be paid out in a readiness for consensus and obedience that goes beyond any single situation" (TCA I, 179). Yet in his enthusiasm for discursive redemption of all such claims he fails to grasp that this "advance" is a key component of every process of persuasion and influence. He calls this phenomenon "trivial."

7 I am referring here to Habermas' repeated use of the term *eingelöst*, generally translated as "redeemed," in such phrases as "rational argument must be redeemed in discourse." Since argument is often presented in abridged, token form, and since the English word "token" takes the verb "redeem" to refer to turning in tokens for something of value, there is a resonant parallel between Habermas' usage and mine.

8 In *Justification and Application* (1993) [1991]) Habermas discusses the view of several critics, especially Alasdair McIntyre (1988), Charles Taylor (1989; 1991), Thomas McCarthy (1992), who, either in direct opposition to Habermas or by implication, have objected to detached conceptions of rational discourse. See also Lukes (1982), Boyte (1992) and Warner (1992). Note, however, Habermas' (1996) treatment of the institutions of law, through which legally established compromises can be redeemed through their place within a larger discursive order.

9 "Self-created societies" was George Washington's term for the backers of the Whiskey Rebellion. Leaders of the emergent anti-Federalist party were so concerned about the pejorative use of this phrase as to devote several days of passionate debate to it, an incident symptomatic of the ambivalence of eighteenth-century attitudes about private groups' participation in public affairs (Elkins and McKitrick 1993, 474–88).

10 Schwartz is referring to the renown "daisy commercial" that he developed for Lyndon Johnson's presidential campaign of 1964. Exploiting Goldwater's reputation as trigger-happy (a vulnerability discovered through market research), the commercial presented a young girl tearing the petals from a daisy; a second voice is heard giving a backwards countdown leading to a nuclear explosion. The presentation was entirely connotative and made no attempt at exposition of its meaning or argument for its validity. That Schwartz's early support for "resonance" as a proper foundation for public debate remains alive, is apparent in a

recent defense of the "Henry and Louise" commercials employed in an advertising campaign against the Clinton health-care plan. An industry spokesperson, answering questions on CNN, explained that what Henry and Louise said "presents issues that resonate with the American people; we didn't make them up."

11 For a review of the issue of exogeneity and a balanced view of the evidence for two-way effects between voter preference and legislative action, casting doubt on the proposition that public preferences are given, see Gerber and Jackson (1993).

12 The distinction between the public and the public sphere is not always easy to specify because the German word that Habermas uses, *Offentlichkeit*, can be (and is) translated as either "public" or "public sphere." Thomas Berger, the English translator of *Structural Transformation of the Public Sphere*, believes that it is better to render *Offentlichkeit* as a public sphere wherever possible. See Habermas (1989 [1962], translator's note, xv).

13 *Bürgerliche Gesellschaft*, the traditional German term for civil society, has come to have strong connotations of "bourgeois" society and to imply a Marxist interpretation. *Civilsocietät* was coined in about 1980 (to capture a fresh and more inclusive meaning for the term) and introduced to academic discourse by Arato (Ely 1992, 175–7). The rapid spread of the new German term is one index of the rise of civil society theory in Europe.

14 Cohen and Arato, like Habermas and other civil society theorists, exclude political parties and other frankly political organizations as too directly involved in direct political governance. The public sphere, then, is organized into a political sector and a strictly civil sector, *civil society*, which is engaged in influential discourse rather than in establishing and implementing law and regulation.

15 Cohen has wavered on the matter of institutional deficit in Habermas, starting by calling attention to it (1979; 1982, 194–228), then noting that the beginnings of an institutional theory in Habermas' emergent concept of civil society might be teased from Habermas' idea of colonization and defense of the lifeworld (1985). See also Cohen and Arato (1992, 389–410) and Habermas' (1996) massive response to the charge of blindness to institutional realities.

### 6 The differentiation of rhetorical solidarity

1 Aristotle defended rhetoric on the grounds that without command of its uses, one would be helpless in the public courts.

2 The nature and impact of civic humanism in the Renaissance has been documented and interpreted in a justly renowned series of monographs: Baron (1955); Garin (1965); Seigel (1968); and Pocock (1975).

3 The demand, by preachers and laymen alike, for a "Godly preaching ministry" was one of the war cries of the militant Puritan movement. Puritan objections to emphasis upon sacrament over sermon, as well as to absentee pastors and

similar ecclesiastical abuses, reflect strong hunger for continuous communications lest, as a Puritan might put it, "the Spirit be quenched." (See Haller 1938, 3–48; Haller 1955, 3–31; Hill 1967, 3–123; Wilson 1969; Seaver 1970.)

4 Milton set forth his ideas regarding church discipline in *The Reason of Church Government* (1957 [1642]). His conception is not entirely original. It is a restatement of the ideal means of enforcing the norms of Christian community by the mechanisms of community itself, as set forth by Calvin, Knox, Field, Cartwright and other sixteenth-century divines (McGinn 1949; Walzer 1965, 199–232).

5 The centrality of communication in the Puritan conception of order was well appreciated even by its contemporary critics. Hooker (1954 [1594], 103–4) denied that the Puritan "way" was founded on eternal principles, either of God's word or of reason, arguing that it was attributable to Puritans' mere "taste" (albeit passionate) for intense communication. Puritans were so anxious about their spiritual state, so afraid of losing their conviction, that they felt the need to testify to each other. "This maketh them diligent hearers" and gives them "an unweariable desire of receiving instruction." Perhaps Hooker's social psychological explanation of the origins of Puritan preoccupation with communication anticipates by 300 years Weber's argument that the social effects of the doctrine of predestination was mediated by the insecurity it produced among its adherents, who could not be sure of their salvation. Anxiety about the state of the soul produced not only rigorous self discipline but also a need for regular mutual reassurance through intense communication.

6 Goodwin developed this argument in *Theomachia* and again in 1654 in *A Fresh Discovery*. This line of thought was specifically tied to Calvin's doctrine of communion in John Spencer's (1641) *A Short Treatise Concerning the Lawfullnesse of Every Mans Exercising his Gift*.

7 On Condorcet's view of public opinion in the social order see Schapiro (1963, 136–55).

8 I am adopting here Wuthnow's (1989) phrase "community of discourse" to denote a group that regularly communicates within a common symbolic field. I do not mean to suggest that this discourse community met Habermas' criteria for discursive action.

9 Zaret denies that the transformation of the petition had Protestant roots. Leaving that issue aside, the subsequent role of the petition in the legitimation of freedom of association was significant. Knights (1993) believes that Locke's *Second Treatise* owed much to his participation in the "Monster" petition drive of 1789–90, and it is well known that American constitutional protection of freedom of association derives from the notion of freedom to petition for redress of grievance.

10 For such explicit discussion of the public has crept to the surface of seventeenth-century thought, see Gunn (1969, 293–6) and Zagorin (1970).

11 According to Robinson (1643, 17), "Writing . . . may be better dispersed, and more freely enjoyed at all times, places and opportunities, besides, that controversies and businesses of intricacie, are far better and more methodically stated

and explained in writing or in print than can possibly be delivered by word of mouth." His argument clearly anticipated (by 150 years) Condorcet's enlightened regard for the cool reason embodied in the printed word.

12 The foregoing analysis of attitudes towards writing and public discussion is based on the sources cited and on other pamphlets from the 1640s, including Greville (1641); E. Brown (1642); Robinson (1643); Overton (1645); Saltmarsh (1646); and Biddle (1647). For an explicit link of this line of thought to Calvin's doctrine of communion, see Spencer (1641).

13 Italian writers on the government of the republican city had also distinguished between the common good and the partial interests of factions, arguing that in discord lies the seeds of the city's loss of its liberty (Pocock 1975; Skinner 1978).

14 Pocock does recognize that the earlier polarization of English politics around "court" and "country" created fertile ground for the later rhetoric of virtue and corruption (Pocock 1975, 407–9). On court and country in the seventeenth century, see Zagorin (1970).

15 References to Jacobson are to his edited versions of *The Independent Whig* and *Cato's Letters*.

16 This is a summary of a dense Puritan argument made in the course of Milton's defense of freedom of the press in *Areopagitica* (1957 [1644], 733) and of political liberty in *The Tenure of Kings and Magistrates* (1957 [1649], 754). His liberal essays are constructed on a theologically animated, ethical theory of rights, not on any notion of freeing people from the bondage of communal responsibility.

17 Sinopoli's approach allows him to assess the founders as fundamentally liberal, despite their frequent rhetorical use of the concept of virtue, and yet concede that virtue played a definable, if subordinate, role in their overall conception of government.

18 By the 1760s, 60,000 people held shares in the public debt (Brewer 1989, 204).

19 The "Bubble" refers to the collapse of a scheme on the part of the South Sea Company to secure control of the public debt by persuading annuitants of public debts to sell their interests to the Company in exchange for Company shares. Sellers paid wildly inflated, speculative prices for company stock and incurred heavy losses.

20 Lord Acton is commonly cited to this effect (Speier 1950). See also Palmer (1953). French public debt is generally treated as paradigmatic. Jacques Necker, Louis XVI's Finance Minister, publicly recognized the regime's dependence on public confidence in the solvency and financial good faith of the crown. His *Compte rendu au Roi* of 1781 presented an accounting of the royal finance to the nation. Despite its duplicitous accounting, as a precedent in public finance, it marked the recognition of public opinion as an inescapable force. For a more recent summary, see Doyle (1989, 44–65).

21 The canonical line of cases is US v Cruickshank 92 US 543 (1876); Hague v C10 317 US 996 (1939); NAACP v Alabama 357 US 449 (1958); NAACP v Button 371 US 415 (1963). In 1876, the first construction of the assembly clause by the

Supreme Court (US v Cruickshank), assembly was held to be subordinate to the petition clause and not to establish a general right. The Court reverted to the language of 1788, regarding "a right on the part of its citizens to meet peacably for consultation in respect of public affairs." Public deliberation and petitioning were protected, but not assembly and association as such. Cruickshank was not overthrown until 1939, when the right of assembly was extended to labor unions.

### 7 The emergence of the New Public

1 Joseph Rowntree may have been influenced by his son, Seebohm Rowntree, whose work in York included important early English social surveys (Abrams 1951, 41–4).

2 This testimony has been collected by Francesco Nicosia as *Advertising, Management, and Society: A Business Perspective* (1974). For Demsetz' contribution, see pp. 214–30. The intellectual history of Demsetz' perspective can be traced to Stigler (1961) and to subsequent elaborations by Nelson (1970; 1974) and others. It is consistent with a popular pardigm for training students of marketing presented in *Consumer Behavior* (Engel, Blackwell, and Miniar 1968), now (1990) in its sixth edition, which assumes consumers to be rational, information-using, problem solvers.

3 The career in advertising of John B. Watson is a case in point. He enhanced the public relations of his firm rather than accomplishing advertising studies (Kreshel 1990a, b).

4 Abrams (1951) makes a similar argument for the close relation between market research and public opinion studies in the United Kingdom. His own private polling firm did research in both genres.

5 Gallup's success was largely a matter of daring and publicity, not of techniques well in advance of his competitors in polling and market research such as Crossley, Roper, and Nielson, some of whom also correctly predicted the 1936 election (Converse 1987). Indeed, Alfred Politz (a former Roper associate) foresaw that polls predicting that Dewey would defeat Truman would fail for want of strict probability sampling (Hardy 1990, 280–90). Gallup's incorrect prediction of this election had immediate and serious adverse consequences for his market research operations (Ohmer 1991).

6 With the demise of ARI, Gallup's film surveys were discontinued by the end of the decade, but the innovations that he brought to marketing research in film making were adopted by the industry and remain standard practice today.

7 Ivy Lee's failure to live up to his famous 1906 "Declaration of Principles," which promised "to supply to the press and the public of the United States prompt and accurate information concerning subjects which it is of value and interest to the public to know about," is documented in Cutlip (1994, 45, 119–23).

8 Some US corporations employ 50 to 100 middle- and upper-level public relations officials.

9 The continuing prestige of science is manifest in Wal-Mart's public relations manager's supposition that his purchased research is possible only because the president of the research company was trained as an engineer!

## 8 Political communication in the New Public

1 In February of 1995, *Campaigns and Elections* also published a directory of consultants, using comparable but not identical categories of specialization. The numbers of listed firms offering particular types of service are generally consistent with the lists published in the *Political Resource Directory*.

2 The term "lobbying" is an Americanism and was not coined until the 1820s, but the practice emerged in England as early as the seventeenth-century Interegnum.

3 The London lobbies that provided *de facto* representation of North American interests ironically illustrate that appeals to information-based, universalistic standards of discourse were contingent on these lobbyists' weakness. Lacking adequate resources to enter the high stakes arena of bribery, they chose the high road (A. Olson 1991).

4 Loomis and Sexton (1995, 195) cite this estimate from a 1989 report by Paul Vogel. Birnbaum's (1992) comparable estimate for Washington DC is 80,000. Congressional Quarterly (1987, 3), employing a more restrictive definition, reports a much lower range – 10,000 to 20,000 in the mid 1980s. Hunter, Wilson, and Break (1991) have estimated the magnitude of lobbying at the state level by aggregating registered lobbying *efforts*, rather than counting the number of people involved. More than 39,000 such *efforts* were registered under state laws in 1985–87.

5 Rosenthal (1993, 190) concludes that "Today's lobbyist will almost invariably have to make an argument on the merits . . . A lobbyist can no longer rely on simply approaching a legislator friend and saying, 'I need this.' On most issues today, the weight of the argument is what matters."

6 Schlozman and Tierny (1983) reported that 63 percent of their sample of lobbyists reported using more research and the technical information in their lobbying than in the past, despite the rise of new "outside" approaches to lobbying.

7 See Cigler and Loomis (1995, 397–8). My 1995 interviews of party leaders and political professionals in Washington confirmed that efforts to use grassroots techniques in the service of party organization and support are underway.

8 For an enlightening collection of essays on the Clinton health care debate, see Mann and Ornstein (1995). See also Johnson and Broder (1996).

9 Audits are necessarily cursory in relation to the amount of detailed data that could be checked. Accordingly, auditing statements do not purport to guarantee perfect accuracy. Certifications are hedged in disclaimers: the accountant affirms an "opinion" based on examining, "on a test basis," evidence allowing "reasonable assurance as to whether financial statements are free of material misstatement."

10 In the United States this committee is called the Financial Accounting Standards Board (FASB); FASB establishes the standards referred to in certification statements as "generally accepted auditing procedures."

11 Schulz (1996), also features an account of Fenton's more recent efforts on behalf of the Environmental Work Group's questionable studies of drinking water. See also Lacey and Llewellyn (1995).

12 When media campaigns are intended to seek legitimacy for media outlets by selecting topics, particularly issues of health and safety, that demonstrate concern for the public, there is little incentive to make an issue seem controversial by showing two sides.

13 Moore does not attempt to prove that serum cholesterol is without danger; he shows that the process was opaque to the general public. It ultimately rested on capturing the right to certify facts. Even when substantial scientific evidence is available, the translation of scientific study into medical policy and public opinion involves a contested process among researchers who bring other than strictly scientific interests to the arena.

14 The extent of the organized American research enterprise bearing on issues of politics and public concerns is suggested by the following data. Of 13,800 university-based or non-profit research centers in the United States and Canada, 770 are devoted to research on government and public affairs, 640 to business and economics, and many others to scientific topics affected with a substantial public interest such as health and environmental studies (Gerring 1995). Nearly 300 consulting firms engage in political research (Political Resources 1995). The number of think tanks in the United States has been estimated at 1000, of which 100 are located in Washington DC (Smith 1991; National Journal 1995); of the 250 leading public interest organizations described in *Public Interest Profiles* (Foundation for Public Affairs 1992), nearly all participate in research to some degree, many undertaking substantial programs of publication.

15 The expression "policy entrepreneur" has become a term of art in recent writing, sometimes as a pejorative term for persons who are not qualified experts but mere hawkers of simplistic political and economic solutions (Krugman 1994; Newhouse 1995). Others emphasize the entreprenurial activity of intellectual innovators who go beyond expressing new ideas to building support among networks of writers, activists, and officials (Smith 1991, 194; Roberts and King 1991; Ricci 1993, 197–8).

16 Radical thinkers also saw strong links between the think tanks and elite policy makers and sought to create institutions for policy studies that would approach issues from an independent, uncompromised stance. This was the motive behind the formation of the Institute for Policy Studies in 1963 (Ricci 1993, 152–4).

17 Policy communities are sometimes called "issue networks" (Heclo 1978). Bykerk and Maney (1995) have delineated a particular policy community, that of advocates and officials interested in consumer issues, by mapping concentric circles of the organizations working in this area. The size and complexity of policy

communities is apparent. Their map requires locating 102 organizations, including core consumer groups in the inner circle, additional consumer groups, closely related organizations (including government agencies) that create a policy environment, and an outer ring of groups not primarily devoted to consumer issues, but sharing a common interest in policies affecting consumers.

### 9  Forums for the redemption of influence

1  "Today Show," May 12, 1995.
2  Campaign expenditures for the US Congress increased from $118 million in 1972 to $445 million in 1990 (H. Alexander 1992, 118). Regens and Gaddie (1995, 19) report expenditures in constant 1992 dollars rather than nominal dollars and still report that campaign expenditures for Senate races increased from $123 million to $195 million between 1982 and 1992.
3  For additional sources and estimates of voter turnout, see Conway 1991; Teixeira 1992. Voter turnout is not easily measured. Is the proper denominator for measures of voter turnout the *entire voting age population* or *registered voters*? The latter denominator shows participation to have remained at nearly 90 percent in every presidential election between 1964 and 1988. Turnout rates in the southern states are remarkably different than those in non-southern states, which makes nationally aggregated statistics potentially misleading (Kleppner 1982).
4  Ansolabehere et al. (1994) have produced turnout data and experimental evidence that political attack advertising demobilizes the electorate, weakens the sense of political efficacy and promotes cynicism.
5  These quotations are taken from Richard C. Harwood's account of the Harwood Group's study of citizen discontent (Harwood Group 1991, 19–25). This report should be read with some caution for it is clearly animated by a strong political agenda: democratic participation is necessary and the people want it.
6  See Twentieth Century Fund (1993, 5, 82). The group also noted several more substantive signs of improvement: less reliance on photo opportunities; increased issue coverage; critiques of campaign commercials; the rise of call-in talk shows.
7  Putnam's conclusions are based on controlling rates of participation by age and education, but Ladd's counter evidence includes a showing of high rates among today's teenagers.
8  Quoted in the *Dallas Morning News*, September 7, 1995, 8A.
9  Before the first launch of a Fishkin deliberative poll in January of 1996, the institution most akin to the Fishkin format was the Granada 500 program in England (MacDonald 1986). Since 1974, Granada Television has assembled samples of 500 electors in the Northwest of England, in general election years. Over the course of the election campaign, the group questions independent experts and party leaders. Since little opportunity is allowed for discussion and

the participants are not polled, the program is neither deliberative nor a poll, yet Fishkin has referred to Granada 500 as "a pathbreaking experiment that lays the groundwork for the national telecast of deliberative opinion polls" (Fishkin 1991, 96). The authors found little to support the hypothesis that participation in Granada 500 affected either the substance or the quality of the participants' attitudes and beliefs (Denver, Hands, and Jones 1995).

## 10 The rhetoric of presentation

1 Aristotle labeled "inartistic" ready-made means of persuasion not invented by the speaker. Signed contracts or written testimony are thus excluded from the category of rhetoric. Today we would not exclude the exhibit of "facts" attested to by others from the category of rhetorical argument. Such presentation is an art form in its own right.

2 For other influential concepts of spectacle, see Debord (1970) and Edelman (1988). Dayan and Katz (1992) present a more positive view of the integrative and adaptive possibilities of spectacle.

3 When spectacle enacts lateral conflict or protest, hierarchy remains an element within the overall display, for status orders *within* the parties or movements are enacted through the prominence accorded to leaders. Such spectacle establishes and reinforces the leadership and influence of those who are, or aspire to be, pro-locutors. Note, for example, that the Million Man March was perceived by many to be a bid by Louis Farrakhan for a larger prolocutorial role in the Black community.

4 The team was heartened by the release in April of the annual report of the Medicare trustees which reported that the Medicare hospital trust fund faced bankruptcy by the year 2002. Such warnings had long been commonplace, and the chronically overextended system had always found ways of staving off bankruptcy with less than radical surgery, but the wordsmiths were then in possession of information to make their linguistic strategy credible.

5 The issues raised in this exchange (Searle 1977; Derrida 1977; Norris 1987) are more complicated than my limited exposition implies. I focus on one aspect of the argument: "[Derrida] is not denying that language possesses an 'intentional' aspect that allows us, again – *for all practical purposes* – to interpret various kinds of performative utterances in keeping with the relevant conventions" (Norris (1987, 179), emphasis supplied).

# References

Abbott, Andrew. 1988. *The System of Professions: Essay on the Division of Expert Labor*. Chicago, Ill.: University of Chicago Press.

Abrams, Mark. 1951. *Social Surveys and Social Action*. London: William Heinemann.

Aho, James A. 1985. "Rhetoric and the Invention of Double-Entry Bookkeeping." *Rhetorica*, 3:21–43.

Ainsworth, Scott and Itai Sened. 1993. "The Role of Lobbyists: Entrepreneurs with Two Audiences." *American Journal of Political Science*, 37: 834–66.

Akerlof, George A. 1970. "The Market for Lemons." *Quarterly Journal of Economics*, 84:488–500.

Alexander, Herbert. 1992. *Financing Politics: Money, Elections, and Political Reform*. 4th edn. Washington, DC: CQ Press.

Alexander, Jeffrey C. 1983. *Theoretical Logic in Sociology, IV: The Reconstruction of Classical Thought in Talcott Parsons*. Berkeley and Los Angeles: University of California Press.

1990a. "Differentiation Theory: Problems and Prospects." In Jeffrey C. Alexander and Paul Colomy, eds., *Differentiation Theory and Social Change: Comparative and Historical Perspectives*, pp.1–15. New York: Columbia University Press.

1990b. "The Mass Media in Systematic, Historical, and Comparative Perspective." In Jeffrey C. Alexander and Paul Colomy, eds., *Differentiation Theory and Social Change: Comparative and Historical Perspectives*, pp. 295–366. New York: Columbia University Press.

1991. "Habermas and Critical Theory: Beyond the Marxian Dilemma?" In Axel Honneth and Hans Joas, eds., *Communicative Action: Essays on Jürgen Habermas's "The Theory of Communicative Action,"* pp. 49–73. Cambridge: Polity Press.

1992. "Citizen and Enemy as Symbolic Classification: On the Polarizing Discourse of Civil Society." In Michèl Lamont and Marcel Fournier, eds., *Cultivating Differences: Symbolic Boundaries and the Making of Inequality*, pp. 289–308. Chicago, Ill.: University of Chicago Press.

Alexander, Jeffrey C. and Giuseppe Sciortino. 1996. "On Choosing Ones' Intellectual Predecessors: The Reductionism of Camic's Treatment of Parsons and the Institutionalists." *Sociological Theory*, 14: 154–71.

Alexander, Jeffrey C. and Philip Smith. 1993. "The Discourse of American Civil Society: A New Proposal for Cultural Studies." *Theory and Society*, 22:151–207.

Anderson, Benedict. 1983. *Imagined Communities: Reflections on the Origin and Spread of Nationalism*. London: Verso.

Ansolabehere, Stephen, Roy Behr, and Shanto Iyengar. 1993. *The Media Game: American Politics in the Television Age*. New York: Macmillan.

Ansolabehere, Stephen and Shanto Iyengar. 1996. "Can the Press Monitor Campaign Advertising? An Experimental Study." *Harvard International Journal of Press/Politics*, 1: 72–86.

Ansolabehere, Stephen et al. 1994. "Does Attack Advertising Demobilize the Electorate?" *American Political Science Review*, 88: 829–38.

Aristotle. 1991. *On Rhetoric: A Theory of Civic Discourse*. Trans. and Introduction by George A. Kennedy. New York: Oxford University Press.

Arnason, Johann P. 1991. "Modernity as Project and as Field of Tensions." In Axel Honneth and Hans Joas, eds., *Communicative Action: Essays on Jürgen Habermas's "The Theory of Communicative Action,"* pp. 181–213. Trans. Jeremy Gaines and Doris L. Jones. Cambridge: Polity Press.

Aronson, Eliott. 1995. *The Social Animal*. 7th edn. New York: Harcourt Freeman.

Ash, Simeon. 1647. *Gods Incomparable Goodnesse*. Wing A3995.

Austen-Smith, David. 1990. "Information Transmission in Debate." *American Journal of Political Science*, 34: 124–52.

1993. "Information and Influence: Lobbying for Agendas and Votes." *American Journal of Political Science*, 37: 799–833.

Bagdikian, Ben H. 1990. *The Media Monopoly*. 3rd edn. Boston: Beacon Press.

Bailyn, Bernard. 1967. *The Ideological Origins of the American Revolution*. Cambridge, Mass.: The Belknap Press of Harvard University.

Banfield, Edward C. 1961. *Political Influence*. New York: Free Press of Glencoe.

Barber, Benjamin. 1984. *Strong Democracy: Participatory Politics for a New Age*. Berkeley and Los Angeles: University of California Press.

Barber, James David. 1980. *The Pulse of Politics: Electing Presidents in the Media Age*. New York: W. W. Norton & Company.

Baron, David P. 1994. "Electoral Competition with Informed and Uninformed Voters." *American Political Science Review*, 88: 33–47.

Baron, Hans. 1955. *The Crisis of the Early Italian Renaissance*. Princeton, NJ: Princeton University Press.

Bartels, Robert. 1976. *The History of Marketing Thought*. Columbus, Ohio: Grid.

Baudrillard, Jean. 1983. "The Ecstacy of Communication." Trans. John Johnston. In Hal Foster, *The Anti-Aesthetic: Essays on Postmodern Culture*, pp. 126–34. Port Townsend, Wash.: Bay Press.

1994 [1981]. *Simulacra and Simulation*. Trans. Sheila Faria Glaser. Ann Arbor, Mich.: University of Michigan Press.

Baum, Rainer C. 1976a. "Introduction to Part IV." In Jan J. Loubser et al., eds., *Explorations in General Theory in Social Science: Essays in Honor of Talcott Parsons*, pp. 448–59. New York: Free Press.

1976b. "Communication and the Media." In Jan J. Loubser et al., eds., *Explorations in General Theory in Social Science: Essays in Honor of Talcott Parsons*, pp. 533–56. New York: Free Press.

1976c. "On Societal Media Dynamics." In Jan J. Loubser. et al., eds., *Explorations in General Theory in Social Science: Essays in Honor of Talcott Parsons*, pp. 579–608. New York: Free Press.

Bauman, Zygmunt. 1987. *Legislators and Interpreters*. Cambridge: Polity Press.

1992. *Intimations of Postmodernity*. London and New York: Routledge.

Baus, Herbert and William B. Ross. 1968. *Politics Battle Plan*. New York: Macmillan.

Beck, Peter Allen. 1991. "Voter's Intermediation Environments in the 1988 Presidential Contest." *Public Opinion Quarterly*, 55:371–94.

Beniger, James R. 1992. "The Impact of Polling on Public Opinion: Reconciling Foucault, Habermas, and Bourdieu." *International Journal of Public Opinion Research*, 4: 204–19.

Berelson, Bernard, Paul Lazarsfeld, and William N. McPhee. 1954. *Voting: A Study of Opinion Formation During a Presidential Campaign*. Chicago: University of Chicago Press.

Bernays, Edward L. 1928. "Manipulating Public Opinion: The Why and the How." *American Journal of Sociology*, 33: 958–71.

Biddle, John. 1647. *Twelve Arguments*. Wing B5107.

Bessette, Joseph M. 1994. *The Mild Voice of Reason: Deliberative Democracy and American National Government*. Chicago, Ill.: University of Chicago Press.

Birnbaum, Jeffrey H. 1992. *The Lobbyists: How Influence Peddlers Get Their Way in Washington*. New York: Times Books, Random House.

Blain, Michael. 1995. "Power War, and Melodrama in the Discourses of Political Movements." *Theory and Society*, 23: 805–37.

Blumenthal, Sidney. 1980. *The Permanent Campaign: Inside the World of Elite Political Operatives*. Boston: Beacon Press.

1994 "The Candidate." *New Yorker* (October 10), 54–62.

Blumer, Herbert. 1946. "The Mass, the Public, and Public Opinion." In Alfred McClung Lee, ed., *New Outline of the Principles of Sociology*, pp. 185–93. New York: Barnes and Noble.

1948 "Public Opinion and Public Opinion Polling." *American Sociological Review*, 13:342–54.

Boorstin, Daniel. 1973. *The Americans: The Democratic Experience*. New York: Random House.

Boot, Arnaud W. A., Stuart I. Greenbaum, and Anjan V. Thakor. 1993. "Reputation and Discretion in Financial Contracting." *American Economic Review*, 83: 1,165–84.

Bourdieu, Pierre. 1979. "Public Opinon Does Not Exist." In Armand Mattelart and Seth Siegelaub, eds., *Communication and Class Struggle*, I, pp. 124–30. New York: International General.

1984 [1979]. *Distinction: A Social Critique of the Judgement of Taste*. Trans. Richard Nice. Cambridge, Mass.: Harvard University Press.

Boyte, Harry C. 1992. "The Pragmatic Ends of Popular Politics." In Craig Calhoun, ed., *Habermas and the Public Sphere*, pp. 340–55. Cambridge, Mass.: MIT Press.

Braaten, Jane. 1991. *Habermas's Critical Theory of Society*. Albany, New York: State University of New York Press.

Bradley, James E. 1990. *Religion, Revolution, and English Radicalism: Non-conformity in Eighteenth-Century Politics and Society*. Cambridge: Cambridge University Press.

Breed, Warren. 1955. " Social Control in the Newsroom: A Functional Analysis." *Social Forces*, 33:326–35.

Brewer, John. 1989. *The Sinews of Power: War, Money and the English State, 1688–1783*. London: Unwin Hyman.

Brooke, Robert (Lord Greville). 1641. *A Discourse Opening the Nature of that Episcopacie, Which is Exercised in England*. Reproduced in William Haller, ed., *Tracts on Liberty in the Puritan Revolution 1638–1647*, I, pp. 35–164. New York: Columbia University Press, 1933.

Brown, Courtney. 1995. *Serpents in the Sand: Essays on the Nonlinear Nature of Politics and Human Destiny*. Ann Arbor, Mich.: University of Michigan Press.

Brown, Edwards. 1642. *Sir James Cambels Clarks Disaster*. Wing B5107.

Brown, Richard D. 1989. *Knowledge is Power: The Diffusion of Information in Early America, 1700–1865*. New York and Oxford: Oxford University Press.

Bruck, Connie. 1995. "The Politics of Perception." *New Yorker* (October 9), 50–76.

Burke, Kenneth. 1950. A Rhetoric of Motives. New York: Prentice Hall.

1953. *Counterstatement*. 2nd edn., Los Altos, Calif.: Hermes Publications.

1961. *The Rhetoric of Religion: Studies in Logology*. Boston: Beacon Press.

1968 "Interaction: Dramatism." In David A. Sills, ed., *International Encyclopedia of the Social Sciences*, VII, pp. 445–52. New York: Macmillan and the Free Press.

Bykerk, Loree and Ardith Maney. 1995. "Consumer Groups and Coalition Politics on Capitol Hill." In Allan J. Cigler and Burdett A. Loomis, eds., *Interest Group Politics*. 4th edn., pp. 259–280. Washington DC: CQ Press.

Calkins, Earnest Elmo. 1928. *Business the Civilizer*. Boston: Little, Brown.

Calvin, John. 1960 [1536]. *Institutes of the Christian Religion*. Trans. Ford Lewis Battles. Ed. John T. McNeill. Philadelphia, Penn.: Westminster Press.

Camic, Charles, ed. 1991. *Talcott Parsons: The Early Essays*. Chicago: University of Chicago Press.

Cantril, Hadley and Research Associates in the Office of Opinion Research, Princeton University. 1947. *Gauging Public Opinion*. Princeton, NJ: Princeton University Press.

Carmines, Edward G. and James H. Kuklinski. 1990. "Incentives, Opportunities, and the Logic of Public Opinion in American Political Representation." In John J. Ferejohn and James H. Kuklinsky, eds., *Information and Democratic Processes*, pp. 240–68. Urbana,Ill.: University of Illinois Press.

Caro, Robert A. 1990. *The Years of Lyndon Johnson: The Means of Ascent*. New York: Alfred A. Knopf.

Carruthers, Bruce G. and Wendy Nelson Espeland. 1991. "Accounting for Rationality: Double-Entry Bookkeeping and the Rhetoric of Economic Rationality." *American Journal of Sociology*, 97:31–69.

Carver, Robert M. Jr. and Thomas E. King. 1990. "An Analysis of the Economic Impact of the Anticipated Reactions of Clients to Management Consultants' Defections from Public Accounting Firms." *Akron Business and Economic Review*, 21: 53–63.

Chase, Stewart and F. J. Schlink. 1927. *Your Money's Worth: A Study of the Waste of the Consumer's Dollar*. New York: Macmillan.

Cicero, Marcus Tullius. 1970. *Cicero on Oratory and Orators. [De oratore]* Trans. and ed. J. S. Watson. Carbondale, Ill.: University of Southern Illinois Press.

Cigler, Allan J. and Burdett A. Loomis, eds. 1995. *Interest Group Politics*. 4th edn. Washington DC: CQ Press.

Cigler, Allan J. and Anthony J. Nownes. 1995. "Public Interest Entrepreneurs and Group Patrons." Allan J. Cigler and Burdett A. Loomis, eds., *Interest Group Politics*. 4th edn., pp. 77–100. Washington DC: CQ Press.

Citrin, Jack and Donald Phillip Green. 1990. "The Self-Interest Motive in American Public Opinion." In Samuel Long, ed., *Research in Micropolitics: A Research Annual: Public Opinion*, pp.1–27. Greenwich, Conn: JAI.

Clark, Gregory. 1994. *Government Debt and Private Capital Markets: England, 1727–1837*. Davis, Cal.: Agricultural History Center, University of California, Davis.

Cmiel, Kenneth. 1990. *Democratic Eloquence: The Fight over Popular Speech in Nineteenth Century America*. Berkeley and Los Angeles: University of California Press.

Cohen, Jean L. 1979. "Why More Political Theory? *Telos*, 40:70–94.

1982. *Class and Civil Society: The Limits of Marx's Critical Theory*. Amherst,, Mass.: University of Massachussets Press.

1983. "Rethinking Social Movements." *Berkeley Journal of Sociology*, 28: 97–113.

Cohen, Jean L. and Andrew Arato. 1992. *Civil Society and Political Theory*. Cambridge, Mass.: MIT Press.

Coleman, James S. 1990. *Foundations of Social Theory*. Cambridge, Mass.: Belknap Press of Harvard University Press.

1993. "The Rational Reconstruction of Society." *American Sociological Review*, 58:1–15.

Collins, Randall. 1979. *The Credential Society: An Historical Sociology of Education and Stratification*. New York: Academic Press.

Condorcet. 1933 [1793]. *Esquisse d'un tableau historique des progrès de l'esprit humaine*. Paris: Boivin.

Conley, Thomas M. 1990. *Rhetoric in the European Tradition*. New York and London: Longman.

Converse, Jean M. 1987. *Survey Research in the United States: Roots and Emergence, 1890–1960*. Berkeley and Los Angeles: University of California Press.

Conway, M. Margaret. 1991. *Political Particpation the United States*. 2nd edn., Washington DC: CQ Press.

Crawford, Vincent P. and Joel Sobel. 1982. "Strategic Information Transmission." *Econometrica*, 50:1,431–51.

Curran, James. 1991. "Rethinking the Media as a Public Sphere." In Peter Dahlgren and Colin Sparks, eds., *Communication and Citizenship: Journalism and the Public Sphere in the New Media Age*, pp. 27–57. London and New York: Routledge.

Cutlip, Scott. 1994. *The Unseen Power: Public Relations. A History*. Hillsdale, NJ: Lawrence Erlbaum Associates.

Dayan, Daniel and Elihu Katz. 1992. *Media Events: The Live Broadcasting of History*. Cambridge, Mass. and London: Harvard University Press.

Debord, Guy. 1970 [1967]. *Society of the Spectacle*. Detroit, Mich.: Black and Red.

Denver, David, Gordon Hands, and Bill Jones. 1995. "Fishkin and the Deliberative Opinion Poll: Lessons from a Study of the *Granada 500* Television Program." *Political Communication*, 12: 147–56.

Derrida, Jacques. 1976 [1967]. *Of Grammatology*. Trans. Gayatri Chakravorty Spivak. Baltimore, Md.: Johns Hopkins University Press.

1977. "Limited Inc abc." *Glyph II*, pp. 162–254. Baltimore, Md.: Johns Hopkins University Press.

Derthick, Martha and Paul J. Quirk. 1985. *The Politics of Regulation*. Washington, DC: The Brookings Institution.

Dewey, John. 1927. *The Public and its Problems: An Essay in Political Inquiry*. New York: Henry Holt.

Diamond, Edwin and Stephen Bates. 1992. *The Spot: The Rise of Political Advertising on Television*. 3rd edn. Cambridge, Mass.: MIT Press.

Dillon, J. T., ed. 1994. *Deliberation in Education and Society*. Norwood, NJ: Ablex Publishing.

DiMaggio, Paul J. and Walter Powell. 1983. "The Iron Cage Revisited: Instititutional Isomorphism and Collective Rationality." *American Sociological Review*, 48:147–60.

Downs, Anthony. 1957. *An Economic Theory of Democracy*. New York: Harper & Brothers.

Doyle, William. 1989. *The Oxford History of the French Revolution*. Oxford: The Clarendon Press at Oxford University Press.

Duncan, Hugh Dalziel. 1962. *Communication and the Social Order*. New York: Bedminster Press.

Durkheim, Emile. 1933 [1893]. *The Division of Labor In Society*. Trans. George Simpson. New York: Macmillan.

Edelman, Murray. 1988. *Constructing the Political Spectacle*. Chicago: University of Chicago Press.

Eisenstein, Elizabeth L. 1979. *The Printing Press as an Agent of Change: Communication and Cultural Transformation in Early Modern Europe*. Cambridge: Cambridge University Press.

Elkins, Stanley and Eric McKitrick. 1993. *The Age of Federalism*. New York and London: Oxford University Press.

Elster, Jon. 1989. *The Cement of Society: A Study of Social Order*. Cambridge and New York: Cambridge University Press.

Ely, John. 1992. "The Politics of Civil Society." *Telos*, 93: 173–91.

Enelow, James and Melvin Hinich. 1984. *The Spatial Theory of Voting*. Cambridge, Mass.: Harvard University Press.

Engel, James F., Roger D. Blackwell, and Roger Miniard. 1990. *Consumer Behavior*. 6th edn. Chicago: Dryden Press.

Entman, Robert E. and Andrew Rojecki. 1993. "Freezing Out the Public: Elite and Media Framing and the U.S Anti-Nuclear Movement." *Political Communication*, 10:155–73.

Epstein, Edward Jay. 1973. *News from Nowhere: Television and the News*. New York: Random House.

Faucheux, Ron. 1995. "The Grassroots Explosion." *Campaigns and Elections* (December/January), 20–5, 53–6, 66–7.

Festinger, Leon, Henry W. Riecken, and Stanley Schacter. 1956. *When Prophesy Fails*. New York: Harper and Row.

Fishkin, James S. 1991. *Democracy and Deliberation: New Directions for Democratic Reform*. New Haven, Conn.: Yale University Press.

Fishman, Mark. 1980. *Manufacturing the News*. Austin, Texas: University of Texas Press.

Forester, John. 1985. "Critical Theory and Planning Practice." In John Forester, ed., *Critical Theory and Public Life*, pp. 202–30. Cambridge, Mass. and London: MIT Press.

Foucault, Michel. 1972. *The Archaeology of Knowledge*. Trans. A. M. Sheridan Smith. New York: Pantheon.

1977. *Discipline and Punish: The Birth of the Prison*. Trans. A. M. Sheridan Smith. New York: Pantheon.

Foundation for Public Affairs. 1992. *Public Interest Profiles*. Washington DC: Congressional Quarterly Inc.

Fox, Stephen. 1984. *The Mirror Makers: A History of American Advertising and its Creators*. New York: Morrow.

Foxe, John. 1965 [1563]. *Actes and Monuments*: New York: AMS Press.

Fraser, Nancy. 1989. *Unruly Practices: Power, Discourse, and Gender in Contemporary Social Theory*. Minneapolis, Minn.: University of Minnesota Press.

Freidson, Eliot. 1970. *Profession of Medicine*. New York: Dodd Mead.

Gadamer, Hans-Georg. 1989 [1960]. *Truth and Method*. 2nd rev. edn. Trans. Joel Weinsheimer and Donald G. Marshall. New York: Crossroad.

1990 [1971]. "Reply to My Critics." Trans. George H. Leiner. In Gayle L. Ormiston and Alan D. Schrift, eds., *The Hermeneutic Tradition: From Ast to Ricoeur*, pp. 273–97. Albany, New York: State University of New York Press.

Gallup, George Jr. 1989. *The Gallup Poll: Public Opinion,1988*. Wilmington, Del.: Scholarly Resources.

Galston, William A. 1991. *Liberal Purposes*. Cambridge: Cambridge University Press.

Gambetta, Diego, ed. 1988. *Trust: Making and Breaking Cooperative Relations*. New York and Cambridge: Basil Blackwell.

Gamson, William A. 1992. *Talking Politics*. Cambridge and New York: Cambridge University Press.

Gans, Herbert J. 1979. *Deciding What's News: A Study of CBS Evening News, NBC Nightly News, Newsweek and Time*. New York: Pantheon Books.

Garin, Eugenio. 1965. *Italian Humanism: Philosophy and Civic Life in the Renaisance*. Trans. Peter Munz. New York: Harper and Row.

Gastil, John. 1994. "A Definition and Illustration of Democratic Leadership." *Human Relations*, 47: 953–75.

Gates, Henry Louis Jr. 1988. *The Signifying Monkey: A Theory of Afro- American Literary Criticism*. New York: Oxford University Press.

Gerber, Elizabeth and John E. Jackson. 1992. "Endogenous Preferences and the Study of Institutions." *American Political Science Quarterly*, 87: 639–56.

Germond, Jack W. and Julius Witcover. 1989. *Whose Broad Stripes and Bright Stars: The Trivial Pursuit of the Presidency*. New York: Warner Books.

Gerring, Anthony L., ed. 1995. *Research Centers Directory*. 20th edn., 1996. Detroit, Mich.: Gayle Research.

Gilbert, Felix. 1965. *Machiavelli and Guicciardini: Politics and History in Sixteenth Century Florence*. Princeton, NJ: Princeton University Press.

Gitlin, Todd. 1978. "Media Sociology: The Dominant Paradigm." *Theory and Society*, 6: 205–53.

Goffman, Erving. 1974. *Frame Analysis: Essay on the Organization of Experience*. New York: Harper and Row.

Good, David. 1988. "Individuals, Interpersonal Relations, and Trust." In Diego Gambetta, ed., *Trust: Making and Breaking Cooperative Relations*, pp. 31–48. New York and Cambridge: Basil Blackwell.

Goodall, Francis. 1986. "Marketing Consumer Products Before 1924, Rowntrees and Elect Cocoa." In R. P. T. Davenport-Hines ed., *Markets and Bagmen: Studies in the History of Marketing and British Industrial Performance, 1830–1939*, pp. 16–57. Aldershot, Hants: Gower Publishing Company.

Goodnight, G. Thomas. 1992. "Habermas, the Public Sphere and Controversy." *International Journal of Public Opinion Research*, 4: 243–55.

Goodwin, John. 1933 [1644]. *Theomachia.* Reproduced in William Haller, ed., *Tracts on Liberty in the Puritan Revolution 1638–1647*, III, pp. 3–58. New York: Columbia University Press.

1654. *A Fresh Discovery.* Wing G1167.

Goodwin, John, et al. 1933 [1644]. *An Apologeticall Narration.* Reproduced in William Haller, ed., *Tracts on Liberty in the Puritan Revolution 1638–1647*, I, pp. 305– 99. New York: Columbia University Press.

Gould, Roger. 1993. "Trade Cohesion, Class Unity, and Urban Insurrection: Artisanal Activity in the Paris Commune." *American Journal of Sociology*, 98: 721–44.

Gouldner, Alvin W. 1960. "The Norm of Reciprocity: A Preliminary Statement." *American Sociological Review*, 25: 161–78.

Grassi, Ernesto. 1976. "The Priority of Common Sense and Imagination: Vico's Philosophical Relevance Today." Trans. Azizeh Azodi. *Social Research*, 43: 553– 75.

1980. *Rhetoric as Philosophy: The Humanist Tradition.* Trans. John Michael Krois and Azizeh Azodi. University Park, Penn.: Pennsylvania State University Press.

Greville, Robert, Lord Brooke. 1933 [1641]. *A Discourse Concerning the Nature of that Episcopacie, Which is Exerscised in England.* Reproduced in William Haller, ed., *Tracts on Liberty in the Puritan Revolution*, I, pp. 35–164. New York: Columbia University Press.

Gunn, J. A. W. 1969. *Politics and the Public Interest in the Seventeenth Century.* London: Routledge & Keegan Paul.

Gusfield, Joseph R. 1976. "The Literary Rhetoric of Science: Comedy and Pathos in Drinking Driver Research." *American Journal of Sociology*, 41: 16–34.

1989. *Kenneth Burke: On Symbols and Society.* Chicago: University of Chicago Press.

Habermas, Jürgen. 1970 [1968–9]. *Toward a Rational Society: Student Protest, Science, and Politics.* Trans. Jeremy J. Shapiro. Boston: Beacon Press.

1971 [1968]. *Knowledge and Human Interests.* Trans. Jeremy J. Shapiro. Boston: Beacon Press.

1979 [1976]. *Communication and the Evolution of Society.* Trans. Thomas McCarthy. Boston: Beacon Press.

1980 [1973]. "The Hermeneutic Claim to Universality." Trans. Josef Bleicher. In Josef Bleicher, ed., *Contemporary Hermeneutics: Hermeneutics as Method, Philosophy and Critique*, pp. 181–211. London: Routledge & Kegan Paul.

1981. "Modernity versus Postmodernity." *New German Critique*, 22: 3–14.

1982. "A Reply to Critics." In John B. Thompson and David Held, eds., *Habermas: Critical Debates*, pp. 219–84. Cambridge, Mass.: MIT Press.

1984 [1981]. *The Theory of Communicative Action, I. Reason and the Rationalization of Society.* Trans. Thomas McCarthy. Boston: Beacon Press.

1985 "Civil Disobedience: Litmus Test for the Democratic Constitutional State." *Berkeley Journal of Sociology*, 30: 95–113.

1987 [1981]. *The Theory of Communicative Action, II. Lifeworld and System: A Critique of Functionalist Reason.* Trans. Thomas McCarthy. Boston: Beacon Press.

1987 [1985]. *The Philosophical Discourse of Modernity: Twelve Lectures.* Trans. Thomas McCarthy. Cambridge, Mass.: MIT Press.

1989 [1962]. *The Structural Transformation of the Public Sphere: An Inquiry into a Category of Bourgeois Society.* Trans. Thomas Burger. Cambridge, Mass.: MIT Press.

1990 [1983]. *Moral Consciousness and Communicative Action.* Trans. Christian Lenhardt and Shierry Weber Nicholsen. Cambridge, Mass.: MIT Press.

1993 [1991]. *Justification and Application: Remarks on Discourse Ethics.* Trans. Ciaran P. Cronin. Cambridge, Mass.: MIT Press.

1993 [1981]. "Modernity – An Incomplete Project." In Thomas Docherty, ed., *Postmodernism: A Reader*, pp. 98–109. New York: Columbia University Press.

1994. "Three Normative Models of Democracy." *Constellations*, 1: 1–10.

1996. *Between Facts and Norms: Contributions to a Discourse Theory of Law and Democracy.* Trans. William Rehg. Cambridge, Mass.: MIT Press.

Hall, Stuart. 1981. "Encoding and Decoding in Television Discourse." In Stuart Hall et al., eds. *Culture, Media, Language.* London: Hutchinson.

Haller, William. 1938. *The Rise of Puritanism.* New York: Columbia University Press.

1955. *Liberty and Reformation in the Puritan Revolution.* New York: Columbia University Press.

Hammond, Henry. 1649. *Mysterium Religionis Recognitum.* Wing H546.

Hardy, Hugh S. 1990. *The Politz Papers: Science and Truth in Marketing Research.* Chicago Ill.: American Marketing Association.

Harwood Group. 1991. *Citizens and Politics: A View from Main Street America.* Dayton, Ohio: Kettering Foundation.

1993. *Meaningful Chaos: How People Form Relationships with Public Concerns.* Dayton, Ohio: Kettering Foundation.

Heard, Alexander. 1960. *The Costs of Democracy.* Chapel Hill, NC: The University of North Carolina Press.

Heclo, Hugh. 1978. "Issue Networks and the Executive Establishment." In Anthony King, ed., *The New American Political System*, pp. 87–124. Washington, DC: American Enterprise Institute.

Herbst, Susan. 1992. "Surveys in the Public Sphere: Applying Bourdieu's Critique of Opinion Polls." *International Journal of Public Opinion Research*, 4: 220–29.

Herman, Edward S. and Noam Chomsky. 1988. *Manufacturing Consent: The Political Economy of the Mass Media.* New York: Pantheon Books.

Hertsgaard, Mark. 1988. *On Bended Knee: The Press and the Reagan Presidency.* New York: Farrar Straus Giroux.

Hill, Christopher. 1961. *Century of Revolution, 1603–1714.* New York: Norton.

1964. *Puritanism and Revolution.* New York: Schocken Books.

1967. *Society and Puritanism in the Puritan Revolution.* New York: Schocken Books.

1977. *Milton and the English Revolution*. Harmondsworth: Penguin.

Hill, Thomas. 1642. *The Trade of Truth Advanced*. Wing H2031.

Hinich, Melvin J. and Michael C. Munger. 1994. *Ideology and the Theory of Political Choice*. Ann Arbor, Mich.: University of Michigan Press.

Hoadley, John F. 1986. *Origins of American Political Parties, 1789–1803*. Lexington, Ken.: University of Kentuckey Press.

Hooker, Richard. 1954 [1594]. *Of the Laws of Ecclesiastical Polity*. London: J. M. Dent and Sons.

Horkheimer, Max and Theodor W. Adorno. 1972 [1947]. *Dialectic of Enlightenment*. Trans. John Cumming. New York: Herder and Herder.

Hower, Ralph M. 1949. *The History of an Advertising Agency: N. W. Ayer & Sons at Work, 1869–1949*. Rev. edn. Cambridge, Mass: Harvard University Press.

Huckfeldt, Robert and John Sprague. 1990. "Social Order and Political Chaos: The Structural Setting of Political Information." In John A. Ferejohn and James H. Kuklinsky, eds., *Information and Democratic Processes*, pp. 23–58. Urbana and Chicago: University of Illinois Press.

1995. *Citizens, Politics, and Social Communication: Information and Influence in an Election Campaign*. Cambridge and New York: Cambridge University Press.

Hunter, Kennith G., Laura Ann Wilson, and Gregory C. Break. 1991. "Societal Complexity and Interest Group Lobbying in the American States." *Journal of Politics*, 53: 488–503.

Iverson, Torben. 1994. "Political Leadership and Representation in Western European Democracies: A Test of Three Models of Voting." *American Journal of Political Science*, 38:45–74.

Jacobson, David L., ed. 1965. *The English Libertarian Heritage: From the Writings of John Trenchard and Thomas Gordon in the Independent Whig and Cato's Letters*. Indianapolis, Ind.: Bobbs-Merrill Company.

Jameson, Fredric. 1991. *Postmodernism, or the Cultural Logic of Late Capitalism*. Durham, NC: Duke University Press.

Johnson, Haynes and David Broder. 1996. *The System: The American Way of Politics at the Breaking Point*. Boston and New York: Little, Brown and Company.

Jones, D. G. Brian and David D. Manieson. 1990. "Early Development of the Philosophy of Marketing Thought." *Journal of Marketing*, 54:102–13.

Joyce, Patrick. 1991. *Visions of the People: Industrial England and the Question of Class*. Cambridge: Cambridge University Press.

Jurkowitz, Mark. 1996. "From the Citizen Up." *Media Critic*, 3: 75–83.

Karpoff, Jonathan and John R. Lott, Jr. 1993. "The Reputational Penalty Firms Bear for Committing Fraud." *Journal of Law and Economics*, 36: 757–802.

Katz, Elihu and Paul F. Lazarsfeld. 1955. *Personal Influence: The Part Played by People in the Flow of Mass Communication*. Glencoe, Ill.: The Free Press of Glencoe.

Kelley, Stanley, Jr. 1956. *Professional Public Relations and Political Power.* Baltimore, Md.: Johns Hopkins University Press.

Kemp, Ray. 1985. "Planning, Public Hearings, and the Politics of Discourse." In John Forester, ed., *Critical Theory and Public Life.* Cambridge, Mass.: MIT Press.

Kernell, Samuel. 1986. *Going Public: New Strategies of Presidential Leadership.* Washington DC: CQ Press.

Klapper, Joseph. 1960. *The Effects of Communication.* New York: Free Press.

Kleppner, Paul. 1982. *Who Voted? The Dynamics of Electoral Turn Out.* New York: Praeger.

Knights, Mark. 1993. "Petitioning and the Political Theorists: John Locke, Algernon Sidney and London's 'Monster' Petition of 1680." *Past and Present,* 36: 94–111.

Kolberg, Elizabeth. 1992. "Test-Marketing a President: How Focus Groups Pervade Campaign Politics." *New York Times Magazine* (August 30), 18–21, 60, 68, 72.

1995. "The Vocabulary of Votes: Frank Luntz." *New York Times Magazine,* 46–9.

Kreshel, Peggy J. 1990a. "The 'Culture' of J. Walter Thomson, 1915–25." *Public Relations Review,* 16: 80–93.

1990b. "John B. Watson at J. Walter Thomson: The Legitimation of Science in Advertising." *Journal of Advertising,* 19(2): 49–59.

Krugman, Paul. 1994. *Peddling Prosperity: Economic Sense and Nonsense in the Age of Diminished Expectations.* New York: W. W. Norton.

Kubiak, Greg D. 1994. *The Gilded Dome: The U.S. Senate and Campaign Finance Reform.* Norman, Ok.: University of Oklahoma Press.

Kurtz, Howard. 1996. "In Search of the People's Voice." *Washington Post,* " Weekly Edition, June 10–15, 34.

Lacey, Jamie Press and John T. Llewellyn. 1995. "The Engineering of Outrage: Mediated Constructions of Risk in the Alar Controversy." In William N. Ellwood, ed., *Public Relations Inquiry as Rhetorical Criticism: Case Studies of Corporate Discourse and Social Influence,* pp. 47–68. Westport, Conn.: Praeger.

Ladd, Everett Carl. 1996a. "Fishkin's 'Deliberative Poll' is Flawed Science and Dubious Democracy." *The Public Perspective* (December/January), 7: 41–5.

1996b. "The Data Just Don't Show Erosion of America's Social Capital." *The Public Perspective* (June/July), 7: 1–6.

Lang, Kurt and Gladys Lang. 1953. "The Unique Perspective of Television and Its Effect: A Pilot Study." *American Sociological Review,* 18: 3–12.

Larson, Magali S. 1977. *The Rise of Professionalism.* Berkeley, Calif.: University of California Press.

Lazarsfeld, Paul F., Bernard Berelson, and Hazel Gaudet. 1948. *The People's Choice.* New York: Columbia University Press.

Leach, William. 1993. *Land of Desire: Merchants, Power, and the Rise of a New American Culture.* New York: Pantheon Books.

Leland, Heyn and David H. Pyle. 1977. "Informational Asymmetries, Financial Structure, and Financial Intermediation." *Journal of Finance*, 32: 371–87.

Lichter, S. Robert and Richard E. Noyes. 1995. "The Unmaking of the Mainstream Media." *Media Critic*, 3: 79–86.

Liebes, Tamar and Elihu Katz. 1990. *The Export of Meaning: Cross-Cultural Readings of Dallas*. New York and Oxford: Oxford University Press.

Lippmann, Walter. 1922. *Public Opinion*. New York: Harcourt, Brace.

Litoff, J. B. 1978. *American Midwives*. Westport, Conn.: Greenview.

Lockley, Lawrence C. 1974. "History and Development of Marketing Research." In Robert Ferber, ed., *Handbook of Marketing Research*, Part One, pp.1–15. New York: McGraw Hill.

Lodge, Milton, Marco R. Steenbergen, and Shawn Brau. 1995. "The Responsive Voter: Campaign Information and the Dynamics of Candidate Evaluation." *American Political Science Review*, 89:309–26.

Lohmann, Suzanne. 1993. "A Signaling Model of Informative and Manipulative Political Action." *American Political Science Review*, 87: 319–33.

Loomis, Burdett A. and Allan J. Cigler. 1995. "Introduction: The Changing Nature of Interest Group Politics." In Allan J. Cigler and Burdett A. Loomis, eds., *Interest Group Politics*. 4th edn., pp. 1–31. Washington, DC: CQ Press.

Lowi, Theodore J. 1979. *The End of Liberalism: The Second Republic of the United States*. 2nd edn. New York: Norton.

Lukacs, Georg. 1971 [1922]. *History and Class Consciousness: Studies in Marxist Dialectic*. Trans. Rodney Livingston. Cambridge. Mass.: MIT Press.

Lukes, Steven. 1973. *Emile Durkheim: His Life and Works*. New York: Harper and Row.

1982. "Of Gods and Demons: Habermas and Practical Reason." In John B. Thompson and David Held, eds., *Habermas: Critical Debates*, pp.134–48. Cambridge, Mass.: MIT Press.

Luntz, Frank L. 1988. *Candidates, Consultants, and Campaigns: The Style and Substance of American Electioneering*. Oxford and New York: Basil Blackwell.

Lupia, Arthur. 1994. "Shortcuts Versus Encyclopedias: Information and Voting Behavior in California Insurance Reform Elections." *American Political Science Review*, 88: 63–76.

Luther, Martin. 1960 [1519]. "The Blessed Sacraments of the Holy and True Body of Christ, and the Brotherhoods." Trans. Jeremiah J. Schindel. In E. Theodore Bachman, ed., *Luther's Works*, XXXV, pp. 45–73. Philadelphia, Penn.: Muhlenberg Press.

Lyotard, Jean Francois. 1984 [1979]. *The Postmodern Condition: A Report on Knowledge*. Trans. Geoff Bennington and Brian Massumi. Minneapolis, Minn.: University of Minnesota Press.

McAdam, Doug and Ronnelle Paulsen. 1993. "Specifying the Relationship between Social Ties and Activism." *American Journal of Sociology*, 99:640–77.

McCarthy, Thomas. 1978. *The Critical Theory of Jürgen Habermas*. Cambridge, Mass.: MIT Press.

1991. "Complexity and Democracy: or the Seducements of Systems Theory." In Axel Honneth and Hans Joas, eds., *Communicative Action: Essays on Jürgen Habermas's "The Theory of Communicative Action,"* pp. 119–39. Cambridge: Polity Press.

1992. "Practical Discourse: On the Relation of Morality to Politics." In Craig Calhoun, ed,. *Habermas and the Public Sphere*, pp. 51–72. Cambridge, Mass.: MIT Press.

MacDonald, Gus. 1986. "Election 500." In Ivor Crewe and Martin Harrop, eds., *Political Communication: The General Election Campaign of 1983*. Cambridge: Cambridge University Press.

McGerr, Michael E. 1986. *The Decline of Popular Politics: The American North,1865–1928*. New York and Oxford: Oxford University Press.

McGinn, Donald. 1949. *The Admonition Controversy*. New Brunswick, NJ: Rutgers University Press.

McGinniss, Joe. 1969. *The Selling of the American President, 1969*. New York: Random House.

MacIntyre, Alisdair. 1988. *Whose Justice? Which Rationality?* Notre Dame, Ind.: Notre Dame University Press.

McKelvey, Richard D. and Peter C. Ordeshook. 1985. "Elections with Limited Information: A Fulfilled Expectations Model Using Contemporaneous Poll and Endorsement Data as Informational Sources." *Journal of Economic Theory*, 36: 55–85.

Macpherson, C. B. 1962. *The Political Theory of Possessive Individualism: Hobbes to Locke*. London: Oxford University Press.

Magleby, David B. and Kelly D. Patterson. 1994. "Congressional Reform." *Public Opinion Quarterly*, 58: 419–27.

Maltese, John Anthony. 1994. *The White House Office of Communications and the Management of Presidential News*. 2nd edn. Chapel Hill, NC: The University of North Carolina Press.

Mann, Thomas N. and Norman J. Ornstein. 1995. *Intensive Care: How Congress Shapes Health Policy*. Washington DC: American Enterprise Institute and The Brookings Institution.

Marchand, Roland. 1985. *Advertising the American Dream: Making Way for Modernity, 1920–1940*. Berkeley and Los Angeles: University of California Press.

1987. "The Fitful Career of Advocacy Advertising: Protection, Client Cultivation, and Corporate Morale." *California Management Review*, 29: 128–56.

1991. "The Corporation Nobody Knew: Bruce Barton, Alfred Sloan, and the Founding of the General Motors 'Family.'" *Business History Review*, 65: 825–75.

Mathews, David. 1994. *Politics for People: Finding a Responsible Voice*. Urbana and Chicago, Ill.: University of Illinois Press.

Mauser, Gary A. 1983. *Political Marketing: An Approach to Campaign Strategy*. New York: Praeger.

Mayhew, Leon. 1968. *Law and Equal Opportunity: A Study of the Massachusetts Commission Against Discrimination*. Cambridge, Mass.: Harvard University Press.

1968. "Ascription in Modern Society." *Sociological Inquiry*, 38: 105–20.

1971. *Society: Institutions and Activities*. Glenview, Ill: Scott Foresman.

1982. *Talcott Parsons: On Institutions and Evolution*. Chicago: University of Chicago Press.

1984a. "In Defense of Modernity: Talcott Parsons and the Utilitarian Tradition." *American Journal of Sociology*, 89:1,273–305.

1984b. "The Public Spirit: On the Origins of Liberal Thought." Davis, Calif.: Library Associates, University of California, Davis.

1990. "The Differentiation of the Solidary Public." In Jeffrey C. Alexander and Paul Colomy, eds., *Differentiation Theory and Social Change: Comparative and Historical Perspectives*, pp. 294–322. New York: Columbia University Press.

1992 "Political Rhetoric and the Contemporary Public." In Paul Colomy, ed., *The Dynamics of Social Systems*, pp. 190–213. London: Sage Publications.

Meadow, Bob, et al. 1995. "Oregon's Prop 13: How Conservative Values Were Used to Defeat an Anti-Gay Rights Measure." *Campaigns and Elections*, 36–38, 66–67.

Mendelsohn, Harold and Irving Crespi. 1970. *Polls, Television, and the New Politics*. Scranton, Penn.: Chandler.

Merton, Robert K. 1968. *Social Theory and Social Structure*. Enlarged edn. New York: Free Press.

Miller, J. Hillis. 1992. *Ariadne's Thread: Story Lines*. New Haven and London: Yale University Press.

Mills, C. Wright. 1956. *The Power Elite*. New York: Oxford University Press.

Milton, John. 1957 [1642]. *The Reason of Church Government Urged Against Prelacy*. Merritt Y. Hughes, ed., *John Milton: Complete Poetry and Major Prose*, pp. 640–89. New York: Odyssey Press.

1957 [1644]. *Areopagitica*. In Merritt Y. Hughes, ed., *John Milton: Complete Poetry and Major Prose*, pp. 716–49. New York: Odyssey Press.

1957 [1649]. *On the Tenure of Kings and Magistrates*. In Merritt Y. Hughes, ed., *John Milton: Complete Poetry and Major Prose*, pp. 750–80. New York: Odyssey Press.

Mitchell, Greg. 1992. *The Campaign of the Century: Upton Sinclair's Race for Governor of California and the Birth of Media Politics*. New York: Random House.

Mitofsky, Warren J. 1996. "It's Not Deliberative and It's Not a Poll." *The Public Perspective* (December/January), 7: 4–6.

Molotch, Harvey and Marilyn Lester. 1974. "News as Purposive Behavior: On the Strategic Use of Routine Events, Accidents and Scandals." *American Sociological Review*, 39: 101–12.

1975. "Accidental News: The Great Oil Spill as Local Occurrence and National Event." *American Journal of Sociology*, 81:235–60.

Moore, Kelly. 1996. "Organizing Integrity: American Science and the Creation of Public Interest Organizations." *American Journal of Sociology*, 101: 1,592–627.

Moore, Thomas. 1989. *Heart Failure. A Critical Inquiry into American Medicine and the Revolution in Health Care.* New York: Random House.

Morris, Dwight and Murielle E. Gamache. 1994. *Gold-Plated Politics: The 1992 Congressional Races.* Washington DC: Congressional Quarterly Inc.

Negrine, Ralph and Stylianus Papathanassopoulos. 1996. "The 'Americanization' of Political Communication: A Critique." *Harvard International Journal of Press/Politics*, 1: 45–62.

Nelson, Phillip. 1970. "Information and Consumer Behavior." *Journal of Political Economy*, 79:311–329.

1974. "Advertising and Information." *Journal of Political Economy*, 82:729–54.

Newhouse, Joseph P. 1995. "Economists, Policy Entrepreneurs, and Health Care Reform." *Health Affairs*, 14:182–198.

Newman, Bruce I. 1994. *The Marketing of the President: Political Marketing as a Campaign Strategy.* Thousand Oaks, Calif.: Sage Publications.

Nicosia, Francesco M. 1974. *Advertising, Management, and Society: A Business Point of View.* New York: McGraw-Hill Book Company.

Nielson, Arthur C. 1951. *Evolution of Factual Techniques in Marketing Research.* Chicago: A. C. Nielson Company.

Nimmo, Dan. 1970. *The Political Persuaders: The Techniques of Modern Election Campaigns.* Englewood Cliffs, NJ: Prentice Hall.

Nimmo, Dan and James E. Combs. 1983. *Mediated Political Realities.* New York: Longmans.

Nolte, Lawrence W. 1979. *Fundamentals of Public Relations: Professional Guidelines, Concepts and Integrations.* 2nd edn. Elmsford, New York: Pergamon Press.

Norris, Christopher. 1987. *Derrida.* Cambridge, Mass.: Harvard University Press.

Nownes, Anthony J, and Grant Neeley. 1996. "Public Interest Group Entrepreneurship and Theories of Mobilization." *Political Research Quarterly*, 49:119–46.

O'Connell, Daniel and Robert A. McKenzie. 1995. "Teaching the Art of Public Deliberation." *PS: Political Science and Politics*, 28: 230–2.

Ogilvie, David. 1963. *Confessions of an Advertising Man.* New York: Macmillan.

Ohmer, Susan. 1991. "Measuring Desire: George Gallup and Audience Research in Hollywood." *Journal of Film and Video*, 43: 3–28.

Olson, Alison Gilbert. 1991. "Coffee House Lobbying." *History Today*, 41: 35–41.

1992a. "The Eighteenth-Century Empire: The London Dissenters' Lobbies and the American Colonies." *Journal of American Studies*, 26: 41–58

1992b. *Making the Empire Work: London and American Interest Groups, 1690–1790.* Cambridge, Mass.: Harvard University Press.

1993. "The Lobbying of London Quakers for Pennsylvania Friends." *The Pennsylvania Magazine of History and Biography*, 117: 131–52.

Olson, Kathryn. 1995. The Function of Form in Newspapers' Political Conflict Coverage: *The New York Times*' Shaping of Expectations in the Bitburg Controversy." *Political Communication*, 12: 43–64.

Olson, Mancur Jr. 1971. *The Logic of Collective Action*. Cambridge, Mass.: Harvard University Press.

Overton, Richard. 1645. *Martins Echo*. Wing O630.

Ozment, Steven. 1992. *Protestants: The Birth of a Revolution*. New York: Doubleday.

Padgett, John F. and Christopher K. Ansell. 1993. "Robust Action and the Rise of the Medici." *American Journal of Sociology*, 86:1,259–319.

Page, Benjamin I. and Robert Y. Shapiro. 1992. *The Rational Public: Fifty Years of Trends in American's Policy Preferences*. Chicago. Ill.: University of Chicago Press.

Page, Benjamin I., Robert Y. Shapiro, and Glenn R. Dempsey. 1987. "What Moves Public Opinion?" *American Political Science Review*, 81: 23–43.

Palmer, Paul A. 1953. "The Concept of Public Opinion in Political Theory." In Bernard Berelson and Morris Janowitz, eds., *Reader in Public Opinion and Communication*, pp. 3–13. Glencoe, Ill. Free Press.

Parker, Henry. 1640. *The Case of the Shipmony Briefly Discoursed*. STC 19215.

Parsons, Talcott. 1937. *The Structure of Social Action*. New York: Macmillan.

  1951. *The Social System*. Glencoe, Ill. Free Press.

  1954a. "The Professions and Social Structure." In *Essays in Sociological Theory*. Rev. edn., pp. 34–49. Glencoe, Ill: Free Press.

  1954b. "A Revised Analytical Approach to the Theory of Social Stratification." In *Essays in Sociological Theory*. Rev. edn., pp. 386–439. Glencoe, Ill: Free Press.

  1954c. "Propaganda and Social Control." In *Essays in Sociological Theory*. Rev. edn., pp. 162–198. Glencoe, Ill: Free Press.

  1959. "An Approach to the Sociology of Knowledge." *Transactions of the Fourth World Congress of Sociology*. International Sociological Association, 4: 25–49, Milan, Italy.

  1961. "Some Considerations on the Theory of Social Change." *Rural Sociology*, 26: 219–39.

  1966. *Societies: Comparative and Evolutionary Perspectives*. Englewood Cliffs, NJ: Prentice-Hall.

  1967a. *Sociological Theory and Modern Society*. New York: Free Press.

  1967b. "On the Concept of Influence." In *Sociological Theory and Modern Society*, pp. 355–82. New York: Free Press.

  1967c. "On the Concept of Political Power." In S*ociological Theory and Modern Society*. pp. 297–354. New York: Free Press.

  1967d. "Voting and the Equilibrium of the American Political System." In *Sociological Theory and Modern Society*, pp. 223–63. New York: Free Press.

  1967e. "Full Citizenship for the Negro American." In *Sociological Theory and Modern Society*, pp. 422–65. New York: Free Press.

  1968. "On the Concept of Value Commitment." *Sociological Inquiry*, 38: 135–60.

  1970. "'The Intellectual': A Social Role Category." In Philip Rieff, ed., *On Intellectuals*, pp. 3–26. New York: Doubleday Books, Anchor Editions.

1971. *The System of Modern Societies*. Inglewood Cliffs, NJ: Prentice-Hall.

1977a. "Law as an Intellectual Stepchild." *Sociological Inquiry*, 47: 11–57.

1977b. "Robert Mangabeira Unger, *Law in Modern Society*." *Law & Society Review*, 12 145–9.

1978. *Action Theory and the Human Condition*. New York: Free Press.

Parsons, Talcott and Gerald A. Platt. 1973. *The American University*. Cambridge, Mass.: Harvard University Press.

Parsons, Talcott and Neil J. Smelser. 1956. *Economy and Society*. New York: Free Press.

Patterson, Kelly D. and David B. Magleby. 1992. "Public Support for Congress." *Public Opinion Quarterly*, 56: 339–51.

Pease, Otis. 1958. *The Responsibilities of American Advertising: Private Control and Public Influence, 1920–1940*. New Haven, Conn.: Yale Univerity Press.

Peer, Limor. 1992. "The Practice of Opinion Polling as a Disciplinary Mechanism: A Foucauldian Perspective." *International Journal of Public Opinion Research*, 4: 230–42.

Perelman, Chaim. 1982 [1977]. *The Realm of Rhetoric*. Trans. William Kluback. Notre Dame, Indiana: University of Notre Dame Press.

Perelman, Chaim and L. Olbrechts-Tyteca. 1969 [1958]. *The New Rhetoric: Treatise on Argumentation*. Trans. John Wilkinson and Purcell Weaver. Notre Dame, Indiana: University of Notre Dame Press.

Perkins, William. 1595. *An Exposition of the Symbole or Creed of the Apostles*. STC 19703.

1603. "A Treatise of the Vocations or Callings." In William Perkins, *Works*, pp. 909–39. STC 19647.

Plato. 1960. *Gorgias*. Trans. with an introduction by Walter Hamilton. London: Penguin Books.

Pocock, J. G. A. 1975. *The Machiavellian Moment: Florentine Political Thought and the Atlantic Republican Tradition*. Princeton, NJ: Princeton University Press.

1977. *The Political Works of James Harrington*. Cambridge: Cambridge University Press.

1987. "Between Gog and Magog: The Republican Thesis and the *Ideologia Americana*." *Journal of the History of Ideas*, 48:305–46.

1981. "*The Machiavellian Moment* Revisited: A Study in History and Ideology." *Journal of Modern History*, 53: 49–72.

*Political Resource Directory: National Edition*. 1995. Ed. Carol Hess. Burlington, Vermont: Political Resources Inc.

Pope, Whitney and Barclay D. Johnson. 1983. "Inside Organic Solidarity." *American Sociological Review*, 48:681–92.

Poster, Mark. 1990. *The Mode of Information: Poststructuralism and Social Context*. Chicago, Ill.: University of Chicago Press.

1994. "Critical Theory and the Technoculture: Habermas and Baudrillard." In Douglas Kellner, ed., *Baudrillard: A Critical Reader*, pp. 68–88. London and Cambridge, Mass: Basil Blackwell.

Powell, Walter W. and Paul J. DiMaggio. 1991. *The New Institutionalism in Organizational Analysis*. Chicago, Ill.: University of Chicago Press.

Proctor, Robert N. 1995. *Cancer Wars: How Politics Shapes What We Know and Don't Know About Cancer*. New York: Basic Books.

Putnam, Robert D. 1995a. "Bowling Alone, Revisited." *The Responsive Community*, 4:18–33.

　1995b. "Tuning In, Tuning Out: The Strange Disappearance of Social Capital in the United States." *PS: Political Science and Politics*, 28: 664–83.

Quirk, Paul J. 1990. "Deregulation and the Politics of Ideas in Congress." In Jane J. Mansbridge, ed., *Beyond Self Interest*, pp. 183–99. Chicago: University of Chicago Press.

Rasmusen, Eric. 1993. "Lobbying When the Decision Maker Can Acquire Independent Information." *Public Choice*, 77: 899–913.

Raucher, Alan R. 1968. *Public Relations and Business, 1900–1929*. Baltimore, Md: Johns Hopkins University Press.

Regens, James L. and Ronald Keith Gaddie. 1995. *The Economic Realities of Political Reform: Elections and the U.S. Senate*. Cambridge: Cambridge University Press.

Remini, Robert V. 1981. *Andrew Jackson and the Course of American Freedom, 1822–1832*, II. New York: Harper and Row Publishers.

Ricci, David M. 1993. *The Transformation of American Politics: The New Washington and the Rise of Think Tanks*. New Haven, Conn: Yale University Press.

Richards, I. A. 1936. *The Philosophy of Rhetoric*. New York: Oxford University Press.

Ricoeur, Paul. 1981. *Hermeneutics and the Human Sciences: Essays on Language, Action, and Interpretation*. Trans. John B. Thompson. Cambridge: Cambridge University Press.

　1981 [1973]. "Hermeneutics and the Critique of Ideology." *In Hermeneutics and the Human Sciences: Essays on Language, Action, and Interpretation*. Trans. John B. Thompson, 1981, pp. 63–100. Cambridge: Cambridge University Press.

Roberts, Nancy C. and Paula J. King. 1991. "Policy Entrepreneurs: Their Activity, Structure, and Function in the Policy Process." *Journal of Public Administration Research and Theory*, a 147–74.

Robinson, Henry. 1643. *Liberty of Conscience*. Reproduced in William Haller, ed., *Tracts on Liberty in the Puritan Revolution 1638–1647*, I, pp. 105–78. New York: Columbia University Press, 1933.

Rosenbloom, David Lee. 1973. *The Election Men: Professional Campaign Managers and American Democracy*. New York: Quadrangle Books.

Rosenstone, Steven J. and John Mark Hansen. 1993. *Mobilization, Participation, and Democracy in America*. New York: Macmillan.

Rosenthal, Alan. 1993. *The Third House: Lobbyists and Lobbying in the States*. Washington, DC: CQ Press.

Rothenberg, Lawrence. 1992. *Linking Citizens to Government: Interest Group Politics at Common Cause*. Cambridge: Cambridge University Press.

Sabato, Larry J. 1981. *The Rise of Political Consultants*. New York: Basic Books.

Salisbury, Robert H. 1969. "An Exchange Theory of Interest Groups." *Midwest Journal of Political Science*, 13: 1–32.

1991. "Putting Interests Back into Interest Groups." In Allan J. Cigler and Burdett A. Loomis, eds., *Interest Group Politics*. 3rd edn., pp. 371–84. Washington DC: CQ Press.

Saltmarsh, John. 1646. *Reasons for Unity*. Wing R2011.

Schapiro, Salwyn. 1963. *Condorcet and the Rise of Liberalism*. New York: Octagon.

Schlesinger, Arthur M. Jr., ed., 1994. *Running for President: The Candidates and Their Images*, I. Simon and Schuster: New York.

Schlozman, Kay Lehman. 1984. "More of the Same: Washington Pressure Group Activity in a Decade of Change." *Journal of Politics*, 45:351–75.

Schlozman, Kay Lehman and John T. Tierney. 1983. "What Accent the Heavenly Choir? Political Equality and the American Pressure System." *Journal of Politics*, 46:1,006–32.

Schnädelbach, Herbert. 1991. "The Transformation of Critical Theory." In Axel Honneth and Hans Joas, eds., *Communicative Action: Essays on Jürgen Habermas's "The Theory of Communicative Action."* Trans. Jeremy Gaines and Doris L. Jones, pp. 7–22. Cambridge: Polity Press.

Schonhardt-Bailey, Cheryl. 1991. "Lessons on Lobbying for Free Trade 19th-Century Britain: To Concentrate or Not." *American Political Science Review*, 85: 37–58

Schudson, Michael. 1978. *Discovering the News: A Social History of American Newspapers*. New York: Basic Books.

1992. "Was There Ever A Public Sphere? If So, When? Reflections on the American Case." In Craig Calhoun, ed., *Habermas and the Public Sphere*, pp. 143–63. Cambridge, Mass.: MIT Press.

1995a. "How News Becomes News." *Media Critic* (Summer), 2: 76–85.

1995b. *The Power News*. Cambridge, Mass.: Harvard University Press.

Schulz, Max. 1996. "Spin Cycle." *Media Critic* (Winter), 3: 86–9.

Schwartz, Tony. 1973. *The Responsive Chord*. New York: Basic Books.

Sciulli, David. 1985. "The Practical Groundwork of Critical Theory: Bringing Parsons to Habermas (and Vice Versa)." In Jeffrey C. Alexander, ed. *Neofunctionalism*, pp. 21–50. Beverly Hills, Calif.: Sage Publications.

1990. "Differentiation and Collegial Formations: Implications of Societal Constitutionalism." In Jeffrey C. Alexander and Paul Colomy, eds., *Differentiation Theory and Social Change: Comparative and Historical Perspectives*, pp. 323–405. New York: Columbia University Press.

1992. *Theory of Societal Constitutionalism: Foundations of a Non-Marxist Critical Theory*. Cambridge: Cambridge University Press.

Searle, John R. 1977. "Reiterating the Differences." *Glyph I*, pp. 198–208. Baltimore, Md.: Johns Hopkins University Press.

Sears, David O. and Carolyn L. Funk. 1990. "Self Interest in American's Political Opinions." Jane J. Mansbridge, ed., *Beyond Self Interest*, pp. 147–70. Chicago: University of Chicago Press.

Seaver, Paul S. 1970. *The Puritan Lectureships: The Politics of Religious Dissent. 1560–1662*. Palo Alto, Calif.: Stanford University Press.

Seigel, Jerrold E. 1968. *Rhetoric and Philosophy in Renaissance Humanism: The Union of Eloquence and Wisdom, Petrarch to Valla*. Princeton, NJ: Princeton University Press.

Selznik, Philip. 1992. *The Moral Commonwealth: Social Theory and the Promise of Community*. Berkeley and Los Angeles: University of California Press.

Sethi, S. Prakesh. 1978. "Alternative Viewpoint: Should Business Aid the Opposition? *Public Relations Journal*, November, 18–20.

Shaiko, Ronald G. 1991. "More Bang for the Buck: The New Era of Full-Service Organizations." In Allan J. Cigler and Burdett A. Loomis, eds., *Interest Group Politics*. 3rd edn., pp. 109–30. Washington DC: CQ Press.

Shalin, Dimitry. 1992. "Critical Theory and the Pragmatist Challenge." *American Journal of Sociology*, 98: 237–79.

Shapiro, Carl. 1982. "Consumer Information, Product Quality, and Seller Reputation." *Bell Journal of Economics*, 13: 20–35.

Shinkle, Don E. 1994. "PR Measurement is the Answer." *Public Relations Quarterly*, 39: 16–17.

Sigal, Leon V. 1973. *Reporters and Officials: The Organization and Politics of Newsmaking*. Lexington, Mass.: D.C. Heath.

Simmons, Robert E. 1990. *Communications Campaign Management: A Systems. Approach*. White Plains, New York: Longmans.

Simon, Herbert A. 1961 [1947]. *Administrative Behavior*. 2nd edn. New York: Macmillan.

Sinopoli, Richard C. 1992. *The Foundations of American Citizenship: Liberalism, the Constitution, and Civic Virtue*. New York and Oxford: Oxford University Press.

Skinner, Quentin. 1978. *The Foundations of Modern Political Thought*. Cambridge: Cambridge University Press.

Smith, James Allen. 1991. *The Idea Brokers: Think Tanks and the Rise of the New Policy Elite*. New York: Free Press.

Sniderman, Paul M., Richard Brody, and Philip E. Tetlock. 1991. *Reasoning and Choice: Explorations in Political Psychology*. Cambridge: Cambridge University Press.

Snow, David A. et al. 1986. "Frame Alignment Processes, Mobilization, and Movement Participation." *American Sociological Review*, 51: 464–81.

Sobel, George. 1985. "A Theory of Credibility." *Review of Economic Studies*, 557–73.

Somers, Margaret R. 1993. "Citizenship and the Place of the Public Sphere: Law, Community, and Political Culture in the Transition to Democracy." *American Sociological Review*, 58: 587–620.

Speier, Hans. 1950. "Historical Development of Public Opinion." *American Journal of Sociology*, 55: 376–88.

Spence, Michael. 1973. "Job Market Signaling." *Quarterly Journal of Economics*, 87:355–74.

Spencer, John. 1641. *A Short Treatise Concerning the Lawfullnesse of Every Mans Exercising his Gift*. Wing S4954.

Stigler, George. 1961. "The Economics of Information." *Journal of Political Economy*, 69:213–25.

Stimson, James A. 1991. *Public Opinion in America: Moods, Cycles, Swings*. Boulder, Col.: Westview Press.

Taylor, Charles. 1989. *Sources of the Self: the Making of Modern Identity*. Cambridge, Mass.: Harvard University Press.

  1991. "Language and Society." In Axel Honneth and Hans Joas, eds., *Communicative Action: Essays on Jürgen Habermas's "The Theory of Communicative Action,"* pp. 23–35. Cambridge: Polity Press.

Teixeira, Ruy A. 1992. *The Disappearing American Voter*. Washington, DC: The Brookings Institution.

Thompson, Margaret Susan. 1985. *The "Spider Web": Congress and Lobbying in the Age of Grant*. Ithaca, NY: Cornell University Press.

Toennies, Ferdinand. 1940 [1887]. *Fundamental Concepts of Sociology*. Trans. C. P. Loomis. New York: American Books.

Toulmin, Stephen. 1958. *The Uses of Argument*. Cambridge: Cambridge University Press.

Tuchman, Gaye. 1972. "Objectivity as Strategic Ritual: Examination of Newsmen's Notions of Objectivity." *American Journal of Sociology*, 77: 660–79.

  1978. *Making News: A Study in the Construction of Reality*. New York: Free Press.

Turner, Terrence S. 1968. "Parsons' Concept of 'Generalized Media of Social Interaction' and its Relevance for Social Anthropology." *Sociological Inquiry*, 38: 121–34.

Twentieth Century Fund. 1993. *1–800–PRESIDENT: The Report of the Twentieth Century Fund Task Force on Television and the Campaign of 1992*. New York: Twentieth Century Fund Press.

Vattimo, Gianni 1988 [1985]. *The End of Modernity: Nihilism and Hermeneutics in Postmodern Culture*. Trans. Jon R. Snyder. Cambridge: Polity Press.

Walker, Jack L. 1991. *Mobilizing Group Interests in America: Patrons, Professions, and Social Movements*. Ann Arbor, Mich.: University of Michigan Press.

Waller-Zuckerman, Mary Ellen. 1989. "'Preconceived Notions' and the Historian's Dilemma: Market Research by Women's Magazine Publishers in the Interwar Years." In Terence Nevett, Kathleen R. Whitney, and Stanley C. Hollander, eds., *Marketing History: The Emerging Discipline*, pp. 331–53. (Proceedings of the Fourth Conference on Historical Research in Marketing and Marketing Thought.) East Lansing, Mich.: Graduate School of Business Administration, Michigan State University.

Walzer, Michael. 1965. *The Revolution of the Saints*. Cambridge, Mass.: Harvard University Press.

Warner, Michael. 1992. "The Mass Public and the Mass Subject." In Craig Calhoun, ed., *Habermas and the Public Sphere*, pp. 377–401. Cambridge, Mass.: MIT Press.

Weatherford, M. Stephen. 1982. "Interpersonal Networks and Political Behavior." *American Journal of Political Science*, 26: 117–43.

Weber, Max. 1930 [1904]. *The Protestant Ethic and the Spirit of Capitalism*. Trans. Talcott Parsons. New York: Scribner.

1968 [1922]. *Economy and Society*. Trans. Guenther Roth and Claus Wittich. New York: Bedminster Press.

Wedgwood, C. V. 1970. "The Trial of Charles I." In R. H. Parry, ed., *The English Civil War and After, 1642–1658*, pp. 41–58. Berkeley: University of California Press.

Weimann, Gabriel. 1994. *The Influentials: People Who Influence People*. Albany, NY: State University of New York Press.

Weisskopf, Michael and David Maraniss. 1995. "Gingrich's War of Words." *Washington Post* (Weekly Edition, November 6–12), 6–8.

Westbrook, Robert B. 1991. *John Dewey and American Democracy*. Ithaca, NY: Cornell University Press.

White, Stephen K. 1988. *The Recent Work of Jürgen Habermas*. Cambridge: Cambridge University Press.

Wilson, John F. 1969. *Pulpit in Parliament: Puritanism During the English Civil Wars 1640–1648*. Princeton, NJ: Princeton University Press.

Wood, Gordon S. 1969. *The Creation of the American Republic, 1776–1787*. Chapel Hill, NC: University of North Carolina Press.

Wood, James Playsted. 1962a. "Raymond Rubicam." *Journal of Market Research*, 26 (2): 77–9.

1962b. "George H. Gallup." *Journal of Market Research*, 26(4): 78–80.

Woodhouse, A. S. P. 1951. *Puritanism and Liberty*. Chicago: University of Chicago Press.

Wuthnow, Robert. 1989. *Communities of Discourse: Ideology and Social Structure in the Reformation, the Enlightenment, and European Socialism*. Cambridge, Mass.: Harvard University Press.

1994. *Sharing the Journey: Support Groups and America's New Quest for Community*. New York: Free Press.

Yankelovich, Daniel. 1991. *Coming to Public Judgment: Making Democracy Work in a Complex World*. Syracuse, NY: Syracuse University Press.

Zagorin, Perez. 1954. *A History of Political Thought in the English Revolution*. London: Routledge and Kegan Paul.

1970. *The Court and the Country: The Beginning of the English Revolution*. New York: Atheneum.

Zaller, John. 1993. *The Nature and Origins of Mass Opinion*. Cambridge: Cambridge University Press.

Zaret, David. 1996. "Petitions and the 'Invention' of Public Opinion in the English Revolution." *American Journal of Sociology*, 101: 1,497–555.

# Index

Achenbaum, A. A., 194–5
accounting
  influence on tax policy, 227–8
  rhetoric of, 39
action
  communicative, 12–18, 35–6, 91, 110,
    111
  frame of reference, 26–7, 33, 35–6, 85
active vs contemplative life, 170
Adorno, Theodore W., 3–4
advertising, 191–9
  and civic ideals, 192–4
  and creating wants, 191, 195
  critique of, 194
  justification of, 194–6
  and modernity, 191–2
Akerlof, George, 66
Alexander, Jeffrey C., 10, 32, 167, 288n,
    290n
American Association of Advertising
    Agencies, 194
American colonists
  pamphlets by, 113
  rights vs virtue, 176–8
Arato, Andrew, 144–5, 152–3
Aristotle, 21, 22, 24, 169–72, 270–1
Association of National Advertisers, 194
Audience Research Inc. (ARI), 200–1
Audit Bureau of Circulation, 199
Ayer and Son, 196

Banning, Lance, 176
Barbour, Haley, 276
bargaining and compromise, 116, 139, 255
Baudrillard, Jean, 277–82
Baum, Rainer, 96, 292n
Bauman, Zygmunt, 282, 284–5
Bernays, Edward, 128–9, 203
Blain, Michael, 34–5

Blumer, Herbert, 139–42
Bourdieu, Pierre, 140–1
Bradley, James E., 182
Burke, Kenneth, 13, 30–5, 69, 122, 167

Calkins, Earnest Elmo, 191
Calvin, John, 158
campaign finance, 238–9
Carruthers, Bruce G., 39
certification of knowledge, 5, 300n
  and economists, 229
  of facts, 227–32
  and inflation of interest, 227
  and public accountants, 227–8
  and public interest groups, 229–32
Chase, Stewart, 194
Cherington, Paul, 197, 198
Churchill, Winston, 195
Cicero, 22
citizenship, 115
  as inclusion, 115, 147
  and information, 253–5
civic humanism, 157, 170–1
civic virtue
  and citizen armies, 171–2
  in classical thought, 169–70
  and communication, 171, 174
  and corruption, 172
  and republican ideals, 172–8, 230
civil society, 142–6, 149
  Cohen and Arato on, 144–5
  founded in solidarities, 125, 154
  Habermas on, 18, 145–6, 152–3
  and public sphere, 142–4
  and social movements, 152–3,
  and societal community, 146–8
Clinton, William J., 237
Cohen, Jean L., 144–5, 152–3
Commons, John R., 197